ANNUAL EDITIONS

World History
Volume 1—Prehistory to 1500
Tenth Edition

EDITORS

Joseph R. Mitchell
History Instructor, Howard Community College

Joseph R. Mitchell is a history instructor at Howard Community College in Columbia, Maryland, and a popular regional speaker. He received a MA in history from Loyola College in Maryland and a MA in African American History from Morgan State University, also in Maryland. He is the principal coeditor of *The Holocaust: Readings and Interpretations* (McGraw-Hill/Dushkin, 2001). He also co-authored (with David L. Stebenne) *New City Upon a Hill: A History of Columbia, Maryland* (The History Press, 2007).

Helen Buss Mitchell
Professor of Philosophy, Howard Community College

Helen Buss Mitchell is a professor of philosophy and director of the women's studies program at Howard Community College in Columbia, Maryland. She is the author of *Roots of Wisdom* and *Readings from the Roots of Wisdom*. Both books were published by Wadsworth Publishing Company and are now in their fourth and third editions respectively. She has also created, written, and hosted a philosophy telecourse, *For the Love of Wisdom,* which is distributed throughout the country by Dallas TeleLearning. She has earned several degrees, including a PhD in intellectual and women's history from the University of Maryland.

 **Higher Education**

Boston   Burr Ridge, IL   Dubuque, IA   New York   San Francisco   St. Louis
Bangkok   Bogotá   Caracas   Kuala Lumpur   Lisbon   London   Madrid   Mexico City
Milan   Montreal   New Delhi   Santiago   Seoul   Singapore   Sydney   Taipei   Toronto

ANNUAL EDITIONS: World History, Volume 1—Prehistory to 1500, Tenth Edition

1 2 3 4 5 6 7 8 9 0 QPD/QPD 0 9

ISBN 978–0–07812778–6
MHID 0–07–812778–5
ISSN 1054–2779

Managing Editor: *Larry Loeppke*
Senior Managing Editor: *Faye Schilling*
Developmental Editor: *Debra Henricks*
Editorial Coordinator: *Mary Foust*
Editorial Assistant: *Nancy Meissner*
Production Service Assistant: *Rita Hingtgen*
Permissions Coordinator: *Lenny Behnke*
Senior Marketing Manager: *Julie Keck*
Marketing Communications Specialist: *Mary Klein*
Marketing Coordinator: *Alice Link*
Project Manager: *Sandy Wille*
Design Specialist: *Tara McDermott*
Senior Production Supervisor: *Laura Fuller*
Cover Graphics: *Kristine Jubeck*

Compositor: Laserwords Private Limited
Cover Images: © 2006 Glowimages, Inc., All Rights Reserved (inset); © Brand X Pictures/PictureQuest/RF (background)

Library in Congress Cataloging-in-Publication Data
Main entry under title: Annual Editions: World History, Volume 1—Prehistory to 1500, 10/e
  1. World History 2. Civilization, Modern—Periodicals 3. Social Problems—Periodicals. I. Mitchell, Joseph R.,
  Mitchell, Helen Buss *comp*. II. Title: World History, Volume 1—Prehistory to 1500, 10/e
658'.05

www.mhhe.com

Editors/Advisory Board

Members of the Advisory Board are instrumental in the final selection of articles for each edition of ANNUAL EDITIONS. Their review of articles for content, level, currentness, and appropriateness provides critical direction to the editor and staff. We think that you will find their careful consideration well reflected in this volume.

Editors/Advisory Board

Preface

In publishing ANNUAL EDITIONS we recognize the enormous role played by the magazines, newspapers, and journals of the public press in providing current, first-rate educational information in a broad spectrum of interest areas. Many of these articles are appropriate for students, researchers, and professionals seeking accurate, current material to help bridge the gap between principles and theories and the real world. These articles, however, become more useful for study when those of lasting value are carefully collected, organized, indexed, and reproduced in a low-cost format, which provides easy and permanent access when the material is needed. That is the role played by ANNUAL EDITIONS.

History is a dialogue between the past and the present. As we respond to events in our own time and place, we bring the concerns of the present to our study of the past. It has been said that where you stand determines what you see. Those of us who stand within the Western world have sometimes been surprised to discover peoples and cultures long gone that seem quite "modern" and even a bit "Western." Other peoples and cultures in the complex narrative of World History can seem utterly "foreign."

At times, the West has felt that its power and dominance made only its own story worth telling. History, we are reminded, is written by the winners. For the Chinese, the Greeks, the Ottoman Turks, and many other victors from the past, the stories of other civilizations seemed irrelevant, and certainly less valuable than their own triumphal saga. From our perspective in the present, however, all these stories form a tapestry. No one thread or pattern tells the whole tale, and all seem to be equally necessary for assembling a complete picture of the past.

As we are linked by capital, communications, and conflict with cultures whose histories, value systems, and goals challenge our own, World History can offer keys to understanding. As businesspeople and diplomats have always known, negotiations require a deep knowledge of the other's worldview. In an increasingly interconnected world, we ignore other civilizations at our own peril. As the dominant world power, we touch the lives of millions by decisions we make in the voting booth. Once powerful cultures that have fallen can offer cautionary advice. Those that survived longer than their neighbors offer hints.

When we read the newspaper or surf the Internet, we find confusing political, economic, religious, and military clashes that make sense only within the context of lived history and historical memory. The role of the United States in Afghanistan and Iraq, the perennial conflicts in the Middle East, China's emerging role as an economic superpower, the threat posed by religious fundamentalism, Africa's political future, the possibility of viral pandemics—these concerns of the global village have roots in the past.

Understanding the origins of conflicts offers us the possibility of envisioning their solutions. Periodization, or the marking of turning points in history, cannot be done universally. Cultures mature on different timetables and rise and fall independently. We have followed a somewhat traditional structure, beginning with natural history, considering early civilizations to 500 B.C.E., later civilizations to 500 C.E., and the world to 1500, pausing to examine the origins of the world's religions, and ending with exploration. Within this structure, one can read revisionist views of Nubians and Maya. Warfare and methods of surviving it; the origins of hospitals, writing, cash, and gold artwork; engineering marvels and planned cities—all of these commonplaces of modern life have ancient historical roots. The lives of women and female deities in ancient Sumer are juxtaposed with those of men. We see Jews, Christians, and Muslims playing their parts on the world stage, as partners or adversaries.

The articles have been selected for balance, readability, and interest. They are offered to the instructor to broaden and deepen material in the assigned text as well as to provide a variety of focuses and writing styles. Our intention has been to offer the most current articles available. If you know of good articles that might be used in future editions, please use the prepaid *article rating form* at the back of this book to make your suggestions. The topic guide will help instructors navigate the volume and choose the readings that best complement a unit of study.

Joseph R. Mitchell
Editor

Helen Buss Mitchell
Editor

Contents

UNIT 1
Natural History and the Spread of Humankind

1. **Stand and Deliver: Why Did Early Hominids Begin to Walk on Two Feet?,** Ian Tattersall, *Natural History,* November 2003

   What got **humankind** started on its unique **evolutionary** trajectory? The ability to walk upright on two feet—**bipedalism** is what it's called—allowed **hominids** to outshine their **prehistoric** cousins. As their environment changed, they adapted. Once they had the ability to hunt and taste red meat, the competition was over. Bipedalism was here to stay! So was meat!

2. **Gone but Not Forgotten,** Richard Monastersky, *The Chronicle of Higher Education,* December 1, 2006

   A recent advertising campaign and an ill-fated television sit-com have brought **cavemen** to a wider audience. Recently, **geneticists,** using **DNA** samples from Neanderthals, have concluded that their relationship with **Homo sapiens** was much closer than originally thought. Will the Neanderthal cavemen finally get the respect they deserve?

3. **Out of Africa,** Spencer Wells, *Vanity Fair,* July 2007

   By examining **human genomes,** obtained through **DNA** samples, scientists have learned that all of us can trace our existence back to **Africa**. Since that continent's peoples saved humankind from **extinction,** do we not have an obligation to assist Africans in their time of need?

4. **Mapping** *the* **Past,** Adam Goodheart, *Civilization,* March/April 1996

   Genetic historians are using **DNA analysis** to track the migration of human beings. **American Indians,** for example, can be traced to a region of Mongolia, and **Polynesians** have been tracked to southeast Asia. DNA markers may eventually provide a "map" of the entire human species.

5. **First Americans,** Karen Wright, *Discover,* February 1999

   Long thought that the **first humans** in the New World crossed the **Bering Strait** at the end of the **Ice Age,** recent **archaeological** evidence seems to indicate that none of this may be true. Scientists continued to search for clues pertaining to who, how, and when the earliest **Americans** arrived.

UNIT 2
The Beginnings of Culture, Agriculture, and Cities

6. **Dawn of the City: Excavations Prompt a Revolution in Thinking about the Earliest Cities,** Bruce Bower, *Science News,* February 9, 2008

   The **excavation** of **Tell Brak** in northern Syria has cast new light on the history of **urban development** in ancient **Mesopotamia.** It also provides an interesting case study involving the rise and fall of Tell Brak, including the reasons for both.

The concepts in bold italics are developed in the article. For further expansion, please refer to the Topic Guide.

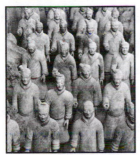

UNIT 3
The Early Civilizations to 500 B.C.E.

The concepts in bold italics are developed in the article. For further expansion, please refer to the Topic Guide.

UNIT 4
The Later Civilizations to 500 C.E.

The concepts in bold italics are developed in the article. For further expansion, please refer to the Topic Guide.

UNIT 5
The Great Religions

The concepts in bold italics are developed in the article. For further expansion, please refer to the Topic Guide.

UNIT 6
The World of the Middle Ages, 500–1500

UNIT 7
1500: The Era of Global Expansion

The concepts in bold italics are developed in the article. For further expansion, please refer to the Topic Guide.

The concepts in bold italics are developed in the article. For further expansion, please refer to the Topic Guide.

Correlation Guide

The *Annual Editions* series provides students with convenient, inexpensive access to current, carefully selected articles from the public press. **Annual Editions: World History, Volume 1: Prehistory to 1500, 10/e** is an easy-to-use reader that presents articles on important topics such as *ancient civilizations, religion, warfare,* and many more. For more information on *Annual Editions* and other *McGraw-Hill Contemporary Learning Series* titles, visit www.mhcls.com.

This convenient guide matches the units in **World History, Volume 1, 10/e** with the corresponding chapters in one of our best-selling McGraw-Hill World History textbooks by Bentley et al.

Annual Editions: World History, Volume 1, 10/e	Traditions & Encounters: A Brief Global History, Volume I: From The Beginning to 1500, 2/e by Bentley et al.
Unit 1: Natural History and the Spread of Humankind	**Chapter 1:** The Foundations of Complex Societies **Chapter 4:** Early Societies in the Americas and Oceania
Unit 2: The Beginnings of Culture, Agriculture, and Cities	**Chapter 1:** The Foundations of Complex Societies **Chapter 2:** Early African Societies and the Bantu Migrations
Unit 3: The Early Civilizations to 500 B.C.E.	**Chapter 2:** Early African Societies and the Bantu Migrations **Chapter 3:** Early Societies in South and East Asia **Chapter 4:** Early Societies in the Americas and Oceania **Chapter 6:** The Unification of China
Unit 4: The Later Civilizations to 500 C.E.	**Chapter 5:** The Rise and Fall of the Persian Empires **Chapter 8:** Mediterranean Society under the Greeks and Romans
Unit 5: The Great Religions	**Chapter 7:** State, Society, and the Quest for Salvation in India **Chapter 8:** Mediterranean Society under the Greeks and Romans **Chapter 11:** The Expansive Realm of Islam
Unit 6: The World of the Middle Ages, 500–1500	**Chapter 4:** Early Societies in the Americas and Oceania **Chapter 8:** Mediterranean Society under the Greeks and Romans **Chapter 10:** The Commonwealth of Byzantium **Chapter 14:** The Foundations of Christian Society in Western Europe **Chapter 15:** Nomadic Empires and Eurasian Integration **Chapter 16:** States and Societies of Sub-Saharan Africa
Unit 7: 1500: The Era of Global Expansion	**Chapter 19:** Reaching Out: Cross-Cultural Interactions

Topic Guide

This topic guide suggests how the selections in this book relate to the subjects covered in your course. You may want to use the topics listed on these pages to search the Web more easily.

On the following pages a number of Web sites have been gathered specifically for this book. They are arranged to reflect the units of this Annual Editions reader. You can link to these sites by going to *http://www.mhcls.com*.

All the articles that relate to each topic are listed below the bold-faced term.

Africa
1. Stand and Deliver: Why Did Early Hominids Begin to Walk on Two Feet?
3. Out of Africa
15. Empires in the Dust
16. Black Pharaohs
38. 1492: The Prequel

Agriculture
13. Indus Valley, Inc.
15. Empires in the Dust
33. The New Maya

Americas
5. First Americans
19. Beyond the Family Feud
24. Woman Power in the Maya World
33. The New Maya

Asian civilization
13. Indus Valley, Inc.
14. Uncovering Ancient Thailand
18. China's First Empire
27. Ancient Jewel
38. 1492: The Prequel

Buddhism
27. Ancient Jewel

Christianity
29. The Dome of the Rock: Jerusalem's Epicenter
30. First Churches of the Jesus Cult
31. Women in Ancient Christianity: The New Discoveries
34. The Ideal of Unity
37. The Fall of Constantinople
39. The Other 1492: Jews and Muslims in Columbus's Spain

Economics
11. The Cradle of Cash
40. The Far West's Challenge to the World, 1500–1700 A.D.
41. A Taste of Adventure: Kerala, India, and the Molucca Islands, Indonesia

Egyptian civilization
12. How to Build a Pyramid
15. Empires in the Dust
16. Black Pharaohs

Environment
1. Stand and Deliver: Why Did Early Hominids Begin to Walk on Two Feet?
13. Indus Valley, Inc.
15. Empires in the Dust

Europe
7. The Dawn of Art
20. In Classical Athens, a Market Trading in the Currency of Ideas

21. Alexander the Great: Hunting for a New Past?
22. Sudden Death: Gladiators Were Sport's First Superstars, Providing Thrills, Chills, and Occasional Kills
23. Vox Populi: Sex, Lies, and Blood Sport
32. The Survival of the Eastern Roman Empire
34. The Ideal of Unity
35. The Arab Roots of European Medicine
36. The Age of the Vikings
37. The Fall of Constantinople
39. The Other 1492: Jews and Muslims in Columbus's Spain
40. The Far West's Challenge to the World, 1500–1700 A.D.
41. A Taste of Adventure: Kerala, India, and the Molucca Islands, Indonesia
42. After Dire Straits, an Agonizing Haul across the Pacific
43. The Significance of Lepanto

Geography
1. Stand and Deliver: Why Did Early Hominids Begin to Walk on Two Feet?
4. Mapping *the* Past
15. Empires in the Dust
32. The Survival of the Eastern Roman Empire
37. The Fall of Constantinople
40. The Far West's Challenge to the World, 1500–1700 A.D.
42. After Dire Straits, an Agonizing Haul Across the Pacific

Greek civilization
20. In Classical Athens, a Market Trading in the Currency of Ideas
21. Alexander the Great: Hunting for a New Past?
37. The Fall of Constantinople

Historiography
5. First Americans
9. Writing Gets a Rewrite
15. Empires in the Dust
16. Black Pharaohs
19. Beyond the Family Feud

Hinduism
27. Ancient Jewel

Indian civilization
13. Indus Valley, Inc.
15. Empires in the Dust
27. Ancient Jewel

Islamic civilization
28. What Is the Koran?
29. The Dome of the Rock: Jerusalem's Epicenter
35. The Arab Roots of European Medicine
37. The Fall of Constantinople
43. The Significance of Lepanto

Judaism
26. It Happened Only Once in History!
29. The Dome of the Rock: Jerusalem's Epicenter
39. The Other 1492: Jews and Muslims in Columbus's Spain

Internet References

The following Internet sites have been selected to support the articles found in this reader. These sites were available at the time of publication. However, because Web sites often change their structure and content, the information listed may no longer be available. We invite you to visit http://www.mhcls.com for easy access to these sites.

Annual Editions: World History, Volume I

General Sources

History of Science, Technology, and Medicine
http://echo.gmu.edu/center/

A database of information on science, technology, and medicine with alphabetical listing of resources, this site has search features and multiple links.

Humanities Links
http://www-sul.stanford.edu/depts/hasrg/

Philosophical, cultural, and historical worldwide links, including archives, history sites, and an electronic library of full texts and documents are included on this Web site. The resources are useful for research in history and the humanities.

Hyperhistory on Line
http://www.hyperhistory.com

At this Web site, click on "hyperhistory" and navigate through 3,000 years of world history. Links to important historical persons, events, and maps are also here.

International Network Information Systems at University of Texas
http://inic.utexas.edu

This gateway has pointers to international study sites for Africa, India, China, Japan, and many other countries.

UNIT 1: Natural History and the Spread of Humankind

The Ancient World
http://www.omnibusol.com/ancient.html

The first part of this online book, *The Amazing Ancient World of Western Civilization,* begins with the dinosaurs and moves to Stonehenge.

Fossil Hominids
http://www.talkorigins.org/faqs/homs

Information and links concerning hominid fossils and paleoanthropology can be found on this page created by The Talk Origins Archive. Visit here to investigate the diversity of hominids.

The Human Origins Program at the Smithsonian
http://anthropology.si.edu/humanorigins/

This site contains the Smithsonian's Human Origins Program, which is dedicated to furthering scientific knowledge about the evolutionary origin of human beings and our relationship with the natural world.

The Origin and Evolution of Life
http://cmex-www.arc.nasa.gov/VikingCD/Puzzle/EvoLife.htm

This site contains NASA's Planetary Biology Program, which is chartered to investigate the origin and evolution of life.

Talk-Origins
http://www.talkorigins.org

This is the site of a newsgroup devoted to debate on the biological and physical origins of the world. Many articles are archived here, and there are links to other Web sites. Be sure to click on "The Origin of Humankind," a comprehensive source for students of human evolution, which has the latest news about new discoveries, a link to an exhibition of human prehistory, and links to many other related sites, including Yahoo's creation/evolution material.

WWW-VL Prehistoric Web Index
http://easyweb.easynet.co.uk/~aburnham/database/index.htm

An index to prehistoric, megalithic, and ancient sites in Europe can be accessed on this site.

UNIT 2: The Beginnings of Culture, Agriculture, and Cities

Civilization of the Olmec
http://loki.stockton.edu/~gilmorew/consorti/1bcenso.htm

Robert Knaak is the curator of this complete Olmec site, which includes history and origins, achievements, and archaeological sites of this "hearth culture" of Central America, whose traditions have carried over through the centuries.

Diotima: Women and Gender in the Ancient World
http://www.stoa.org/diotima

Historical information about women in the ancient world is available at this site, which also includes search possibilities.

Oriental Institute
http://www.etana.org/abzu

Click on *ABZU.htm* in the index of the University of Chicago's Oriental Institute for information about ancient Near East archaeology and a bibliographic reference on women in the areas covered.

Tell Brak Homepage
http://www.learningsites.com/Brak/Tell-Brak_home.html

This site provides information on the excavation of Tell Brak, ancient Nagar, located in northeastern Syria.

UNIT 3: The Early Civilizations to 500 B.C.E.

Ancient Indus Valley
www.harappa.com/har/har0.html

This site references the most recent discoveries about the Indus Civilization.

Civilization of the Olmecs
http://www.ancientsudan.org/

Contains information on Nubia, which is located in Northeast Africa within the political boundaries of modern Sudan.

Internet References

Exploring Ancient World Cultures
http://eawc.evansville.edu

Eight ancient world cultures can be explored from this starting point. They include Ancient China, Egypt, India, Greece, Rome, Near East, Early Islam, and Medieval Europe.

Nubia Museum
http://www.numibia.net/nubia/history.htm

Comprehensive website that includes information on Nubian history, culture, and current status

Reeder's Egypt Page
http://www.egyptology.com/reeder

Click on the tomb opening to reveal a wealth of historical and archaeological information about Egypt, including a tour of the tombs of Niankhkhnum and Khnumhotep.

UNIT 4: The Later Civilizations to 500 C.E.

Alexander the Great
http://1stmuse.com/frames/

This historical site describes the life and accomplishments of Alexander the Great.

Ancient City of Athens
http://www.stoa.org/athens

Look in the Index for images of ancient Athens as well as insights into Greek history and links to other Greek historical sites

Cracking the Maya Code
www.pbs.org/wgbh/nova/mayacode

Watch the story of the decipherment of ancient Mayan hieroglyphs online.

Illustrated History of the Roman Empire
http://www.roman-empire.net

Visit this site for information about the Roman Empire.

Internet Ancient History Sourcebook
http://www.fordham/halsall/ancient/asbook9.html

Contains primary source materials covering Rome from the Etruscans to its own decline and fall.

Internet East Asian Sourcebook
http://www.fordham/halsall/eastasia/eastasiasbook.html

Excellent website that provides primary source documents on Asian civilizations.

Reconstructing Petra
http://www.smithsonianmag.com/history-archaeology/petra.html

Visit this site to find out what archaeologists are discovering about ancient Petra.

UNIT 5: The Great Religions

Cultural India
www.culturalindia.net

This site contains information on the unique and varied aspects of Indian culture.

Major World Religions
http://www.omsakthi.org/religions.html

Information at this site provides short introductions to the major world religions. There are also links to great books on religion and spirituality.

Religion Search Engines: Christianity and Judaism
http://www.suite101.com/article.cfm/search_engines/13501/

Paula Dragutsky's collection of search engines will lead to a wide-ranging directory of Christian Web sites. Shamash is a comprehensive search engine for Jewish information.

Religion Search Engines: Islam, Hinduism, Buddhism and Baha'i
http://www.suite101.com/article.cfm/search_engines/14603

Specialized search engines reviewed on this page can be very helpful in leading to original and interpretive documents that explain the philosophy and practices of Islam, Hinduism, Buddhism, and Baha'i.

UNIT 6: The World of the Middle Ages, 500–1500

Labyrinth Home Page to Medieval Studies
http://www.georgetown.edu/labyrinth/

Complete information about medieval studies on the Web can be found here. Site also has a search capability.

Lords of the Earth: Maya/Aztec/Inca Exchange
http://www.mayalords.org/

History, geography, and art about the indigenous inhabitants of the Americas before the arrival of Columbus is available here.

The Maya Astronomy Page
http://www.michielb.nl/maya/astro_content.html?t2_1021391248914

The focus here is on Mayan civilization, especially astronomy, mathematics, and the Mayan calendar. There are also links to other Maya-related sites. Click on the "Maya Astronomy Page."

WWW Medieval Resources
http://ebbs.english.vt.edu/medieval/medieval.ebbs.html

This site has links to different resources concerning medieval times.

UNIT 7: 1500: The Era of Global Expansion

Gander Academy's European Explorers Resources on the World Wide Web
http://www.stemnet.nf.ca/CITE/explorer.htm

Access to resources for each of the European explorers of the "new world" can be made here. It is organized by country that each explored.

The Great Chinese Mariner Zheng He
www.chinapage.com/zhenghe.html

Visit this site to learn about Zheng He, China's most famous navigator, who sailed from China to many places throughout South Pacific, Indian Ocean, Taiwan, Persian Gulf and distant Africa years before Columbus's voyages.

Internet References

Internet Medieval Sourcebook
http://wwwfordham.edu/halsall/Sbook12.html

Primary source website with documents on a variety of subjects related to the Age of Exploration.

Magellan's Voyage Around the World
www.fordham.edu/halsall/mod/1519magellan.html

Learn more about how Ferdinand Magellan set sail on a voyage around the world in 1519–1522 CE.

NOVA Online: The Vikings
http://www.pbs.org/wgbh/nova/vikings/

This is a companion site to NOVA's two-hour "The Vikings" program. It contains a video, a map, a time line, information on the runes, and discussion on who the Vikings were and the secrets of Norse ships.

UNIT 1
Natural History and the Spread of Humankind

Unit Selections

1. **Stand and Deliver: Why Did Early Hominids Begin to Walk on Two Feet?,** Ian Tattersall
2. **Gone but Not Forgotten,** Richard Monastersky
3. **Out of Africa,** Spencer Wells
4. **Mapping *the* Past,** Adam Goodheart
5. **First Americans,** Karen Wright

Key Points to Consider

- Why was bipedalism such a crucial factor in the evolutionary survival game?

- What evidence is offered to support the claim that the Neanderthals made a substantial contribution to the modern gene pool of Europe? How might this change the way we view them?

- What evidence is offered to prove that Africa was the birthplace of humankind? What implication does this have for the modern world?

- How has DNA analysis affected the study of archaeology? What new findings might be possible as a result of its continued use?

- How have recent discoveries changed the answer to the question, "Who were the First Americans?" What effect has this had on the archaeological world?

Student Web Site
www.mhcls.com

Internet References

The Ancient World
http://www.omnibusol.com/ancient.html
Fossil Hominids
http://www.talkorigins.org/faqs/homs
The Human Origins Program at the Smithsonian
http://anthropology.si.edu/humanorigins/
The Origin and Evolution of Life
http://cmex-www.arc.nasa.gov/VikingCD/Puzzle/EvoLife.htm
Talk-Origins
http://www.talkorigins.org
WWW-VL Prehistoric Web Index
http://easyweb.easynet.co.uk/~aburnham/database/index.htm

The late astronomer Carl Sagan, in his famous book *The Dragons of Time* (1970), imagined all of time compressed into a single year. New Year's Day began fifteen billion years ago with the Big Bang, a moment when the universe emerged from an enormously powerful explosion of compressed matter and anti-matter. The Earth formed in mid-September and life began near the end of that month. In Sagan's scenario, humans do not make an appearance until 10:30 P.M. on December 31st. The Akkadian Empire, the first we know about, formed in the last nine seconds of the year. When we think in cosmic time, as Sagan invites us to do, human existence seems both recent and fragile. It is this human story, nonetheless, that is the chief focus of world history.

During our hour and a half of cosmic time, humans of various kinds have lived and flourished on our wet, green planet. Many of the branches of our family tree, however, have led to dead ends. What happened to Neanderthals, who shared Europe with more modern Cro-Magnons? Was it predators, environmental conditions, or warfare that ended their history? Only one species survived, but the story of its survivability is incomplete and some of it is lost in mystery. Bipedal locomotion—the ability to walk upright on two legs—was a huge advantage to some of our distant relatives. They saw expanded possibilities, and began a migration that now spans the globe.

Access to sophisticated tools of analysis has allowed anthropologists and genetic historians to peel back some of the layers of mystery. Studying dental records and styles of tool making has allowed us to trace the spread of peoples and cultures throughout the world. DNA analysis focusing on mitochondrial DNA (passed directly from mothers) and the Y-chromosome (inherited only from fathers) now permits people to trace their genetic ancestry into the distant past. These same techniques can shed light on where the first Americans began their long journey. Was it Mongolia, Southeast Asia, or somewhere else? And, did they cross a land bridge from Siberia into modern-day Alaska or arrive by boats, as many legends insist? Was there a single migration, or were there multiple ones with different starting points?

The answers to questions such as these might affect how we feel about ourselves. Individually, we might be thrilled or appalled to discover who some of our distant ancestors were. And, larger language groups can have the same reactions. If we share blood with those who have become our traditional enemies, does this make warfare or negotiation easier or more difficult? Linguistic analysis can be increasingly precise on these points. So can DNA patterning. In the most general sense, we all share the same common ancestors. As our species has spread across the Earth, we have become quite diverse. Thousands of years of history have chronicled our cooperation and competition. In Carl Sagan's year, all of this has been accomplished in less than a minute.

Stand and Deliver

Why Did Early Hominids Begin to Walk on Two Feet?

Ian Tattersall

Ask any paleoanthropologist what got humankind started on its unique evolutionary trajectory, and the reflex answer will almost certainly be "the adoption of upright bipedalism." And whatever the exact characteristics of the most ancient hominid may have been, there is no question that the adoption of upright locomotion on the ground was an epoch-making event for our hominid family.

The idea that *Homo sapiens* might be descended from some ancient apelike animal that walked around on its two hind legs goes back at least as far as Jean-Baptiste Lamarck's great *Philosophie Zoologique,* which appeared in the opening decade of the nineteenth century. And Darwin famously expressed a similar viewpoint in *The Descent of Man,* published in 1871. Darwin speculated that the importance of bipedalism was that it freed the hands from the demands of locomotion, thereby opening the way for toolmaking and other manual activities that make us uniquely human. If so, it took some time for our precursors to realize the potential of their upright posture: it is now clear that the origin of stone toolmaking postdated the acquisition of bipedalism by millions of years. Still, it is hard to resist the idea that bipedalism was a necessary condition for all that followed, even if it might not have been a sufficient one.

Since Darwin's day, paleoanthropologists have energetically sought the key to hominid erectness in many different places. Nearly always, though, these scientists have sought the Holy Grail of a single critical function: what exactly was it about being upright that gave early hominids the edge? For, given that teetering along on a single pair of feet is, to all appearances, hardly an optimal solution for a hominid whose ancestors almost certainly got around using four limbs, isn't it intuitively obvious that the particular advantage of walking upright on two limbs must have been an overwhelming one? And, at the very least, it's clear that upright bipedalism is not an automatic primate response to descending from the trees to live on the ground. Even patas monkeys, apart from ourselves the most committed-to-ground-dwelling of all living primates, have accomplished that shift by becoming even more specialized quadrupeds than their more arboreal ancestors had been before them.

So just what was going on when our ancient forebears, in a period of climate change that transformed their ancestral forested habitats in Africa into one of trees, shrubs, and grasses, started opting for upright, two-legged locomotion on the ground? There has been no dearth of suggestions, all based on adaptation to some aspect or another of ground-dwelling life. I have to confess here that I have long been suspicious of the profligate use of "adaptation" to simultaneously explain any and all evolutionary innovations. After all, any individual is made up of a whole host of features that one could describe as adaptations, whereas natural selection can only vote up and down on the whole thing, warts and all. Still, there is no doubt that paleoanthropologists have come up with a whole host of terrific stories on the subject.

The first to describe a truly ancient biped was the Australian-born physical anthropologist and paleontologist Raymond Dart, in 1925. Dart understood that life on the predator-ridden open savannas would have been pretty dangerous for the relatively small, slow, and defenseless early hominids. He suggested that standing up would have enabled the creatures to peer over tall grass and spot dangerous animals at a distance. Other investigators have pointed out that an animal looks bigger when it stands up, which might help discourage predators from attacking it. Corroborating that idea, contemporary studies do seem to show that the predatory interest of big cats is more readily triggered by horizontal silhouettes than by vertical ones.

Those who prefer to look upon even our remotest ancestors as bush-league versions of ourselves have tended to side with Darwin. They see bipedalism as a mechanism for freeing the hands to carry food and other objects back to home base, or as a way of making it easier for mothers to tote babies around. The most recent wrinkle in this hypothesis has been the suggestion (by male paleoanthropologists) that bipedal early hominid males used their free hands to carry food back to hapless females, whose baby-toting activities had dramatically curtailed their food seeking. This social behavior supposedly led in turn to such far-reaching consequences as pair-bonding, concealed ovulation, and the prominence of female breasts. The story has the undeniable attraction of tying bipedalism to a variety of human physical and social peculiarities, but it is no less controversial for that, and it has recently come under attack on a variety of grounds. Feminist anthropologists, for example, perhaps in retaliation for the perceived sexual slight, have directly blamed erect bipedalism on the appalling exhibitionist tendencies of males.

Lately, the bulk of the debate on the subject has focused on what might be called the thermoregulatory hypothesis. When you're out of the forest, the argument goes, you're out of the shade. With direct exposure to the tropical Sun, you need some way to cool down your body—particularly your heat-sensitive brain. Lacking specialized means for such cooling, hominids might have discovered that by standing up, they absorbed less of the Sun's heat (by minimizing the surface area exposed directly to the Sun's vertical rays). Furthermore, standing exposed the heat-radiating portions of their bodies to the cooling breezes that blow above ground-level vegetation. The idea is persuasive. The cooling effects dovetail nicely with such special human characteristics as sweating and the drastic reduction—compared with our ape ancestors—of body hair.

But the thermoregulatory hypothesis has by no means met with universal acclaim. An opposing camp argues that bipedalism is simply the most energy-efficient way for a hominid to get around on a flat surface. Careful calculations show that, under certain plausible conditions, ground-living hominids expend less energy moving around on two legs than they do on four. And the less energy you expend, the less food you need to find—another clear advantage.

Will the Real Reason for Bipedalism Please Stand Up?

In light of all the competing theories, some cautious weighing of their relative merits is clearly welcome. With excellent timing, here now are two books that, from rather different perspectives, devote themselves to the question of why hominids became upright, and to exploring exactly how that event may have shaped subsequent human evolutionary history. Intriguingly, both authors at least partly avoid the Holy Grail trap by developing quite complex scenarios. Each book, moreover, is a work of advocacy, with a clear and well-defined story to tell. That approach has the advantage of making both books highly readable. At the same time, though, it leaves readers with little choice but to embrace or to spurn the arguments in their entirety, instead of offering readers a chance to shop around among the various components of each story.

Jonathan Kingdon commands a unique position at the interface of science and art. Not only has he made a substantial contribution to the scientific understanding of African mammal evolution and diversity; he has also enhanced our aesthetic appreciation of these animals through his graceful drawings and paintings. Predictably, his book *Lowly Origin* (a title drawn from Darwin's concluding statement in *The Descent of Man*) is enlivened by a generous selection of engaging illustrations. After listing at least thirteen distinct explanations that have been advanced at one time or another for hominid bipedalism (including all the ones mentioned above, and many more besides), Kingdon plumps for a multicausal argument, drawing on his extensive knowledge of African ecology and biogeography.

His scenario is a gradualist one. At first an ancestral quadrupedal "ground ape" slowly but smoothly progresses to a long-lasting squat-feeding phase. Whenever the creature forages on the forest or woodland floor, the trunk is held upright. Over millions of years the hind legs gradually assume the support of the upper body's weight. The resulting reduction of upper-body bulk improves the balance of the vertical trunk, until "four-legged movement cease[s] to be as efficient as simple straightening of the legs." At the same time, the pressure from predators on the ground becomes greater than it ever was in the trees, and so survival dictates greater social cooperation and more complex behaviors than ever before. Those developments enable the hominids to explore an increasingly broad range of environments, until they occupy the open savanna.

Governing this proposed sequence of events is the African environment in which the early hominids lived. Somewhat controversially, Kingdon contends that apelike human ancestors from Eurasia, originally of African ancestry, crossed back into Africa from Arabia about 10.5 million years ago. At that time the ancient Tethys Sea, which preceded the Mediterranean, was closing, permitting intercontinental contact between Africa and Eurasia. These apelike ancestors ultimately evolved to become chimpanzees and gorillas in the dense rainforests of central Africa, while, isolated on the other side of a relatively arid, treeless barrier, another group of descendants occupied the drier littoral forests of the African continent's eastern edge. Those latter primates eventually gave rise to the early hominids: creatures who were forced to change their ancestral feeding habits as a result of a changing environment. More specifically, they had to supplement the food resources available in the forest canopy with nutrients found on the forest floor.

Such a bald statement of Kingdon's complex and nuanced argument—which actually reaches back to explore our remotest primate origins, and beyond—does little justice to his elegant and thoughtful, if somewhat idiosyncratic, book. Whether or not Kingdon manages to convince you of his larger thesis, you will be provoked along the way by the many connections he makes. And just as important, Lowly Origin is a landmark for its thoroughness in integrating the story of human evolution (which he brings up to the present day) with that of the evolving landscapes and habitats of the African continent. What's more, Kingdon doesn't shy away from extrapolating the past to the future, painting an unattractive portrait of our species as a "niche thief" whose past success has depended on invading the ecological niches of others, but whose rapacious activities now threaten even its own future survival.

Craig Stanford, the author of *Upright,* is an accomplished primatologist who has specialized in studying the behaviors of African apes. His knowledge of chimpanzees, and, in particular, his field experience with them, inform much of his new book. Stanford points out that bipedal locomotion is a pretty bizarre way of getting around, with the clear implication that it calls for a pretty special explanation. He looks for that explanation in all the usual places, notably in the energetics of walking and the cooling of the brain, but he finds problems with them all.

One of the pleasures of Stanford's book is its splendidly gossipy account of recent research into the early history of hominid

3

bipedalism. It dwells lovingly, for instance, on the prolonged sniping that went on between two groups of scientists, one based in the Midwest and the other on the East Coast, over the interpretation of the famous 3.2-million-year-old skeleton from Ethiopia known as Lucy. Stanford places himself somewhere in the middle. Reasonably, he rejects the East Coast scientists' assertion that Lucy's locomotor adaptation was "transitional." Just as reasonably, he accepts their (totally correct) conclusion that Lucy's bipedalism differed significantly from that of her successors of the genus Homo.

Oddly, in view of what Stanford has to say later on in his book, he also takes time to trash the idea that bipedalism was driven by environmental change. More significant, he argues, was that from the beginning hominids appear to have been ecological generalists. The key to their success was, and is, their ability to thrive in diverse environments. Yet despite his emphasis on environmental adaptability, he is still convinced that the hominids' unusual and implication-ridden form of locomotion was a response to something, and he is clearly concerned to discover a single underlying explanation for it. He finds it in meat eating.

Between 7 million and 8 million years ago, at the beginning of the scenario he reconstructs, some very early hominids "shuffled across the ground a bit between fruit trees." But as the climate became increasingly seasonal, and the grasslands expanded at the expense of the forest, natural selection would have favored those individuals who shuffled most efficiently across the enlarging open areas. That would have laid the groundwork for the success of the archaic bipedal hominids. They were the animals that could most effectively scavenge meat from carcasses they encountered in increasingly open areas, even as they hunted smaller game in forests and woodlands—much as some chimpanzees do today. Thus, despite Stanford's earlier insistence that hominids succeeded because they were generalists, he eventually falls back on environmental change as at least the initial external impetus for the multistage sequence of events that led to bipedalism.

Once a taste for meat had been acquired, everything else followed. "By three million years ago," he writes, "the whole equation of foraging energetics and diet had begun a fundamental shift." A "virtuous circle" had been established. More efficient upright walking fed back into increasing intelligence and social complexity, and those attributes led to ever more effective hunting. The last part of Stanford's short book is devoted to a once-over-lightly of the later hominid fossil record, illustrating how that dynamic has played out over the past couple of million years.

Two very different books, then, presenting radically different scenarios for the origin of bipedalism in our lineage. But, significantly, what both books have in common is a firm belief in the gradual environmental molding of lineages, generation by generation, through natural selection. Indeed, both authors see natural selection as a driving force in human evolution—though Stanford correctly emphasizes that natural selection promotes the diversity of species, and stoutly denies that evolution is toward anything.

Yet natural selection can only work on novelties presented to it spontaneously; it cannot call anatomical innovations into being, however desirable they might appear. In nature, form has to precede function, for without form there can be no function. Yes, in retrospect bipedalism opened up a huge range of radical new possibilities for hominids. But evolutionists can hardly invoke those possibilities and their exploitation as explanations for the appearance of the new behavior.

So what can be said about how this fateful innovation came to pass? Well, it is clear that bipedalism arose quite early in hominid history, even if no one can be certain, in the strictest genealogical sense, that the earliest hominid was an upright biped. It is also pretty safe to conclude that the adoption of bipedalism was a formative event, with the profoundest possible consequences for later hominid evolution.

And there is a simple explanation, potentially testable by future fossil discoveries, for why early hominids began to move upright on the ground as their ancestral forests started to fragment. The explanation is that their own ancestors already favored upright postures in the trees, keeping their trunks erect during foraging, as many other primates do today. In other words, the early hominids were bipedal because they were already creatures that would have been most comfortable (if initially not totally at ease) moving upright on the ground.

If that was indeed the case, paleoanthropologists don't need to make difficult choices from the extensive menu of potential advantages that upright locomotion may or may not have offered the early hominids. Once our precursors had begun to descend from the trees, at the very least encouraged to do so by a changing milieu, they stood and moved upright simply because it was the most natural thing for them to do. Of course, once they had made this move, all the advantages of this new posture were theirs. And all of the liabilities too, for that matter.

IAN TATTERSALL is a curator in the Division of Anthropology at the American Museum of Natural History, and the author of numerous books, most recently, *The Monkey in the Mirror* (Harcourt, 2002).

Gone but Not Forgotten

Richard Monastersky

Neanderthals, those long-lost cousins of modern humans, will not remain lost for long, at least from the prying eyes of geneticists.

Two teams of scientists announced in November that for the first time they had analyzed DNA from the nuclei of cells preserved in 37,000-year-old Neanderthal fossils. That, they say, lays the groundwork for determining the entire sequence of the Neanderthal genome within the next two years.

Because Neanderthals, who disappeared 28,000 years ago, are the closest relatives of modern humans, obtaining the genetic blueprint for those extinct people could reveal important clues about how our own species evolved, the researchers say.

The genetic evidence could also solve mysteries that have plagued anthropologists since the first Neanderthal skeleton was found 150 years ago: namely, what did the ancient people look like, could they speak, and why did they ultimately vanish? After successfully weathering ice ages in Europe for more than 150,000 years, Neanderthals went extinct soon after modern humans appeared there around 40,000 years ago. Some researchers have argued that modern humans wiped out the stockier Neanderthals. Others contend, however, that the two groups intermingled and that the more numerous modern humans simply engulfed the smaller Neanderthal populations.

The DNA sequences will profoundly alter studies of the enigmatic ancient people, said one of the team leaders, Edward M. Rubin, of the Lawrence Berkeley National Laboratory, a federal facility managed by the University of California. "Instead of it being a data-poor field largely based on bones and associated artifacts, it will be a data-rich field, associated with enormous amounts—billions of bits—of data available on the Internet," he says.

In an era when scientists are routinely publishing the genetic sequences of living animals and plants, Mr. Rubin and his colleagues said they would soon manage that feat for the extinct people. "We're going to be able to learn about their biology and learn about things we could never learn from the bones and the artifacts we have," says Mr. Rubin.

The results announced this week go far beyond previous work on Neanderthal DNA, which has focused exclusively on genetic material from mitochondria, the power plants inside cells. They carry their own snippets of DNA, which is passed down from mother to child, with no contribution from the father. In the new work, Mr. Rubin's team and a group led by Svante Paabo of the Max Planck Institute for Evolutionary Anthropology, in Leipzig, Germany, studied Neanderthal DNA that came from the nuclei of cells, where most of an organism's genetic information is housed.

Mr. Rubin's group published its analysis in *Science,* and Mr. Paabo's team published its paper in *Nature* in November. "These papers are perhaps the most significant contributions published in this field since the discovery of Neanderthals," according to a commentary in *Nature* written by David M. Lambert of Massey University and Craig D. Millar of the University of Auckland, both in New Zealand.

Finding the Right Bone

DNA degrades with time, and Mr. Paabo's team has searched for years to find bones that have preserved enough Neanderthal genetic material and are not contaminated by DNA from modern people. After testing 70 bone and tooth samples from fossils collected around Europe and Western Asia, the researchers eventually found a small bone from a cave in Croatia.

"One thing that is fortunate about this particular bone: It's rather small and uninteresting," Mr. Paabo says. "It was thrown in a big box of uninteresting bones and not handled very much." That kept it from being contaminated by the DNA of researchers.

Mr. Paabo and Mr. Rubin used different methods to sequence the Neanderthal DNA, but they came to generally similar conclusions about how recently the ancestors of modern humans and Neanderthals split apart, roughly 400,000 to 500,000 years ago.

DNA consists of long chains of nucleotide bases, the letters that make up the genetic code. Mr. Paabo's group sequenced one million bases of Neanderthal DNA, a tiny fraction of the total. People today have three billion bases. But he says he could complete a rough draft of the entire Neanderthal genome in two years, using less than one-tenth of an ounce of fossil material.

The researchers say their data do not support much mixing of Neanderthal genes into the modern human population during the time the two populations overlapped in Europe.

But supporters of that theory say the new data do not kill off the idea that Neanderthals and humans were interbreeding. In fact, they cite some evidence, reported by Mr. Paabo's team, that indicates human males might have been mating with Neanderthals and contributing DNA to that gene pool. "That's a very convincing demonstration of interbreeding between Neanderthals and humans," says Milford H. Wolpoff, a professor of anthropology at the University of Michigan at Ann Arbor.

Evidence for such interbreeding comes from two recent studies that looked at the genetic variation present in modern humans. In one paper, published in November in the Proceedings of the National Academy of Sciences, Bruce T. Lahn, a professor of human genetics at the University of Chicago, and his colleagues studied a gene called microcephalin that is involved in guiding brain formation. Mr. Lahn's group found that the gene comes in many variations, or alleles, with one class that differs markedly from the others. The degree of difference suggests that the unusual allele was introduced into the human population 37,000 years ago from a group of people that had been separated from humans for roughly a million years.

"We speculate that Neanderthals might have been the source for that new variant," says Mr. Lahn. "We know that 37,000 years ago, Neanderthals and humans coexisted." And the researchers have found more of this variant allele among people in Europe and Asia, where Neanderthals lived.

Mr. Lahn's group has looked at other genes and found one other possible set that might have come from interbreeding, which he takes as evidence that there was limited gene flow between the two groups. If interbreeding had happened commonly, the human genome would harbor more of these unusual genes, he says.

In another study, researchers from the University of California at Los Angeles looked at sequences of 135 genes in people today and estimated that 5 percent of the gene pool represents ancient admixture, meaning it came from extinct populations of people. "If the signal we observe is indeed the result of an admixture event, then these results would change our understanding of the origins of modern humans," the researchers write in the journal *Public Library of Science Genetics*. "it would argue that archaic populations such as Neanderthals must have made a substantial contribution to the modern gene pool in Europe."

Out of Africa

Somewhere between 80,000 and 50,000 years ago, Africa saved *Homo sapiens* from extinction. Charting the DNA shared by more than six billion people, a population geneticist—and director of the Genographic Project—suggests what humanity "owes" its first home.

SPENCER WELLS

Do you think you know who you are? Maybe Irish, Italian, Jewish, Chinese, or one of the dozens of other hyphenated Americans that make up the United States melting pot? Think deeper—beyond the past few hundred years. Back beyond genealogy, where everyone loses track of his or her ancestry—back in that dark, mysterious realm we call prehistory. What if I told you every single person in America—every single person on earth—is African? With a small scrape of cells from the inside of anyone's cheek, the science of genetics can even prove it.

Here's how it works. The human genome, the blueprint that describes how to make another version of you, is huge. It's composed of billions of sub-units called nucleotides, repeated in a long, linear code that contains all of your biological information. Skin color, hair type, the way you metabolize milk: it's all in there. You got your DNA from your parents, who got it from theirs, and so on, for millions of generations to the very beginning of life on earth. If you go far enough back, your genome connects you with bacteria, butterflies, and barracuda—the great chain of being linked together through DNA.

What about humanity, though? What about creatures you would recognize as being like you if they were peering over your shoulder right now? It turns out that every person alive today can trace his or her ancestry back to Africa. Everyone's DNA tells a story of a journey from an African homeland to wherever you live. You may be from Cambodia or County Cork, but you are carrying a map inside your genome that describes the wanderings of your ancestors as they moved from the savannas of Africa to wherever your family came from most recently. This is thanks to genetic markers—tiny changes that arise rarely and spontaneously as our DNA is copied and passed down through the generations—which serve to unite people on ever older branches of the human family tree. If you share a marker with someone, you share an ancestor with him or her at some point in the past: the person whose DNA first had the marker that defines your shared lineage. These markers can be traced to relatively specific times and places as humans moved across the globe. The farther back in time and the closer to Africa we get, the more markers we all share.

What set these migrations in motion? Climate change—today's big threat—seems to have had a long history of tormenting our species. Around 70,000 years ago it was getting very nippy in the northern part of the globe, with ice sheets bearing down on Seattle and New York; this was the last Ice Age. At that time, though, our species, *Homo sapiens,* was still limited to Africa; we were very much homebodies. But the encroaching Ice Age, perhaps coupled with the eruption of a super-volcano named Toba, in Sumatra, dried out the tropics and nearly decimated the early human population. While *Homo sapiens* can be traced to around 200,000 years ago in the fossil record, it is remarkably difficult to find an archaeological record of our species between 80,000 and 50,000 years ago, and genetic data suggest that the population eventually dwindled to as few as 2,000 individuals. Yes, 2,000—fewer than fit into many symphony halls. We were on the brink of extinction.

And then something happened. It began slowly, with only a few hints of the explosion to come: The first stirrings were art—tangible evidence of advanced, abstract thought—and a significant improvement in the types of tools humans made. Then, around 50,000 years ago, all hell broke loose. The human population began to expand, first in Africa, then leaving the homeland to spread into Eurasia. Within a couple of thousand years we had reached Australia, walking along the coast of South Asia. A slightly later wave of expansion into the Middle East, around 45,000 years ago, was aided by a brief damp period in the Sahara. Within 15,000 years of the exodus from Africa our species had entered Europe, defeating the Neanderthals in the process. (Neanderthals are distant cousins, not ancestors; our evolutionary lineages have been separate for more than 500,000 years.) We had also populated Asia, learning to live in frigid temperatures not unlike those on the Moon, and around 15,000 years ago we walked across a short-lived, icy land bridge to enter the Americas—the first hominids ever to set foot on the continents of the Western Hemisphere. Along the way we kept adapting to new climates, in some cases lost our dark tropical skin pigmentation, developed different languages, and generated the complex tapestry of human diversity we see around the world today, from Africa to Iceland to Tierra del Fuego. But the thing that set it all in motion, the thing that saved us from extinction, happened first in Africa. Some anthropologists call it the Great Leap Forward, and it marked the true origin of our species—the time when we started to behave like humans.

Africa gave us the tool we needed, in the form of a powerful, abstract mind, to take on the world.

Africa gave us the tool we needed, in the form of a powerful, abstract mind, to take on the world (and eventually to decode the markers in our DNA that make it possible to track our amazing journeys). Perhaps just a few small genetic mutations that appeared around 50,000 years ago gave humans the amazing minds we use to make sense of the confusing and challenging world around us. Using our incredible capacity to put abstract musing into practice, we have managed to populate every continent on earth, in the process increasing the size of our population from a paltry few thousand to more than six billion. Now, 50 millennia after that first spark, times have changed. A huge number of things have contributed to Africa's relative decline on the world stage, perhaps most important geography. As Jared Diamond describes in his masterly book *Guns, Germs, and Steel,* Eurasia, with its East-West axis, allowed the rapid latitudinal diffusion of ideas and tools that would give its populations a huge advantage after the initial leap out of Africa. Couple that with the results of colonial exploitation over the past five centuries, and Africa, despite many strengths and resources, is once again in need, as it was 70,000 years ago. This time, though, things are different.

The world population that was spawned in Africa now has the power to save it. We are all alive today because of what happened to a small group of hungry Africans around 50,000 years ago. As their good sons and daughters, those of us who left, whether long ago or more recently, surely have a moral imperative to use our gifts to support our cousins who stayed. It's the least we can do for the continent that saved us all thousands of years ago.

Mapping *the* Past

ADAM GOODHEART

Ancestors have always been hard to keep track of. We all have them, of course, but most of us can trace our families back only four or five generations. Even the oldest lineages are fairly new on the grand scale of human history; Prince Charles, with his 262,142 recorded ancestors, has a family tree little more than 1,500 years old. (Only one reliable pedigree in the world—that of the Bagratid kings of Georgia—stretches back into classical antiquity, petering out in 326 B.C.) "As each of us looks back into his or her past," wrote E. M. Forster, "doors open upon darkness."

Writing in 1939, Forster was arguing the futility of ever tracing the genetic history of a nation. Indeed, if ancestral accounts are muddled and incomplete at the level of individual families, the genealogies of entire nations and peoples are impossibly confused. Historians who refer to "the Irish" or "the Jews" as though they were well-defined groups have only the vaguest idea of their origins, of how they fit into the family tree of the human race. And when it comes to the origins and fate of long-vanished peoples like the ancient Egyptians, the darkness is almost complete. "A common language, a common religion, a common culture all belong to the present, evidence about them is available, they can be tested," Forster wrote. "But race belongs to the unknown and unknowable past. It depends upon who went to bed with whom in the year 1400 . . . and what historian will ever discover that?"

Yet scientists are now discovering just that—not just who went to bed with whom in 1400, but an entire family history of our species stretching far into the past. It's in an archive we've been carrying with us all along: the coiled molecules of our DNA. "Everybody alive today is a living fossil who contains their own evolutionary history within themselves," says Steve Jones, head of the genetics department at University College, London. Genetics has recently made headlines with the pronouncements of scientists looking ahead, toward medical breakthroughs and moral dilemmas. A far less publicized group of geneticists is looking backward, using new technology to analyze deoxyribonucleic acid, molecule by molecule—and trace the migrations, conquests, expansions and extinctions of ancient peoples.

Using new genetic techniques, scientists are solving the ancient mysteries of mankind's origins and migrations.

Genes are often described as a blueprint. That's only a partial analogy. For besides its role in mapping out the makeup of our bodies (and perhaps our personalities), DNA serves as an internal archive handed down from generation to generation. Every individual's genetic code, though unique, contains sequences that have been passed down from parent to child, not just since the beginning of human history, but reaching back over a billion years of evolution.

Picture the human genome, then, not as a blueprint but as an elaborate medieval coat of arms, perhaps the family crest of some inbred princeling of the Holy Roman Empire. To most people, such a heraldic device would look like a mass of meaningless symbols: dots, bars and crosshatchings, rampant lions quartered with screaming eagles. But an expert in heraldry could read in it an entire family history, tracing the prince's forebears as they married Hapsburgs, fathered bastards, conquered duchies, far back through time. Similarly, the genome looks like gibberish: an endless repetition of four chemicals, represented by the letters *A, C, G* and *T.* But geneticists are beginning to recognize sequences that identify specific human lineages, and are using them to reconstruct the family history of the species. Recent technology is also enabling them to unearth fragments of DNA from the remains of our long-dead ancestors. Using these two approaches, one scientist says, researchers are undertaking "the greatest archaeological excavation in history."

Ever since early explorers of the new world announced that they had discovered the lost tribes of Israel, the origin of the Native Americans has been the subject of intense debate. Experts now agree that the Indians' ancestors crossed into Alaska over a land bridge from Siberia. Yet no one knows exactly when or how. Even the vaguest legends of that time have been long forgotten, and the land that the hunters crossed, with whatever faint traces their passage left, is hidden beneath the waters of the North Pacific.

Far to the south, Connie Kolman was following the ancient immigrants' track when she drove out into western Panama in the fall of 1991. A molecular biologist with the Smithsonian Institute, Kolman was conducting a study of the genes of some of the New World's most ancient populations. Archaeologists had known for many years that despite Panama's location on a narrow causeway between two continents, many of the tribes who lived there had been isolated from outsiders for many millenniums—perhaps almost since their hunter-gatherer ancestors arrived.

Kolman's scientific team set up their equipment in the small cinder-block schoolhouse that served an entire community of Ngöbé Indian farmers. Just past dawn, the Ngöbé started to arrive: dozens of them, coming down over the hillsides in single file, the traditional ruffled dresses of the women and girls standing out in vivid reds and purples against the tall grass. As the Indians gathered, the visitors explained their mission and asked for volunteers. A medic collected a small vial of blood from each Indian's arm. Over the next few months, back at their lab in Panama City, Kolman and her colleague Eldredge Bermingham broke down the blood cells in the samples and decoded the ancient historical text that they contained. The text, it turned out, read something like this: TGGGGAGCAC- GCTGGC . . .

Genetic historians have begun to read the vast archive in our DNA directly, molecule by molecule.

The work that genetic historians like Connie Kolman have started to do—reading the DNA archive directly, molecule by molecule—relies on technology that is little more than 10 years old, so their conclusions are often controversial. Like medievalists poring over a newly unearthed manuscript, geneticists argue about every fresh interpretation, every cryptic passage and variant reading.

By the mid-1980s, scientists had begun to identify the specific genetic markers common to all Native Americans, which are similar to sequences found in present-day Asians, as one would expect. What was surprising, however, was that American Indians seemed to be divided into three distinct genetic groups. One lineage included most of the native tribes of North and South America, from northern Canada down to Patagonia. Another comprised the Eskimo and Aleut peoples of the far north. The third group included a number of tribes in northwestern Canada, as well as the Navajos and Apaches of the southwestern United States. These genetic lines corresponded with the three major Indian linguistic groups.

Some scientists, particularly a group from Emory University, have suggested that several different waves of migration crossed the Bering land bridge at different times, not the single migration most scientists envisioned. And in order to account for the genetic differences among modern Indians, these researchers maintain, their ancestors must have begun to arrive around 27,000 B.C.—more than twice as long ago as most archaeologists believe. That would mean that humans were living in North America even before the last ice age, in the days when Neanderthals and woolly rhinoceros still roamed the European continent. "Another migration about 9,000 to 10,000 years ago . . . into northwestern North America gave us the Na-Dene speaking peoples, who about 1,000 years ago went down to become the Apaches and the Navajo," says Douglas Wallace, head of the genetics department at Emory. "Finally, there was a recent migration out of Siberia to the northern part of America that gave us the Eskimos and Aleuts."

Could such a radically new version of American history be correct? This is what Kolman hoped to learn from the Ngöbé

blood samples. Her research turned up an unanticipated answer: The same kind of separation that existed among the three major Indian genetic groups also divided the Ngöbé from neighboring tribes in Panama. Yet archaeological evidence showed it was impossible that the Panamanian Indians had come over the land bridge in more than one migration. Therefore, she concluded, the genetic difference between Indian groups is the result of their separation from one another over the centuries after their arrival in the New World. Based on her own research, she says, "there doesn't appear to be any support for three waves of migration." The most likely scenario, Kolman argues, is that all of today's Native Americans, from Canada to Patagonia, are the descendants of one hardy group of prehistoric pioneers. In fact, researchers have pinpointed a region of Mongolia where the genetic patterns are similar to those of all three major Indian groups. Some modern Mongolians, then, appear to be remnants of the same population that settled the New World.

Slowly but surely, researchers like Kolman are rewriting history. In the Pacific, scientists are tracing the genetic trail left by the ancient mariners who settled Polynesia, finding evidence of a journey that began in Southeast Asia nearly 4,000 years ago—and sinking for good the widely publicized theories of Thor Heyerdahl, who sailed the balsa raft *Kon-Tiki* from Peru to the Tuamotu Archipelago to "prove" that American Indians had settled the Pacific. And in disproving Heyerdahl, the geneticists have found evidence of the Polynesians' traditional sagas, which speak of their ancestors' frequent voyages between Hawaii and Tahiti in huge oceangoing canoes. "Archaeologists kept saying it was impossible, that it was just a story people told," says Rebecca Cann, a geneticist at the University of Hawaii. "But by doing a very fine analysis of the DNA, we've seen that there is in fact one very common cosmopolitan lineage that's spread throughout the Pacific, [which] could only have happened if people were in constant physical contact. The idea that these islands were so isolated is really a foreign invention. The Polynesians used the ocean as a superhighway."

The great archaeological dig into the human genome began in the villages of northern Italy. In the 1950s, a young Italian geneticist named Luigi Luca Cavalli-Sforza traveled among the towns near Parma, taking blood samples in the sacristies of parish churches after Sunday Mass. He began with the prosperous communities in the river valley, then worked his way up into the smaller towns in the hills until he reached the mountain villages with 100 or fewer inhabitants. As he gathered blood samples, Cavalli-Sforza also began another investigation that, for a geneticist at least, was quite unorthodox: He pored over the parishes' manuscript books of births, marriages and deaths, records dating as far back as the 1500s.

Cavalli-Sforza was investigating the theory of genetic drift, which had never been conclusively proved. Genetic drift proposes that Charles Darwin's law of "survival of the fittest" doesn't suffice to explain all the differences among species, or among peoples. Certain changes just happen naturally over time, independent of the mechanisms of natural section—especially when populations are isolated from one another for many generations. Sometimes the changes can be quite noticeable, as in the case of remote Alpine valleys where many of the inhabitants are albinos. But more typically the effects of genetic drift are neutral and invisible: For instance, the people in an isolated region will have high percentages of an uncommon blood type. Barring extensive marriage with outsiders, every population will develop a distinctive genetic profile. (This is the same phenomenon that Connie Kolman found among the Panamanian Indians.)

In the 1950s, of course, the technology didn't exist that would allow Cavalli-Sforza to read the DNA directly. But he was able to test for blood type, and what he found confirmed the presence of genetic drift. In the large valley towns, where the parish books recorded many marriages with people from different communities, the blood-group profile was typical of that entire region of Italy. But as Cavalli-Sforza moved up into the small, isolated mountain villages, the genetic "distances" between the various settlements increased. The longer a population had been isolated, the more it differed from its neighbors. If the principle worked for villages in Italy, why shouldn't it work for the rest of the world? "My supposition was this: if enough data on a number of different genes are gathered, we may eventually be able to reconstruct the history of the entire human species," Cavalli-Sforza later wrote. And so he embarked on a decades-long project to study thousands of gene markers in hundreds of indigenous peoples around the world.

Of course, scientists had tried before to establish the relationships among the world's populations, often using methods that they claimed were based on strict Darwinian science. They traveled the world with calipers and charts, measuring the bone structure and skin color of the "natives." (One Victorian geneticist even created a "beauty map" of Britain, grading the women of various regions on a scale of 1 to 5. The low point was Aberdeen.) If you trusted such findings, the Australian aborigines, with their dark skin and flat noses, were closely related to sub-Saharan Africans. Cavalli-Sforza didn't believe it. Those visible similarities, he reasoned, might just be the result of similar adaptation to hot climates. To gauge relationships accurately, one had to measure factors that were genetically neutral, immune to the mechanisms of natural selection.

Genetically, each of us represents not only ourself but, in a certain sense, all of our ancestors.

One of the most elegant aspects of Cavalli-Sforza's approach is that there is no need to sample huge numbers of people in each group under examination. Genetically, after all, each of us represents not only ourself but all of our ancestors. (Long before genome mapping, Henry Adams explained this principle quite well. "If we could go back and live again in all of our two hundred and fifty million arithmetical ancestors of the eleventh

century," he wrote, speaking of those with Norman blood, "we should find ourselves . . . ploughing most of the fields of the Cotentin and Calvados; going to mass in every parish church in Normandy; [and] rendering military service to every lord, spiritual or temporal, in all this region.")

In 1994, Cavalli-Sforza, along with Paolo Menozzi and Alberto Piazza, published his magnum opus, *The History and Geography of Human Genes*—a sort of combination atlas and family tree. Cavalli-Sforza's genealogy places Africans at the root of the tree, with the Europeans and Asians branching off from them, and American Indians branching off in turn from the Asians. He finds the genetic traces of the Mongol invasions of China, the Bantus' sweep across Africa and the Arabs' spread through the Middle East under the successors of Muhammad.

In his analysis of Europe's genetic landscape, Cavalli-Sforza has shaken the foundations of conventional history. Nine thousand years ago, a technological and cultural revolution swept Europe. From the Balkans to Britain, forests sparsely dotted with the campfires of hunter-gatherers gave way to a patchwork of cultivated fields and burgeoning settlements. In the course of a few thousand years, as the practice of agriculture spread from southeast to northwest, Europeans abandoned the way of life they had led for tens of thousands of years. That much is agreed upon. But Cavalli-Sforza suggests that the agricultural revolution was a genetic revolution as well. It wasn't merely that the Europeans gradually learned about farming from their neighbors to the southeast. Instead, the Middle Eastern farmers actually migrated across Europe, replacing the existing population. This wasn't a case of prehistoric genocide, Cavalli-Sforza emphasizes: The farmers simply multiplied far more rapidly than the hunters, and, as they sought new land to cultivate, they pushed their frontiers to the northwest.

Today's Europeans, Cavalli-Sforza argues, are almost wholly the descendants of these interlopers—with the exception of the Basques, whose gene patterns are so anomalous that he believes they are the last close relatives of the Cro-Magnon hunters. Furthermore, Cavalli-Sforza believes, there was a *second* genetic invasion of Europe around 4000 B.C.—this time from the steppes of Central Asia. His maps show that an important component of the European gene pool spreads out from the area north of the Black Sea like ripples in a pond. Cavalli-Sforza connects this to a controversial archaeological theory: the idea that nomadic herdsmen swept in from the east, bringing with them domesticated horses, bronze weapons and the Indo-European language that would become the basis for all major European tongues.

Cavalli-Sforza's ideas have drawn criticism as well as praise. "All genetic data has a time depth of one generation back from the past," says Erik Trinkaus, an anthropologist at the University of New Mexico: Cavalli-Sforza's maps only prove that present-day Europeans demonstrate genetic divergences that occurred at some point in the past. All the rest is interpretation. Some scholars have argued that these patterns could be explained by more recent migrations, such as the barbarian invasions that toppled the Roman Empire. Even Alberto Piazza, who collaborated with

Cavalli-Sforza, admits that "it's important to try to get the dates. If we find that we're talking about 6,000 or 7,000 years ago, as we believe, then it's justifiable to say that we're talking about Indo-Europeans. But if we discover instead that the dates are more recent—2,000 or 3,000 years ago—we could be talking about the Huns."

What was needed, obviously, was a more direct route into the past. As it happened, by the time Cavalli-Sforza's genetic atlas appeared, scientists were already starting to catch glimpses of the DNA in our ancestors' cells.

Since the 19th century, scientists have been studying fossils to reconstruct our past. But there was no evidence to tell them definitely whether these represented our direct ancestors or were merely dead branches on the family tree. So scientists did the logical thing: They arranged them with the oldest and most dissimilar hominids first, leading up to the most recent and close-to-human types. It was a convenient time line, familiar from textbook illustrations and museum dioramas. And then came Eve.

She debuted before the world in the winter of 1988: a naked woman holding an apple on the cover of *Newsweek*. The article explained that a team of biochemists at Berkeley had discovered the single female ancestor of the entire human race. The scientists, led by Rebecca Cann, had done so by looking at the DNA found in a specific part of the cell called the mitochondria. Unlike other DNA, mitochondrial DNA isn't a combination of both parents' genes; it is inherited only from the mother. This means that the only changes to the mitochondrial genes, as they pass from generation to generation, are occasional mutations. By calculating the rate of these mutations, and comparing the mitochondrial DNA of people from around the world, the Berkeley researchers had come up with a surprisingly young common ancestress: Eve, as the scientists dubbed her, was only 200,000 years old. "Genetically speaking," writes James Shreeve in *The Neanderthal Enigma*, "there was not all that much difference between a [modern] New Guinean highlander, a South African !Kung tribeswoman, and a housewife from the Marin County hills. . . . Whatever appearances might suggest, they simply hadn't had time enough to diverge."

The Eve discovery shocked evolutionary historians. It meant the hominids that spread out of Africa 1.2 million years ago were not modern humans' direct ancestors. Instead they and their descendants had been supplanted by a far more recent out-of-Africa migration—perhaps only 100,000 years ago. That would mean that all the old standbys of the museum diorama—Peking Man, Java Man, Neanderthal Man—were evolutionary dead ends.

Not surprisingly, traditional paleontologists have attacked Eve with vigor, arguing that Cann's sample was skewed, her computer program flawed, and that even if all humans share a recent female ancestor, it doesn't mean there weren't other contributions to our gene pool. Eve's partisans counterattacked: A number of independent researchers have looked at different parts of the DNA and arrived at similar dates for our divergence from a common ancestor. Last fall, a geneticist at the University of Arizona claimed to have found a common male ancestor who lived 188,000 years ago.

Now scientists are tying to resolve the Eve debate by looking in the most logical place of all: ancient DNA. "If we had even one Neanderthal DNA sample we could be sure of, it would quickly emerge how closely related it was to modern *Homo sapiens,*" says Sir Walter Bodmer, former president of the Human Genome Organisation. Just a few years ago, the idea of finding a sample of Neanderthal DNA would have seemed about as probable as the idea of finding a live Neanderthal living deep in some cave, since scientists believed that the fragile DNA molecule decayed rapidly after death. But now geneticist are reading DNA recovered from ancient human remains. Despite skepticism from many scientists, their results are winning acceptance.

In 1984, a group of Berkeley scientists announced that they had sequenced the DNA of a quagga, an African animal, similar to the zebra, that was hunted to extinction in the late 19th century. They had accomplished this using the polymerase chain reaction (PCR), a chemical method for amplifying tiny DNA sequences. This is the same technique that scientists like Cann and Kolman use on fresh DNA from blood samples; the Berkeley team simply applied it to a fragment of quagga skin that was preserved in a German museum.

Quickly, other researchers began applying PCR to ancient specimens—and reporting spectacular results. Scientists claimed to have cloned DNA from Egyptian mummies, woolly mammoths, even a 120-million-year-old weevil trapped in amber, à la *Jurassic Park*. There was only one problem: The PCR process is extremely vulnerable to contamination, so nearly all these results turned out to be false—the mammoth's DNA, for instance, was that of a lab technician.

However, a few ancient-DNA laboratories have started to produce credible and verifiable work. Last year, two labs independently sequenced genes from the Ice Man, the Stone Age hunter whose frozen body was found high in the Italian Alps in 1991, and both arrived at the same results. Many of the best samples, oddly enough, have come from bones and teeth. "Now people generally accept that you can get DNA from hard tissues," says Oxford geneticist Bryan Sykes, who is generally considered one of the most careful ancient-DNA researchers. "I suppose the oldest we've ever got to was about 15,000 years—that was for some animal bones from a limestone cave in England. But I think most people wouldn't be too surprised if one were to report recovery of DNA from well-preserved bone up to maybe even 100,000 years ago."

That implies that Neanderthal DNA should be waiting to be discovered in the collections of museums around the world. The treasure hunt is now in full swing. No lab yet claims publicly to have sequenced Neanderthal genes (although Sykes, when asked if he has obtained results, hesitates and replies, "Nothing I could reveal to you"). "It's only a matter of time," says Andrew Merriwether of the University of Pittsburgh, who is looking for Neanderthal DNA in some 35,000-year-old teeth from a Croatian cave. "There are a lot of Neanderthal remains around."

Once the treasure hunters find their quarry, they'll use it to put the Eve hypothesis to a powerful test. And that's not all they'll learn. "One particularly burning question just begs to be answered," writes Walter Bodmer in *The Book of Man*. "Exactly what evolutionary advantage did *Homo sapiens* have over this hominid competitors, and in particular over our nearest evolutionary brothers and sisters, the Neanderthals? What genetic gifts made *Homo sapiens* so special and allowed us to inherit the Earth, while other hominids conspicuously failed?"

In the meantime, scientists are using more recent ancient DNA to answer less profound questions. Scott Woodward of Brigham Young University is working with the royal mummies of Egypt's 18th dynasty, trying to chart the pharaohs' complex family tree. Sykes is using Neolithic bones from Europe to test Cavalli-Sforza's ideas about the spread of agriculture. Merriwether and Kolman are comparing DNA from ancient American specimens with that of modern Indians, hoping to resolve conclusively the history of the peopling of the New World.

Ancient DNA may allow scientists to establish a continuum from very early times to the present.

Scientists hope that, bit by bit, ancient DNA samples will allow them to interpret more accurately the history encoded in modern genes. "What ancient DNA will allow us to do is establish a continuum from very early times up to the present," says Woodward. "Right now, all we can look at is a single snapshot. If we go back to 500 years ago, 1,000 years ago, 1,500 years ago, it will give us snapshots of the past. And as we fill in the gaps, soon there will be a motion picture and we'll be able to watch history unfold."

Southwest of Cairo, on the edge of the great Fayum oasis, the desert sand teems with thousands upon thousands of graves. Here ancient Egyptians buried their dead, the bodies wrapped in linen cloth, with only a few possessions—a reed mat, a cup, a loaf of bread—to accompany them into the afterlife. For these were common folk, and although they lived in the shadow of the pyramids, the age of the pharaohs was already past. The Fayum cemetery was in use from the middle of the first millennium B.C. to the middle of the first millennium A.D., during the period of Greek and Roman dominion over Egypt.

Still, Scott Woodward is unearthing treasure from the simple burials: clues to the identity of the Egyptian, and to the spread of Christianity. The cemetery's history spans the time when the Egyptians abandoned paganism for the new faith, and the graves reflect the change. Until late in the first century A.D., the dead were buried facing west. Then, suddenly, they were oriented facing east—reflecting the Christian belief that the resurrected Christ would return from the east, according to Woodward and

his collaborators. Woodward is analyzing the bodies' DNA to find out just who these early Christians were—native converts or immigrants. "We're [also] trying to answer the question of how much sub-Saharan African influence there was in the ancient Egyptians," Woodward says. "Egypt was probably a very cosmopolitan place, as much of a melting pot as the United States is today. . . . My guess is that we'll see African, we'll see Asian, we'll see Caucasian markers." In time, he says, it will be possible to get a genetic picture of the entire population of the cemetery.

So far, Woodward only has results from a half-dozen burials, none of which shows the typically African DNA marker. Even so, his investigation suggests how DNA research can confirm or question disputes over the identity of a particular people, like the modern Coptic Christians, who claim that they are the sole descendants of the ancient Egyptians, or those of sub-Saharan African origin, especially in the United States, who derive ethnic pride from the theory that the pharaohs were black.

Sometimes, such research can turn up unwelcome results. "Judaism is without doubt the most genetic of all religions—it depends on descent," says Steve Jones. "Orthodox Jews are very much of the opinion that Judaism is a huge pedigree of individuals who descend from Abraham." Yet studies of Jewish DNA indicate extensive mixing with outsiders. The Yemenite Jews, Jones notes, who have been accepted without question into Israeli society, appear to be almost entirely the descendants of Arab converts. Meanwhile, members of the black Lemba tribe of South Africa, who claim to be one of the lost tribes of Israel, have never been accepted as Jews. But their genes, Jones says, seem to support their claim: They show patterns typical of Middle Eastern origin.

"The genome pushes us to redefine ourselves," says Howard University immunogeneticist Georgia Dunston. Dunston plans a major genetic study to trace the origins of American blacks back to the lands from which their ancestors were taken. "At this point in the history of African-Americans, we are seeking to make connections to roots that extend beyond slavery," she says.

Our genes cannot wholly account for our diversity. In fact, the work of genetic historians would be far easier were it not for the fact that the peoples of the world are so similar under the skin. "It is because they are external that . . . racial differences strike us so forcibly, and we automatically assume that differences of similar magnitude exist below the surface, in the rest of our genetic makeup," Cavalli-Sforza has written. "This is simply not so: the remainder of our genetic makeup hardly differs at all." Indeed, research has shown that culture usually drives the spread of genes and not vice versa. "In the history of human development," Cavalli-Sforza says, "whenever there has been a major expansion geographically or demographically, it has been because one people has had an increase in food or power or transportation. . . . Whenever I see an expansion, I start looking for the innovation that made it." The invention of agriculture or the wheel makes history; genes only reflect it.

13

Even so, the story that the genes' tiny gradations tells is altering the way we think about the past. "Genetics changed something fundamental about our view of history," says Jones. "It shows us that history is largely the story of love, not war." The genetic historians suggest that it's time we started asking, with E. M. Forster: Who *did* go to bed with whom in the year 1400? And as we consider the possibilities—a Mongol chieftain and his Chinese bride, say; an Aztec woman and her husband; a fumbling pair of teenagers on a French hillside—it is pleasing to think that those ancient acts of love left their mark somewhere within each of us.

ADAM GOODHEART, an associate editor at *Civilization* and author of its Lost Arts column, has also written for *The New York Times, The Washington Post* and other publications.

First Americans

Not long ago we thought the first humans in the New World were mammoth hunters from Siberia who crossed the Bering Strait at the end of the Ice Age. Now, we are learning, none of that may be true—not the *who,* not the *where,* not the *how,* and certainly not the *when.*

KAREN WRIGHT

You don't expect someone who has been dead for more than 9,000 years to have any odor left—let alone a strong one. But you don't expect him to have any hair or skin or clothes left, either, and Spirit Cave Man has all of those: long, soft brown hair, gray skin the texture of parchment, shoes crafted from animal hide and lined with bulrushes. Though little of his flesh remains, his smell—a musty, thick sweetness that clings to the back of your throat—is wholly intact.

On the day I visited Spirit Cave Man, in a museum laboratory on the outskirts of Carson City, Nevada, that smell served as a pungent reminder that I was not inspecting just another Paleo-Indian artifact, a spearpoint or a pendant or a stone-flaking tool. I was in the presence of a human being whose story, along with that of his ancestors, is as intriguing as his mummified remains—and so far, just as incomplete.

Spirit Cave Man is one of a dozen or so early Americans who are helping rewrite the prehistory of human habitation in the New World. A small cohort of skeletons and skull fragments up to 11,500 years in age, they are the oldest human remains known in North and South America. While some of these individuals, like Washington State's notorious Kennewick Man, are new finds, most were discovered decades ago and were preserved in museum collections. Only in the last few years, however, have anthropologists made a systematic effort to determine the antiquity and ancestry of these remains.

When Spirit Cave Man was unearthed in 1940 from a dry rock-shelter in western Nevada, his discoverers assumed that he had been buried a couple of thousand years ago at most. But in 1994 radiocarbon dating of his bones and hair put his age closer to 9,400 years. That was a big surprise, but his way of life—and suspected ancestry-proved even more surprising.

"The traditional textbook interpretation has the first human populations coming over into the New World about 11,500 years ago," says Doug Owsley, a physical anthropologist at the National Museum of Natural History in Washington, D.C. At that time low sea levels had exposed a land bridge between Siberia and Alaska, where the Bering Strait now lies, and Ice Age

glaciers were just beginning to melt. The first Americans, the story goes, trekked across the Bering land bridge from the Old World into the New in search of happier hunting grounds, then made their way south between retreating sheets of ice. "When you think of this time period, you imagine those people running around chasing big game, wearing skins, throwing spears, looking like today's Siberians," says Owsley. "That probably isn't true."

For Spirit Cave Man, it certainly isn't true: not the skins, not the spears, and not the modern Siberian looks. He did not wear primitive skin clothing; instead he wore a carefully constructed blanket woven from thin, twisted strips of rabbit pelt and cords of hemp. The contents of his abdominal cavity reveal that he last dined on fish, not game; apparently he gleaned his meals from netting fish in the marshes that once filled desert basins, rather than from grueling hunts on the plains.

And Spirit Cave Man doesn't look like the Siberians of today, either. From the shape of his skull, it's clear that he had a longer, narrower head, flatter cheekbones, and a more prominent chin than those typical of both northern Asians and Native Americans today. In fact, in recent analyses of some ten early American skulls, anthropologists have found just two individuals who could pass as kin of either contemporary northern Asians or Native Americans.

But Spirit Cave Man and his contemporaries aren't the only ones challenging old textbook scenarios. In 1997 a renegade archeologist published convincing evidence of human occupation in southern Chile that predates by a thousand years any well-established site in North America—in particular, the site in Clovis, New Mexico, that has long been the oldest undisputed human settlement this side of the Pacific. Other recent archeological findings hint that the first Americans may have arrived by sea rather than by land. Studies of Native American genes suggest that people have called the New World home for 20,000 years or longer—maybe much longer. And archeologists working in North and South America claim to have found signs of these proto-pioneers. In light of new lines of evidence, the traditional model of the peopling of the Americas, a tale as simple and satisfying as any Native American creation story, seems just about as likely.

The Models that describe the migration into the New World used to be based on relatively simple evidence—sites, spear-points, and soil layers, like the ones at Clovis. Because of researchers' respect for the sanctity of human remains, skeletons generally weren't tampered with. But recent techniques for radiocarbon dating allow researchers to retrieve age estimates from minuscule samples of organic material—like human bones—without doing much damage. And personal computers enable anthropologists to perform mathematically sophisticated quantitative comparisons of skull shapes among different populations. Unlike physical traits such as height and vigor, skull shape is distinctive, highly heritable, and mostly impervious to environmental influences such as diet. Hence these comparisons, known as craniometric analyses, could be used to trace a population's ancestry.

A second impetus for dating early American remains was not technological but political. In 1990, Congress enacted the Native American Graves Protection and Repatriation Act in response to long-standing concerns over the treatment of Native American remains and artifacts. This legislation required museums and universities to return to the affiliated Native American tribes any relevant materials—including thousands of poorly identified skeletons—that had been found on federal land.

For remains of recent vintage (which the vast majority are), tribal affiliations can usually be deduced from the locations of burial sites, historical records, and physical examination. If the provenance of a skeleton isn't clear, museums call in Owsley and his colleague Richard Jantz of the University of Tennessee in Knoxville. Owsley and Jantz have spent 20 years compiling a database of craniometric profiles of modern Native American tribes in the Great Plains, Great Basin, and Southwest regions of the United States. By comparing the dimensions of a given skull—some 90 measurements per skull—with these profiles, they can often tell which people the departed most resembles, whom, in effect, he is ancestor to.

But when Owsley and Jantz examined some of the oldest North American remains, the skulls didn't provide the kinship clues they expected. Measurements from Spirit Cave Man and two Minnesota skulls—one 7,900 and the other 8,700 years old—were off the charts. "We were impressed with how different the older skulls are from any of the modern-day groups," says Owsley. "They do not have the broad faces, they do not have the big, prominent cheekbones that you think of as the more traditional features of the Chinese and American Indians." Instead they looked more like the inhabitants of, say, Indonesia, or even Europe.

Owsley and Jantz weren't the first to notice this discrepancy. In the early 1990s anthropologists Gentry Steele of Texas A&M University and Joseph Powell of the University of New Mexico at Albuquerque had collected craniometric data from four North American skulls between 8,000 and 9,700 years old. They found the same puzzling differences between those subjects and modern Native Americans, the same puzzling affinities

with southern Asians rather than northern Asians. A survey of prehistoric South Americans by anthropologist Walter Neves of the University of Sao Paolo yielded similar findings. Then Kennewick Man appeared in an eroded bank of the Columbia River. Based on his facial features, he was identified as a nineteenth-century European trapper until a CT scan revealed an ancient spearpoint embedded in his hip.

"I began to feel that what we were seeing was definitely not just sampling error," says Steele. And last year Neves reported that the oldest American, an 11,500-year-old skeleton from central Brazil, also shares the appearance of southern Asians and Australians.

But the fact is, most prehistoric Americans don't really look like anyone alive today, and they don't all look like each other, either. According to Owsley, Spirit Cave Man's closest match might be found among the Ainu, the indigenous people of Japan. But Kennewick Man has been likened to the ultra-Caucasoid British actor Patrick Stewart. And there are a couple of prehistoric Americans whose features actually do resemble those of modern Native Americans. One is Buhl Woman, a 10,700-year-old Idaho skeleton that was reburied in 1992. Another is 9,200-year-old Wizards Beach Man, whose remains were found in Nevada less than 100 miles to the northwest of Spirit Cave Man's rock-shelter. It seems that thousands of years before the arrival of Columbus, America was already something of a melting pot.

Needless to say, the variability among Paleo-Indian remains raises some interesting questions. Where did these people with the distinctively long heads and narrow faces come from? And if they aren't the ancestors of modern Native Americans, what happened to them? In the past few years, some anthropologists have come up with the following model: The founding populations of first Americans came from somewhere in Asia more than 8,000 years ago. They were small bands of hunter-gatherers, a few dozen strong at most, who followed the Bering land bridge in search of food and established scattered outposts in the New World. The "modern looking" or "roundheaded" northeast Asian face, by contrast, is probably evidence of fairly recent immigration from Korea or China into Siberia around 8,000 years ago. Eventually these populations expanded into the Americas or began infiltrating in greater numbers than they had before. With the waves of new immigrants, some of the earlier arrivals were wiped out, others assimilated.

"They could've made war or they could've made love," says Steele. "They probably did both." Either way, their influence on subsequent generations waned.

This patchwork colonization would explain some of the discrepancies in skull shapes. Unfortunately, that scenario may account for only the last third or so of the actual human habitation of the New World. There is evidence of far earlier immigration into the Americas, and it doesn't come from skulls.

Southern Chile is home to an extraordinary archeological site called Monte Verde. Excavated by Tom Dillehay of the University of Kentucky at Lexington, the Monte Verde artifacts include hundreds of stone tools; bone, wood, and ivory implements; food caches of leaves, seeds, nuts, fruits, crayfish bones; the butchered remains of birds, an extinct form of camel, and a mastodon; the remnants of huts and hearths; and even a child's footprint. Dillehay's exhaustive documentation of the site has in the past few years convinced most archeologists that humans set up camp in the nether regions of South America some 12,500 years ago. Monte Verde is roughly 10,000 miles from the Bering Strait. "People obviously didn't walk there overnight," says Owsley.

Genetic analyses have even provided an estimated time of arrival for pre-Clovis immigrants. Nearly all Native American groups carry one of four distinct DNA lineages in cellular structures called mitochondria. These mtDNA lineages vary somewhat among tribes, and though they are similar to lineages found in the populations of Asia and Siberia, they bear signatures that are unique to the New World natives. Genes diversify at a predictable rate—mtDNA changes between 2 and 3 percent every million years. So genetic differences between populations provide a gauge of how long they have been apart—the theory being that the more variation you find between two groups, the longer they've been apart. In the mid-1990s Theodore Schurr, a molecular anthropologist at Emory University in Atlanta, compared the genetic variation among new-world natives with the variation between them and their old-world kin. He calculated that 20,000 to 40,000 years had elapsed since new-world and old-world groups shared a common ancestor.

Schurr's results support the notion of pre-Clovis settlement of the New World. But they conflict with the melting-pot scenario. Only four mtDNA lineages characterize over 95 percent of all modern Native American populations. That implies a relatively limited number of founding groups from Asia spreading over a vast geographic area. Indeed, some geneticists, including Andrew Merriwether of the University of Michigan, have used the mtDNA data to argue that there was but one founding population for all living Native American tribes after all.

Many different peoples may have colonized the Americas, with only one ethnic subset surviving. It's also possible, though unlikely, that the diversity in skull shapes conceals an underlying kinship.

But Schurr's findings do not rule out the possibility of physical diversity among the ancient Americans. It could be that many different peoples colonized the Americas but were winnowed out over time, leaving only one ethnic subset of survivors. Perhaps those with the anomalous longish skulls were vanquished by disease, famine, or pestilence; or perhaps the balance of lovemaking to warmaking was tipped in favor of war, and the broad-faced, rounder-headed group always won. It's also possible, though unlikely, that the diversity in skull shapes conceals an underlying kinship: perhaps both skull types existed within the same tribe. To resolve this issue, researchers would have to do both craniometric and genetic analyses on the same ancient remains. So far no one has.

In any event, subsequent mtDNA studies may support the notion that some of the genes of these vanished predecessors worked their way into the Native American bloodlines. In the past few years a fifth mtDNA lineage, called X, has turned up both in living Native American groups and in prehistoric remains. Though variants of the first four mtDNA lineages have been found in Siberian, Mongolian, and Tibetan populations, the origins of the X lineage are downright mysterious. "It doesn't seem to appear in any East Asian or North Asian populations—which are the putative progenitors, or at least the potential sister groups, of the Native Americans," says Schurr. "The source area for the X lineage is not clear, but it doesn't appear to be Asia." In fact, the first variant of X mtDNA was identified in Europeans. Schurr speculates that the X lineage originated somewhere in Eurasia, with its carriers then going their separate ways: some west in the Old World, some east all the way to the New.

Schurr's evidence for prolonged human presence in the New World is provocative but lamentably indirect. It would be nice if the data were backed up by some hard physical evidence like tools or human bone. In the Old World, signs of habitation by modern humans go back at least 40,000 and possibly 100,000 years. Why does the New World record stop at a paltry 12,500?

One reason may be that, before 12,000 years ago, immigrants from Asia arrived in fits and starts. "It probably wasn't like a continuous highway of people moving in," Dillehay says. "They were probably very few and far between, leaving tiny little specks of activity on the earth, the equivalent of your going out and having a family picnic somewhere and hauling most of your garbage away." These transients had what Dillehay calls "low archeological visibility: a fiber-wood-skin-hide kind of material culture. The chances of finding those earliest traces are minimal, I would think."

Yet Dillehay thinks he may have found such traces in a second excavation at Monte Verde. On a promontory overlooking what used to be a lagoon, 200 feet from his 12,500-year-old village, Dillehay named up what appears to be an even more ancient settlement. He found old charcoal, a suite of stone tools, and clay-lined pits that could be hearths—all buried six feet deep in a soil layer more than 30,000 years old. "In terms of strict empirical evidence, as scant as it is, it's hard to reject," he says. Still, Dillehay wants to explore the site more thoroughly before he makes any definitive statements. "It's very hard to step out there on the plank and say, 'Here's the evidence for people in the Americas at 33,000 years ago,' without anything else in that time range that serves as a strong candidate."

There are other candidates; they just aren't strong ones. A few daring archeologists have staked their reputations on sites they believe are considerably older than Clovis. In light of recent developments, skeptics may reconsider these claims. One site sure to be revisited is the immaculately excavated Meadowcroft Rock-shelter in Pennsylvania; its chief proponent, James Adovasio of Mercyhurst College in Erie, has long contended that Meadowcroft is at least 17,000 years old. Richard MacNeish's Pendejo Cave in New Mexico might also get a closer look. MacNeish, who is at the Andover Foundation for Archeological

Research in Massachusetts, has maintained that the artifacts and human fingerprints in the cave are 30,000 years old or more. In the mid-1980s, French-Brazilian archeologist Niede Guidon published evidence that cave paintings at Pedra Furada in Brazil were 17,000 years old and that stone tools from the site were 32,000 years old. Her findings attracted interest but not much credulity.

Maybe the first Americans came not by land but by sea, hugging the ice-age coast in a wide arc from Fiji to Tierra del Fuego.

One of the biggest barriers to accepting pre-Clovis sites has been geographical. During the last ice age, the New World was pretty much closed to pedestrian traffic. Some 30,000 years ago, the northwest corridor in Canada would have been filled with glacier, and much of the Bering land bridge would also have been covered with ice. Though ancient humans might have mastered the prehistoric crampon, mastodons almost certainly did not, and finding food and shelter under those circumstances would have been difficult at best. But the latest idea circulating among archeologists and anthropologists has people ditching their crampons and spears for skin-covered boats. Maybe the first Americans came not by land but by sea, hugging the ice-age coast in a wide arc from Fiji to Tierra del Fuego.

When the seafaring theory was proposed in the mid-1970s, it sank for lack of evidence. Any shoreline outposts of an ancient maritime culture would probably have been submerged when sea levels rose some 300 feet about 12,000 years ago at the end of the Ice Age. But as the timeline for new-world occupation has changed, the theory seems downright sensible, if not quite provable. The Pacific Rim has vast resources of salmon and sea mammals, and people need only the simplest of tools to exploit them: nets, weirs, clubs, knives. Whereas ancient landlubbers would have had to reinvent their means of hunting, foraging, and housing as they passed through different terrains, ancient mariners could have had smooth sailing through relatively unchanging coastal environments. And recent geologic studies show that even when glaciers stretched down into North America, there were thawed pockets of coastline in northwest North America where people could take refuge and gather provisions. "Most archeologists have a continental mindset," says Robson Bonnichsen, an anthropologist at the Center for the Study of the First Americans at the University of Oregon in Eugene. "But the peopling of the Americas is likely to be tied very much to the development and spread of maritime adaptation."

As for evidence, the situation isn't entirely hopeless. Archeological finds in Australia, Melanesia, and Japan suggest that coastal peoples have used boats for at least 25,000 to 40,000 years and maybe much longer. Indeed, humans could hardly have reached Australia—which they did, 55,000 years ago—without trusty watercraft and navigational skills. In the Americas, however, traces of maritime cultures are much younger than the

proposed time of arrival from 20,000 to 40,000 years. A cave on San Miguel Island, about 25 miles off the coast of California, was inhabited 13,000 years ago, and artifacts retrieved from a roughly 9,000-year-old site near Miami indicate that its occupants were eating reef fish that could only have been caught from seaworthy vessels. Last year, archeologists announced the discovery of two 12,000-year-old sites in coastal Peru whose residents regularly dined on seabirds, clams, and anchovies.

Like Spirit Cave Man, the early Americans suggested by these sites are forcing experts to revise their model of the spear-chucking Clovis types of textbook lore. The possibility of maritime immigration is also turning the model for new-world settlement upside down. According to the new thinking, anyone who paddled across the northern Pacific during the last ice age could have moseyed south along the coast until reaching balmy climes. The newcomers would have colonized Central and South America first, then expanded north on the heels of the glacial retreat. While the archeological evidence for this pattern is still slim, there is another kind of proof that supports it. Johanna Nichols, a linguist at the University of California at Berkeley, has analyzed the 150 language families of the New World, and her work suggests that North American tongues are a subset of South American ones. The languages seem to have formed around the Gulf Coast, Mexico, or the Caribbean and then moved north on the lips of migrating people.

If humans came to the Americas by boat rather than foot, then what was to stop them from crossing the Atlantic, à la Columbus?

There's one more aspect of the seafaring hypothesis, though, that's bothersome: if humans came to the Americas by boat rather than foot, then what was to stop them from crossing the Atlantic, a la Columbus? Dennis Stanford, an archeologist at the Smithsonian Institution, didn't set out to answer that question, but more than two decades of research have led him to pose it. In 1976, Stanford began to look for precursors to the Clovis spearpoints—the weapons that earned early Americans their reputation as mammoth-killing hunters. Named Clovis because of where they were first found, the fluted stone points are in fact scattered throughout North and South America in soil layers up to 11,500 years in age. Stanford wanted to locate the forerunners to this technology to trace the migration patterns of the Clovis culture. He looked in all the obvious places—Canada, Alaska, Siberia—but found nothing.

"I came to the conclusion that Clovis is a new-world invention," he says. Moreover, it seemed that Clovis was an East Coast invention, since many significant—and possibly older—Clovis sites were clustered in the southeastern United States.

Then, several years ago, some unusual spearpoints turned up in a dig 50 miles south of Richmond, Virginia. Preliminary dating suggested that the points could be about 15,000 years old. More intriguing still, they were created using Clovis-like methods but lacked the classic Clovis fluting. Stanford had finally found his Clovis precursors, and they even looked a lot like old-world spearpoints. But the old-world artifacts they most resemble were not from Siberia—they were from Spain. In particular, the Virginia spearpoints resembled stone tools crafted by a people called the Solutreans who lived in western Europe between 24,000 and 16,500 years ago. Stanford has since examined those tools and found striking similarities between them and the stateside ones. The two cultures also share bone-shaping techniques, pebble-decorating artistry, and the unusual habit of burying exquisitely fashioned stone tools in caches filled with red ocher. Last year another pre-Clovis site was discovered on the Savannah River; its artifacts, too, are in the Solutrean vein.

Similarities between Solutrean and Clovis cultures had been noted before but had not been thought worth pursuing. There was simply too much water—and too many centuries—separating the two.

"It's quite possible that a Clovis-like technology developed in Latin America and then spread up around the Gulf Coast and into the southeastern part of the United States," says Stanford. "There's absolutely no evidence to support that, but it's possible. Then there's always the possibility that folks may have been going across the Atlantic Ocean. That would explain Madame X in the gene pool. The question is, how the hell did they get across?"

Stanford speculates that ancient ocean currents might have hastened a transatlantic trip. Or Europeans may have rowed along the edge of an ice bridge that extended from England to Nova Scotia in glacial times, much as seafaring Asians followed the coast of the Bering land bridge. It's not clear that such a journey could succeed, however, without those handy coastal refuges for rest stops. As with so many explanations for the peopling of the Americas, Stanford's research presents more problems than it solves. The first Americans, whoever they were, left a confounding heritage, one that makes even the most modern analytical techniques look primitive.

"How they got here is up in the air completely. When they got here is up in the air completely. And whether they're related to modern Native Americans is up in the air completely," gripes Owsley. The New World may have been settled long ago, but the way it happened is still uncharted territory.

KAREN WRIGHT is a freelance writer and editor. "It seems to me that in archeology, when you lack direct evidence, whoever tells the best story wins," she says. "The best story is often the simplest, like the idea that the first Americans all came across the Bering land bridge 11,000 years ago, or the Native American claim that they've been here forever. The problem archeologists face now is that none of the new stories are simple. Until the dust settles, this question is going to be surrounded by chaos." In the October 1998 *Discover,* Wright reported on the practice of buying and selling body parts and products.

UNIT 2

The Beginnings of Culture, Agriculture, and Cities

Unit Selections

Key Points to Consider

- How has the discovery of the ancient city of Tell Brak forced scientists to rethink how urbanism originated in the Near East?

- Swabia today is a thriving, prosperous area in Germany. Is it possible that its early history and development are responsible for its modern success?

- To what extent was warfare prevalent during the prehistoric era? What proof is offered to support the article's thesis?

- What is the significance of writing for societies? What significance does writing hold for the study of history?

- Was Sumerian society male-dominated or gender-friendly? What proof is offered to support the latter argument?

- Can there be urban life without money as a medium of exchange? Why, or why not?

- What theories have been offered regarding how the Egyptians were able to build pyramids? Which theory offers the most likely explanation?

Student Web Site

www.mhcls.com

Internet References

Civilization of the Olmec
http://loki.stockton.edu/~gilmorew/consorti/1bcenso.htm

Diotima: Women and Gender in the Ancient World
http://www.stoa.org/diotima

Oriental Institute
http://www.etana.org/abzu

Tell Brak Homepage
http://www.learningsites.com/Brak/Tell-Brak_home.html

© Hisham F. Ibrahim/Getty Images

Most of what we take for granted as essential to human flourishing had its beginnings during this time period. As our distant ancestors moved from a hunter-gatherer, nomadic lifestyle to horticulture, the intentional planting and harvesting of plants, and the domestication of animals, rather than the hunt, culture became possible. With this shift came permanent settlements, usually near water, as we see in the Fertile Crescent of Mesopotamia—literally, the place between two rivers, the Tigris and Euphrates. As farmers remained close by to tend crops and raise animals, cities were born, beginning some 10,000 years ago.

Culture arises when people observe the natural environment around them and imagine ways to shape it. The annual flooding of the Nile River in Egypt made a rich civilization possible, and it sharpened the skills of those who "read" the heavens to find the star Sirius that signaled the river's rise and the beginning of the harvest season. When humans discovered ways to manipulate their environment, a great transformation was under way. Trial and error probably led to the establishment of the great grain crops—corn in the Western Hemisphere, wheat in the Middle East, and rice in Asia. Each seems to have developed independently.

Peaceful coexistence is much more likely when resources are plentiful. Scarcity creates competition and can lead to warfare.

Myths and stories, honed and embellished over time, establish what is vital and worth protecting. What circumstances would have been extreme enough to cause a culture to make war on a neighbor? And, who would have had the power to make such a decision? Nomads can always move on. In a city, major decisions touch everyone. So, collective decision making would have been required for anything affecting the common good.

Windows into these ancient cultures open once writing is established. Sumerians were among the first to experiment with, first, business transactions and, later, poetry and prayer, using their characteristic cuneiform style. Prominent in myth and story, the Goddess Innana ruled the heavens, and made powerful roles for human women seem "natural." Humans who share gender with divine figures find it easy to claim earthly power as well.

As cities mature and cultures exchange goods, barter or trade of one item for another works for a while. Eventually, however, a marketplace of many items of differing values requires what economists call a medium of exchange—something with a fixed value, against which a wide range of goods can be priced.

Precious metals such as gold and silver served as the first money, making possible sophisticated transfers of good and services as early as 2500 B.C.E. Agriculture and cash had created new possibilities for early humans.

Dawn of the City

Excavations Prompt a Revolution in Thinking about the Earliest Cities

Bruce Bower

A massive earthen mound rises majestically and rather mysteriously above agricultural fields in northeastern Syria. From a distance, the more than 130-foot-tall protrusion looks like a jagged set of desolate hills. But up close, broken pottery from a time long past litters the mound's surface. The widespread debris vividly testifies to the large number of people, perhaps as many as 10,000, who once congregated on and around this raised ground.

Known as Tell Brak, the mound and its surrounding fields contain the remnants of the world's oldest known city. The word *tell* refers to an ancient Near Eastern settlement consisting of numerous layers of mud-brick construction. Generation after generation of residents cut down, leveled, and replaced each layer with new buildings, eventually creating an enormous mound.

At the city of Brak, the first *tell* layers were built more than 6,000 years ago. At that time, the settlement emerged as an urban center with massive public structures, mass-produced crafts and daily goods, and specially made prestige items for socially elite citizens.

Surprisingly, the evidence for Brak's rise as a major city predates, by as many as 1,000 years, evidence for comparable urban centers hundreds of miles to the south, in what's now southern Iraq. Like those southern cities, Brak lay between the Tigris and Euphrates rivers in the ancient land of Mesopotamia. But scholars have long assumed that southern Mesopotamia's fertile crescent, blessed with rich soil and copious water, represented the "cradle of civilization." In the traditional scenario, fast-growing southern cities established colonies that led to a civilization of the north. Southern immigrants sought timber, metal, and other resources that were absent in their homeland.

Excavations at Tell Brak and at the nearby remains of a comparably ancient city, Hamoukar, may turn that model on its head. New discoveries indicate that the world's first cities either arose in northern Mesopotamia or developed independently and at roughly the same time in the region's northern and southern sectors. The idea that urbanites radiated out of the south and triggered the construction of major northern settlements now rests on shaky ground.

"As yet, no other large site, indeed no other Near Eastern site, has yielded evidence of early urban growth comparable to that at Tell Brak," says archaeologist Augusta McMahon of the University of Cambridge in England. McMahon directs excavations at the Syrian site.

Researchers have also discovered dramatic signs of ancient warfare at Brak and Hamoukar. Further analysis of these discoveries may illuminate the nature of contacts and conflict between northern and southern Mesopotamians.

"Excavations at Brak and Hamoukar are the biggest thing to happen in Mesopotamian research in a long time," comments archaeologist Guillermo Algaze of the University of California, San Diego.

Urban sprawl Excavations at Tell Brak started modestly enough about 70 years ago. Archaeologist Max Mallowan, husband of author Agatha Christie, led a team that uncovered the ruins of a religious temple. Thousands of small stone idols depicting eyes littered its floor. The investigators dubbed the poorly dated structure the Eye Temple.

A husband-and-wife team from Cambridge, David Oates and Joan Oates, initiated a new series of Tell Brak excavations in 1976. At the time, they suspected that the site held remnants of urban development from perhaps as early as 5,000 years ago, when, evidence suggested, the Eye Temple had been built.

But as years of field work accumulated, unexpectedly deep tell levels came to light. By 2006, the investigators realized that they were digging into something special. Sediment from 6,000 years ago or more, when the earliest known southern Mesopotamian cities had not yet been built, started to surrender the remains of huge public buildings.

In the September 2007 *Antiquity,* McMahon, Joan Oates, and their colleagues describe these discoveries. (David Oates is now deceased.)

The oldest structure found so far, dating to about 6,400 years ago, featured a massive entrance framed by two towers and an enormous doorsill made of a single piece of basalt. Excavations revealed parts of two large rooms inside, a group of small rooms near the front, and a pair of guard rooms just outside the entrance. Despite its size, it was likely not a temple, but rather an administrative center, McMahon says. With a central room and several satellite areas, its layout is not that of a standard Mesopotamian temple.

"Whatever its formal functions, this is the earliest Mesopotamian example of a genuinely secular monumental building," McMahon says.

A second ancient structure, with red mud-brick walls surrounding three floors, housed potters and other artisans. These workers had access to several large, clay ovens inside the building.

Pottery finds include large, open bowls, small bowls with incised craftsman's marks, and a basic type of mass-produced bowl.

The scientists also uncovered huge piles of raw flint, obsidian, and a variety of colored stones used to make beads and other stone objects. Some areas contained caches of clay spindle whorls situated near the bones of sheep or possibly goats. These finds resulted from wool weaving, according to the investigators.

To their surprise, this building also yielded an unusual obsidian and white marble chalice. A piece of obsidian had been hollowed out to form a drinking vessel and attached with sticky bitumen to a white marble base. This fancy cup contrasts with mass-produced bowls found throughout the building and points to the presence of at least a small number of social elites in ancient Brak, McMahon holds.

Workshop rooms also contained numerous clay stamp seals, including one bearing the impression of a lion and another showing a lion caught in a net. Such seals signified a ruler's total ownership or control in southern Mesopotamian cities, and probably meant much the same at Brak.

The researchers refer to a third huge structure from roughly 6,000 years ago as "the feasting hall." It contained several large ovens for grilling or baking huge amounts of meat. The bones of goats and other medium-sized game, as well as pieces of mass-produced plates, littered the floors of adjacent rooms.

Either this building was designed for feasting or it served as a kind of ancient cafeteria for nearby workers and bureaucrats, the scientists speculate.

One of the most intriguing insights at Tell Brak came not from excavations but from an analysis of how pottery fragments accumulated across the entire site, from the city center to adjacent suburbs. Brak's urban expansion began more than 6,000 years ago in a set of small settlements that now surround the central mound, according to the pottery study (SN: 9/15/07, p. 174). As these villages ballooned in size, they expanded inward. Construction of the city center's massive buildings followed.

In other words, Brak's urban ascent was not planned and directed by a ruling class that first built an imposing group of core structures, as happened at southern Mesopotamian sites. McMahon's team argues that decentralized growth characterized the northern city, as inhabitants of nearby settlements interacted to cultivate a metropolis without necessarily planning to do so.

Brak attack Sometimes archaeologists make major finds serendipitously. In 2006, local residents bulldozed a grain-storage trench along the mound's border. The shocked farmers dug into a pit crammed with human skeletons, pottery, and animal bones. They had uncovered a mass grave.

Last year, McMahon's team excavated the area and found two mass graves containing parts of at least 70 bodies.

Radiocarbon measurements and assessments of pottery scattered among the bones place their age at about 5,800 years, a time of intense growth at Brak.

These graves probably held the victims of warfare, McMahon says. The bodies primarily come from young and middle-aged adults who apparently died at the same time. Many individuals lack hands and feet, possibly due to scavenging of the dead by rats and dogs on the battlefield.

Skirmish survivors apparently dumped dead bodies of their comrades, or perhaps of their enemies, into the pits. It wasn't an entirely haphazard operation, however. In one cavity, a pile of human skulls rises from the skeletal carnage.

Animal bones that held choice pieces of meat were thrown into one burial pit after ancient residents held some sort of ceremonial feast on top of it, McMahon adds.

"It's a little bit gruesome, but very exciting," she says. "It's also frustrating that we don't yet know anything about normal ways of death at Brak."

The unearthing of mass burials at Brak follows the 2005 discovery of an ancient war zone at Hamoukar. A major battle destroyed the city around 5,500 years ago, says archaeologist and excavation codirector Clemens Reichel of the University of Chicago.

Reichel's team noted extensive destruction of a 10-foot-high mud-brick wall that protected Hamoukar. Bombardment by thousands of inch-long clay bullets shot out of slings weakened the wall, which then collapsed in a fire.

Southerners likely contributed to the attack on Hamoukar, Reichel says. Destruction debris strewn across the site contains numerous large pits stocked with southern Mesopotamian pottery. Southerners either led the charge against the northern city or assumed control of it afterward, in Reichel's view.

Investigators have also discovered a site for making obsidian tools on Hamoukar's outskirts, dating to more than 6,000 years ago. The nearly 800-acre site roughly equals the size of Uruk, the largest known southern Mesopotamian city.

Hamoukar residents built this enormous workshop primarily to export tools, Reichel proposes. It sits on an ancient trade route that led to southern Mesopotamia.

"Urbanism in northern Mesopotamia started much earlier than we previously realized and wasn't imposed by the south," Reichel says.

Southern secrets Ironically, new insights into northern Mesopotamian cities gleaned from work at Brak and Hamoukar highlight huge gaps in what researchers know about urban origins in the south.

No archaeological projects have occurred in southern Iraq for nearly 20 years because of political instability and war. Moreover, periodic flooding in that region has covered ancient sites in layers of river sediment.

"I don't believe we're seeing earlier urban development in the north than in the south," Reichel remarks. "We don't know what happened in the south at the time of Brak and Hamoukar."

UCSD's Algaze agrees. He formerly advanced the view that urbanism spread from southern Mesopotamia to the rest of the Near East, but he has changed his mind in light of the new northern discoveries.

Ancient urban centers in the north and south likely developed at roughly the same time, Algaze theorizes. For now, much more data exist for early northern cities, making regional comparisons difficult.

"Tell Brak is an archaeological gold mine," Algaze says. "The picture of Mesopotamian urbanism is now more complex and interesting than ever."

Consider the puzzle of the decline of northern cities such as Brak beginning around 5,000 years ago, accompanied by continued growth of southern settlements. No one knows why urbanism initially reached massive heights in both regions only to wither in the north and flower in the south.

For that matter, it remains a mystery why northern Mesopotamian cities emerged in the first place, Reichel adds.

New hypotheses for when and how Brak transformed into a major city need to be tested in further work, including excavations of additional northern and southern Mesopotamian cities, according to Algaze.

"We need to go back to the drawing board," Algaze remarks, "and rethink how urbanism originated in the Near East."

The Dawn of Art

A controversial scholar claims modern culture was born in the foothills of the Alps.

ANDREW CURRY

The search for the origins of civilization has taken archaeologists to less pleasant places than Swabia. Nestled between France, Switzerland, and Bavaria, the German region is the heart of Baden-Württemburg, a state that markets itself as a center for creativity and innovation. It's no idle boast. Hundreds of small high-tech firms dot the region. Giants such as Mercedes-Benz, Porsche, and Zeiss are all based in the gleaming, modern state capital, Stuttgart.

American archaeologist Nicholas Conard is convinced Swabia's tradition of innovation goes back a long way: 40,000 years, give or take a few thousand. Excavating in caves east of Tübingen, a medieval town 20 miles south of Stuttgart, Conard has unearthed expertly carved figurines and the oldest musical instruments in the world. The finds are among the earliest art ever discovered, and they're extremely sophisticated in terms of craftsmanship, suggesting a surprising degree of cultural complexity.

Conard claims his finds are evidence of an intense flowering of art and culture that began in southwestern Germany more than 35,000 years ago. Although older art and decorations have been found—including geometric patterns on stones and personal ornaments in South Africa, as well as drilled shell beads on the shores of the Mediterranean—the figurines and instruments in Conard's caves are symbolic representations that reflect a state of mind with which modern humans can easily identify. "Figurative art began in Swabia, music began in Swabia," he says. "It couldn't have developed elsewhere, because the dates are just later elsewhere."

If he's right, it could change the way we look at the development of humanity. But Conard's conclusions have been controversial from the start, and he's still fighting an uphill battle to convince colleagues that the evidence backs him up.

The Swabian Jura, a limestone plateau about the size of Rhode Island, forms part of the foothills of the Alps. The Danube's headwaters are in the nearby Black Forest, and over the last 50 million years the river and its tributaries carved narrow, high-walled canyons that are dotted with thousands of caves.

Archaeologists believe the Danube, sweeping west across Europe, was the path of least resistance for early humans migrating north. Searching for open space and new hunting grounds, they followed the receding glaciers. Eventually, they would have reached the Swabian Jura and stopped. "If modern humans are coming up the Danube, at some point the Danube ends," Conard says. "That happens to be here."

Forty thousand years ago, glaciers a mile or more thick still covered northern Europe. Present-day Swabia was at the edge of the habitable world. In the region's caves, archaeologists have found animal remains—bones from woolly mammoths, woolly rhinoceroses, reindeer, snow hares, and arctic lemmings—that indicate a tundra-like environment.

Researchers have been systematically working in Swabia's Lone and Ach valleys since the early 1880s. In the 1930s, excavators found hundreds of stone and bone tools, as well as small figurines carved from mammoth ivory. When World War II began, hundreds of artifacts were put in storage at regional museums and essentially forgotten about until the 1960s. If not for a career-making stroke of luck, the artifacts might still be there.

In 1969, Tübingen archaeologist Joachim Hahn began rummaging through uninventoried finds. From more than 200 fragments of mammoth ivory, he reconstructed a half-man, half-lion sculpture almost a foot tall: the "Löwenmensch," or "Lion Man." Hahn spent the next 25 years working on the Swabian caves, until his death in 1997.

After Hahn died, Conard, who has been chair of the archaeology department at the University of Tübingen since 1995, took over work in the Swabian Jura. He quickly attracted motivated young researchers from Germany, France, the United States, and elsewhere and led them in a hunt for more evidence of the area's prehistoric inhabitants.

The results have been impressive. In 2003, Conard announced three finds from a cave called Höhle Fels, sophisticated and artful, the ivory sculptures—a horse head, bird, and mysterious humanoid figurine—each fit in the palm of a hand. According to Conard, they were carved at least 30,000 and perhaps as many as 40,000 years ago, making them the oldest figurines in the world. "Nobody imagined the earliest representational art could be so perfect," Conard says.

At Geißenklösterle, a cave not far from Höhle Fels, his team uncovered a carved mammoth-ivory flute almost seven inches long. Reconstructed from 31 fragments, the three-hole flute was both the oldest musical instrument ever found and an unparalleled example of craftsmanship. Hahn had discovered flutes made from hollow swan bones at Geißenklösterle, but this one was carved from solid ivory. The instrument, Conard announced, was between 30,000 and 37,000 years old.

Höhle Fels is a 15-minute walk from the tiny town of Schelklingen, past the Heidelberger Cement plant and up a dirt path that winds around the local swimming pool. The cave entrance is gated with steel bars. Inside, a metal walkway is suspended over a floodlit pit in the cave's entrance passageway. The pit walls, made of sand and loose limestone pebbles, are reinforced by sandbags.

Despite warm weather outside, the cave is wet and chilly. Clad in jackets, boots, and long pants, a half-dozen researchers from the United States, Germany, and South Africa are at work in the pit. Conard arrives wearing a wrinkled plaid shirt, khakis, and battered green Converse sneakers, and swings into the pit to inspect the day's work.

The Höhle Fels dig is divided into three layers. At the bottom, a sheet of paper in a plastic sleeve reads "Middle Paleolithic," marking the cave's lowest, and therefore oldest, layer. It contains tools and bones left by Neanderthals, who occupied Europe for about 200,000 years before modern humans arrived. A barren, or sterile, layer sits atop the Middle Paleolithic.

About four feet higher, a sheet labeled "Aurignacian" modestly marks a critical shift in human history. Across Europe, the beginning of the Aurignacian marked a significant step forward: art, sophisticated bone and ivory tools, jewelry, cave paintings, musical instruments, and other "hallmarks of modernity" all appear for the first time in this layer. Although the definition of "modernity" is hotly debated, Conard sees it as a state of mind that people today would recognize. "If you were transported back in time, you'd have to learn a new language, you'd have to learn how to knap flint and maybe hunt mammoth, but you and those people are the same" he says. "That's certainly the case with the Aurignacian in Swabia." The final level is the Gravettian, an era best known for Venus figurines found at sites in France and elsewhere.

Although Conard had been working on European Paleolithic sites for more than 20 years, he wasn't an expert on the Swabian Jura until he took over Hahn's work in the late 1990s. The first thing he did was review data from local digs, including dozens of radiocarbon dates.

Conard says the timing of the Aurignacian and Gravettian artifacts found in the Swabian caves immediately leapt out at him. While most archaeologists think that the Aurignacian began about 36,000 years ago, Conard is convinced that the Swabian Aurignacian began thousands of years before it emerged elsewhere in Europe—perhaps even 10,000 years before. "The Aurignacian developed here, the Gravettian developed here," he says now.

A significantly older Aurignacian might overlap with the Neanderthal era, or Middle Paleolithic. But when Conard reopened digs at Höhle Fels and Geißenklösterle, he found a sterile layer between the Middle Paleolithic and the Aurignacian levels, a critical indicator of the lack of human occupation as clear as a roadside motel's blinking neon "vacancy" sign. "Judging by the low artifact density in the Middle Paleolithic and sterile layers, we conclude modern people came into a nearly empty region," says Michael Bolus, a German archaeologist who works closely with Conard. "In our region there's no continuity between Neanderthals and modern humans."

As Conard, Bolus, and others dug deeper into the caves and sifted through Hahn's decades of data, they came up with a daring theory to explain the Swabian Jura's sophisticated tools and incredible carved figurines. "Looking at it from a physics background, if you have a vacuum, something's going to get sucked in," Conard says.

As humans followed the Danube into the region, the theory goes, they found an area at once abundant with animal life and virtually empty of competitors—so they began to settle it. The cold climate forced early inhabitants to be creative in order to survive. In response, they developed new tools and hunting strategies. The modern human population then surged, prompting still more innovation, including what Conard and his colleagues believe is the world's earliest representational art.

Conard and Bolus say the region served first as an incubator and then as a sort of piston, pushing its cultural and technological innovations out into the rest of Europe. They have dubbed the theory "Kulturpumpe," or culture pump. "Swabians may have been inventors all these years ago," Bolus says. "People sitting here got ideas from outside, but developed new things and spread them to other regions. It's a point our French colleagues don't want to accept."

The Kulturpumpe theory means more than just bragging rights for Swabia. On one level it's a bold claim to a set of prehistoric "firsts." But it's also a controversial vision of the beginnings of cultural modernity: all at once, and all in one place, rather than in slow evolutionary steps across Africa and Europe over tens of thousands of years.

When you're talking about the issue of where human beings come from, who's going to answer that except for a paleoarchaeologist? You can talk to a priest, or you can talk to us.

The theory is an ambitious stab at one of the most important questions only archaeology can answer: When, how, and where did anatomically modern humans make the mental leap to true modernity? As Conard puts it, "When did people become like ourselves? When you're talking about the issue of where human beings come from, who's going to answer that except for a paleoarchaeologist? You can talk to a priest, or you can talk to us."

You'll certainly get a more straightforward answer from a priest. While Conard was making waves in the popular press for a string of "firsts" for the Swabian Jura, a storm was building in the world of paleoanthropology. Conard's colleagues read the publications flooding out of Tübingen with admiration—and consternation. "I think Nick is doing a great job in Tübingen," says João Zilhão, a paleoanthropologist at Bristol University who is one of Conard's main sparring partners. "He's going back to the sites and extracting data we can all use—even to disagree with him."

Zilhão says the Kulturpumpe theory has been controversial from the start. Critics have attacked everything from the accuracy of the radiocarbon dates to Conard's interpretation of the stratigraphy layers at key sites such as Höhle Fels and Geißenklösterle. More than five years after he floated the idea, few outside Conard's Tübingen department are willing swallow his argument. "The whole Kulturpumpe thing is very heated. Everybody has their belief in how things were, and they tend to stick to the beliefs pretty strongly," says Laura Niven, a researcher at the Max Planck Institute for Human Evolution in Leipzig (and one of Conard's former students).

If you look at the layers of an ideal excavation, the radiocarbon dates of the finds should match their physical locations, with the youngest pieces on top and the oldest at the bottom. Geißenklösterle, the first cave to be systematically excavated by Conard's team, has the best chronological evidence for the Kulturpumpe—and yet the site's layering is far from ideal. Deer bones that Conard dated to 41,000 years ago, for example, were uncovered above pieces that are only 29,000 years old.

Meanwhile, artifacts from the Middle Paleolithic layers came back with dates thousands of years younger than pieces from the Aurignacian. Bones with cut marks and other clear signs of human use are sometimes mixed with "unmodified" bones that seem much older. And the pieces themselves can't be directly tested. Even if Conard was willing to pulverize parts of the world's oldest sculptures to date them, mammoth ivory has very little organic matter to extract.

Conard's explanation relies on the intricacies of radiocarbon (C-14) dating. Especially with older artifacts, C-14 dates don't always correspond to the calendar. Climate change, rising and lowering sea levels, the earth's magnetic field, and cosmic rays can all change C-14 levels, making artifacts seem older or younger than they actually are. So scientists must calibrate radiocarbon dates, comparing them to tree rings, glacial ice cores, and lake sediments.

In the critical period Conard is investigating—between 30,000 and 50,000 years ago—some radiocarbon experts have observed wildly fluctuating levels of C-14 in the earth's atmosphere. Conard and Bolus argue that the fluctuations explain the odd dates at Geißenklösterle. "In some cases," Conard wrote last year, "these production spikes can lead to younger dates stratigraphically underlying older dates from secure contexts."

Ordinarily, Conard would cross-reference results with other local sites. But many of the caves that could corroborate his theory were excavated in the 1930s, before modern archaeological techniques were developed. "So many of these dates depend on old sites, and there are so many problems with old sites," says Niven. In 1931, for example, all 170 square meters of Vogel-herd Cave were excavated in 10 weeks flat by 31-year-old German archaeologist Gustav Riek, who employed mostly local laborers with shovels and pickaxes. None of his field notes survived.

Without other sites to back him up, Conard is vulnerable to another charge. Some suggest that the odd dates aren't the result of cosmic rays, but something more mundane. "German sites are used by carnivores as much as by humans," Zilhão points out. A restless bear could have dug into the coarse limestone rubble of a cave floor, churning up pieces of bone from lower layers and creating dating havoc.

If that's the case, the artifacts supporting the Kulturpumpe idea could simply be in the wrong place. Conard concedes the difficulties—and dismisses them. "Overall, the mixing is not so great" he says.

Critics say Conard based his estimates of each layer's age on the oldest artifacts—rather than looking at the finds as a whole. "There are dozens of dates in Europe for the Aurignacian, nothing older than 36,500 [years]. This is the only case with a date of 40,000. It seems unlikely that people bearing the same culture were at Geißenklösterle 4,000 years ahead of the rest of Europe," says Francesco d'Errico, an archaeologist at the University of Bordeaux. "If you really work on the dates and the site stratigraphy, you come up with the conclusion that this Aurignacian is 35,000–33,000 years old, the same as the rest of Europe."

Conard refuses to give any ground on his interpretations. "They're willfully misunderstanding the data," he says, frustrated. "That's just ignorance on their part."

But Conard refuses to give any ground on his interpretations. "They're willfully misunderstanding the data," he says, frustrated. "That's just ignorance on their part." When it comes to radiocarbon dating, there's no shaking his confidence: Conard's entire career has been based on the technique. As an undergraduate at the University of Rochester in the early 1980s, one of his mentors was Harry Gove, a nuclear physicist who was in the process of inventing the accelerated mass spectrometry (AMS) method of carbon dating.

The technique, capable of accurately dating a few milligrams of organic matter, was a breakthrough for archaeologists. And Conard was the first person to apply AMS to an archaeological find. His undergraduate thesis on radiocarbon dating of prehistoric horticulture in Illinois was published in *Nature* in 1984 and his background in the natural sciences continues to inform his work today. "An excavation's like a laboratory," Conard says. "My role models are physicists—in physics, what you do and your experimental data carry the day."

Yet many colleagues feel Conard's faith in radiocarbon dating is too strong. "Data produced from the natural sciences is often seen as more solid. But errors can happen," says archaeologist Olaf Jöris of the Roman-Germanic Museum in Mainz, Germany. "I highly esteem the work he's doing, but you can't just take dates for granted."

Two years ago, Conard decided to take another look at Vogelherd, the cave Gustav Riek excavated in 1931. The cave sits atop a steep hill, and spilling down from its mouth are the remains of Riek's dig—more than 4,000 bags worth of soil from the cave hastily pushed down the hill by workmen. Sifting the dirt, Tübingen graduate students trained in a more patient era have uncovered thousands of fragmentary artifacts missed during the first excavation.

This summer, Conard announced the first finds: fragments of an ivory flute, four fragmentary sculptures, and a complete carving of a mammoth. "This doesn't change anything, it just reinforces my position," he says. "People here dealt with figurative representations in ordinary life and routinely created music. From my point of view, that's overwhelming evidence of modernity."

It remains to be seen whether Conard can convince his colleagues that Swabian modernity came first. In the meantime, he hasn't stopped looking. "We're very much in the new data line of work here," Conard says. "We're dealing with a giant landscape, and all we've got is a few square meters. We haven't seen the whole picture."

ANDREW CURRY is a freelance writer in Berlin, Germany, and a frequent contributor to *Archaeology*.

Prehistory *of* Warfare

Humans have been at each others' throats since the dawn of the species.

STEVEN A. LEBLANC

In the early 1970s, working in the El Morro Valley of west-central New Mexico, I encountered the remains of seven large prehistoric pueblos that had once housed upwards of a thousand people each. Surrounded by two-story-high walls, the villages were perched on steep-sided mesas, suggesting that their inhabitants built them with defense in mind. At the time, the possibility that warfare occurred among the Anasazi was of little interest to me and my colleagues. Rather, we were trying to figure out what the people in these 700-year-old communities farmed and hunted, the impact of climate change, and the nature of their social systems—not the possibility of violent conflict.

One of these pueblos, it turned out, had been burned to the ground; its people had clearly fled for their lives. Pottery and valuables had been left on the floors, and bushels of burned corn still lay in the storerooms. We eventually determined that this site had been abandoned, and that immediately afterward a fortress had been built nearby. Something catastrophic had occurred at this ancient Anasazi settlement, and the survivors had almost immediately, and at great speed, set about to prevent it from happening again.

Thirty years ago, archaeologists were certainly aware that violent, organized conflicts occurred in the prehistoric cultures they studied, but they considered these incidents almost irrelevant to our understanding of past events and people. Today, some of my colleagues are realizing that the evidence I helped uncover in the El Morro Valley is indicative warfare endemic throughout the entire Southwest, with its attendant massacres, population decline, and area abandonments that forever changed the Anasazi way of life.

When excavating eight-millennia-old farm villages in southeastern Turkey in 1970, I initially marveled how similar modern villages were to ancient ones, which were occupied at a time when an abundance of plants and animals made warfare quite unnecessary. Or so I thought. I knew we had discovered some plaster sling missiles (one of our workmen showed me how shepherds used slings to hurl stones at predators threatening their sheep). Such missiles were found at many of these sites, often in great quantities, and were clearly not intended for protecting flocks of sheep; they were exactly the same size and shape as later Greek and Roman sling stones used for warfare.

The so-called "donut stones" we had uncovered at these sites were assumed to be weights for digging sticks, presumably threaded on a pole to make it heavier for digging holes to plant crops. I failed to note how much they resembled the round stone heads attached to wooden clubs—maces—used in many places of the world exclusively for fighting and still used ceremonially to signify power. Thirty years ago, I was holding mace heads and sling missiles in my hands, unaware of their use as weapons of war.

We now know that defensive walls once ringed many villages of this era, as they did the Anasazi settlements. Rooms were massed together behind solid outside walls and were entered from the roof. Other sites had mud brick defensive walls, some with elaborately defended gates. Furthermore, many of these villages had been burned to the ground, their inhabitants massacred, as indicated by nearby mass graves.

Certainly for those civilizations that kept written records or had descriptive narrative art traditions, warfare is so clearly present that no one can deny it. Think of Homer's *Iliad* or the Vedas of South India, or scenes of prisoner sacrifice on Moche pottery. There is no reason to think that warfare played any less of a role in prehistoric societies for which we have no such records, whether they be hunter-gatherers or farmers. But most scholars studying these cultures still are not seeing it. They should assume warfare occurred among the people they study, just as they assume religion and art were a normal part of human culture. Then they could ask more interesting questions, such as: What form did warfare take? Can warfare explain some of the material found in the archaeological record? What were people fighting over and why did the conflicts end?

Scholars should assume warfare occurred among the people they study, just as they assume religion was a normal part of human culture. Then they would ask more interesting questions, such as: What form did warfare take? Why did people start and stop fighting?

Today, some scholars know me as Dr. Warfare. To them, I have the annoying habit of asking un-politic questions about their research. I am the one who asks why the houses at a particular site were jammed so close together and many catastrophically burned. When I suggest that the houses were crowded behind defensive walls that were not found because no one was looking for them, I am not terribly appreciated. And I don't win any popularity contests when I suggest that twenty-mile-wide zones with no sites in them imply no-man's lands—clear evidence for warfare—to archaeologists who have explained a region's history without mention of conflict.

Virtually all the basic textbooks on archaeology ignore the prevalence or significance of past warfare, which is usually not discussed until the formation of state-level civilizations such as ancient Sumer. Most texts either assume or actually state that for most of human history there was an abundance of available resources. There was no resource stress, and people had the means to control population, though how they accomplished this is never explained. The one archaeologist who has most explicitly railed against this hidden but pervasive attitude is Lawrence Keeley of the University of Illinois, who studies the earliest farmers in Western Europe. He has found ample evidence of warfare as farmers spread west, yet most of his colleagues still believe the expansion was peaceful and his evidence a minor aberration, as seen in the various papers in Barry Cunliffe's *The Oxford Illustrated Prehistory of Europe* (1994) or Douglas Price's *Europe's First Farmers* (2000). Keeley contends that "prehistorians have increasingly pacified the past," presuming peace or thinking up every possible alternative explanation for the evidence they cannot ignore. In his *War Before Civilization* (1996) he accused archaeologists of being in denial on the subject.

Witness archaeologist Lisa Valkenier suggesting in 1997 that hilltop constructions along the Peruvian coast are significant because peaks are sacred in Andean cosmology. Their enclosing walls and narrow guarded entries may have more to do with restricting access to the *huacas,* or sacred shrines, on top of the hills than protecting defenders and barring entry to any potential attackers. How else but by empathy can one formulate such an interpretation in an area with a long defensive wall and hundreds of defensively located fortresses, some still containing piles of sling missiles ready to be used; where a common artistic motif is the parading and execution of defeated enemies; where hundreds were sacrificed; and where there is ample evidence of conquest, no-man's lands, specialized weapons, and so on?

A talk I gave at the Mesa Verde National Park last summer, in which I pointed out that the over 700-year-old cliff dwellings were built in response to warfare, raised the hackles of National Park Service personnel unwilling to accept anything but the peaceful Anasazi message peddled by their superiors. In fact, in the classic book *Indians of Mesa Verde,* published in 1961 by the park service, author Don Watson first describes the Mesa Verde people as "peaceful farming Indians," and admits that the cliff dwellings had a defensive aspect, but since he had already decided that the inhabitants were peaceful, the threat must have been from a new enemy—marauding nomadic Indians. This, in spite of the fact that there is ample evidence of Southwestern warfare for more than a thousand years before the cliff dwellings were built, and there is no evidence for the intrusion of nomadic peoples at this time.

Of the hundreds of research projects in the Southwest, only one—led by Jonathan Haas and Winifred Creamer of the Field Museum and Northern Illinois University, respectively—deliberately set out to research prehistoric warfare. They demonstrated quite convincingly that the Arizona cliff dwellings of the Tsegi Canyon area (known best for Betatakin and Kiet Siel ruins) were defensive, and their locations were not selected for ideology or because they were breezier and cooler in summer and warmer in the winter, as was previously argued by almost all Southwestern archaeologists.

For most prehistoric cultures, one has to piece together the evidence for warfare from artifactual bits and pieces. Most human history involved foragers, and so they are particularly relevant. They too were not peaceful. We know from ethnography that the Inuit (Eskimo) and Australian Aborigines engaged in warfare. We've also discovered remains of prehistoric bone armor in the Arctic, and skeletal evidence of deadly blows to the head are well documented among the prehistoric Aborigines. Surprising to some is the skeletal evidence for warfare in prehistoric California, once thought of as a land of peaceful acorn gatherers. The prehistoric people who lived in southern Californian had the highest incident of warfare deaths known anywhere in the world. Thirty percent of a large sample of males dating to the first centuries A.D. had wounds or died violent deaths. About half that number of women had similar histories. When we remember that not all warfare deaths leave skeletal evidence, this is a staggering number.

There was nothing unique about the farmers of the Southwest. From the Neolithic farmers of the Middle East and Europe to the New Guinea highlanders in the twentieth century, tribally organized farmers probably had the most intense warfare of any type of society. Early villages in China, the Yucatán, present-day Pakistan, and Micronesia were well fortified. Ancient farmers in coastal Peru had plenty of forts. All Polynesian societies had warfare, from the smallest islands like Tikopia, to Tahiti, New Zealand (more than four thousand prehistoric forts), and Hawaii. No-man's lands separated farming settlements in Okinawa, Oaxaca, and the southeastern United States. Such societies took trophy heads and cannibalized their enemies. Their skeletal remains show ample evidence of violent deaths. All well-studied prehistoric farming societies had warfare. They may have had intervals of peace, but over the span of hundreds of years there is plenty of evidence for real, deadly warfare.

When farmers initially took over the world, they did so as warriors, grabbing land as they spread out from the Levant through the Middle East into Europe, or from South China down through Southeast Asia. Later complex societies like the Maya, the Inca, the Sumerians, and the Hawaiians were no less belligerent. Here, conflict took on a new dimension. Fortresses, defensive walls hundreds of miles long, and weapons and armor expertly crafted by specialists all gave the warfare of these societies a heightened visibility.

There is a danger in making too much of the increased visibility of warfare we see in these complex societies. This is especially true for societies with writing. When there are no texts, it is easy to see no warfare. But the opposite is true. As soon as societies can write, they write about warfare. It is not a case of literate societies having warfare for the first time, but their being able to write about what had been going on for a long time. Also, many of these literate societies link to European civilization in one way or another, and so this raises the specter of Europeans being warlike and spreading war to inherently peaceful people elsewhere, a patently false but prevalent notion. Viewing warfare from their perspective of literate societies tells us nothing about the thousands of years of human societies that were not civilizations—that is, almost all of human history. So we must not rely too much on the small time slice represented by literate societies if we want to understand warfare in the past.

The Maya were once considered a peaceful society led by scholarly priests. That all changed when the texts written by their leaders could be read, revealing a long history of warfare and conquest. Most Mayanists now accept that there was warfare, but many still resist dealing with its scale or implications. Was there population growth that resulted in resource depletion, as throughout the rest of the world? We would expect the Maya to have been fighting each other over valuable farmlands as a consequence, but Mayanist Linda Schele concluded in 1984 that "I do not think it [warfare] was territorial for the most part," this even though texts discuss conquest, and fortifications are present at sites like El Mirador, Calakmul, Tikal, Yaxuná, Uxmal, and many others from all time periods. Why fortify them, if no one wanted to capture them?

Today, more Maya archaeologists are looking at warfare in a systematic way, by mapping defensive features, finding images of destruction, and dating these events. A new breed of younger scholars is finding evidence of warfare throughout the Maya past. Where are the no-man's lands that almost always open up between competing states because they are too dangerous to live in? Warfare must have been intimately involved in the development of Maya civilization, and resource stress must have been widespread.

Demonstrating the prevalence of warfare is not an end in itself. It is only the first step in understanding why there was so much, why it was "rational" for everyone to engage in it all the time. I believe the question of warfare links to the availability of resources.

Demonstrating the prevalence of warfare is not an end in itself. It is only the first step in understanding why there was so much of it, why it was "rational" for everyone to engage in it all the time. I believe the question of warfare links to the availability of resources.

During the 1960s, I lived in Western Samoa as a Peace Corps volunteer on what seemed to be an idyllic South Pacific Island—exactly like those painted by Paul Gauguin. Breadfruit and coconut groves grew all around my village, and I resided in a thatched-roof house with no walls beneath a giant mango tree. If ever there was a Garden of Eden, this was it. I lived with a family headed by an extremely intelligent elderly chief named Sila. One day, Sila happened to mention that the island's trees did not bear fruit as they had when he was a child. He attributed the decline to the possibility that the presence of radio transmissions had affected production, since Western Samoa (now known as Samoa) had its own radio station by then. I suggested that what had changed was not that there was less fruit but that there were more mouths to feed. Upon reflection, Sila decided I was probably right. Being an astute manager, he was already taking the precaution of expanding his farm plots into some of the last remaining farmable land on the island, at considerable cost and effort, to ensure adequate food for his growing family. Sila was aware of his escalating provisioning problems but was not quite able to grasp the overall demographic situation. Why was this?

The simple answer is that the rate of population change in our small Samoan village was so gradual that during an adult life span growth was not dramatic enough to be fully comprehended. The same thing happens to us all the time. Communities grow and change composition, and often only after the process is well advanced do we recognize just how significant the changes have been—and we have the benefit of historic documents, old photographs, long life spans, and government census surveys. All human societies can grow substantially over time, and all did whenever resources permitted. The change may seem small in one person's lifetime, but over a couple of hundred years, populations can and do double, triple, or quadruple in size.

The consequences of these changes become evident only when there is a crisis. The same can be said for environmental changes. The forests of Central America were being denuded and encroached upon for many years, but it took Hurricane Mitch, which ravaged most of the region in late October 1998, to produce the dramatic flooding and devastation that fully demonstrated the magnitude of the problem: too many people cutting down the forest and farming steep hillsides to survive. The natural environment is resilient and at the same time delicate, as modern society keeps finding out. And it was just so in the past.

These observations about Mother Nature are incompatible with popular myths about peaceful people living in ecological balance with nature in the past. A peaceful past is possible only if you live in ecological balance. If you live in a Garden of Eden surrounded by plenty, why fight? By this logic, warfare is a sure thing when natural resources run dry. If someone as smart as Sila couldn't perceive population growth, and if humans all over Earth continue to degrade their environments, could people living in the past have been any different?

A study by Canadian social scientists Christina Mesquida and Neil Wiener has shown that the greater the proportion of a society is composed of unmarried young men, the greater the likelihood of war. Why such a correlation? It is not because the young men are not married; it is because they cannot get married. They are too poor to support wives and families. The idea that poverty breeds war is far from original. The reason poverty exists has remained the same since the beginning of time: humans have invariably overexploited their resources because they have always outgrown them.

From foragers to farmers to more complex societies, when people no longer have resource stress they stop fighting. When climate greatly improves, warfare declines. The great towns of Chaco Canyon were built during an extended warm—and peaceful—period.

There is another lesson from past warfare. It stops. From foragers to farmers, to more complex societies, when people no longer have resource stress they stop fighting. When the climate greatly improves, warfare declines. For example, in a variety of places the medieval warm interval of ca. 900–1100 improved farming conditions. The great towns of Chaco Canyon were built at this time, and it was the time of archaeologist Stephen Lekson's *Pax Chaco*—the longest period of peace in the Southwest. It is no accident that the era of Gothic cathedrals was a response to similar climate improvement. Another surprising fact is that the amount of warfare has declined over time. If we count the proportion of a society that died from warfare, and not the size of the armies, as the true measure of warfare, then we find that foragers and farmers have much higher death rates—often approaching 25 percent of the men—than more recent complex societies. No complex society, including modern states, ever approached this level of warfare.

If warfare has ultimately been a constant battle over scarce resources, then solving the resource problem will enable us to become better at ridding ourselves of conflict.

There have been several great "revolutions" in human history: control of fire, the acquisition of speech, the agricultural revolution, the development of complex societies. One of the most recent, the Industrial Revolution, has lowered the birth rate and increased available resources. History shows that peoples with strong animosities stop fighting after adequate resources are established and the benefits of cooperation recognized. The Hopi today are some of the most peaceful people on earth, yet their history is filled with warfare. The Gebusi of lowland New Guinea, the African !Kung Bushmen, the Mbuti Pygmies of central Africa, the Sanpoi and their neighbors of the southern Columbia River, and the Sirionno of Amazonia are all peoples who are noted for being peaceful, yet archaeology and historical accounts provide ample evidence of past warfare. Sometimes things changed in a generation; at other times it took longer. Adequate food and opportunity does not instantly translate into peace, but it will, given time.

The fact that it can take several generations or longer to establish peace between warring factions is little comfort for those engaged in the world's present conflicts. Add to this a recent change in the decision-making process that leads to war. In most traditional societies, be they forager bands, tribal farmers, or even complex chiefdoms, no individual held enough power to start a war on his own. A consensus was needed; pros and cons were carefully weighed and hotheads were not tolerated. The risks to all were too great. Moreover, failure of leadership was quickly recognized, and poor leaders were replaced. No Hitler or Saddam Hussein would have been tolerated. Past wars were necessary for survival, and therefore were rational; too often today this is not the case. We cannot go back to forager-band-type consensus, but the world must work harder at keeping single individuals from gaining the power to start wars. We know from archaeology that the amount of warfare has declined markedly over the course of human history and that peace can prevail under the right circumstances. In spite of the conflict we see around us, we are doing better, and there is less warfare in the world today than there ever has been. Ending it may be a slow process, but we are making headway.

© 2003 by **Steven A. LeBlanc.** Portions of this article were taken from his book *Constant Battles,* published in April 2003 by St. Martin's Press. LeBlanc is director of collections at Harvard University's Peabody Museum of Archaeology and Ethnology.

Writing Gets a Rewrite

Recent discoveries in the Near East and Pakistan are forcing scholars to reconsider traditional ideas about writing's evolution. But a lack of fresh data is making their task difficult.

ANDREW LAWLER

The inventor of writing, according to Mesopotamian legend, was a high priest from the great city of Uruk who one day began making marks on wet clay. Five thousand years later, German archaeologists triumphantly discovered the oldest examples of writing—called cuneiform—200 kilometers south of here in a long-buried Uruk temple, providing what seemed to be scientific confirmation of the ancient myth.

But that heroic story is quietly being shelved by scholars as new finds in Egypt and Pakistan over the past decade, and a radical reinterpretation of clay objects found in Mesopotamia's heartland and its periphery—today's Iraq, Syria, and Iran—have necessitated a different account. Most researchers now agree that writing is less the invention of a single talented individual than the result of a complex evolutionary process stretching back thousands of years before the first hard evidence of writing surfaced in Mesopotamia, Egypt, and the Indus River valley about 3300 B.C. "The prehistoric communication revolution began some 9000 years ago," says Joan Oates, an archaeologist at the University of Cambridge, U.K. "In a sense, writing appears as the last step in the long line of evolution of communication systems."

The revised text on writing's history, however, is far from complete. Scholars say they are hampered by a lack of fresh data from Near Eastern sites, the reluctance of museum curators to allow potentially destructive testing of critical artifacts, and the limitations of radiocarbon dating. Moreover, the 1989 discovery in Egypt of an ancient and sophisticated writing system has fueled a new debate: Did Mesopotamia's literacy trigger that of Egypt, as is traditionally supposed, or was it the other way around—or neither? More recent finds showing that the Indus script likely was evolving around 3300 B.C.—at about the same time as its Near East counterparts began to coalesce—have deepened the mystery. Some researchers, pondering the near-simultaneous appearance of seemingly separate protowriting systems in three distinct civilizations, suggest that they may have developed independently in response to similar circumstances.

But tracing the predecessors of cuneiform, hieroglyphics, and Indus River valley script becomes increasingly tricky the farther back in prehistory researchers probe. "We really have very little information prior to 3500 B.C.," says Piotr Michalowski, a cuneiform scholar at the University of Michigan, Ann Arbor. "It comes down to a matter of faith."

Token Theory

For decades, archaeologists in Iraq, Syria, and Iran dug up curious ceramic pieces—numerous small tokens in diverse geometric shapes. They also found hollow clay spheres with markings on the outside from later periods and with these same small ceramic pieces inside. Those ranged in age from about 9000 to 4000 years old but were dismissed by most researchers as ancient games and relegated to museum storage bins.

But Pierre Amiet, an archaeologist at the Louvre in Paris, suspected as early as the 1960s that the mysterious objects were actually used to count goods. Since then, his student Denise Schmandt-Besserat, now at the University of Texas, Austin, has elaborated on that theory. After studying thousands of tokens, she proposed in the 1980s that different shapes signified different commercial objects—a cone shape, for example, represented a measure of grain; a cylinder connoted an animal. The number of tokens indicated quantity. "It was the first visual code, the first system of artifacts created for the sole purpose of communicating information," she says.

Despite her colleagues' skepticism, Schmandt-Besserat went on to theorize that the system grew and evolved over thousands of years. By the end of the fourth millennium B.C., tokens represented different animals; processed foods such as oil, trussed ducks, or bread; and manufactured and imported goods such as textiles and metal, she says. By about 3500 B.C., concurrent with the growth of major cities like Uruk, the tokens were often found in hollow clay spheres, like envelopes; markings on the outside indicated the sorts and quantities of tokens within.

Ultimately, the tokens were dispensed with altogether, and the clay spheres became clay tablets with impressed marks representing objects—marks that evolved into early cuneiform, according to Schmandt-Besserat. By 3100 B.C., someone—perhaps indeed an Uruk priest—began to use a reed stylus on wet clay to make the more precise markings that comprise cuneiform. This form of writing continued at Uruk and other Mesopotamian sites until the latter days of the Roman Empire, much as Latin survived as an elite and holy language in Europe for more than 1000 years after Rome's fall.

The token theory, according to some scholars, helps solve a nagging puzzle. "The great mystery until now was how a full-fledged system emerged so suddenly," says William Hallo, an Assyriologist at Yale University. "Now we can see a progression of successive steps [over] a fairly extended time."

But many Assyriologists say Schmandt-Besserat goes too far in postulating a sophisticated representational system before 3500 B.C. Oates prefers to call the tokens "a means of remembering rather than a genuine recording device." Eleanor Robson, an Assyriologist at Oxford University, U.K., says the later arrangements of tokens in spheres clearly are "a coherent system"; even so, she says, it is hard to identify the inside objects definitively from before 3500 B.C. "Most are little blobby lumps," she says, "and it's hard to know which are tokens and which are beads or weights."

Skeptics also insist that there is little evidence that cuneiform grew directly out of this system, as Schmandt-Besserat maintains. Token shapes and the impressions made on the spheres, she says, inspired cuneiform's representations for objects such as sheep and oil. But others are not so sure. "I accept the tokens as the earliest form of writing, but I see no good evidence that incised tokens are precursors" to cuneiform, says Robert Englund, a Sumerian scholar at the University of California, Los Angeles. Paul Zimansky, a Boston University archaeologist, agrees. "There's no indication of linkage," he says.

A few scholars take a harder line. Michalowski holds to the idea that cuneiform is a separate development that may have been influenced by tokens and cylinder seals—also widely used in ancient Mesopotamia—but that is unique and distinct. "I joke that cuneiform had to be invented by one person because it was too good to be invented by a committee," he says, arguing that the system is the result of a "quantum leap" that drew on many traditions.

More data would clearly be welcome. Englund and Robson assert that more research should be done on the sealed hollow spheres, more than 100 of which are in museums around the world. Englund and his colleagues have already done x-rays and computerized tomography scans on these objects at the University of Heidelberg in Germany, but, they say, the time, expense, and low resolution of these procedures make them a poor substitute for splitting open the spheres and studying them directly. Curators, however, are reluctant to see their artifacts tampered with and possibly destroyed. "It's an unpleasant situation," Englund says.

Dating Troubles

Egypt is only 1000 kilometers west of Mesopotamia, and there is a long history of trade between the two great civilizations. So scholars have long accepted the idea that

hieroglyphics—which were thought to have appeared a century or so after cuneiform—were inspired by the Uruk concept of storing information.

But a 1989 discovery by Gunther Dreyer of Cairo's German Archeological Institute and his subsequent findings at Abydos in upper Egypt have threatened Mesopotamia's ancient claim as the source of the first writing system. Opening a royal tomb dubbed U-j in 1989, Dreyer's team found a large trove of objects bearing inscriptions that are more than a century older than the oldest written materials previously discovered in Egypt. The finds, which include nearly 200 small bone and ivory objects, are from roughly the same era as Uruk's earliest tablets—around 3200 B.C. A rougher set of similar inscriptions was found on nearby vessels. About 50 signs seem to represent humans, animals, and a palace façade. Later findings nearby included pot marks dating to about 3500 B.C.

Dreyer argues that the symbols represent a single well-developed system that led to hieroglyphics. But other researchers are skeptical of this claim. "The pot marks can't be interpreted," and so the data "are insufficient" to draw wide-ranging conclusions, says John Baines, an Egyptologist at Oxford University, although he agrees that the inscriptions on bone and ivory clearly are writing.

Meanwhile, attempts to accurately date materials from both Egypt and Mesopotamia have proven inconclusive. Recent radiocarbon dating in Heidelberg of charcoal from both an Uruk temple, where early cuneiform tablets were found, and the Abydos tomb showed a date of approximately 3450 B.C. for Uruk and 3320 B.C. for Abydos—pushing back the previous dates, based on well-known Egyptian chronologies, about 150 years.

Margarete van Ess of Berlin's German Archeological Institute, for one, accepts those dates, which push the origin of cuneiform back by a century or so, giving Mesopotamia the edge. But other scholars say such precision is not possible in radiocarbon dating. Researchers are looking for additional clues, both in situ and on the tablets and vessels that record the early writing; Van Ess, for example, recently began digging at Uruk after the decade-long hiatus resulting from international sanctions against Iraq.

Those clues are hard to come by, however. Because builders at Uruk often used old tablets as fill, pinpointing their date and context is difficult. "Uruk is such a mess," says Englund. "The stratigraphic record is really quite horrible." And Dreyer—who continues his excavations—has yet to find significant material at Abydos that may shed more light on hieroglyphic evolution.

Three at Once?

Archaeologists in Pakistan have had more luck in recent years. A team of U.S. researchers discovered compelling evidence in the late 1990s that the script from the Indus River valley also has a long and complex history. The Harappan civilization flourished there from 2800 B.C. to 1700 B.C. before collapsing; its script ceased to be used afterward, and the meanings of the signs remain a mystery. But although it never attained the complexity of the Mesopotamian or Egyptian writing systems, the Indus script nevertheless developed into a formidable grouping of signs.

The recent finds suggest that the script arose more than half a millennium earlier than previously believed. Pottery discovered at the site of Harappa includes markings that date from 3500 B.C. to 3300 B.C. and that appear to be precursors to that script. "I wouldn't call these signs writing," says Richard Meadow, a Harvard archaeologist who works at the site. "But these could be seen as part of an evolution of signs that continue to the Harappan period."

The Harappan and Abydos finds pose a major challenge to the traditional theory that writing diffused gradually from Mesopotamia to Egypt and perhaps to the Indus. All three areas were linked by trade in pre-history—Egypt to Mesopotamia through the Levant, and Mesopotamia to the Indus through modern-day Iran and the Persian Gulf coast. But the dominance of Mesopotamia is now in question.

"That the idea [of writing] passed from Egypt to Mesopotamia is quite a possibility now," maintains Dreyer. Others are not so quick to make that leap. "I'm undecided," says Baines, "but I don't think that's likely." Still other Mesopotamian scholars largely adhere to the old school of east-to-west influence, given what they say is the long evolution apparent from cylinder seals and the clay spheres.

Baines, however, posits a third possibility: that the two systems developed independently at about the same time. And if Harappa is included, then the evidence suggests that three separate systems with their own evolutionary paths began to mature nearly simultaneously. That would appear a stunning coincidence, but some researchers say contact with other groups, combined with an indigenous need to convey more complex information, might have been the not-so-coincidental common ingredients that made the Near East and the Indus advance so quickly.

"Writing develops in areas where people are interacting," says Jonathan Kenoyer, an archaeologist at the University of Wisconsin, Madison, who has dug along the Indus. "Yet these regions also developed their own unique forms of expression." This is true not only for the scripts, which are unrelated, but also for their function. In Egypt, for example, writing typically was focused on ceremonial uses, while accounting dominated Mesopotamian tablets.

However writing matured, scholars are left with the more daunting mystery of who laid the foundation for the artisans at Abydos, priests at Uruk, and the unknown makers of Indus script. "No one expected writing had such deep roots in prehistory," says Schmandt-Besserat. Deciphering that long and complex story is proving a formidable and controversial task, with no Rosetta Stone in sight.

Poets and Psalmists
Goddesses and Theologians

SAMUEL NOAH KRAMER

Let us now turn . . . to an anthropological inquiry relating to the Sumerian counterpart of one of modern man's more disturbing social ills: the victimization of woman in a male-dominated society. At the *XVIII Rencontre assyriologique internationale* held in Munich in 1970, I read a paper entitled "Modern Social Problems in Ancient Sumer," that presented evidence in support of the thesis that Sumerian society, not unlike our own rather tormented society, had its deplorable failings and distressing shortcomings: it vaunted utopian ideals honored more in the breach than in observance; it yearned for peace but was constantly at war; it preferred such noble virtues as justice, equity and compassion, but abounded in injustice, inequality, and oppression; materialistic and shortsighted, it unbalanced the ecology essential to its economy; it was afflicted by a generation gap between parents and children and between teachers and students; it had its "drop-outs," "cop-outs," hippies and perverts.

This highly competitive, and in some ways hypocritical, unjust, oppressive, genocidal Sumerian society, resembled our own sick society in one other significant aspect—it was male dominated: men ran the government, managed the economy, administered the courts and schools, manipulated theology and ritual. It is not surprising to find therefore, that by and large, women were treated as second-class citizens without power, prestige, and status, although there are some indications that this was predominantly true only of later Sumerian society, from about 2000 B.C. on; in earlier days the Sumerian woman may have been man's equal socially and economically, at least among the ruling class. Moreover, in the religious sphere, the female deity was venerated and worshiped from earliest times to the very end of Sumer's existence; in spite of some manipulative favoritism on the part of the male theologians, God in Sumer never became all-male.

Woman in Early Sumer

We begin our inquiry with the little that is known about women's rights and status in early Sumer. Some time about 2350 B.C., a king by the name of Urukagina reigned for a brief period in Lagash, one of Sumer's important city-states. Many of his inscriptions were excavated by the French almost a century ago and have since been deciphered and translated. Among them is a "reform" document in which Urukagina purports to depict the evil "of former days," that is, of the times preceding his reign, as well as the measures he introduced to alleviate them. One of these reforms reads as follows: "The women of former days used to take two husbands, but the women of today (when they attempted to do this) were stoned with stones inscribed with their evil intent." To judge from this rather strident boast, women in pre-Urukagina days practiced polyandry, which hardly smacks of a male-dominated society.

Or, take the case of Baranamtarra, the wife of Urukagina's predecessor, Lugalanda. Quite a number of administrative documents concerned with this lady have been uncovered, and these indicate that she managed her own estates, and even sent diplomatic missions to her counterpart in neighboring city-states, without consulting her husband.

Even Urukagina who, because of his uptight reaction to polyandry, might perhaps be stigmatized as the first "sexist" known to history, was not all antifeminine. His wife Shagshag, for example, like her predecessor Baranamtarra, was the mistress of vast estates, and ran her affairs every bit her husband's equal. In fact Urukagina might well be acclaimed as the first known individual to favor "equal pay for equal work" regardless of sex. One of the remedial measures he proudly records in the above-mentioned reform document, concerns the bureaucratic gouging of the bereaved by officials in charge of a funeral. In pre-Urukagina days, reads the document, when a citizen was brought to rest "among the reeds of Enki," a cemetery that was deemed more desirable than an ordinary burial ground, there were on hand three male officials who received a considerable amount of beer, bread, and barley, as well as a bed and a chair, as compensation for their services. But Urukagina decreed that the food rations of the three male attendants be reduced considerably and that the furniture "bonus" be eliminated altogether. At the same time he ordered that a woman designated as *nin-dingir*, "Lady Divine," who formerly had received no remuneration, be given a headband and a *sila*-jar (about one-fifth of a gallon) of scented ointment as compensation for her services—a payment that compared not unfavorably with that received by her male colleagues.

Enheduanna: The First Woman Poet on Record

Nor was the *nin-dingir* the only priestess who played a significant role in the cult. A more prominent and important lady was the *en,* a Sumerian word that may be rendered "high priestess" as well as "high priest." According to Sumerian religious practice, the main temple in each large city had its *en* who was male if the deity worshipped in that temple was female, and was female if the deity worshipped there was male. Quite a number of these high-priestesses are known to us by name, beginning with about 2300 B.C., a generation or two after the days of Urukagina. The first of these is Enheduanna, the daughter of Sargon the Great, one of the first empire-builders of the ancient world, whom her father appointed to be high-priestess of great moon-god temple in the city of Ur. But not only was she the spiritual head of one of Sumer's largest temples, she was also a poet and author of renown. Quite recently it has been demonstrated that at least three poetic compositions—a collection of temple hymns and two hymnal prayers to the Goddess Inanna, are at least in part, the imaginative literary creation of this Enheduanna. Here, in Sumer, therefore, some 4300 years ago, it was possible for a woman, at least if she was a princess, to hold top rank among the literati of the land, and to be a spiritual leader of paramount importance.

Woman in Later Sumer

From the three centuries following the days of Enheduanna, little is known about Sumerian society and the status of woman. But from about 2000 B.C. there have been recovered legal documents and court decisions of diverse content, and from these we learn that the role of woman had deteriorated considerably, and that on the whole it was the male who ruled the roost. Marriage, for example, was theoretically monogamous, but the husband was permitted one or more concubines, while the wife had to stay faithful to her one and only spouse. To be sure, a married woman could own property and other possessions, could sometimes buy and sell without consulting her husband, and on rare occasions, could even set special conditions in her marriage contract. In case of divorce, however, the husband had very much the upper hand—he could divorce his wife virtually at will, although if he did so without good cause, he had to pay her as much as *mina* (about a pound) of silver, no mean sum in those days.

Female Deities: Victimization and Resentment

But it was not only on the human plane that women had lost some of their rights and prerogatives in the course of the centuries—it also happened on the divine plane. Some of the female deities that held top rank in the Sumerian pantheon, or close to it, were gradually forced down the hierarchical ladder by the male theologians who manipulated the order of the divinities

in accordance with what may well have been their chauvinistic predilections. The goddesses, however, were no "pushovers"; more determined and aggressive than their human counterparts, they struggled to hold or regain at least part of their deprived supremacy to the very end of Sumer's existence. What is more, at least one of the goddesses, Inanna, "Queen of Heaven," continued to be predominant and preeminent to the very last, although the theologians ranked her only seventh in the divine hierarchy. The available texts are not explicit on the subject, but with a bit of between-the-lines reading and burrowing, it is possible to follow the struggling career of at least two important female deities, and to trace some of their ups and downs in myth and cult.

Nammu, Goddess of the Primeval Sea

The female deity that seems to have suffered the sharpest decline was Nammu, the goddess of the primeval sea who, according to several texts, was the creator of the universe and the mother of all the gods. By all genealogical rights, therefore, had the theologians played it fair, she should have had top billing in the pantheon. But in the god-lists where the deities are arranged in hierarchical order, she is rarely mentioned, and never at the head of the list. Moreover, her vast powers as goddess of the sea were turned over to the male deity Enki, who was designated by the theologians as the son of Nammu, in an apparent attempt to mitigate and justify this bit of priestly piracy. Even so, the king who founded the Third Dynasty of Ur, and ushered in a political and cultural Sumerian renaissance about 2050 B.C., chose as his royal name *Ur-Nammu,* "Servant of Nammu," which indicates that the goddess was still worshipped and adored by the mighty of the land.

Ki, Mother Earth

But it is Nammu's daughter Ki, "(Mother) Earth," whose gradual decline can be followed almost step by step with the help of the ancient texts. As noted above, the sea-goddess Nammu was conceived as the creator of the universe. Now the Sumerian word for universe is the compound *an-ki,* where *an* means both "heaven," and "(Father) Heaven," and *ki* means both "earth," and "(Mother) earth." It was the sexual union of Father Heaven with Mother Earth, that according to the Sumerian theologians, ushered in the birth of the gods unto their generations. The first to be born of this Heaven-Earth union, was the airgod Enlil, "Lord Air," and it was he who, by making use of his atmospheric power, succeeded in separating Heaven from Earth, thus preparing the way for the creation of vegetation and all living things including man. In view of these theological premises and postulates, the leading deities of the pantheon, once Nammu had been deprived of her supremacy, should have been ranked by the theologians in the order An (Heaven), Ki (Earth), and Enlil (Lord Air), and this may have been so in very early times. But by 2400 B.C., when the relevant inscriptional evidence first becomes available, we find the leading deities of the pantheon usually arranged in the order An (Heaven), Enlil (Lord Air), Ninhursag (Queen of the Mountain), and Enki (Lord of the Earth). What had evidently happened was, that the theologians, uncomfortable and unhappy with a female deity as the ruler of so important a cosmic entity as earth, had taken this power away from her and transferred it to the male deity Enlil who, as one poet puts it, "carried off the earth," after he had separated it from heaven. Moreover, after taking away from the goddess the rulership over the earth, the theologians also deprived her of the name *Ki*, (Mother) Earth," since it no longer accorded with her reduced status. Instead they called her by one of her several epithets, Ninhursag, that means "Queen of the Mountain," and demoted her to third place in the pantheon.

But the worst was yet to come—even third place was deemed too high by male "chauvinistic" theologians, and she was finally reduced to fourth place, third going to Enki, "Lord of the Earth." This god's name was actually a misnomer, since he had charge only of the seas and rivers, and even this power, as noted earlier, he usurped from the Goddess Nammu. But the theologians of Eridu, a city not far from Ur, which was the God's main seat of worship, were consumed with ambition. As the name "Lord of the Earth" indicates, the devotees of this God were really out to topple the God Enlil who had become the ruler of the earth after he had separated it from heaven. To achieve their goal, they went so far as to have their God Enki confound the speech of man and turn it into a "babel" of tongues, in order to break up Enlil's universal sway over mankind that worshipped him "in one tongue." In spite of this, however, they failed to dethrone Enlil from second place, since his bailiwick was Nippur, Sumer's holy city, whose priests were too powerful to overcome. Disappointed and frustrated the Eridu theologians turned upon the female deity Ninhursag (originally named Ki) whose devotees were evidently too weak to prevent her victimization. And so, by 2000 B.C., when the pertinent texts become available once again, the order of the four leading deities of the pantheon is no longer An, Enlil, Ninhursag, Enki, but An, Enlil, Enki, and Ninhursag.

Still, as already noted, the Sumerian goddesses did not take male-domination "lying down," and not infrequently, according to the mythographers, they registered their resentment in no uncertain terms, and showed the male "victors" who was really "boss." As of today, for example, we have two myths in which Ninhursag and Enki are the main protagonists, and in both it is Ninhursag who dominates the action, with Enki "playing second fiddle."

The scene of one of these myths is Dilmun, the Sumerian "Paradise" land, where both Ninhursag and Enki are at home. Here, after considerable maneuvering, Ninhursag contrived to make eight different plants sprout. But when Enki sees them, they tempt his appetite, and he sends his vizier to pluck them and bring them to him. After which, he proceeds to eat them one at a time. This so enrages Ninhursag that she pronounces against him the "curse of death." And mighty male though he was, eight of his organs become sick, one for each of the plants he had eaten without permission from the goddess. The failing Enki would surely have died in due course, had not the goddess finally taken pity on

him, and created eight special deities, each of whom healed one of Enki's ailing organs.

In the other available myth, we find Ninhursag and Enki acting as partners in the creation of man from the "clay that is over the Deep." In the course of a banquet of the gods, however, the two deities become tipsy, and the partnership turns into a competition. First Ninhursag fashions six malformed creatures whom Enki dutifully blesses and for whom he even finds useful "jobs" in spite of their handicaps. Then it was Enki's turn. But the creature he fashions displeased Ninhursag who proceeds to rebuke Enki bitterly for his clumsy effort, a reproach that the god accepts as his due, in language that is obsequious and flattering.

Prestigious Female Deities

Nor was Ninhursag the only female deity who, in spite of occasional victimization by the theologians, continued to be revered and adored in the land. There was Nidaba, the patroness of writing, learning, and accounting, whom the theologians provided with a husband by the name of Haia, who seemed to be no more than a shadowy reflection of the goddess. There was the goddess of medicine and healing who was worshipped in Lagash under the name of Bau, and in Isin under the name of Ninisinna. In Lagash, it is true, the theologians did succeed in making her husband Ningirsu paramount in cult and adoration. Even so, there are indications that originally Bau was of higher rank than her spouse. Moreover, when it came to the naming of their children, the people of Lagash preferred by far to include Bau rather than Ningirsu in the chosen theophoric name—clear evidence of the popularity of the goddess, no matter what the theological dogma. As for Ninisinna, it was she who was venerated as the heroic tutelary deity of Isin, while her husband Pabilsag is a far less impressive figure. Most interesting is the case of the Lagashite goddess Nanshe who was acclaimed and adored as Sumer's social conscience, and who was depicted as judging mankind every New Year. Her spouse Nindara, a far less significant figure, did not participate in this solemn and fateful procedure; it was her bailiff, the male deity Hendursagga, who carried out obediently and faithfully the verdict of his deeply revered mistress.

Inanna, "Queen of Heaven"

But the goddess that should be soothing balm to the resentful wounds of liberated women the world over, is the bright, shining Inanna, the brave, crafty, ambitious, aggressive, desirable, loving, hating "Queen of Heaven," whose powers and deeds were glorified and extolled throughout Sumer's existence in myth, epic, and hymn. No one, neither man nor god, dared oppose her, stand in her way, or say her nay. Early in her career, perhaps about 3000 B.C., she virtually took over the divine rulership of the important city, Erech, from the theoretically and theologically all powerful heaven-god An. In an effort to make her city Erech the center of civilized life, she braved a dangerous journey to the *Abzu*, "the Deep," where the cosmic and cultural divine laws were guarded by its King Enki. When this same Enki organized the universe and somehow failed to assign her the insignia and prerogatives she felt were her due, he had to defend himself apologetically and contritely against her angry complaint. When the rebellious highland, Ebih, failed to show her due honor, she virtually destroyed it with her fiery weapons, and brought it to its knees. Raped by the gardener Shukalletuda while sleeping wearily after a long cosmic journey under one of his shade-trees, she pursued him relentlessly and finally caught up with him and put him to death, but was gracious enough to console him with the promise to make his name endure in story and song.

The role that no doubt delighted Inanna most, one that guaranteed her the affection and veneration of every Sumerian heart, was that which she played in the New Year "Sacred Marriage" rite, that celebrated her sexual union with the King of Sumer in order to ensure the fertility of the soil and the fecundity of the womb. The first king whom the goddess selected as her mortal spouse was Dumuzi (Biblical Tammuz), who reigned early in the third millennium B.C. From then on, many, if not most of the rulers of Sumer, celebrated their marriage to the goddess as avatars, or incarnations of Dumuzi. Throughout the "Sacred Marriage" ceremony, it was the goddess who was the active, dominant protagonist; the king was but the passive, ecstatic recipient of the blessings of her womb and breasts, and of just a touch of her immortality. And when—so tell the mythographers—Dumuzi, with typical male arrogance, became weary of being subordinate to the goddess, and, in her absence, began to play high and mighty, she fastened upon him her "eye of death," and had him carried off to the Nether World. There he would have remained forever, had not his loving sister offered herself as his substitute, thus allowing him to return to earth for half the year.

Monotheism: Death-Knell of the Female Deity

So much for the Goddess Inanna, the feared and beloved "Holy Terror" of the ancients. The female deity, as is clear from what was said above, had her ups and downs in Sumerian religion, but she was never really licked or totally eclipsed by her male rivals. Even in much later days, when Sumer had become generally known as Babylonia, and the Sumerian language was superseded by the Semitic Akkadian, the poets continued to compose hymns and psalms to the female deities, and especially to the Goddess Inanna under her Semitic name Ishtar. The death-knell of the female deity in Near Eastern religious worship came with the birth of monotheism, and especially the Jahwistic monotheism propagated by the Hebrew prophets. For them, Jahweh was the one and only, omniscient, omnipotent and all-male—there was no room for any goddess no matter how minimal her power, or how irreproachable her conduct. Still, even in Jahwistic Judaism there are faint echoes of the female divinities of earlier days, and it is not altogether surprising to find that the Hebrew mystics, the Kabbalists, spoke of a feminine element in Jahweh designated as the "Shekinah," opposed to a masculine element designated as the "Holy One, Blessed Be He." And at least one passage in the renowned Kabbalistic book, the Zohar, states that Moses, the son of God, actually had intercourse with the "Shekinah,"—a distant but not so faint reminder of the "Sacred Marriage" between Dumuzi and Inanna, that provides us with one more example of the far, gossamer, reach of the "legacy of Sumer."

From *The Legacy of Sumer:* Goddesses and Theologians by Samuel Noah Kramer, (1976, pp. 12–17). Copyright © 1976 by Undena Publications. Reprinted by permission.

The Cradle of Cash

When money arose in the ancient cities of Mesopotamia, it profoundly and permanently changed civilization.

HEATHER PRINGLE

The scene in the small, stifling room is not hard to imagine: the scribe frowning, shifting in his seat as he tries to concentrate on the words of the woman in front of him. A member of one of the wealthiest families in Sippar, the young priestess has summoned him to her room to record a business matter. When she entered the temple, she explains, her parents gave her a valuable inheritance, a huge piece of silver in the shape of a ring, worth the equivalent of 60 months' wages for an estate worker. She has decided to buy land with this silver. Now she needs someone to take down a few details. Obediently, the scribe smooths a wet clay tablet and gets out his stylus. Finally, his work done, he takes the tablet down to the archive.

For more than 3,700 years, the tablet languished in obscurity, until late-nineteenth-century collectors unearthed it from Sippar's ruins along the Euphrates River in what is now Iraq. Like similar tablets, it hinted at an ancient and mysterious Near Eastern currency, in the form of silver rings, that started circulating two millennia before the world's first coins were struck. By the time that tablet was inscribed, such rings may have been in use for a thousand years.

When did humans first arrive at the concept of money? What conditions spawned it? And how did it affect the ancient societies that created it? Until recently, researchers thought they had the answers. They believed money was born, as coins, along the coasts of the Mediterranean in the seventh or sixth century B.C., a product of the civilization that later gave the world the Parthenon, Plato, and Aristotle. But few see the matter so simply now. With evidence gleaned from such disparate sources as ancient temple paintings, clay tablets, and buried hoards of uncoined metals, researchers have revealed far more ancient money: silver scraps and bits of gold, massive rings and gleaming ingots.

In the process, they have pushed the origins of cash far beyond the sunny coasts of the Mediterranean, back to the world's oldest cities in Mesopotamia, the fertile plain created by the Tigris and Euphrates rivers. There, they suggest, wealthy citizens were flaunting money at least as early as 2500 B.C. and perhaps a few hundred years before that. "There's just no way to get around it," says Marvin Powell, a historian at Northern Illinois University in De Kalb. "Silver in Mesopotamia functions like our money today. It's a means of exchange. People use it for a storage of wealth, and they use it for defining value."

Many scholars believe money began even earlier. "My sense is that as far back as the written records go in Mesopotamia and Egypt, some form of money is there," observes Jonathan Williams, curator of Roman and Iron Age coins at the British Museum in London. "That suggests it was probably there beforehand, but we can't tell because we don't have any written records."

Just why researchers have had such difficulties in uncovering these ancient moneys has much to do with the practice of archeology and the nature of money itself. Archeologists, after all, are the ultimate Dumpster divers: they spend their careers sifting through the trash of the past, ingeniously reconstructing vanished lives from broken pots and dented knives. But like us, ancient Mesopotamians and Phoenicians seldom made the error of tossing out cash, and only rarely did they bury their most precious liquid assets in the ground. Even when archeologists have found buried cash, though, they've had trouble recognizing it for what it was. Money doesn't always come in the form of dimes and sawbucks, even today. As a means of payment and a way of storing wealth, it assumes many forms, from debit cards and checks to credit cards and mutual funds. The forms it took in the past have been, to say the least, elusive.

From the beginning, money has shaped human society. It greased the wheels of Mesopotamian commerce, spurred the development of mathematics, and helped officials and kings rake in taxes and impose fines. As it evolved in Bronze Age civilizations along the Mediterranean coast, it fostered sea trade, built lucrative cottage industries, and underlay an accumulation of wealth that might have impressed Donald Trump. "If there were never any money, there would never have been prosperity," says Thomas Wyrick, an economist at Southwest Missouri State University in Springfield, who is studying the origins of money and banking. "Money is making all this stuff happen."

Ancient texts show that almost from its first recorded appearance in the ancient Near East, money preoccupied estate owners and scribes, water carriers and slaves. In Mesopotamia, as early

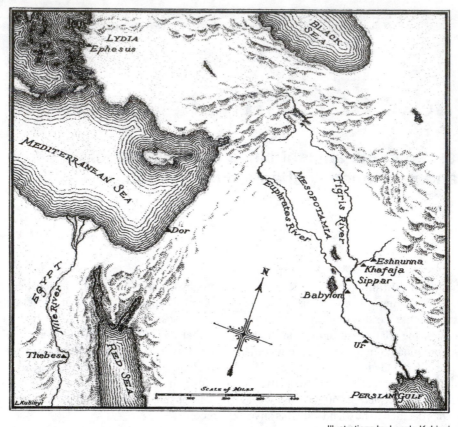

Illustrations by Laszlo Kubinyi

Figure 1 Cash first appeared in Mesopotamia then spread westward to the Mediterranean.

as 3000 B.C., scribes devised pictographs suitable for recording simple lists of concrete objects, such as grain consignments. Five hundred years later, the pictographs had evolved into a more supple system of writing, a partially syllabic script known as cuneiform that was capable of recording the vernacular: first Sumerian, a language unrelated to any living tongue, and later Akkadian, an ancient Semitic language. Scribes could write down everything from kingly edicts to proverbs, epics to hymns, private family letters to merchants' contracts. In these ancient texts, says Miguel Civil, a lexicographer at the Oriental Institute of the University of Chicago, "they talk about wealth and gold and silver all the time."

Ancient texts show that almost from its first recorded appearance in the ancient Near East, money preoccupied estate owners and scribes, water carriers and slaves.

In all likelihood, says Wyrick, human beings first began contemplating cash just about the time that Mesopotamians were slathering mortar on mud bricks to build the world's first cities. Until then, people across the Near East had worked primarily on small farms, cultivating barley, dates, and wheat, hunting gazelles and other wild game, and bartering among themselves

for the things they could not produce. But around 3500 B.C., work parties started hauling stones across the plains and raising huge flat-topped platforms, known as ziggurats, on which to found their temples. Around their bases, they built street upon twisted street of small mud-brick houses.

To furnish these new temples and to serve temple officials, many farmers became artisans—stonemasons, silversmiths, tanners, weavers, boatbuilders, furniture makers. And within a few centuries, says Wyrick, the cities became much greater than the sum of their parts. Economic life flourished and grew increasingly complex. "Before, you always had people scattered out on the hillsides," says Wyrick, "and whatever they could produce for their families, that was it. Very little trade occurred because you never had a large concentration of people. But now, in these cities, for the first time ever in one spot, you had lots of different goods, hundreds of goods, and lots of different people trading them."

Just how complex life grew in these early metropolises can be glimpsed in the world's oldest accounting records: 8,162 tiny clay tokens excavated from the floors of village houses and city temples across the Near East and studied in detail by Denise Schmandt-Besserat, an archeologist at the University of Texas at Austin. The tokens served first as counters and perhaps later as promissory notes given to temple tax collectors before the first writing appeared.

By classifying the disparate shapes and markings on the tokens into types and comparing these with the earliest known

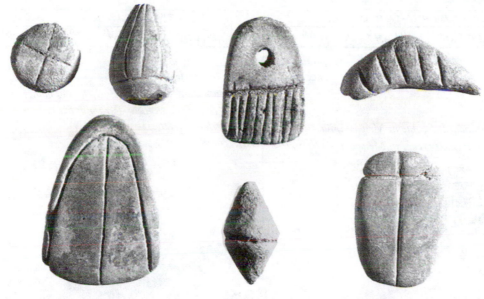

Courtesy Denise Schmandt-Besserat

Figure 2 These clay tokens from Susa, Iran, around 3300 B.C., represent (clockwise from top left): one sheep, one jar of oil, one garment, one measure of metal, a mystery item, one measure of honey, and one garment.

written symbols, Schmandt-Besserat discovered that each token represented a specified quantity of a particular commodity. And she noticed an intriguing difference between village tokens and city tokens. In the small communities dating from before the rise of cities, Mesopotamians regularly employed just five token types, representing different amounts of three main goods: human labor, grain, and livestock like goats and sheep. But in the cities, they began churning out a multitude of new types, regularly employing 16 in all, with dozens of subcategories representing everything from honey, sheep's milk, and trussed ducks to wool, cloth, rope, garments, mats, beds, perfume, and metals. "It's no longer just farm goods," says Schmandt-Besserat. "There are also finished products, manufactured goods, furniture, bread, and textiles."

Faced with this new profusion, says Wyrick, no one would have had an easy time bartering, even for something as simple as a pair of sandals. "If there were a thousand different goods being traded up and down the street, people could set the price in a thousand different ways, because in a barter economy each good is priced in terms of all other goods. So one pair of sandals equals ten dates, equals one quart of wheat, equals two quarts of bitumen, and so on. Which is the best price? It's so complex that people don't know if they are getting a good deal. For the first time in history, we've got a large number of goods. And for the first time, we have so many prices that it overwhelms the human mind. People needed some standard way of stating value."

In Mesopotamia, silver—a prized ornamental material—became that standard. Supplies didn't vary much from year to year, so its value remained constant, which made it an ideal measuring rod for calculating the value of other things. Mesopotamians were quick to see the advantage, recording the prices of everything from timber to barley in silver by weight in shekels. (One shekel equaled one-third of an ounce, or just a little more than the weight of three pennies.) A slave, for example, cost

between 10 and 20 shekels of silver. A month of a freeman's labor was worth 1 shekel. A quart of barley went for three-hundredths of a shekel. Best of all, silver was portable. "You can't carry a shekel of barley on your ass," comments Marvin Powell (referring to the animal). And with a silver standard, kings could attach a price to infractions of the law. In the codes of the city of Eshnunna, which date to around 2000 B.C., a man who bit another man's nose would be fined 60 shekels of silver; one who slapped another in the face paid 10.

How the citizens of Babylon or Ur actually paid their bills, however, depended on who they were. The richest tenth of the population, says Powell, frequently paid in various forms of silver. Some lugged around bags or jars containing bits of the precious metal to be placed one at a time on the pan of a scale until they balanced a small carved stone weight in the other pan. Other members of the upper crust favored a more convenient form of cash: pieces of silver cast in standard weights. These were called *har* in the tablets, translated as "ring" money.

At the Oriental Institute in the early 1970s, Powell studied nearly 100 silver coils—some resembling bedsprings, others slender wire coils—found primarily in the Mesopotamian city of Khafaje. They were not exactly rings, it was true, but they matched other fleeting descriptions of *har*. According to the scribes, ring money ranged from 1 to 60 shekels in weight. Some pieces were cast in special molds. At the Oriental Institute, the nine largest coils all bore a triangular ridge, as if they had been cast and then rolled into spirals while still pliable. The largest coils weighed almost exactly 60 shekels, the smallest from one-twelfth to two and a half shekels. "It's clear that the coils were intended to represent some easily recognizable form of Babylonian stored value," says Powell. "In other words, it's the forerunner of coinage."

The masses in Mesopotamia, however, seldom dealt in such money. It was simply too precious, much as a gold coin would

41

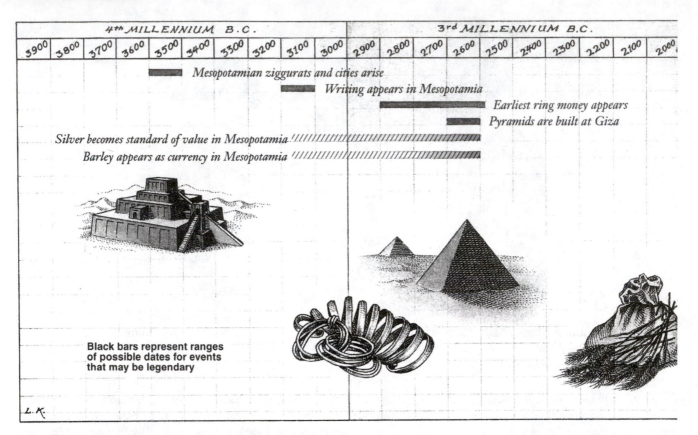

Figure 3

have been for a Kansas dirt farmer in the middle of the Great Depression. To pay their bills, water carriers, estate workers, fishers, and farmers relied on more modest forms of money: copper, tin, lead, and above all, barley. "It's the cheap commodity money," says Powell. "I think barley functions in ancient Mesopotamia like small change in later systems, like the bronze currencies in the Hellenistic period. And essentially that avoids the problem of your being cheated. You measure barley out and it's not as dangerous a thing to try to exchange as silver, given weighing errors. If you lose a little bit, its not going to make that much difference."

Measurable commodity money such as silver and barley both simplified and complicated daily life. No longer did temple officials have to sweat over how to collect a one-sixth tax increase on a farmer who had paid one ox the previous year. Compound interest on loans was now a breeze to calculate. Shekels of silver, after all, lent themselves perfectly to intricate mathematical manipulation; one historian has suggested that Mesopotamian scribes first arrived at logarithms and exponential values from their calculations of compound interest.

"People were constantly falling into debt," says Powell. "We find reference to this in letters where people are writing to one another about someone in the household who has been seized for securing a debt." To remedy these disastrous financial affairs, King Hammurabi decreed in the eighteenth century B.C. that none of his subjects could be enslaved for more than three years for failing to repay a debt. Other Mesopotamian rulers, alarmed at the financial chaos in the cities, tried legislating moratoriums on all outstanding bills.

While the cities of Mesopotamia were the first to conceive of money, others in the ancient Near East soon took up the torch. As civilization after civilization rose to glory along the coasts of the eastern Mediterranean, from Egypt to Syria, their citizens began abandoning the old ways of pure barter. Adopting local standards of value, often silver by weight, they began buying and selling with their own local versions of commodity moneys: linen, perfume, wine, olive oil, wheat, barley, precious metals—things that could be easily divided into smaller portions and that resisted decay.

And as commerce became smoother in the ancient world, people became increasingly selective about what they accepted as money, says Wyrick. "Of all the different media of exchange, one commodity finally broke out of the pack. It began to get more popular than the others, and I think the merchants probably said to themselves, 'Hey, this is great. Half my customers have this form of money. I'm going to start demanding it.' And the customers were happy, too, because there's more than just one merchant coming around, and they didn't know what to hold on to, because each merchant was different. If everyone asked for barley or everyone asked for silver, that would be very convenient. So as one of these media of exchange becomes more popular, everyone just rushes toward that."

What most ancient Near Easterners rushed toward around 1500 B.C. was silver. In the Old Testament, for example, rulers of the Philistines, a seafaring people who settled on the Palestine coast in the twelfth century B.C., each offer Delilah 1,100 pieces of silver for her treachery in betraying the secret of Samson's immense strength. And in a well-known Egyptian tale from

Moneyfact

The Bartering Ape

William Hopkins and Charles Hyatt at Yerkes Regional Primate Center report that chimpanzees were observed swapping items for food from humans. First, a human experimenter knelt down and begged in front of a chimp cage (chimpanzees customarily beg from one another in the wild). At the same time, the experimenter also pointed at an item—an empty food case—in the chimp's cage and held out desirable food, like an apple or half a banana. Of 114 chimpanzees, nearly half caught the trading spirit and pushed the item out. Some even traded much faster for more desirable food—taking just 15 seconds to trade for a banana versus nearly 3 minutes to trade for typical fare. And some chimpanzees negotiated on their own terms, notes Hopkins. He has worked with four who refused to cooperate in experiments for their usual food reward when other, more preferable food was in sight.

the eleventh century B.C., the wandering hero Wen-Amon journeys to Lebanon to buy lumber to build a barge. As payment, he carries jars and sacks of gold and silver, each weighed in the traditional Egyptian measure, the deben. (One deben equals 3 ounces.) Whether these stories are based on history or myth, they reflect the commercial transactions of their time.

To expedite commerce, Mediterranean metalsmiths also devised ways of conveniently packaging money. Coils and rings seem to have caught on in some parts of Egypt: a mural painted during the fourteenth century B.C. in the royal city of Thebes depicts a man weighing a stack of doughnut-size golden rings. Elsewhere, metalsmiths cast cash in other forms. In the Egyptian city of el-Amarna, built and briefly occupied during the fourteenth century B.C., archeologists stumbled upon what they fondly referred to as a crock of gold. Inside, among bits of gold and silver, were several slender rod-shaped ingots of gold and silver. When researchers weighed them, they discovered that some were in multiples or fractions of the Egyptian deben, suggesting different denominations of an ancient currency.

All these developments, says Wyrick, transformed Mediterranean life. Before, in the days of pure barter, people produced a little bit of everything themselves, eking out a subsistence. But with the emergence of money along the eastern Mediterranean, people in remote coastal communities found themselves in a new and enviable position. For the first time, they could trade easily with Phoenician or Syrian merchants stopping at their harbors. They no longer had to be self-sufficient. "They could specialize in producing one thing," says Wyrick. "Someone could just graze cattle. Or they could mine gold or silver. And when you specialize, you become more productive. And then more and more goods start coming your way."

The wealth spun by such specialization and trade became the stuff of legend. It armed the fierce Mycenaean warriors of Greece in bronze cuirasses and chariots and won them victories. It outfitted the tomb of Tutankhamen, sending his soul in grandeur to the next world. And it filled the palace of Solomon with such magnificence that even the Queen of Sheba was left breathless.

But the rings, ingots, and scraps of gold and silver that circulated as money in the eastern Mediterranean were still a far cry from today's money. They lacked a key ingredient of modern cash—a visible guarantee of authenticity. Without such a warranty, many people would never willingly accept them at their face value from a stranger. The lumps of precious metal might be a shade short of a shekel, for example. Or they might not be pure gold or silver at all, but some cheaper alloy. Confidence, suggests Miriam Balmuth, an archeologist at Tufts University in Medford, Massachusetts, could be won only if someone reputable certified that a coin was both the promised weight and composition.

Balmuth has been trying to trace the origins of this certification. In the ancient Near East, she notes, authority figures—perhaps kings or merchants—attempted to certify money by permitting their names or seals to be inscribed on the official carved stone weights used with scales. That way Mesopotamians would know that at least the weights themselves were the genuine article. But such measures were not enough to deter cheats. Indeed, so prevalent was fraud in the ancient world that no fewer than eight passages in the Old Testament forbid the faithful from tampering with scales or substituting heavier stone weights when measuring out money.

Clearly, better antifraud devices were needed. Under the ruins of the old city of Dor along northern Israel's coast, a team of archeologists found one such early attempt. Ephraim Stern of Hebrew University and his colleagues found a clay jug filled with nearly 22 pounds of silver, mainly pieces of scrap, buried in a section of the city dating from roughly 3,000 years ago. But more fascinating than the contents, says Balmuth, who recently studied this hoard, was the way they had been packaged. The scraps were divided into separate piles. Someone had wrapped each pile in fabric and then attached a bulla, a clay tab imprinted with an official seal. "I have since read that these bullae lasted for centuries," says Balmuth, "and were used to mark jars—or in this case things wrapped in fabric—that were sealed. That was a way of signing something."

All that remained was to impress the design of a seal directly on small rounded pieces of metal—which is precisely what

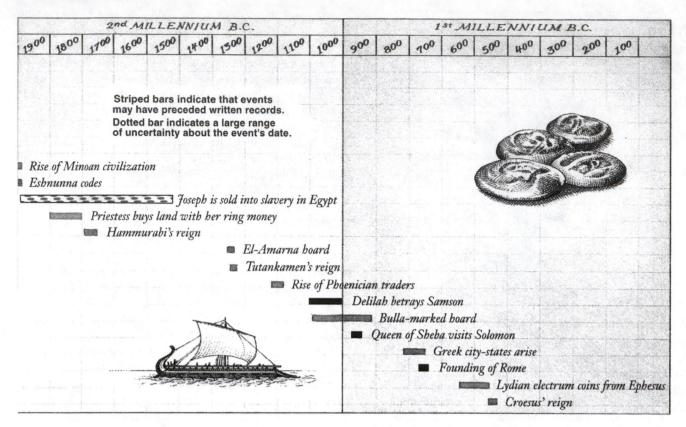

Striped bars indicate that events
may have preceded written records.
Dotted bar indicates a large range
of uncertainty about the event's date.

Rise of Minoan civilization
Eshnunna codes
Joseph is sold into slavery in Egypt
Priestess buys land with her ring money
Hammurabi's reign
El-Amarna hoard
Tutankamen's reign
Rise of Phoenician traders
Delilah betrays Samson
Bulla-marked hoard
Queen of Sheba visits Solomon
Greek city-states arise
Founding of Rome
Lydian electrum coins from Ephesus
Croesus' reign

Figure 4

happened by around 600 B.C. in an obscure Turkish kingdom by the sea. There traders and perfume makers known as the Lydians struck the world's first coins. They used electrum, a natural alloy of gold and silver panned from local riverbeds. (Coincidentally, Chinese kings minted their first money at roughly the same time: tiny bronze pieces shaped like knives and spades, bearing inscriptions revealing places of origin or weight. Circular coins in China came later.)

Such wealth did the newly invented coins bring one Lydian king, Croesus, that his name became a byword for prosperity.

First unearthed by archeologists early this century in the ruins of the Temple of Artemis in Ephesus, one of the Seven Wonders of the ancient world, the Lydian coins bore the essential hallmarks of modern coinage. Made of small, precisely measured pieces of precious metal, they were stamped with the figures of lions and other mighty beasts—the seal designs, it seems, of prominent Lydians. And such wealth did they bring one Lydian king, Croesus, that his name became a byword for prosperity.

Struck in denominations as small as .006 ounce of electrum—one-fifteenth the weight of a penny—Lydia's coinage could be used by people in various walks of life. The idea soon caught on in the neighboring Greek city-states. Within a few decades, rulers across Greece began churning out beautiful coins of varied denominations in unalloyed gold and silver, stamped with the faces of their gods and goddesses.

These new Greek coins became fundamental building blocks for European civilization. With such small change jingling in their purses, Greek merchants plied the western Mediterranean, buying all that was rare and beautiful from coastal dwellers, leaving behind Greek colonies from Sicily to Spain and spreading their ideas of art, government, politics, and philosophy. By the fourth century B.C., Alexander the Great was acquiring huge amounts of gold and silver through his conquests and issuing coins bearing his image far and wide, which Wyrick calls "ads for empire building."

Indeed, says Wyrick, the small change in our pockets literally made the Western world what it is today. "I tell my students that if money had never developed, we would all still be bartering. We would have been stuck with that. Money opened the door to trade, which opened the door for specialization. And that made possible a modern society."

How to Build a Pyramid

Hidden ramps may solve the mystery of the Great Pyramid's construction.

Bob Brier

Of the seven wonders of the ancient world, only the Great Pyramid of Giza remains. An estimated 2 million stone blocks weighing an average of 2½ tons went into its construction. When completed, the 481-foot-tall pyramid was the world's tallest structure, a record it held for more than 3,800 years, when England's Lincoln Cathedral surpassed it by a mere 44 feet.

We know who built the Great Pyramid: the pharaoh Khufu, who ruled Egypt about 2547-2524 B.C. And we know who supervised its construction: Khufu's brother, Hemienu. The pharaoh's right-hand man, Hemienu was "overseer of all construction projects of the king" and his tomb is one of the largest in a cemetery adjacent to the pyramid.

What we don't know is exactly how it was built, a question that has been debated for millennia. The earliest recorded theory was put forward by the Greek historian Herodotus, who visited Egypt around 450 B.C., when the pyramid was already 2,000 years old. He mentions "machines" used to raise the blocks and this is usually taken to mean cranes. Three hundred years later, Diodorus of Sicily wrote, "The construction was effected by mounds" (ramps). Today we have the "space alien" theory—those primitive Egyptians never could have built such a fabulous structure by themselves; extraterrestrials must have helped them.

Modern scholars have favored two basic theories, but deep in their hearts, they know that neither one is correct. A radical new one, however, may provide the solution. If correct, it would demonstrate a level of planning by Egyptian architects and engineers far greater than anything ever imagined before.

The External Ramp and Crane Theories

The first theory is that a ramp was built on one side of the pyramid and as the pyramid grew, the ramp was raised so that throughout the construction, blocks could be moved right up to the top. If the ramp were too steep, the men hauling the blocks would not be able to drag them up. An 8-percent slope is about the maximum possible, and this is the problem with the single ramp theory. With such a gentle incline, the ramp would

have to be approximately one mile long to reach the top of the pyramid. But there is neither room for such a long ramp on the Giza Plateau, nor evidence of such a massive construction. Also, a mile-long ramp would have had as great a volume as the pyramid itself, virtually doubling the man-hours needed to build the pyramid. Because the straight ramp theory just doesn't work, several pyramid experts have opted for a modified ramp theory.

This approach suggests that the ramp corkscrewed up the outside of the pyramid, much the way a mountain road spirals upward. The corkscrew ramp does away with the need for a massive mile-long one and explains why no remains of such a ramp have been found, but there is a flaw with this version of the theory. With a ramp corkscrewing up the outside of the pyramid, the corners couldn't be completed until the final stage of construction. But careful measurements of the angles at the corners would have been needed frequently to assure that the corners would meet to create a point at the top. Dieter Arnold, a renowned pyramid expert at The Metropolitan Museum of Art, comments in his definitive work, *Building in Egypt:* "During the whole construction period, the pyramid trunk would have been completely buried under the ramps. The surveyors could therefore not have used the four corners, edges, and foot line of the pyramid for their calculations." Thus the modified ramp theory also has a serious problem.

The second theory centers on Herodotus's machines. Until recently Egyptian farmers used a wooden, cranelike device called a *shadouf* to raise water from the Nile for irrigation. This device can be seen in ancient tomb paintings, so we know it was available to the pyramid builders. The idea is that hundreds of these cranes at various levels on the pyramid were used to lift the blocks. One problem with this theory is that it would involve a tremendous amount of timber and Egypt simply didn't have forests to provide the wood. Importing so much lumber would have been impractical. Large timbers for shipbuilding were imported from Lebanon, but this was a very expensive enterprise.

Perhaps an even more fatal flaw to the crane theory is that there is nowhere to place all these cranes. The pyramid blocks tend to decrease in size higher up the Great Pyramid. I climbed it dozens of times in the 1970s and '80s, when it was permitted, and toward the top, the blocks sometimes provide only 18 inches of standing room, certainly not enough space for cranes large enough to lift heavy blocks of stone. The crane theory can't explain how the blocks of the Great Pyramid were raised. So how was it done?

The Internal Ramp Theory

A radical new idea has recently been presented by Jean-Pierre Houdin, a French architect who has devoted the last seven years of his life to making detailed computer models of the Great Pyramid. Using state-of-the-art 3-D software developed by Dassault Systemes, combined with an initial suggestion of Henri Houdin, his engineer father, the architect has concluded that a ramp was indeed used to raise the blocks to the top, and that the ramp still exists—inside the pyramid!

The theory suggests that for the bottom third of the pyramid, the blocks were hauled up a straight, external ramp. This ramp was far shorter than the one needed to reach the top, and was made of limestone blocks, slightly smaller than those used to build the bottom third of the pyramid. As the bottom of the pyramid was being built via the external ramp, a second ramp was being built, inside the pyramid, on which the blocks for the top two-thirds of the pyramid would be hauled. The internal ramp, according to Houdin, begins at the bottom, is about 6 feet wide, and has a grade of approximately 7 percent. This ramp was put into use after the lower third of the pyramid was completed and the external ramp had served its purpose.

The design of the internal ramp was partially determined by the design of the interior of the pyramid. Hemienu knew all about the problems encountered by Pharaoh Sneferu, his and Khufu's father. Sneferu had considerable difficulty building a suitable pyramid for his burial, and ended up having to construct three at sites south of Giza! The first, at Meidum, may have had structural problems and was never used. His second, at Dashur—known as the Bent Pyramid because the slope of its sides changes midway up—developed cracks in the walls of its burial chamber. Huge cedar logs from Lebanon had to be wedged between the walls to keep the pyramid from collapsing inward, but it too was abandoned. There must have been a mad scramble to complete Sneferu's third and successful pyramid, the distinctively colored Red Pyramid at Dashur, before the aging ruler died.

From the beginning, Hemienu planned three burial chambers to ensure that whenever Khufu died, a burial place would be ready. One was carved out of the bedrock beneath the pyramid at the beginning of its construction. In case the pharaoh had died early, this would have been his tomb. When, after about five years, Khufu was still alive and well, the unfinished underground burial chamber was abandoned and the second burial chamber, commonly called the Queen's Chamber, was begun. Some time around the fifteenth year of construction Khufu was still healthy and this chamber was abandoned unfinished and the last burial chamber, the King's Chamber, was built higher up—in the center of the pyramid. (To this day, Khufu's sarcophagus remains inside the King's Chamber, so early explorers of the pyramid incorrectly assumed that the second chamber had been for his queen.)

Huge granite and limestone blocks were needed for the roof beams and rafters of the Queen's and King's Chambers. Some of these beams weigh more than 60 tons and are far too large to have been brought up through the internal ramp. Thus the external ramp had to remain in use until the large blocks were hauled up. Once that was done, the external ramp was dismantled and its blocks were led up the pyramid via the internal ramp to build the top two-thirds of the pyramid. Perhaps most blocks in this portion of the pyramid are smaller than those at the bottom third because they had to move up the narrow internal ramp.

There were several considerations that went into designing the internal ramp. First, it had to be fashioned very precisely so that it didn't hit the chambers or the internal passageways that connect them. Second, men hauling heavy blocks of stones up a narrow ramp can't easily turn a 90-degree corner; they need a place ahead of the block to stand and pull. The internal ramp had to provide a means of turning its corners so, Houdin suggests, the ramp had openings there where a simple crane could be used to turn the blocks.

There are plenty of theories about how the Great Pyramid could have been built that lack evidence. Is the internal ramp theory any different? Is there any evidence to support it? Yes.

A bit of evidence appears to be one of the ramp's corner notches used for turning blocks. It is two-thirds of the way up the northeast corner—precisely at a point where Houdin predicted there would be one. Furthermore, in 1986 a member of a French team that was surveying the pyramid reported seeing a desert fox enter it through a hole next to the notch, suggesting that there is an open area close to it, perhaps the ramp. It seems improbable that the fox climbed more than halfway up the pyramid. More likely there is some undetected crevice toward the bottom where the fox entered the ramp and then made its way up the ramp and exited near the notch. It would be interesting to attach a telemetric device to a fox and send him into the hole to monitor his movements! The notch is suggestive, but there is another bit of evidence supplied by the French mentioned earlier that is far more compelling.

When the French team surveyed the Great Pyramid, they used microgravimety, a technique that enabled them to measure the density of different sections of the pyramid, thus detecting hidden chambers. The French team concluded that there were no large hidden chambers inside it. If there was a ramp inside the pyramid, shouldn't the French have detected it? In 2000, Henri Houdin was presenting this theory at a scientific conference where one of the members of the 1986 French team was present. He mentioned to Houdin that their computer analysis of the pyramid did yield one curious image, something they couldn't interpret and therefore ignored. That image showed exactly what Jean-Pierre Houdin's theory had predicted—a ramp spiraling up through the pyramid.

Far from being just another theory, the internal ramp has considerable evidence behind it. A team headed by Jean-Pierre

Houdin and Rainer Stadlemann, former director of the German Archaeological Institute in Cairo and one of the greatest authorities on pyramids, has submitted an application to survey the Great Pyramid in a nondestructive way to see if the theory can be confirmed. They are hopeful that the Supreme Council of Antiquities will grant permission for a survey. (Several methods could be used, including powerful microgravimetry, high-resolution infrared photography, or even sonar.) If so, sometime this year we may finally know how Khufu's monumental tomb was built. One day, if it is indeed there, we might just be able to remove a few blocks from the exterior of the pyramid and walk up the mile-long ramp Hemienu left hidden within the Great Pyramid.

BOB BRIER is a senior research fellow at the C. W. Post Campus of Long Island University and a contributing editor to *Archaeology*.

UNIT 3

The Early Civilizations to 500 B.C.E.

Unit Selections

Key Points to Consider

- To what extent were Harappa and Mohenjo-Daro cosmopolitan urban centers? What made their success possible, and what was responsible for their demise?

- What effect has the work of Charles Higham had on the archaeology of ancient Southeast Asia? What are some of the fruits of his work?

- What proof is offered to support the thesis that drought-like conditions brought an end to several world civilization centers? Is the proof strong enough to support this thesis?

- What effect did Nubian pharaohs have on Egyptian history? On African History?

- Why was Qatna an important city in the ancient Near East? What factors combined to bring about its demise?

- Why was Shi Huangdi able to become China's first emperor? What effects did his rule have on the course of Chinese history?

- What difference of opinion exists between scholars regarding the role of Olmecs on the development of Mesoamerican civilization?

Student Web Site
www.mhcls.com

Internet References

Ancient Indus Valley
   www.harappa.com/har/har0.html
Civilization of the Olmecs
   www.ancientsudan.org/
Exploring Ancient World Cultures
   http://eawc.evansville.edu
Reeder's Egypt Page
   http://www.egyptology.com/reeder

What constitutes a civilization? Some characteristics might include urbanization, complex economic, political, and social systems, sophisticated technology, and literacy. If we use these criteria as a standard, evidence of cities, writing, and metallurgy would indicate the presence of civilization. But suppose one of these ingredients is missing. Would we be willing to conclude, for example, that a group or society that does not write is uncivilized? And, to take this question further, since historians rely on written records, are illiterate people prehistoric?

Judgments about what is a civilization and what is not imply value rankings. And, since world history texts are organized around a history of civilizations, only those societies that are considered civilizations are included in the story. Mesopotamia, the ancient Greek name for the area "between the rivers"—the Tigris and Euphrates in modern Iraq—was home to the Bronze Age civilizations of Assyria, Akkad, and Sumer. In that "cradle of civilization," as well as on the Greek island of Crete, we find systems of writing, decorated pottery, paved streets, elaborate metal working, and sophisticated trading networks.

You know about the Incas because historians broadened the definition of civilization to include this complex society. But, you may know little about the Nubians, a powerful, literate society that once controlled all of ancient Egypt. The Greeks and Romans considered Nubia one of the foremost civilizations of the world, and valued its gold, frankincense, ebony, ivory, and animal skins. Herodotus admired the Nubians for their height, beauty, and longevity.

And, in the Indus River Valley, two of the earliest planned cities—Harappa and Mohenjo-Daro—featured water conduits, toilets, straight streets, and standard-sized building bricks four thousand years ago. Archaeologists have unearthed orderly walled cities and evidence of one of the world's first written languages in a civilization twice the size of Egypt and Mesopotamia that lasted for 700 years. Until the nineteenth century, however, we knew nothing of these peoples or their thriving, prosperous cultures.

Borrowing the methods and findings of archaeology has permitted historians to add to the list of civilizations. Most ancient cities and their civilizations have not survived, conquered either by competing civilizations or by nature. So, what is called material culture is often our only window into the lives

© Getty Images

of ancient peoples. Potsherds and even gold jewelry provide some insights about daily life and wealth, but tell us nothing about the thoughts and attitudes of the people who used these artifacts. Access to the inner life is possible only through the written word. And legacies from these ancient languages endure today, in our use of Assyrian words for many plants and minerals, as well as in our borrowing of the Sumerian system of astronomy and timekeeping, based on the number six. Our 60-second minutes and 60-minute hours have their roots in ancient Sumer.

Indus Valley, Inc.

No golden tombs, no fancy ziggurats. Four thousand years ago city builders in the Indus Valley made deals, not war, and created a stable, peaceful, and prosperous culture.

SHANTI MENON

The railway linking Lahore to Multan in Pakistan is 4,600 years old. In truth, the rails were laid down in the middle of the nineteenth century, but to build the railway bed, British engineers smashed bricks from crumbling buildings and rubble heaps in a town called Harappa, halfway between the two cities. Back in 1856, Alexander Cunningham, director of the newly formed Archaeological Survey of India, thought the brick ruins were all related to nearby seventh-century Buddhist temples. Local legend told a different story: the brick mounds were the remnants of an ancient city, destroyed when its king committed incest with his niece. Neither Cunningham nor the locals were entirely correct. In small, desultory excavations a few years later, Cunningham found no temples or traces of kings, incestuous or otherwise. Instead he reported the recovery of some pottery, carved shell, and a badly damaged seal depicting a one-horned animal, bearing an inscription in an unfamiliar writing.

That seal was a mark of one of the world's great ancient civilizations, but mid-nineteenth-century archeologists like Cunningham knew nothing of it. The Vedas, the oldest texts of the subcontinent, dating from some 3,500 years ago, made no mention of it, nor did the Bible. No pyramids or burial mounds marked the area as the site of an ancient power. Yet 4,600 years ago, at the same time as the early civilizations of Mesopotamia and Egypt, great cities arose along the floodplains of the ancient Indus and Saraswati rivers in what is now Pakistan and northwest India. The people of the Indus Valley didn't build towering monuments, bury their riches along with their dead, or fight legendary and bloody battles. They didn't have a mighty army or a divine emperor. Yet they were a highly organized and stupendously successful civilization. They built some of the world's first planned cities, created one of the world's first written languages, and thrived in an area twice the size of Egypt and Mesopotamia for 700 years.

To archeologists of this century and the last, Harappa and Mohenjo-Daro, a neighboring city some 350 miles to the southwest, posed an interesting, if unglamorous puzzle. Excavations revealed large, orderly walled cities of massive brick buildings, with highly sophisticated sanitation and drainage systems and a drab, institutional feel. The streets of Harappa, remarked British archeologist Mortimer Wheeler, "however impressive quantitatively, and significant sociologically, are aesthetically miles of monotony." The archeologist and popular author Leonard Cottrell, a contemporary of Wheeler's, wrote in 1956, "While admiring the efficiency of Harappan planning and sanitary engineering, one's general impression of Harappan culture is unattractive. . . . One imagines those warrens of streets, baking under the fierce sun of the Punjab, as human ant heaps, full of disciplined, energetic activity, supervised and controlled by a powerful, centralized state machine; a civilization in which there was little joy, much labor, and a strong emphasis on material things."

Superior plumbing and uniform housing, no matter how well designed, don't fire the imagination like ziggurats and gold-laden tombs. "But there's more to society than big temples and golden burials," argues Jonathan Mark Kenoyer, an archeologist at the University of Wisconsin in Madison. "Those are the worst things that ancient societies did, because they led to their collapse. When you take gold and put it in the ground, it's bad for the economy. When you waste money on huge monuments instead of shipping, it's bad for the economy. The Indus Valley started out with a very different basis and made South Asia the center of economic interactions in the ancient world."

Kenoyer, who was born in India to missionary parents, has been excavating at Harappa for the past 12 years. His work, and that of his colleagues, is changing the image of Harappa from a stark, state-run city into a vibrant, diverse metropolis, teeming with artisans and well-traveled merchants.

"What we're finding at Harappa, for the first time," says Kenoyer, "is how the first cities started." Mesopotamian texts suggest that cities sprang up around deities and their temples, and once archeologists found these temples, they didn't look much further. "People assumed this is how cities evolved, but

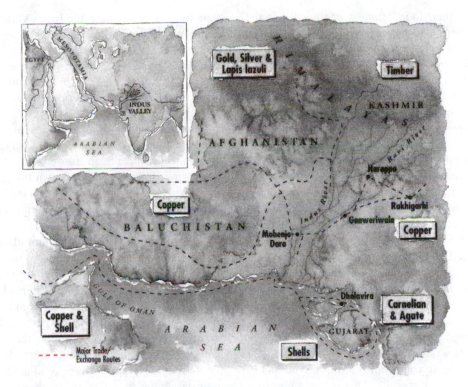

Figure 1　Indus Valley cities lay along major trade routes.

Note: Map by Bette Duke.

we don't know that for a fact," says Kenoyer. At Harappa, a temple of the glitzy Mesopotamian variety has yet to be found.

Kenoyer's archeological evidence suggests that the city got its start as a farming village around 3300 B.C. Situated near the Ravi River, one of several tributaries of the ancient Indus River system of Pakistan and northwestern India, Harappa lay on a fertile floodplain. Good land and a reliable food supply allowed the village to thrive, but the key to urbanization was its location at the crossroads of several major trading routes.

Traders from the highlands of Baluchistan and northern Afghanistan to the west brought in copper, tin, and lapis lazuli; clam and conch shells were brought in from the southern seacoast, timber from the Himalayas, semiprecious stones from Gujarat, silver and gold from Central Asia. The influx of goods allowed Harappans to become traders and artisans as well as farmers. And specialists from across the land arrived to set up shop in the new metropolis.

The city had room to expand and an entrepreneurial spirit driven by access to several sources of raw materials. "You had two sources of lapis, three of copper, and several for shell," says Kenoyer. "The way I envision it, if you had entrepreneurial go-get-'em, and you had a new resource, you could make a million in Harappa. It was a mercantile base for rapid growth and expansion." Enterprising Harappan traders exported finely crafted Indus Valley products to Mesopotamia, Iran, and Central Asia and brought back payment in precious metals and more raw materials. By 2200 B.C., Harappa covered about 370 acres

and may have held 80,000 people, making it roughly as populous as the ancient city of Ur in Mesopotamia. And it soon had plenty of neighbors. Over the course of 700 years, some 1,500 Indus Valley settlements were scattered over 280,000 square miles of the subcontinent.

Unlike Mesopotamian cities, Indus Valley cities all followed the same basic plan, reflecting the people's ritual conception of universal order.

Unlike the haphazard arrangement of Mesopotamian cities, Indus Valley settlements all followed the same basic plan. Streets and houses were laid out on a north-south, east-west grid, and houses and walls were built of standard-size bricks. Even early agricultural settlements were constructed on a grid. "People had a ritual conception of the universe, of universal order," says Kenoyer. "The Indus cities and earlier villages reflect that." This organization, he believes, could have helped the growing city avoid conflicts, giving newcomers their own space rather than leaving them to elbow their way into established territories.

Part of that ritual conception included a devotion to sanitation. Nearly every Harappan home had a bathing platform and a latrine, says Kenoyer, and some Indus Valley cities reached heights of 40 feet in part because of concern about hygiene.

Cities often grow upon their foundations over time, but in the Indus Valley, homes were also periodically elevated to avoid the risk of runoff from a neighbor's sewage, "It's keeping up with the Joneses' bathroom," he quips, "that made these cities rise so high so quickly." Each neighborhood had its own well, and elaborate covered drainage systems carried dirty water outside the city. By contrast, city dwellers in Mesopotamian cities tended to draw water from the river or irrigation canals, and they had no drains.

The towering brick cities, surrounded by sturdy walls with imposing gateways, reminded early researchers of the medieval forts in Delhi and Lahore. But Kenoyer points out that a single wall, with no moat and with no sudden turns to lead enemies into an ambush, would have been ill-suited for defense. He thinks the walls were created to control the flow of goods in and out of the city. At Harappa, standardized cubical stone weights have been found at the gates, and Kenoyer suggests they were used to levy taxes on trade goods coming into the city. The main gateway at Harappa is nine feet across, just wide enough to allow one oxcart in or out. "If you were a trader," he explains, "you wanted to bring goods into a city to trade in a safe place, so bandits wouldn't rip you off. To get into the city, you had to pay a tax. If you produced things, you had to pay a tax to take goods out of the city. This is how a city gets revenues."

The identity of the tax collectors and those they served remains a mystery. Unlike the rulers of Mesopotamia and Egypt, Indus Valley rulers did not immortalize themselves with mummies or monuments. They did, however, leave behind elaborately carved stone seals, used to impress tokens or clay tabs on goods bound for market. The seals bore images of animals, like the humped bull, the elephant, the rhinoceros, and the crocodile, which were probably emblems of powerful clans. The most common image is the unicorn, a symbol that originated in the Indus Valley.

Frustratingly, though, those seals carry inscriptions that no one has been able to decipher. Not only are the inscriptions short, but they don't resemble any known language. From analyzing overlapping strokes, it is clear that the script reads right to left. It is also clear that the script is a mix of phonetic symbols and pictographs. Early Mesopotamian cuneiform, which used only pictographs, was thought to be the world's first written language, says Kenoyer, but the Indus Valley script emerged independently around the same time—at least by around 3300 B.C.

As long as the language remains a mystery, so too will the identities of the Indus Valley elites. Kenoyer thinks each of the large cities may have functioned as an independent city-state, controlled by a small group of merchants, landowners, and religious leaders. "They controlled taxation, access to the city, and communication with the gods," he says. While the balance of power may have shifted between these groups, they seem to have ruled without a standing army. Sculptures, paintings, and texts from Egypt and Mesopotamia clearly illustrate battles between cities and pharaonic wars of conquest. But in the Indus Valley, not a single depiction of a military act, of taking prisoners, of a human killing another human has been found. It's possible these acts were illustrated on cloth or paper or some other perishable and simply did not survive. Yet none of the cities show signs of battle damage to buildings or city walls, and very few weapons have been recovered.

Human remains show no signs of violence either. Only a few cemeteries have been found, suggesting that burial of the dead may have been limited to high-ranking individuals (others may have been disposed of through cremation or river burials). The bones from excavated burials show few signs of disease or malnourishment. Preliminary genetic studies from a cemetery in Harappa have suggested that women were buried near their mothers and grandmothers. Men do not seem to be related to those near them, so they were probably buried with their wives' families. There is evidence that people believed in an afterlife: personal items like amulets and simple pottery have been recovered from a few burials. But true to their practical, businesslike nature, the Harappans didn't bury their dead with riches. Unlike the elites of the Near East, Harappans kept their valuable items in circulation, trading for new, often extraordinary ornaments for themselves and their descendants.

In spite of this practice, excavators have turned up some hints of the wealth an individual could accumulate. Two decades ago, in the rural settlement of Allahdino, near modern Karachi in Pakistan, archeologists stumbled upon a buried pot filled with jewelry, the secret hoard of a rich landowner. Among the silver and gold necklaces and gold bands, beads, and rings was a belt or necklace made of 36 elongated carnelian beads interspersed with bronze beads. Shaping and drilling these long, slender beads out of hard stone is immensely difficult and time-consuming. Indus craftsmen made a special drill for this purpose by heating a rare metamorphic rock to create a superhard material. Even these high-tech drills could perforate carnelian at a rate of only a hundredth of an inch per hour. Kenoyer estimates that a large carnelian belt like the one at Allahdino would have taken a single person 480 working days to complete. It was most likely made by a group of artisans over a period of two or three years.

Such intensive devotion to craftsmanship and trade, Kenoyer argues, is what allowed Indus Valley culture to spread over a region twice the size of Mesopotamia without a trace of military domination. Just as American culture is currently exported along with goods and media, so too were the seals, pottery styles, and script of the Indus Valley spread among the local settlements. Figurines from the Indus Valley also testify to a complex social fabric. People within the same city often wore different styles of dress and hair, a practice that could reflect differences in ethnicity or status. Men are shown with long hair or short, bearded or clean-shaven. Women's hairstyles could be as simple as one long braid, or complex convolutions of tresses piled high on a supporting structure.

Eventually, between 1900 and 1700 B.C., the extensive trading networks and productive farms supporting this cultural integration collapsed, says Kenoyer, and distinct local cultures emerged. "They stopped writing," he says. "They stopped using the weight system for taxation. And the unicorn motif disappeared." Speculation as to the reasons for the disintegration has ranged from warfare to weather. Early archeologists believed that Indo-Aryan invaders from the north swept through and conquered the peaceful Harappans, but that theory has since been disproved. None of the major cities show evidence of warfare, though some smaller settlements appear to have been abandoned. There is evidence that the Indus River shifted, flooding many settlements and disrupting agriculture. It is likely that when these smaller settlements were abandoned, trade routes were affected. In the Ganges River valley to the east, on the outskirts of the Indus Valley sphere of influence, the newly settled Indo-Aryans, with their own customs, grew to prominence while cities like Harappa faded.

But the legacy of the ancient Indus cities and their craftspeople remains. The bead makers of Khambhat in India continue to make beads based on Harappan techniques—though the carnelian is now bored with diamond-tipped drills. Shell workers in Bengal still make bangles out of conch shells. And in the crowded marketplaces of Delhi and Lahore, as merchants hawk the superiority of their silver over the low-quality ore of their neighbors, as gold and jewels are weighed in bronze balances, it's hard to imagine that a 4,000-year-old Harappan bazaar could have been terribly different.

Uncovering Ancient Thailand

Charles Higham's 40-year career has transformed our understanding of prehistoric Southeast Asia.

Tom Gidwitz

Eleven skeletons lie exposed at the bottom of a yawning ten-foot-deep hole in the village of Ban Non Wat, Thailand. Two dozen people swarm over them, troweling the earth in search of more graves, hoisting up the soil bucket by bucket. Workers kneel over the 3,000-year-old bones, coaxing them free with dental picks, still others sketch, bag, and carry them away. A white fabric roof hangs over the 40-foot-square pit; outside its shelter, more workers screen soil, sort artifacts, and reassemble countless sherds into graceful, ancient pots.

One man in shorts, sandals, and floppy gray hat seems to be everywhere. Charles Higham is in charge of this dig, leading his army of archaeologists, villagers, and Earthwatch volunteers by inspiration and example. One moment he's lying in the dirt, scraping at a wrist bone thick with shell bangles, and the next he's huddling over field notes with one of his students or joking with the locals in Thai. When traces of a new grave are discovered, he sometimes darts into the crowd of excavators and, with a few sweeps of his trowel, exposes a pot or a skull.

Higham, 66, an ebullient Englishman with a fringe of graying hair and a ready laugh, is a professor at the University of Otago in Dunedin, New Zealand. Since 1969 he has set his sights on filling in what he calls "the tabula rasa" of Southeast Asian prehistory by probing its most profound transformations: how its hunter-gatherers became farmers, its farmers became metalworkers, and its village elders became kings. His discoveries and books have illuminated a culture that stretches back 30,000 years.

"Until 30 years ago our knowledge of this area was very sparse indeed," Higham says, "but now Southeast Asia has become a major place in the world for understanding human history, not just prehistory, but the history of our species. If anyone is remotely interested in that, then don't ignore Southeast Asia."

Higham has been one of the few English-speaking archaeologists working year after year in the region. "Everybody flocks like lemmings into Maya country and western Europe or the Near East," says Brian Fagan, emeritus professor of anthropology at the University of California, Santa Barbara, but Higham has hunkered down "in one of the seminal areas of early civilization."

"He's very much an archaeologist's archaeologist," says Graeme Barker, of Cambridge University. "What Charles writes we all want to read."

And here at Ban Non Wat, he has found plenty to write about. The village is on the Khorat Plateau, a rolling plain in northeast Thailand with a rich past; occupied since 2100 B.C., the site is only 30 miles from Phimai, once a temple city of the Angkor civilization. Over the past five years, Higham and Thai archaeologist Rachanie Thosarat have returned each dry season. So far, they have unearthed more than 460 Neolithic, Bronze, and Iron Age graves, offering an unparalleled view of the region's prehistoric past. "Every time we dig here," Higham says with relish, "it's a new surprise."

Higham fell in love with archaeology when he was 14 years old, after his aunt gave him W. Ceram's classic *Gods, Graves, and Scholars* for Christmas. The next summer he and his older brother Richard volunteered to dig at Snail Down, an Early Bronze Age cemetery near Stonehenge. By 1959, when Higham entered Cambridge, he had also dug in France and Greece and studied archaeology at the University of London.

The son of an architect, Higham had two burning goals at Cambridge: to win the highest academic honors and thus earn a full scholarship, and to play against Oxford in the annual rugby match. Although only 5'9" tall, he was a star player on the university's unbeaten rugby team and, in its victory over Oxford, put the first points on the board. In the classroom, he shone in a group of gifted young scholars studying under archaeologist Grahame Clark.

Clark pioneered the field of economic prehistory, the study of how early societies survived in their environments using evidence gleaned from the seeds, sticks, bones, and soil that most archaeologists at the time simply threw away. For his doctorate, Higham used domesticated cattle bones to reconstruct prehistoric life in Denmark and Switzerland.

Says Norman Hammond, a fellow student at Cambridge and now professor of archaeology at Boston University, "His natural gift is for seeing promise in an unpromising situation. Nobody really thought of cattle bones in central Europe as being sexy. Charles was able to turn them into a major piece of work." While he researched he shrewdly submitted his findings to local and national journals. "By the time he got his Ph.D., he had a string of publications as long as your arm in six languages, and he was able to walk straight into a job at the University of Otago in New Zealand to teach European prehistory."

The Otago appointment was also due to Clark, who worked hard to spread his influence by placing his students in jobs around the world. "He got it into his head that because I was a rugby player and the [New Zealand] All Blacks were the best rugby team in the world, that I was the right person for New Zealand," Higham says.

Higham, his wife, Polly, and son Tom, the first of four children, arrived in 1967, and Higham swiftly made his mark. New Zealand has no prehistoric pottery, so its past can be difficult to decipher. Higham, with a landmark study, used the shells in an ancient midden to reveal the seasonal migrations of prehistoric Maori tribes. Two years after arriving, at only 28 years old, Higham became the first professor of prehistoric archaeology in Australasia.

Until then, prehistoric excavations in Southeast Asia had been few, and finds meager. Instead, scholars had focused on the stone ruins and inscriptions of ancient kingdoms that arose in the first centuries A.D.—Funan in the Mekong Delta, Champa in coastal Viet Nam, Dvarivati in central Thailand, and above all the magnificent Angkor civilization that thrived in Cambodia, Laos, and Thailand from the ninth to fifteenth centuries. These scholars thought Indian Brahmins and seafaring merchants had brought India's sophisticated Hindu culture to docile, primitive clans.

In the late 1960s, archaeologists began to focus anew on the region's prehistory. In 1969, Higham went to Thailand to meet American archaeologists Wilhelm Solheim, Donn Bayard, and Chester Gorman, who had discovered what were thought to be Asia's oldest bronze artifacts on the Khorat plateau. Soon, he was digging with Gorman in remote Thai caves, looking in vain for the region's first farmers.

In 1974, Higham was with Gorman and Thai archaeologist Prisit Charoenwongsa at Ban Chiang, a Khorat plateau village where looters had been plundering extraordinarily beautiful pots. Thermoluminescence dating suggested the pottery was 6,000 years old, and the University of Pennsylvania sponsored an excavation to rescue what was left. "We were in very heady, exciting times," Higham recalls.

Two years later, Gorman and Charoenwongsa announced Ban Chiang's bronze dated to 3600 B.C. and its iron to 1600 B.C., making them the earliest in the world. Extraordinarily, these advances had arisen in an egalitarian rural village. Elsewhere, metalworking had developed hand in hand with stratified societies, warfare, and specialized labor.

The discovery sparked a sensation. Ban Chiang artifacts appeared in newspapers around the globe, in *Time* and *Newsweek* cover stories, and in a traveling Smithsonian Institution show. But it also featured in heated debate.

"It led to two groups," Higham recalls, "one of which believed it, and one of which said, 'It's a whole lot of hooey, and this can't be the case'."

In 1980 Higham teamed up with Thai archaeologist Amphan Kijngam. At Ban Na Di, 14 miles southwest of Ban Chiang, they uncovered chunks of melted bronze and casting molds from a cultural phase almost certainly contemporary with Ban Chiang's famous bronze. Higham sent the charcoal dating samples to a New Zealand lab.

"When they came back I got quite a shock. They were a thousand, two thousand years later than I imagined." The site's earliest bronze was dated to about only 1300 B.C., which pushed the site's iron to an even more recent date. "Beyond any doubt the radiocarbon results from Ban Chiang were far too early." The charcoal samples from this site, some of which Higham had gathered, had come from grave fill, which can include charcoal unearthed at the time of burial and far older than the graves themselves.

Later tests showed Ban Chiang's earliest pottery to be only about 4,000 years old, and most archaeologists now agree with Higham's dates. He is convinced bronze is a Middle Eastern innovation, carried into China along the Silk Road; the Thais learned it in the later second millennium B.C. from Shang Dynasty merchants who ventured south to swap bronze vessels for local goods.

Early in his career, before he had the resources to lead his own expeditions, Higham published a paper describing how best to explore what he called the "terra incognita" of prehistoric Southeast Asia. "He then moved like a general," says Hammond, "marshalling his forces across the area of central and northern Thailand, identifying a series of problems, and the sites at which they might be resolved, digging them, publishing them in depth, and promptly."

In the 1980s he aimed his sights on the hundreds of mounds that dot rice paddies in Thailand and northeast Cambodia. Often surrounded with ancient moats and banks, with villages perched on top, the mounds can cover 100 acres and reach 30 feet high. They formed during generations of human occupation, in a steady accumulation of cultural debris.

An hour east of Bangkok is a steep mound known as Khok Phanom Di. It was thought to be a natural hill until 1978, when a bulldozer, cutting a new path to the Buddhist temple atop it, unearthed beads, bracelets, and bones. A Thai archaeologist sank a test pit into the mound, and in 1980 showed Higham shellfish, rice, and radiocarbon dates suggesting it had been occupied for thousands of years.

Sea levels have risen and fallen several times over the past ten millennia, and although Khok Phanom Di now lies 14 miles from the Gulf of Siam, the test pit's shellfish were saltwater varieties. The mound seemed an ideal place to study the relationship between the resource-rich coast and early rice cultivation.

In 1984, Higham and Thosarat returned and dug for seven months, down 26 feet to the natural soil, removing 155 skeletons and enough pots, jewelry, stone tools, seeds, and dirt to fill more than five railroad boxcars.

The team subjected the material to an investigation that was unprecedented in Southeast Asia. They performed detailed forensic analyses of all the skeletons, even testing for strontium isotopes in their teeth—which vary depending on one's childhood environment—to spot newcomers to the settlement. They looked at food remains in the ingestive tracts of two especially well-preserved bodies to discover what they had eaten. They drilled the soil around the mound for ancient seeds, pollen, and sediments. The analyses filled seven volumes.

What they discovered was the first settlers arrived in 2000 B.C. at what was then a major river estuary near the open sea. They made a living as hunter-fisher-gatherers, using weighted nets and bone fishhooks to snare crabs, fish, porpoises, sharks, and rays. They were also skillful potters, and since the surrounding mud flats were too salty to farm, they traded ceramics for rice with farmers who lived on higher ground. They suffered from malarial mosquitoes and an inherited anemia that killed most of their children in infancy, but the surviving adults—some lived into their 40s—were generally in good health.

After about six generations sea levels fell, and the surrounding swamps silted up. Women from outside the community joined the site, and the people of Khok Phanom Di began to farm rice on the floodplain, digging with granite hoes, harvesting with shell knives. In time, the sea rose again, the salt marshes returned, and the villagers made their livelihood once more from ceramics.

The team found an astonishing grave dated to roughly 1500 B.C., when a woman was reverently interred under stacked pots and cylinders of raw potter's clay. The team dubbed her "the Princess." She was covered in red ochre and wore a shell headdress and two garments embroidered with more than 120,000 beads. Nearby lay a 15-month-old infant, undoubtedly her child, beneath the same clay forms, in the same red ochre, in a miniature version of her spectacular beaded garments. Beside the Princess's ankle a shell container held a ceramic anvil for shaping pots. Beside the infant, in exactly the same position, was a little anvil no bigger than a thimble.

The Princess died in her mid thirties, a wealthy master potter in the largest prehistoric grave Higham had yet seen. But she was only one of many thriving villagers. The team traced inherited skeletal traits in the clustered graves and discovered that two families endured for 17 generations. These families' fortunes fluctuated, with some generations rich in grave goods, others with little, proof that personal achievement, not inheritance, was the community's key to wealth.

"Only when a mortuary tradition in a single community can be followed over so many generations can we gain such an intimate glimpse into its operating principles," Higham wrote.

In 1994, Higham and Thosarat launched the Origins of Angkor, a multidisciplinary study in search of the region's Iron Age, a time around 500 B.C. when chiefdoms began to coalesce into the civilization of Angkor.

So far, they have excavated four sites in Thailand, and expanded to encompass two Cambodian digs. But the finds at Noen U-Loke, a village three miles from Ban Non Wat, stand out.

Noen U-Loke is a 30-acre mound ringed with five moats jutting 600 feet into the rice fields. The team dug for two seasons, revealing Southeast Asia's longest Iron Age mortuary sequence, more than 120 graves revealing an eight-century-long narrative of growing wealth, power, and eventual strife.

Iron was used at Noen U-Loke from the start, at first primarily for jewelry, then increasingly for farm tools and weapons. The early men and women wore Bronze Age-style shell and marble jewelry, but adopted beads of carnelian, jade, glass, and silver as well as gold earrings, tiger-tooth necklaces, and agate pendants imported from India. As time went on, the settlement grew rich, with some members buried in rice-filled coffins, wearing so many bronze toe rings, finger rings, bangles, and bracelets that they must have blazed in the sun.

Between 1 and 300 B.C., the community's leaders ordered construction of the moats and banks. But not long after, signs of warfare—iron spears and arrowheads—appear in abundance. In the mound's last years, one youth was laid to rest with an iron arrowhead piercing his spine, a victim.

Higham believes the increasingly elaborate burials demonstrate fine emergence of princely elites. And although the site was abandoned early in the first millennium, elsewhere lords like these soon began to construct brick temples, worship Hindu deities, adopt Sanskrit names, and, in time, swear fealty to the Khmer god-kings.

Excavations in southeast asia take place in the dry season from December to March, and to Higham, time is precious. "When we find nothing except soil and potsherds we have to work very hard and fast, like a battlefield, like a war," says Warrachai Wiriyaromp, an associate professor at Bangkok's Kasetsart University, a doctoral student of Higham's who has worked with him since 1979. "But when we reach the skeleton layer, we slow down, and work like hearing an orchestra, slowly, bit by bit."

Now it is March 1, and the diggers at Ban Non Wat have come to the undisturbed soil beneath the mound. This year Higham's team has found Iron Age butchering floors, a collapsed wattle and daub house, and a cemetery with 60 bodies crammed like sardines. The site's Bronze Age layers have yielded what he calls "super burials," high-status individuals interred together in single graves as long as 15 feet, laden with jewelry, beaded garments, bronze tools, and as many as 150 pots. These burials, near relatively poor, unadorned graves, have "revolutionized our thinking on the Bronze Age and its social structure," he says triumphantly, for they offer firm proof that, as elsewhere in the world, "there is a social hierarchy, a marked one, in the Bronze Age of Southeast Asia."

But as the season nears its end, he is encountering new puzzles. Until now the team has found bodies interred flat on their backs, the custom with farming cultures. But for the last two days three adults of unknown gender and a baby cradled in its mother's arms have emerged, buried on their sides with their knees drawn up in the crouching position favored by hunter-gatherers, with pots and shell jewelry unlike any found in the Neolithic graves. They're the first flexed bodies discovered on the Khorat plateau.

"They shouldn't be there. We've never found one before, and now we have five of them," says Higham. "We're nonplused, is the only way to put it."

These flexed burials support a bold theory. In 1987, Higham's former classmate, Cambridge professor Colin Renfrew, proposed that farmers in the Near East moved into new lands occupied by hunter-gatherers, spreading agriculture and Indo-European languages west to Ireland, east to China, and south into India. Linguists and archaeologists have proposed a similar diaspora for the spread of Austroasiatic and Austronesian languages in Asia, as farmers in China's Yangtze River valley began a migration in about 6000 B.C. that took human pioneers to eastern India, the Pacific Islands, and into Southeast Asia around 2500–200 B.C.

Higham notes that agriculture and metalworking arise later and later with further distance from the Yangtze, and that across the region pottery decoration, burial practices, and language are intriguingly similar.

He is already toying with scenarios for the flexed burials. Did Neolithic farmers move onto the mound where a hunter-gatherer cemetery already existed, or did arriving farmers and local, hunter-gatherers intermarry and bury their dead in the hunter-gatherer style?

But as Higham looks down at the gray bones of the clinging infant and its mother, he knows that future excavations could easily prove his theories wrong. "If we were to start opening up an area of this size at another site," he says, "God knows what we'd find."

TOM GIDWITZ is a contributing editor for *Archaeology*.

Empires in the Dust

Some 4,000 years ago, a number of mighty Bronze Age cultures crumbled. Were they done in by political strife and societal unrest? Or by a change in the climate?

KAREN WRIGHT

Mesopotamia: cradle of civilization, the fertile bread-basket of western Asia, a little slice of paradise between the Tigris and Euphrates rivers. Today the swath of land north of the Persian Gulf is still prime real estate. But several millennia ago Mesopotamia was absolutely The Place to Be. There the visionary king Hammurabi ruled, and Babylon's hanging gardens hung. There the written word, metal-working, and bureaucracy were born. From the stately, rational organization of Mesopotamia's urban centers, humanity began its inexorable march toward strip malls and shrink-wrap and video poker bars and standing in line at the DMV. What's more, the emergence of the city-state meant that we no longer had to bow to the whims of nature. We rose above our abject dependence on weather, tide, and tilth; we were safe in the arms of empire. Isn't that what being civilized is all about?

Not if you ask Harvey Weiss. Weiss, professor of Near Eastern archeology at Yale, has challenged one of the cherished notions of his profession: that early civilizations—with their monuments and their grain reserves, their texts and their taxes—were somehow immune to natural disaster. He says he's found evidence of such disaster on a scale so grand it spelled calamity for half a dozen Bronze Age cultures from the Mediterranean to the Indus Valley—including the vaunted vale of Mesopotamia. Historians have long favored political and social explanations for these collapses: disruptions in trade routes, incompetent administrators, barbarian invasions. "Prehistoric societies, single agriculturists—they can be blown out by natural forces," says Weiss. But the early civilizations of the Old World? "It's not supposed to happen."

Yet happen it did, says Weiss, and unlike his predecessors, he's got some data to back him up. The evidence comes from a merger of his own archeological expertise with the field of paleoclimatology, the study of climates past. His first case study concerns a series of events that occurred more than 4,000 years ago in a region of northern Mesopotamia called the Habur Plains. There, in the northeast corner of what is present-day Syria, a network of urban centers arose in the middle of the third millennium B.C. Sustained by highly productive organized agriculture, the cities thrived. Then, around 2200 B.C., the region's new urbanites abruptly left their homes and fled south, abandoning the cities for centuries to come.

Weiss believes that the inhabitants fled an onslaught of wind and dust kicked up by a drought that lasted 300 years. He also believes the drought crippled the empire downriver, which had come to count on the agricultural proceeds of the northern plains. Moreover, he contends, the long dry spell wasn't just a local event; it was caused by a rapid, region-wide climate change whose effects were felt by budding civilizations as far west as the Aegean Sea and the Nile and as far east as the Indus Valley. While the Mesopotamians were struggling with their own drought-induced problems, he points out, neighboring societies were collapsing as well: the Old Kingdom in Egypt, early Bronze Age cities in Palestine, and the early Minoan civilization of Crete. And in the Indus Valley, refugees fleeing drought may have overwhelmed the cities of Mohenjo-Daro and Harappa. The troubles of half a dozen Bronze Age societies, says Weiss, can be blamed on a single event—and a natural disaster at that.

Weiss first presented this scenario in 1993, when soil analyses showed that a period of severe dust storms accompanied the mysterious Habur hiatus. "I was thinking you can't have a microregion drought," he recalls, "because that isn't how climate works. It's got to be much bigger. And I said, 'Wait a minute, didn't I read about this in graduate school? Weren't there those who, 30 years ago, had said that drought conditions were probably the agency that accounts for all these collapses that happened in contiguous regions?'" says Weiss. "Back in the late sixties, we had read this stuff and laughed our heads off about it."

In 1966, British archeologist James Mellaart had indeed blamed drought for the downfalls of a whole spectrum of third-millennium civilizations, from the early Bronze Age communities in Palestine to the pyramid builders of Egypt's Old Kingdom. But when Mellaart first put forth this idea, he didn't have much in the way of data to back him up. Weiss, however, can point to new paleoclimate studies for his proof. These studies suggest that an abrupt, widespread change in the climate of western Asia did in fact occur at 2200 B.C. Samples of old ocean sediments from the Gulf of Oman, for example, show signs of extreme drought just when Weiss's alleged exodus took place. A new model of air-mass movement explains how subtle shifts in atmospheric circulation could have scorched Mesopotamia as well as points east, west, and south. And recent analyses of ice cores from Greenland—which offer the most detailed record of global climate change—reveal unusual climatic conditions at 2200 B.C. that could well have brought drought to the region in question.

I've got some figures I can show you. Figures always help," says paleoclimatologist Peter deMenocal, swiveling his chair from reporter to computer in his office at Columbia University's Lamont-Doherty Earth Observatory, just north of New York City. On the monitor, deMenocal pulls up a graph derived from the research project known as GISP2 (for Greenland Ice Sheet Project 2). GISP2 scientists, he explains, use chemical signals in ice cores to reconstruct past climates. There are two kinds of naturally occurring oxygen atoms, heavy and light, and they accumulate in ice sheets in predictable ratios that vary with prevailing temperatures. In a cool climate, for example, heavy oxygen isotopes are less easily evaporated out of the ocean and transported as snow or rain to northern landmasses like Greenland. In a warm climate, however, more heavy oxygen isotopes will be evaporated, and more deposited in the Greenland ice sheets.

By tracking oxygen-isotope ratios within the ice cores, the GISP2 graph reflects temperatures over Greenland for the past 15,000 years. Near the bottom of the graph, a black line squiggle[s] wildly until 11,700 years ago, when the last ice age ended and the current warm era, the Holocene, began. The line then climbs steadily for a few thousand years, wavering only modestly, until 7,000 years before the present. From then until now, global temperatures appear relatively stable—"then until now" comprising, of course, the entire span of human civilization.

"The archeological community—and actually segments of the paleoclimate community—have viewed the Holocene as being climatically stable," says deMenocal. "And so they imagine that the whole drama of civilization's emergence took place on a level playing field in terms of the environment."

Until he met Harvey Weiss, deMenocal wasn't much interested in studying the Holocene; like most of his peers, he was more drawn to the dynamic climate fluctuations that preceded it. In fact, the Holocene had something of a bad rep among climatologists. "It was thought of as kind of a boring time to study," says deMenocal. "Like, why would you possibly want to? All the action is happening 20,000 years earlier."

Then a few years ago he read an account of Weiss's drought theory and had an epiphany of sorts. It occurred to him that even the smallest variations in climate could be interesting if they had influenced the course of history. What if something was going on in the Holocene after all? He looked up the 1993 paper in which Weiss had laid out the evidence for the Habur hiatus and reported the results of the soil analysis.

"I was pretty skeptical," says deMenocal. "I mean, what would you expect if everyone left a town? It would get dusty. Especially in the world's dustiest place. Big surprise."

Weiss, meanwhile, was getting a similar response from many of his peers. But when he and deMenocal met at a conference in 1994, they hit it off right away—largely because Weiss, too, was dismayed at the paucity of his own evidence. "Peter was immediately sensitive to my moaning about how we needed additional data, different kinds of data," says Weiss. "And he immediately understood where such data could be obtained."

DeMenocal told Weiss that if a large-scale drought had in fact occurred, it would have left a mark in the sediments of nearby ocean floors—the floor of the Gulf of Oman, for example. Lying approximately 700 miles southeast of ancient Mesopotamia, the gulf would have caught any windblown dust that swept down from the Tigris and Euphrates valleys. (The Persian Gulf is closer, but because it's so shallow, its sediments get churned up, thereby confusing their chronology.) And deMenocal just happened to know some German scientists who had a sediment core from the Gulf of Oman.

Analysis of the gulf core is ongoing, but deMenocal has already extracted enough information to confirm Weiss's suspicions. To track dry spells in the sediments, he and his colleague Heidi Cullen looked for dolomite, a mineral found in the mountains of Iraq and Turkey and on the Mesopotamian floodplains that could have been transported to the gulf only by wind. Most of the Holocene section of the core consists of calcium carbonate sediments typical of ocean bottoms.

"And then all of a sudden, at exactly 4,200 calendar years, there's this big spike of dolomite," says deMenocal—a fivefold increase that slowly decays over about three centuries. The chemistry of the dolomite dust matches that of the dolomite in the Mesopotamian mountains and plains, verifying the mineral's source. And not only did deMenocal and his colleagues figure out what happened, they may have figured out how. Studies by Gerard Bond at Lamont-Doherty have shown that the timing of the drought coincided with a cooling period in the North Atlantic. According to a survey by Cullen of current meteorological records, such cooling would have dried out the Middle East and western Asia by creating a pressure gradient that drew moisture to the north and away from the Mediterranean.

"The whole disruption, collapse bit, well, I just have to take Harvey at his word," says deMenocal. "What I tried to do is bring some good hard climate data to the problem." Why hasn't anybody seen this signature of calamity before? Simple, says deMenocal. "No one looked for it."

Weiss's first hints of climate-associated calamity came from a survey of his principal excavation site, a buried city in northeastern Syria called Tell Leilan. Tell Leilan (rhymes with "Ceylon") was one of three major cities on the Habur Plains to be taken over by the Akkadian Empire around 2300 B.C. The city covered more than

200 acres topped by a haughty acropolis, and was sustained by a tightly regulated system of rain-fed agriculture that was co-opted and intensified by the imperialists from the south. Weiss had asked Marie-Agnès Courty of the National Center for Scientific Research in France to examine the ancient soils of Tell Leilan to help him understand the agricultural development of the region. She reported that a section dating from 2200 to 1900 B.C. showed evidence of severe drought, including an eight-inch-thick layer of windblown sand and a marked absence of earthworm tunnels.

In his own excavations of the same period, Weiss had already found evidence of desertion: mud-brick walls that had fallen over clay floors and were covered with, essentially, 300 years' worth of compacted dust. And once he made the drought connection at Tell Leilan, he began turning up clues to the catastrophe everywhere he looked. In 1994, for example, Gerry Lemcke, a researcher at the Swiss Technical University in Zurich, presented new analyses of sediment cores taken from the bottom of Lake Van in Turkey, which lies at the headwaters of the Tigris and the Euphrates. The new results indicated that the volume of water in the lake—which corresponds to the amount of rainfall throughout western Asia—declined abruptly 4,200 years ago. At the same time, the amount of windblown dust in the lake increased fivefold.

Weiss came to believe that the effects of the drought reached downriver to the heart of Mesopotamia, causing the collapse of the Akkadian Empire. The collapse itself is undisputed: written records describe how, soon after it had consolidated power, Akkad crumbled, giving way to the Ur III dynasty in—when else?—2200 B.C. The cause of this collapse has been the subject of considerable speculation. But Weiss's studies of early civilizations have convinced him that their economies—complex and progressive though they may have been—were still fundamentally dependent on agricultural production. In fact, he notes, one hallmark of any civilization is that it requires a life-support system of farming communities toiling away in the fields and turning over the fruits of their labor to a central authority. The drought on the Habur Plains could have weakened the Akkadian Empire by drastically reducing agricultural revenues from that region. People fleeing the drought moved south, where irrigation-fed agriculture was still sustainable. For want of a raindrop, the kingdom was lost.

The curse of Akkad describes "large fields" that "produced no grain" and "heavy clouds" that "did not rain." Scholars had decided that these expressions were mere metaphor.

"Well, believe it or not, all my colleagues had not figured that out," says Weiss. "They actually believed that somehow this empire was based on bureaucracy, or holding on to trade routes, or getting access to exotic mineral resources in Turkey." But the drought itself is documented, Weiss says, in passages of cuneiform texts. Images from a lengthy composition called the Curse of Akkad, for example, include "large fields" that "produced no grain" and "heavy clouds" that "did not rain." Scholars had decided that these expressions were mere metaphor.

And many still stand by their interpretations. "I don't agree with his literal reading of the Mesopotamian texts, and I think he has exaggerated the extent of abandonment in this time period," says Richard Zettler, curator of the Near East section at the University of Pennsylvania's Museum of Archaeology and Anthropology in Philadelphia. Zettler doesn't question the evidence for drought, but he thinks Weiss has overplayed its implications. Although Tell Leilan may well have been deserted during the putative hiatus, for example, nearby cities on the Habur Plains show signs of continuing occupation, he says. As for the Curse and other Mesopotamian passages describing that period, says Zettler, "there are a lot of questions on how to read these texts—how much of it is just literary license, whatever. Even if there is a core of historical truth, it's hard to determine what the core of truth is."

Instead of backing down in the face of such commentary, Weiss has continued to document his thesis. Echoing Mellaart, he points out that 2200 B.C. saw the nearly simultaneous collapses of half a dozen other city-based civilizations—in Egypt, in Palestine, on Crete and the Greek mainland, and in the Indus Valley. The collapses were caused by the same drought, says Weiss, for the same reasons. But because historians and archeologists look for internal rather than external forces to explain civilizations in crisis, they don't communicate among themselves, he says, and many aren't even aware of what's going on next door, as it were.

"Very few people understand that there was a synchronous collapse and probably drought conditions in both Egypt and Mesopotamia," let alone the rest of the Old World, says Weiss.

It didn't help Weiss's extravagant claims for third-millennium cataclysm that his alleged drought didn't appear in the GISP2 oxygen-isotope record. The graph in deMenocal's office, for example, has no spikes or dips or swerves at 2200 B.C., just a nice flat plateau. That graph was drawn from an interpretation of the ice-core data. But according to Paul Mayewski of the University of New Hampshire in Durham, who is chief scientist of GISP2 there are plenty of reasons a drought in western Asia might not make it into the oxygen-isotope record in the Greenland glacier. Greenland might be too far away to "feel" the regional event, or the drought may have left a different kind of chemical signature. Only a climatologist like Mayewski could explain these reasons, however. And no one asked him to.

"As a consequence, a lot of people called Harvey Weiss and said, 'Well, the GISP2 record is the most highly resolved record of Holocene climate in the world. And if it's not in there, you're wrong, Harvey,'" says Mayewski. "I didn't realize that poor Harvey was being abused for not existing in our record."

Fortunately Mayewski, like deMenocal, is a curious sort with interests a bit broader than his own specialty. When he happened upon Weiss's 1993 paper, he'd already lent a hand on a few archeological projects, including one on the disappearance of Norse colonies from Greenland in the mid-1300s. But he figured other scientists had already looked for the Mesopotamian drought in the climate record. When he finally met Weiss in 1996, he learned otherwise. Mayewski began reanalyzing his core data with Weiss's theory in mind, and he uncovered a whole new Holocene.

"We can definitely show from our records that the 2200 B.C. event is unique," says Mayewski. "And what's much more exciting than that, we can show that most of the major turning points in civilization in western Asia also correlate with what we would say would be dry events. We think that we have found a proxy for aridity in western Asia."

Earlier interpretations of the GISP2 data had measured a variety of ions in ice cores that would reveal general information about climate variability. To look for the 2200 B.C. drought in particular, Mayewski used tests based on 2.5-year intervals in the climate record instead of 50- to 100-year intervals. He also collected a broader set of data that allowed him to reconstruct specific patterns of atmospheric circulation—not only over land but over land *and* oceans. When Mayewski focused on the movement of air masses over oceans, he found that air transport from south to north in the Atlantic—so-called meridional circulation—hit a significant winter low some 4,200 years ago.

Mayewski and deMenocal are studying how this event relates to drought in western Asia.

"But it seems on the basis of the paleoclimatic data that there is no doubt about the event at 2200 B.C.," says Weiss. "What the qualities of this event were, and what the magnitude of this event was, that is the current research frontier now."

Trouble is, even though the drought may seem like a sure thing, its effects on Mesopotamia are still unproved, as Zettler points out. They will remain controversial, Weiss admits, until archeologists better understand the contributions of politics, agriculture, and climate in the formation of ancient societies. That mission grows more urgent as more archeologists seem ready to grapple with models of "climatic determinism." In the past few years, drought and flooding have been cited in the demise of several New World civilizations, including the Maya of Central America, the Anasazi of the American Southwest, and the Moche and Tiwanaku of Peru and Bolivia.

"Until climatic conditions are quantified, it's going to be very difficult to understand what the effects of climate changes—particularly controversial, abrupt ones—were upon these societies," says Weiss. The precise constellation of forces that led to the collapse of Bronze Age cultures around 2200 B.C. will probably be debated for a very long time. But paleoclimatology has assured Mother Nature a place in that constellation. And the notion that civilizations are immune to natural disaster may soon be ancient history.

Black Pharaohs

An ignored chapter of history tells of a time when kings from deep in Africa conquered ancient Egypt.

ROBERT DRAPER

I n the year 730 B.C., a man by the name of Piye decided the only way to save Egypt from itself was to invade it. Things would get bloody before the salvation came.

"Harness the best steeds of your stable," he ordered his commanders. The magnificent civilization that had built the great pyramids had lost its way, torn apart by petty warlords. For two decades Piye had ruled over his own kingdom in Nubia, a swath of Africa located mostly in present-day Sudan. But he considered himself the true ruler of Egypt as well, the rightful heir to the spiritual traditions practiced by pharaohs such as Ramses II and Thutmose III. Since Piye had probably never actually visited Lower Egypt, some did not take his boast seriously. Now Piye would witness the subjugation of decadent Egypt firsthand—"I shall let Lower Egypt taste the taste of my fingers," he would later write.

North on the Nile River his soldiers sailed. At Thebes, the capital of Upper Egypt, they disembarked. Believing there was a proper way to wage holy wars, Piye instructed his soldiers to purify themselves before combat by bathing in the Nile, dressing themselves in fine linen, and sprinkling their bodies with water from the temple at Karnak, a site holy to the ram-headed sun god Amun, whom Piye identified as his own personal deity. Piye himself feasted and offered sacrifices to Amun. Thus sanctified, the commander and his men commenced to do battle with every army in their path.

By the end of a yearlong campaign, every leader in Egypt had capitulated—including the powerful delta warlord Tefnakht, who sent a messenger to tell Piye, "Be gracious! I cannot see your face in the days of shame; I cannot stand before your flame, I dread your grandeur." In exchange for their lives, the vanquished urged Piye to worship at their temples, pocket their finest jewels, and claim their best horses. He obliged them. And then, with his vassals trembling before him, the newly anointed Lord of the Two Lands did something extraordinary: He loaded up his army and his war booty, and sailed southward to his home in Nubia, never to return to Egypt again.

When Piye died at the end of his 35-year reign in 715 B.C., his subjects honored his wishes by burying him in an Egyptian-style pyramid, with four of his beloved horses nearby. He was the first pharaoh to receive such entombment in more than 500 years. A pity, then, that the great Nubian who accomplished these feats is literally faceless to us. Images of Piye on the elaborate granite slabs, or stelae, memorializing his conquest of Egypt have long since been chiseled away. On a relief in the temple at the Nubian capital of Napata, only Piye's legs remain. We are left with a single physical detail of the man—namely, that his skin was dark.

Piye was the first of the so-called black pharaohs—a series of Nubian kings who ruled over all of Egypt for three-quarters of a century as that country's 25th dynasty. Through inscriptions carved on stelae by both the Nubians and their enemies, it is possible to map out these rulers' vast footprint on the continent. The black pharaohs reunified a tattered Egypt and filled its landscape with glorious monuments, creating an empire that stretched from the southern border at present-day Khartoum all the way north to the Mediterranean Sea. They stood up to the bloodthirsty Assyrians, perhaps saving Jerusalem in the process.

Until recently, theirs was a chapter of history that largely went untold. Only in the past four decades have archaeologists resurrected their story—and come to recognize that the black pharaohs didn't appear out of nowhere. They sprang from a robust African civilization that had flourished on the southern banks of the Nile for 2,500 years, going back at least as far as the first Egyptian dynasty.

Today Sudan's pyramids—greater in number than all of Egypt's—are haunting spectacles in the Nubian Desert. It is possible to wander among them unharassed, even alone, a world away from Sudan's genocide and refugee crisis in Darfur or the aftermath of civil war in the south. While hundreds of miles north, at Cairo or Luxor, curiosity seekers arrive by the busload to jostle and crane for views of the Egyptian wonders, Sudan's seldom-visited pyramids at El Kurru, Nuri, and Meroë stand serenely amid an arid landscape that scarcely hints of the thriving culture of ancient Nubia.

Now our understanding of this civilization is once again threatened with obscurity. The Sudanese government is building a hydroelectric dam along the Nile, 600 miles upstream from the Aswan High Dam, which Egypt constructed in the 1960s, consigning much of lower Nubia to the bottom of Lake Nasser (called Lake Nubia in Sudan). By 2009, the massive Merowe Dam should be complete, and a 106-mile-long lake will flood the terrain abutting the Nile's Fourth Cataract, or rapid, including thousands of unexplored sites. For the past nine years, archaeologists have flocked to the region, furiously digging before another repository of Nubian history goes the way of Atlantis.

The ancient world was devoid of racism. At the time of Piye's historic conquest, the fact that his skin was dark was irrelevant. Artwork from ancient Egypt, Greece, and Rome shows a clear awareness of racial features and skin tone, but there is little evidence that darker skin was seen as a sign of inferiority. Only after the European powers colonized Africa in the 19th century did Western scholars pay attention to the color of the Nubians' skin, to uncharitable effect.

Explorers who arrived at the central stretch of the Nile River excitedly reported the discovery of elegant temples and pyramids—the ruins of an ancient civilization called Kush. Some, like the Italian doctor Giuseppe Ferlini—who lopped off the top of at least one Nubian pyramid, inspiring others to do the same—hoped to find treasure beneath. The Prussian archaeologist Richard Lepsius had more studious intentions, but he ended up doing damage of his own by concluding that the Kushites surely "belonged to the Caucasian race."

Even famed Harvard Egyptologist George Reisner—whose discoveries between 1916 and 1919 offered the first archaeological evidence of Nubian kings who ruled over Egypt—besmirched his own findings by insisting that black Africans could not possibly have constructed the monuments he was excavating. He believed that Nubia's leaders, including Piye, were light-skinned Egypto-Libyans who ruled over the primitive Africans, That their moment of greatness was so fleeting, he suggested, must be a consequence of the same leaders intermarrying with the "negroid elements."

For decades, many historians flip-flopped: Either the Kushite pharaohs were actually "white," or they were bumblers, their civilization a derivative offshoot of true Egyptian culture. In their 1942 history, *When Egypt Ruled the East,* highly regarded Egyptologists Keith Seele and George Steindorff summarized the Nubian pharaonic dynasty and Piye's triumphs in all of three sentences—the last one reading: "But his dominion was not for long."

The neglect of Nubian history reflected not only the bigoted worldview of the times, but also a cult-like fascination with Egypt's achievements—and a complete ignorance of Africa's past. "The first time I came to Sudan," recalls Swiss archaeologist Charles Bonnet, "people said: 'You're mad! There's no history there! It's all in Egypt!'"

That was a mere 44 years ago. Artifacts uncovered during the archaeological salvage campaigns as the waters rose at Aswan in the 1960s began changing that view. In 2003, Charles Bonnet's decades of digging near the Nile's Third Cataract at the abandoned settlement of Kerma gained international recognition with the discovery of seven large stone statues of Nubian pharaohs. Well before then, however, Bonnet's labors had revealed an older, densely occupied urban center that commanded rich fields and extensive herds, and had long profited from trade in gold, ebony, and ivory. "It was a kingdom completely free of Egypt and original, with its own construction and burial customs," Bonnet says. This powerful dynasty rose just as Egypt's Middle Kingdom declined around 1785 B.C. By 1500 B.C. the Nubian empire stretched between the Second and Fifth Cataracts.

Revisiting that golden age in the African desert does little to advance the case of Afrocentric Egyptologists, who argue that all ancient Egyptians, from King Tut to Cleopatra, were black Africans. Nonetheless, the saga of the Nubians proves that a civilization from deep in Africa not only thrived but briefly dominated in ancient times, intermingling and sometimes intermarrying with their Egyptian neighbors to the north. (King Tut's own grandmother, the 18th-dynasty Queen Tiye, is claimed by some to be of Nubian heritage.)

The Egyptians didn't like having such a powerful neighbor to the south, especially since they depended on Nubia's gold mines to bankroll their dominance of western Asia. So the pharaohs of the 18th dynasty (1539–1292 B.C.) sent armies to conquer Nubia and built garrisons along the Nile. They installed Nubian chiefs as administrators and schooled the children of favored Nubians at Thebes. Subjugated, the elite Nubians began to embrace the cultural and spiritual customs of Egypt—venerating Egyptian gods, particularly Amun, using the Egyptian language, adopting Egyptian burial styles and, later, pyramid building. The Nubians were arguably the first people to be struck by "Egyptomania."

Egyptologists of the latter 19th and early 20th centuries would interpret this as a sign of weakness. But they had it wrong: The Nubians had a gift for reading the geopolitical tea leaves. By the eighth century B.C., Egypt was riven by factions, the north ruled by Libyan chiefs who put on the trappings of pharaonic traditions to gain legitimacy. Once firmly in power, they toned down the theocratic devotion to Amun, and the priests at Karnak feared a godless outcome. Who was in a position to return Egypt to its former state of might and sanctity?

The Egyptian priests looked south and found their answer—a people who, without setting foot inside Egypt, had preserved Egypt's spiritual traditions. As archaeologist Timothy Kendall of Northeastern University puts it, the Nubians "had become more Catholic than the pope."

Under Nubian rule, Egypt became Egypt again. When Piye died in 715, his brother Shabaka solidified the 25th dynasty by taking up residence in the Egyptian capital of Memphis. Like his brother, Shabaka wed himself to the old pharaonic ways, adopting the throne name of the 6th-dynasty ruler Pepi II, just as Piye had claimed the old throne name of Thutmose III. Rather than execute his foes, Shabaka put them to work building dikes to seal off Egyptian villages from Nile floods.

Shabaka lavished Thebes and the Temple of Luxor with building projects. At Karnak he erected a pink granite statue depicting himself wearing the Kushite crown of the double uraeus—the two cobras signifying his legitimacy as Lord of the Two Lands. Through architecture as well as military might, Shabaka signaled to Egypt that the Nubians were here to stay.

To the east, the Assyrians were fast building their own empire. In 701 B.C., when they marched into Judah in present-day Israel, the Nubians decided to act. At the city of Eltekeh, the two armies met. And although the Assyrian emperor, Sennacherib, would brag lustily that he "inflicted defeat upon them," a young Nubian prince, perhaps 20, son of the great pharaoh Piye, managed to survive. That the Assyrians, whose tastes ran to wholesale slaughter, failed to kill the prince suggests their victory was anything but total.

In any event, when the Assyrians left town and massed against the gates of Jerusalem, that city's embattled leader, Hezekiah, hoped his Egyptian allies would come to the rescue. The Assyrians issued a taunting reply, immortalized in the Old Testaments Book of II Kings: "Thou trustest upon the staff of this bruised reed [of] Egypt, on which if a man lean, it will go into his hand, and pierce it: So is Pharaoh king of Egypt unto all that trust on him."

Then, according to the Scriptures and other accounts, a miracle occurred: The Assyrian army retreated. Were they struck by a plague? Or, as Henry Aubin's provocative book, *The Rescue of Jerusalem*, suggests, was it actually the alarming news that the aforementioned Nubian prince was advancing on Jerusalem? All we know for sure is that Sennacherib abandoned the siege and galloped back in disgrace to his kingdom, where he was murdered 18 years later, apparently by his own sons.

The deliverance of Jerusalem is not just another of ancient history's sidelights, Aubin asserts, but one of its pivotal events. It allowed Hebrew society and Judaism to strengthen for another crucial century—by which time the Babylonian king Nebuchadrezzar could banish the Hebrew people but not obliterate them or their faith. From Judaism, of course, would spring Christianity and Islam. Jerusalem would come to be recast, in all three major monotheistic religions, as a city of a godly significance.

It has been easy to overlook, amid these towering historical events, the dark-skinned figure at the edge of the landscape—the survivor of Eltekeh, the hard-charging prince later referred to by the Assyrians as "the one accursed by all the great gods": Piye's son Taharqa.

So sweeping was Taharqa's influence on Egypt that even his enemies could not eradicate his imprint. During his rule, to travel down the Nile from Napata to Thebes was to navigate a panorama of architectural wonderment. All over Egypt, he built monuments with busts, statues, and cartouches bearing his image or name, many of which now sit in museums around the world. He is depicted as a supplicant to gods, or in the protective presence of the ram deity Amun, or as a sphinx himself, or in a warriors posture. Most statues were defaced by his rivals. His nose is often broken off, to foreclose him

returning from the dead. Shattered as well is the uraeus on his forehead, to repudiate his claim as Lord of the Two Lands. But in each remaining image, the serene self-certainty in his eyes remains for all to see.

His father, Piye, had returned the true pharaonic customs to Egypt. His uncle Shabaka had established a Nubian presence in Memphis and Thebes. But their ambitions paled before those of the 31-year-old military commander who received the crown in Memphis in 690 and presided over the combined empires of Egypt and Nubia for the next 26 years.

Taharqa had ascended at a favorable moment for the 25th dynasty. The delta warlords had been laid low. The Assyrians, after failing to best him at Jerusalem, wanted no part of the Nubian ruler. Egypt was his and his alone. The gods granted him prosperity to go with the peace. During his sixth year on the throne, the Nile swelled from rains, inundating the valleys and yielding a spectacular harvest of grain without sweeping away any villages. As Taharqa would record in four separate stelae, the high waters even exterminated all rats and snakes. Clearly the revered Amun was smiling on his chosen one.

Taharqa did not intend to sit on his profits. He believed in spending his political capital. Thus he launched the most audacious building campaign of any pharaoh since the New Kingdom (around 1500 B.C.), when Egypt had been in a period of expansion. Inevitably the two holy capitals of Thebes and Napata received the bulk of Taharqa's attention. Standing today amid the hallowed clutter of the Karnak temple complex near Thebes is a lone 62-foot-high column. That pillar had been one of ten, forming a gigantic kiosk that the Nubian pharaoh added to the Temple of Amun. He also constructed a number of chapels around the temple and erected massive statues of himself and of his beloved mother, Abar. Without defacing a single preexisting monument, Taharqa made Thebes his.

He did the same hundreds of miles upriver, in the Nubian city of Napata. Its holy mountain Jebel Barkal—known for its striking rock-face pinnacle that calls to mind a phallic symbol of fertility—had captivated even the Egyptian pharaohs of the New Kingdom, who believed the site to be the birthplace of Amun. Seeking to present himself as heir to the New Kingdom pharaohs, Taharqa erected two temples, set into the base of the mountain, honoring the goddess consorts of Amun. On Jebel Barkal's pinnacle—partially covered in gold leaf to bedazzle wayfarers—the black pharaoh ordered his name inscribed.

Around the 15th year of his rule, amid the grandiosity of his empire-building, a touch of hubris was perhaps overtaking the Nubian ruler. "Taharqa had a very strong army and was one of the main international powers of this period," says Charles Bonnet. "I think he thought he was the king of the world. He became a bit of a megalomaniac."

The timber merchants along the coast of Lebanon had been feeding Taharqa's architectural appetite with a steady supply of juniper and cedar. When the Assyrian king Esarhaddon sought to clamp down on this trade artery, Taharqa sent troops to the southern Levant to support a revolt against the Assyrian. Esarhaddon quashed the move and retaliated by crossing into Egypt in 674 B.C. But Taharqa's army beat back its foes.

The victory clearly went to the Nubians head. Rebel states along the Mediterranean shared his giddiness and entered into an alliance against Esarhaddon. In 671 the Assyrians marched with their camels into the Sinai desert to quell the rebellion. Success was instant; now it was Esarhaddon who brimmed with bloodlust. He directed his troops toward the Nile Delta.

Taharqa and his army squared off against the Assyrians. For 15 days they fought pitched battles—"very bloody," by Esarhaddon's grudging admission. But the Nubians were pushed back all the way to Memphis. Wounded five times, Taharqa escaped with his life and abandoned Memphis. In typical Assyrian fashion, Esarhaddon slaughtered the villagers and "erected piles of their heads." Then, as the Assyrian would later write, "His queen, his harem, Ushankhuru his heir, and the rest of his sons and daughters, his property and his goods, his horses, his cattle, his sheep, in countless numbers, I carried off to Assyria. The root of Kush I tore up out of Egypt." To commemorate Taharqa's humiliation, Esarhaddon commissioned a stela showing Taharqa's son, Ushankhuru, kneeling before the Assyrian with a rope tied around his neck.

As it happened, Taharqa outlasted the victor. In 669 Esarhaddon died en route to Egypt, after learning that the Nubian had managed to retake Memphis. Under a new king, the Assyrians once again assaulted the city, this time with an army swollen with captured rebel troops. Taharqa stood no chance. He fled south to Napata and never saw Egypt again.

A measure of Taharqa's status in Nubia is that he remained in power after being routed twice from Memphis. How he spent his final years is a mystery—with the exception of one final innovative act. Like his father, Piye, Taharqa chose to be buried in a pyramid. But he eschewed the royal cemetery at El Kurru, where all previous Kushite pharaohs had been laid to rest. Instead, he chose a site at Nuri, on the opposite bank of the Nile. Perhaps, as archaeologist Timothy Kendall has theorized, Taharqa selected the location because, from the vista of Jebel Barkal, his pyramid precisely aligns with the sunrise on ancient Egypt's New Year's Day, linking him in perpetuity with the Egyptian concept of rebirth.

Just as likely, the Nubian's motive will remain obscure, like his people's history.

Robert Draper is the author of *Dead Certain: The Presidency of George W. Bush.* He recently wrote for *National Geographic* about 21st-century cowboys.

Messages from the Dead

Tablets fired in the crucible of a burning city reveal the last days of a Bronze Age kingdom.

MARCO MEROLA

Inscribed on the small, pillow-shaped tablet is a 3,000-year-old warning to Idanda, king of Qatna, from the Hittite general Hanutti, telling him to prepare for war. A small Bronze Age Syrian city-state, Qatna was once under Hittite control, but had been conquered by the Mitanni people from the north. The clay tablet, like others found with it, was fired twice—once just after it was written, to preserve it, and again when the ancient Syrian city was sacked and burned to the ground in 1340 B.C. by the Hittites, who ruled an empire that stretched from northern Turkey to Mesopotamia and Syria.

According to scholars still translating and studying it, the letter is full of anxiety and pathos. "Reading that letter today still makes you shiver," says archaeologist Daniele Morandi Bonacossi of the University of Udine in Italy. Bonacossi is part of a multinational team that excavated the remains of the royal palace of Qatna, where they found intact burial chambers and, in a stone corridor leading to the tombs, a collection of 73 tablets describing the royal life and business of one of the wealthiest and most famous cities in Middle and Late Bronze Age (2000 to 1200 B.C.) Syria. The tablets are inscribed in script that is a hybrid of Akkadian, a Mesopotamian language, and Hurrian, which was probably the original language of what is today eastern Turkey and the Caucasus. They betray—especially in the diplomatic messages from other minor Syrian kings to Idanda—the moods, fears, and hopes of a people anticipating their own end.

In the dawn light, Qatna today is a study in stillness, forgotten by all but the archaeologists. But one can easily imagine the bustling city, once a productive center of pottery manufacture and a key trading center, as well as its heated, violent end. Amid the fragments of walls, a royal palace takes shape. Then, just as quickly, it catches fire.

Qatna originated around 2700 to 2600 B.C. as a small settlement on a rocky plain 130 miles north of modern Damascus. By 2000 B.C., it began to resemble a more organized town, and soon was referred to by name in the royal archives of Mari, a massive collection of cuneiform clay tablets found in the ruins of another ancient Syrian city some 200 miles to the west.

Qatna was in an ideal position along the caravan route that linked the Middle Euphrates with the Mediterranean. According to clay tablets in the Mari archives, white horses, rich fabrics, and fine palm, cypress, and myrtle wood passed through the city. This commercial activity attracted the attention of nearby kingdoms—the Hittites and Mitanni to the north, and the Egyptians to the south—eager to expand their empires and influence. It is perhaps a wonder that Qatna survived as long as it did.

"And the winners were the Hittites," says Bonacossi. "They arrived here in 1340 B.C. and fortunately they burned anything they found." While it may seem odd to praise the Hittites' proclivity for arson, Bonacossi is an archaeologist—when it comes to clay artifacts, fire is his friend. In this case, it ensured the preservation of those 73 clay tablets of royal correspondence.

Since Qatna was often referenced in ancient sources, several mid-nineteenth-century scholars and travelers, such as Sebastien Ronzevalle, Charles Clérmont-Ganneau, and Max Van Berchem tried in vain to track down the remains of the ancient city. In 1924, French archaeology enthusiast Count Robert du Mesnil du Buisson began excavating in Syria. Qatna, however, eluded him—it was covered by Mishrifeh, a modern, densely populated town with concerns more pressing than the history and archaeology beneath its streets. Little happened until 1982, when the Syrian government surprisingly uprooted and relocated the entire population of Mishrifeh—10,000 people at the time—to clear the site for excavation. In 1999, the government allowed three teams to begin excavation: an Italian group directed by Bonacossi, a German team led by Peter Pfälzner of the University of Tübingen, and a local group under Michel Al-Maqdissi of the Syrian Directorate General of Antiquities. By 2002, they had made a series of startling discoveries.

As the team excavated a 40-yard-long corridor that led away from the ruins of the palace's ceremonial room, the archaeologists found a pile of debris that probably had fallen from a room above—perhaps the royal

Desperate Pleas for Help

Qatna is mentioned many times in cuneiform archives, including the royal archives at Mari in Syria and the Egyptian archive at Amarna. Like the tablets found in Qatna itself, some of these records reflect the city's basic insecurity as a small city-state surrounded and often threatened by powerful expanding empires. Letters 52 through 56 (54 is too poorly preserved for translation) of the Amarna archive record the correspondence in 1350 B.C. between Qatna's Prince Akizzi and probably Pharaoh Akhenaten. In the letters, Akizzi swears his loyalty, establishes the aggression of Hittite general Aitukama, and pleads for help. The desperation and obeisance of the letters were greeted only by silence. Qatna found no protector in Egypt and the Hittites eventually destroyed the Syrian city.

Letter 52: The Loyalty of Qatna

Say to the king of Egypt: Message of Akizzi, your servant. I fall at the feet of my lord, my Storm-god, 7 times. . . .

. . . the houses of Qatna belong to my lord alone. . . .

Come, my . . . has abandoned me. . . . I will certainly not rebel against the . . . of my lord . . .

Letter 53: Of the Villain Aitukama

And now, the king of Hatti [the land of the Hittites] has sent Aitukama out against me, and he seeks my life. . . .

May my lord send him . . . that he may come against Aitukama so that my lord . . . he may fear your presence. . . .

My lord, if he makes this land a matter of concern to my lord, then may my lord send archers that they may come here. Only messengers of my lord have arrived here. . . .

I do not fear at all in the presence of the archers or my lord, since the archers belong to my lord . . .

Letter 55: A Plea for Troops

From the time my ancestors were your servants, this country has been your country, Qatna has been your city, and I belong to my lord. My lord, when the troops and chariots of my lord have come here, food, strong drink, oxen, sheep, and goats, honey and oil, were produced for the troops and chariots of my lord. Look, there are my lord's magnates; my lord should ask them. My lord, the whole country is in fear of your troops and chariots. . . .

My lord knows it. My lord . . . his ancestors . . . But now the king of Hatti has sent them up in flames. The king of Hatti has taken bid gods and the fighting men of Qatna. . . .

If it pleases him, may my lord send the ransom money for the men of Qatna, and may my lord ransom them. . . . my lord, the money for their ransom, as much as it may be, so I can hand over the money. . . .

My lord, your ancestors made a statue of Simigi, the god of my father, and because of him became famous. Now the king of Hatti has taken the statue of Simigi, the god of my father. My lord knows what the fashioning of divine statues is like. Now that Simigi, the god of my father, has been reconciled to me, if, my lord, it pleases him, may he give me a sack of gold, just as much as is needed, for the statue of Simigi, the god of my father, so they can fashion it for me. Then my lord will become, because of Simigi, more famous than before. . . .

Letter 56: A Declaration of Trust

I am your servant, and, my lord, you must not let me go from your hand. I, for my part, will not desert my lord. I have put my trust in my lord, his troops, and in his chariots. . . .

—Translations from *The Amarna Letters,* edited and translated by William Moran. Johns Hopkins University Press, 2002.

registry—when the palace was burned by the Hittites. Among the debris were the tablets, each containing information about how the kingdom was run, especially at the time leading up to the Hittite attack.

According to letters in the Egyptian Amarna archive of late-eighteenth-dynasty diplomatic correspondence, influential though Qatna may have been, it was still a small kingdom in a dangerous position—surrounded by heavy-weights. In addition to the tablet warning King Idanda to prepare for war, others found at Qatna contain orders for 18,600 bronze swords and 40,000 mud bricks, probably to reinforce the city walls, as well as inventories that tally 200 gold knives and 200 knives with lapis lazuli handles. Tablets also list the names of 25 captains assigned to distribute the weapons among soldiers.

In the battle—more of a rout, perhaps—the Hittites destroyed the 300-year-old palace, the audience hall of which spread over 1,300 square yards probably covered by a wooden roof supported by columns 20 to 30 feet high. In an area of the site thought to be an ancient underground cistern, the archaeologists also found pieces of frescoes depicting landscapes, animals

(especially fish and turtles), and blue palm trees. "We are trying to reconstruct the original painting cycle through the many fragments we have found," says Pfälzner, who looks more Mediterranean than German and speaks fluent Arabic. "One of the walls of the palace collapsed when the palace was attacked, so the paintings crumbled and fell into the well." So similar are the frescoes to those in the Palace of Knossos in Crete that a number of archaeologists believe they were painted by Minoan artists who had come to Syria on commission.

Following the long corridor containing the tablets, the archaeologists made another major find: royal crypts beneath tons of dirt and bricks that had gone untouched by ancient looters and modern grave robbers alike. At the end of the 2002 field season, the German archaeologists found a shaft guarded by two basalt statues representing deceased sovereigns from the eighteenth and seventeenth centuries B.C. The seated couple, one of whose inlaid limestone eyes were still intact, wears Syrian braided headdresses characteristic of the period and carries bowls for sacrificial offerings. Bones of birds and domestic animals found nearby point to the statues' key symbolic functions as guardians of the tomb, guides for the dead, and counselors for the living seeking advice from their ancestors. Between them is the entrance to the crypts.

Inside, the archaeologists found a large room that included an open sarcophagus with the incomplete remains of three people, as well as four more bodies in the outlines of wooden biers. They also found other artifacts, including a lion-head-shaped box, a golden hand, numerous pots and bowls, and animal bones. The dead were once dressed, but centuries of decay had turned their garments into dust studded with beads of glass, amethyst, and gold. In three side chambers were other bones, both animal and human, and many vessels, some of which were made locally and some of which came from Egypt.

From the abundance of animal bones and vessels, the archaeologists theorize that they found a funerary/banquet hall for the mysterious ritual *kispum,* the banquet of the living to honor the dead. "Relatives would visit the dead at least once a month," says Pfälzner. "They shared food with them, showing their gratitude because they thought the dead would warn and protect them in case of sinister events." The ritual was practiced at that time in other towns of the Middle East, but was never mentioned in connection with Qatna or in any of the tablets found there.

In the west chamber of the tomb, which was probably used for the most significant burial, the archaeologists discovered the only complete skeleton. "The bones were burnt" and had been exposed to a temperature of about 400 degrees Fahrenheit, according to Pfälzner. "This was either the result of sterilization or an unsuccessful attempt at mummification. Or maybe they used this technique to reduce bad odors." This skeleton has helped archaeologists piece together a hypothetical burial ritual for a king of Qatna. The corpse first was heated in some manner, probably during a public ritual outside the tomb, and then stored in a burial chamber. Later, the remains would have been placed in a sarcophagus in another room, and displayed as the centerpiece of a banquet.

But there was probably no such ritual for Idanda. He was likely killed in the siege in 1340 B.C., after which Qatna was no longer significant. As if the ground were somehow cursed, no one inhabited the area for 400 years. In 900 B.C., a smaller settlement with no great ambitions grew at the site and became part of the Princedom of Hamat. Just 200 years later it disappeared as well. Only around A.D. 1850 was the modern town of Mishrifeh established, only to be moved itself so that the ancient, prosperous, imperiled Qatna could be resurrected.

MARCO MEROLA is *Archaeology*'s Naples correspondent.

China's First Empire

Michael Loewe looks at the dynastic, administrative and intellectual background of the Qin empire, which defined how China would be run for more than 2,000 years, and at the life and achievements of the First Emperor Shi Huangdi, one of the greatest state-builders of history, whose tomb was guarded by the famous terracotta army.

Michael Loewe

The kings of Western Zhou ruled from a small part of northwest China (present-day Shaanxi province) from 1045 BC. Their rule was long revered as a Chinese 'golden age' but in 771, overcome by dissension and subject to hostile intrusion, they were forced to forsake their original homeland and settle further east, establishing their centre at the city now known as Luoyang. Although the kings of Zhou actually survived until 256 BC, their territory and powers was severely curtailed through the rise of a number of independent leaders who could control large areas of land and style themselves with titles. As early as 777 BC, one of these leaders from Qin who, like the Zhou, came from the north-west, adopted the title of gong, often translated as duke; this title passed from father to son until 325 BC, when it was changed for the more grandiose one of king (*wang*).

This change was something more than a mere formality, and in what is known as the Warring States period (481–221 BC) six other rulers—Chu, Qi, Yan, Hann, Wei and Zhao—in different parts of China likewise adopted the title of king. The new title indicated that these men did not accept that the kings of Zhou enjoyed a position superior to their own; and it reflected the steady growth of their powers. For Qin, this process of expansion reached its culmination after 250 BC, notably in the reign of Ying Zheng (*r.* 246–210).

By 221 BC, through a combination of adroit diplomacy not necessarily bound by moral scruples, policies that looked beyond the short term gains and success in battle, Ying Zheng (259–210) emerged the triumphant conqueror of the six coexisting kingdoms. He was by now master not only of the west but also of the northern and eastern parts

of present-day China, the lush fertile lands of present-day Sichuan province and the woodlands of the north-east. In the east this area included the fields watered, and all too often flooded, by the Yellow River and the Huai River. With no remaining challengers, in 221 BC he adopted the majestic title of emperor (*Huangdi*), signifying that he claimed authority and wielded power over all lands and all peoples below the skies. He is known to history as Qin Shi Huangdi 'The First Qin Emperor', though his influence is such that he may correctly be termed China's First Emperor.

The First Qin Emperor and his advisers are credited today with having created the means of governing much of the area later known as 'China' as a unity, bequeathing a heritage on which later dynasties modelled their institutions. Even the very name 'China' as known in Western usage itself derives from Qin. The dynasty's heritage should, though, be seen in its historical context. Earlier kingdoms had already been fostering a systematic means of government conducted by trained officials chosen for their ability; and they had experimented with institutions designed to increase their own strength. By adapting such existing institutions, Qin extended their application on a far wider scale. In turn, future rulers of China looked to Qin's single empire and government as a model to which they should aspire. They followed many of Qin's practices, whether over long or short periods, over limited or wide expanses of territory.

We depend for the most part on a single source for the dynastic and political history of the Qin state, the *Records of the Historian* (*Shiji*) of Sima Tan (*d.*110 BC) and his son Sima Qian (145–?86 BC), with no means of external verification of their content. They were officials of Qin's successor the Han dynasty, and were obliged to show that Han had been justified in eliminating Qin with what they claimed were its evil ways, so they are necessarily biased. A few highly valuable archival documents found recently verify some of the historians' statements. As the years pass, new archaeological evidence serves to validate the general picture that we have of Qin and adds to what had been known of the religious activities or mythology that formed a background to so many people's lives.

Some of the statements of the *Shiji* have been subject to question, on the grounds that they were not complete. For example, it was later alleged that Zhuangxiang Wang, king of Qin from 250–247, was not the father of Ying Zheng who succeeded him in 246 BC at the age of thirteen, but such suspicions cannot be confirmed. Ying Zheng himself fathered at least two sons but there is no record of the name of his queen or his empress; nor are there any tales, as there are for later dynasties, of the rivalries and disputes that broke out between the families of various imperial consorts, threatening the stability of the realm. Such threats arose in a different way.

The First Emperor survived perhaps three attempts at assassination, as was portrayed by artists of the succeeding empire. He achieved much. He chose officials to govern large parts of the land as provinces, rather than delegate this task to members of his family. He reorganized the system of defence lines of the north, unifying their different parts into the so-called Great Wall. This was built by conscript and convict labour but it did not follow the same line, nor was it situated in the same area, as that of the later wall of which remnants are seen north of Beijing. In a major advance that was by no means always maintained in later dynasties, the Qin empire stretched far to the south, beyond the Yangzi River; but it is difficult to estimate how effective his government was in the intemperate and unhealthy lands of the tropics, where the way of life differed markedly from that of the north.

The First Emperor died on his way back to the capital city of Xianyang (close to modern Xi'an) from a tour in the east in 210 BC. Li Si, who held the supreme office of Chancellor and was perhaps the most influential adviser at the time, suppressed news of his death, perhaps fearing that it would set off an uprising. But as happened frequently in China's history, the succession was beset by intrigue and rivalry and in this instance by violence. Fusu, son of the emperor and his named heir, was displaced and forced to commit suicide, along with Meng Tian, a military officer who under Shi Huangdi had had responsibility for the defence lines and the manning of the Great Wall

and who was one of Fusu's close supporters. Huhai, a second son of the Emperor, duly took Fusu's place, to reign as the Second Emperor for a short period from 210 BC.

This outcome had been contrived by Li Si himself, in collaboration with Zhao Gao who is described as a eunuch. There is however no record of the emergence of eunuchs in the palace or government of Qin, and it is possible that it was only due to later allegations that Zhao Gao was thus named. Appointed to a senior appointment shortly after Huhai's accession, he exercised commanding powers of government, at times exciting the criticism or protests of Li Si. Clearly there was no room in Xianyang for two men each of whom wished to impose his will on the Emperor and his government, and it was Zhao Gao who emerged as the victor. Accused of disloyalty and subjected to flogging, Li Si took his own life and by way of punishment his family was extirpated (208). Zhao Gao could now dominate the Second Emperor who, in turn, was forced to commit suicide to make way for Zhao Gao's own nominee. In the instability that followed Zhao Gao met his end in 207 BC. The Qin empire closed amid a series of uprisings and open warfare between two protagonists, Xiang Yu and Liu Bang. Claiming the title king of Han in 206, Liu Bang eliminated his rival and proclaimed himself Emperor of Han in 202. The Han empire lasted, with some interruptions, until AD 220.

Under Qin, supreme power rested in the emperor; he was advised by salaried officials many of whose titles and duties derived from earlier usage in pre-imperial Qin or the other kingdoms. At the highest level stood the Chancellor and Imperial Counsellor; ranking immediately below them nine senior ministers were responsible for duties of a specialist nature. These included ceremonial and ritual activities; security of the palace; the emperor's horse and carriages; administration of punishments; treatment of dignitaries from outside the empire; kinship relations within the imperial family; taxation; agricultural production, storage and distribution of staple foods; and products of other types, from the mountains and the lakes. There were other officials who controlled the capital city or commanded forces with which to patrol Xianyang. Others were responsible for constructing imperial buildings such as the palaces and the mausolea or for maintaining the establishments of the Empress and the Heir Apparent. Appointed directly by imperial authority, these senior officials called on the services of a large number of assistants.

In the course of creating the empire, Qin had acquired territories from the other kingdoms. To administer them these kingdoms had been formed into units known either as counties (*xian*) or as commanderies (*jun*). After 221 BC this system was applied throughout the new empire except for Xianyang itself which lay under the control of a special official, governor of the metropolitan area. Outside, there were thirty-six, or perhaps more, commanderies, each in the charge of a governor (*shou*). Junior staff carried out the task of governing an empire efficiently by maintaining order and security, promoting the production of cereal crops and hemp, as used for clothing for most persons in the land, and collecting tax.

There is nothing to show that an abstract concept of law existed in the Qin Empire, which would protect individuals from oppression, define rights and obligations, and stand above an emperor. Commands for action were issued from the emperor either as 'statutes' or as 'ordinances'; officials saw that these were implemented. Manuscripts of some of these 'laws', of 217 BC, discovered in 1975 in Hubei province, inform us of the subjects and depth of detail of these provisions. Many, which lay down approved procedures and activities and the penalties for failure to comply, concern matters such as agriculture, coinage, work of artisans, protection of government property, establishment of officials, control of travel and transmission of official documents. They may regulate the conduct of daily life to the finest detail, such as the method of stacking grain; the removal of marks made by painting, branding or incision on valuable equipment owned by the government, once this was damaged beyond repair; or the amount of lubrication allowed for wheeled vehicles.

Such documents identify crimes such as injury to other persons, robbery, murder or tax evasion, and laid down a scale of punishments ranging from the death penalty—carried out in various, sometimes grim, ways—to terms of hard labour for perhaps five or six years, mutilation by severing a foot, or payment of heavy fines. Set procedures followed arrest of an alleged criminal: interrogation to ascertain the facts; examination of the accused, perhaps after flogging; a search for corroboration; and decision of the action required by the statutes.

Officials of the kingdom of Qin had evolved several instruments to control the population, set up social distinctions, restrain criminal activity and possibly promote the farmers' work in the fields. The gift of one step in a series of eighteen 'orders of honour' conferred status on an individual; and as, with successive bestowals, an individual rose in the scale so too did his or her privileges. These included mitigation of punishment for crime; favourable terms for statutory obligations; and probably an allocation of land with which to make a living.

Provincial and local officials performed an annual task that was fundamental to government: they registered the population according to age, sex and relationship within a family, and the extent of land in various uses, for cereal crops, pasture, orchard or timber. It was on the basis of these records that officials collected taxation in its various forms. That on the land was paid in kind, a *per capita* tax in cash. Able-bodied males were obliged to serve for periods in the armed forces and also in the labour corps, being set to build a palace or a city wall, to construct a canal or perhaps pump water from one level to another; to maintain roads and bridges; and to hump grain from the fields to the designated granaries.

Another institution bore on social cohesion and the repression of crime. Five, or perhaps ten, families were formed into a group whose members were responsible for reporting suspicious activities or crimes of any one of them. A few recorded cases of the trial of a suspected criminal show how an official could require members of a responsibility group to give evidence.

Various systems of weights and measures and different types of coinage had been in use in the pre-imperial kingdoms of the fifth century BC and later. Efficient government empire wide required the collection of tax and distribution of staple products on an equitable basis. Qin therefore took steps to introduce uniformity, by issuing sets of standard weights and units of capacity, and unifying the coinage. Cast in bronze, the coins of the Qin empire were of one denomination as stated in the inscription of 'One half *liang*' (*ban liang*, 7 grams). A square hole in the centre allowed the insertion of a string to tie the coins together in units perhaps of a hundred. Probably an attempt was made to standardize the width of the carts that carried grain or other commodities, sometimes on the narrow paths up and down the hillsides or the tracks that ran between the fields and beside the waterways.

Qin needed armed forces to maintain internal security against would-be dissidents and for protection against potentially hostile peoples of the hills and pasture lands of Central Asia, such as the Xiongnu. Qin's armies drew on the conscripts whom the provincial officials assembled and perhaps to some extent on criminals, but presumably not those who had suffered punishment by mutilation. Some of these forces stood to arms in the garrisons of the north, commanded by provincial officials or officers who may be termed 'generals'. It seems unlikely that these conscripts would have been dressed and equipped as well as the soldiers buried in terracotta effigy around the tomb of the First Emperor. Such was the structure and means of government of the Qin empire and we may look at the emergence of the ideas upon which it rested. The centuries of the Warring States, before the emergence of the Qin empire, had witnessed the first flowering of China's intellectual development. Manuscripts found since the 1970s have revealed a greater diversity of the thoughts of those days than had been recognized and confirmed that these should not be classified into exclusive schools. The writers of those times were individualists quite ready to draw eclectically from the works of their contemporaries. Best known of the writers of the Warring States are those that sought the permanent principles that underlie the universe. Surviving writings known as the *Zhuangzi* and the *Daode jing* (*The Way and its Power,* ascribed to Laozi) show how these mystics saw these principles in *Dao* (the Way) and they are today categorized as Daoist. Other thinkers preferred to fasten on the lessons of the past, the means of instilling order in human activities and stability in social distinctions, and the importance of ethical values; one of these was named Kong Qiu, later known as Kongzi or Confucius (551–479 BC). For over 2,000 years he has been adopted as the model to whom Chinese rulers and officials have looked, his followers being classified by Western, but not Chinese, writers as 'Confucianist'.

But ideas of a different type lay behind Qin's growth to power. Kings and their advisers in the Warring States saw their own survival and the conquest of their enemies as their first priority. Clever men gifted with the powers of persuasion made their way from one kingdom to the next, tendering advice and offering stratagems to kings beset by danger or fired by ambition. Adopting an outlook best described as realistic, they called for measures to gather strength and govern in security. Officials capable of implementing a king's orders had to be chosen on merits rather than on the circumstances of their birth; both they and the population at large had to be trained to obey the acknowledged authority of the kingdom and disciplined to accept the burden of its demands; and kings had to be able to deploy armed forces in sufficient strength to meet emergencies.

Records such as these are ascribed to two men—Shang Yang (c.385–338) and Han Fei (c.280–c.233)—who are credited with fostering Qin's growth and categorized somewhat loosely as 'Legalists'. They both had visited other kingdoms; and both met a violent death thanks to animosities. The essays collected in the *Shangjun shu* and the *Hanfeizi* call on historical precedent and cite principle to emphasize three essential concepts: *fa,* the models of government on which orders or laws should be based; *shu,* the practical methods and expedients with which to attain a ruler's objectives; and *shi,* the visible expression of his authority.

The First Qin Emperor and his advisers took these precepts to heart, as may be evidenced in the decrees and institutions of government. In addition, his authority must be displayed, the scale of his majesty must be apparent to all. As the capital city, Xianyang housed

the Emperor as the fount of all authority and the officials who implemented his orders; his palace was said to include an audience hall that could accommodate no less than 10,000 persons. Outside Xianyang the First Emperor embarked on progresses to distant parts of his realm; inscriptions on the *stelae* that he erected told of his victories over his enemies and his unification of the world under his sole authority. He proclaimed that he was the first of a line of emperors that would be numbered by the thousand. To ensure that his reputation would survive on Earth and perhaps in the hereafter, he ordered the construction of an exceptionally large tomb which would simulate the shape and features of the cosmos. Topped by a tumulus perhaps 100 meters high, the mausoleum stood out as a conspicuous reminder of the Emperor's strength. The tomb itself yet awaits excavation; around it lay buried a large number of clay warriors, drawn up in their serried ranks to guard him from his enemies.

Realistic as the outlook of the Emperor was, he was apparently not entirely disdainful of the call of religion or the force of mythology. In a search for personal immortality he sent a party of youths to put to sea to visit Penglai, a legendary isle where immortal beings live and the elixir of everlasting life may be obtained. In one of his progresses he climbed to the summit of Mount Tai, known perhaps to be the seat of unnamed powers who ruled the universe; precisely what rites the Emperor performed when there are unknown. But whatever the beliefs or hopes that inspired these undertakings, it is unlikely that they rested on a trust in heaven, the almighty power whom the kings of Zhou had worshipped and to whose gift they credited their own charge to rule the world.

Officials of Qin and their clerks wrote special documents on silk, and more routine reports, registers of land and its inhabitants and tax dues, on narrow strips of wood which were bound together to form a scroll. The clerks used a more simplified form of script than their predecessors; this had been emerging in various forms during the Warring States and was perhaps made standard by Li Si. The new form of writing served the needs of the more intensive administration of the time; it may also have helped the government to deflect attention away from the literature of earlier days, in which precepts and ethical principles could be found that might well contradict the purposes and decisions of the realistic government of imperial Qin.

Later historians voiced sharp criticisms of the steps that they said were taken by Qin to reduce attention to writings associated with the leaders and teachers of Zhou. It was claimed that, on imperial orders, copies of such books were burnt and a large number of scholars sent to their deaths; but such accounts may have been exaggerated, and it is by no means certain that these measures were as effective as was claimed.

The primary sources for the history of Qin are in general antagonistic. They therefore tended to paint Qin's government as oppressive and cruel and to blame the severity of its laws for engendering the insurgency that spelt dynastic collapse. Some of these critics of Qin may have been well aware that Han had taken over most of Qin's laws and punishments, with little mitigation of their severity. In later times when a dynasty's strength was on the ebb, an independently minded writer might occasionally press for a reversion to Qin's ways so as to restore a sense of discipline to the body politic.

Overall, by laying the foundations of empire, the First Qin Emperor introduced a radical change in China. Many of its offices and ways of government remained in force, with some adaptations, for perhaps seven centuries, until major social and economic developments required the next major changes, of the Sui (AD 589–618) and Tang (618–907) dynasties. Intellectual advance and religious practice characterized China's brilliant Song dynasty (960–1279); determined government arose with the northern, non-Chinese, emperors, and during the Ming (1368–1644) and Qing (1644–1911) dynasties; but some traces of Qin's concepts and terminology survived even until the establishment of the Republic in 1911.

Beyond the Family Feud

After decades of debate, are younger scholars finally asking the right questions about the Olmec?

ANDREW LAWLER

It's a drizzly autumn morning in the eastern Mexican city of Xalapa, near the heartland of what many scholars say was Mesoamerica's first civilization. At the city's elegant anthropology museum, amid one of the finest Olmec collections in the world, Yale archaeologist Michael Coe points at the giant squat stone head staring sullenly at us. "Look at this," he says enthusiastically. "When it was made, the Maya area didn't even have pottery, and the biggest sculpture from this time in Oaxaca"—an important valley to the west—"could fit in this guy's eye." The Olmec, Coe insists, "were the Sumerians of the New World."

An energetic man even at 77, he is part of an older generation of scholars who have spent a good part of their professional lives arguing among themselves over whether the Olmec birthed the rudiments of Mesoamerican civilization, or whether they were one among many contemporary peoples who contributed art, technology, and religious beliefs to the Aztec, Maya, and other cultures that Cortés and the Spanish encountered 2,500 years later. But that lingering "mother-sister" debate—often vociferous, occasionally unseemly, and sometimes downright nasty—obscures a quiet revolution in research on early Mesoamerica. While the elders bicker, a younger batch of archaeologists is pursuing other questions, asking, for example, how the ordinary Olmec lived and worked, and what they ate.

Such fundamental matters until now were largely neglected amid the academic fracas, which has focused on monumental structures, evidence of kings, and the iconography of the elite. "Everyone is flying a flag from their own valley," sighs Mary Pye, a 40-something archaeologist in Mexico City who is also in Xalapa for a conference on the Olmec. "Forget mother-sister," she says. "It's more complicated." The more nuanced picture emerging of early Mesoamerica does not fit that of either warring camp. Those who back the Olmec as the first civilization traditionally point to the early adoption of maize, the growth of urban centers, and the export of finished goods such as pottery throughout Mesoamerica to clinch their argument. Opponents emphasize the complexity of other cultures in different areas, such as Oaxaca. But the new research shows that during the early critical phase of urbanization the Olmec

may have shunned maize, lived mostly as fishermen, and sought luxury items from distant places, while simultaneously expanding their cultural influence throughout the region.

Unlike the dry valley of Oaxaca or the chilly Basin of Mexico—home today to sprawling Mexico City—the Olmec homeland bordering the Gulf of Mexico is marshy, humid, and hot. It is also remote, and even today traveling to Olmec sites during the rainy season is treacherous. Scholars have long known of this area's famous giant stone heads—massive images of kings, chiefs, and ballplayers as heavy as 20 tons—unearthed in the nineteenth century and long considered remnants of Mesoamerica's heyday in the early centuries A.D., with its sprawling Maya cities. But it was not until the 1940s that researchers realized that the region the Aztecs called "place of wealth" was awash in pre-Maya artifacts.

It was then that, after years of investigation, the Smithsonian Institution's Matthew Stirling and Mexican art historian Miguel Covarrubias drew the startling conclusion that the Olmec heads were in fact the earliest monumental sculptures in Mesoamerica. Radiocarbon dating ultimately backed up their findings, but their further contention that the Olmec created the first Mesoamerican civilization was greeted skeptically, particularly by scholars who had long considered the highlands of the north to be the original source of urbanization.

People were undoubtedly drawn to this area by its rich aquatic resources long before the Olmec, but it was in the second millennium B.C. that the inhabitants began to live in more complex societies. They began, for example, to make pilgrimages to sacred places. Excavators at El Manatí in the 1980s found an extraordinary ritual deposit, dated about 1400 B.C., that included wooden effigies wrapped in vegetation that were preserved in thick mud, along with finely carved axes and stones of jadeite, basalt, and serpentine. They also discovered polished stones carefully laid out along the cardinal directions, and, deep under the muck, rubber balls similar to those used by the Aztec for ritual ballgames when Cortés arrived in 1519—an extraordinarily long history for a sacred sport. There is little evidence for a town at El Manatí, hinting that it was used mainly for religious purposes.

74

But what many consider to be Mesoamerica's first urban center emerged two centuries later just a few miles away. San Lorenzo grew up on a long ridge above a network of rivers on the marshy lowlands that feed into the Gulf of Mexico. The site was easily defended, protected from floods, and blessed with freshwater springs at its summit.

Coe and his colleagues focused on this acropolis during the 1960s, and its ten gigantic stone heads and three carved altars or thrones hint at an impressive processional way. The faces are individualized, and wear what could be leather ballplayers' helmets. Though there are no inscriptions with their identities, most scholars see the heads as representations of generations of rulers. Under the so-called Red Palace—a gravel-floored structure with painted mud walls and stone accents—is a sophisticated basalt drainage system that may have ended in a ritual bath. Stone sculptures of jaguars, serpents, and half-animal, half-human creatures provide the iconography of the Mesoamerican pantheon that reappear for millennia, from the Maya cities of the Yucatán to the Aztec capital Tenochtitlán in the north.

After a 20-year hiatus of digging at San Lorenzo, a new team led by Ann Cyphers of the National Autonomous University of Mexico is now exploring large areas off the acropolis as well, from the terraces below to the small islets surrounding San Lorenzo proper. The terraces were densely packed, mostly with simple houses with earthen floors, pole walls, and thatched roofs. Below, a wide dike or causeway a quarter-mile long was lined with houses as well. Stacey Symonds, a young researcher who is part of Cyphers's team, estimates that an average of 5,500 people may have lived in San Lorenzo proper during its heyday between 1200 and 900 B.C. And an average of 13,000 people may have lived in the city and its 155 square miles of hinterlands.

Cyphers is also exploring the various ways in which the Olmec lived around their capital. The elite resided at San Lorenzo proper and at nine surrounding sites in the immediate neighborhood. Interspersed among these larger towns were 19 smaller villages and 76 small islands built up from the marshy soil only large enough to support a single household. The villages and islands nestled within the twisting river network were ideal locations for transportation by boat and access to seafood. Above them all loomed the ridge of San Lorenzo with its magnificent monuments. Though much of Cyphers's work is yet to be published, scholars are hopeful that her finds will provide the first hard evidence of San Lorenzo's way of life outside the acropolis.

The hierarchical settlement pattern and the population—while modest compared to later Mesoamerican cities—make it clear that something unusual was taking place here. Such well-defined gradations—single households, villages, towns, city—have not yet been found elsewhere in Mesoamerica during this period. "No one can dispute that San Lorenzo is unlike anything else in Mesoamerica," says Philip Arnold, an archaeologist at Loyola University. "It belongs to a way of life that's different from contemporary culture."

Unlike traditional mother-culture advocates, who see maize as the jumpstarter for San Lorenzo, Arnold thinks that the Olmec continued to draw primarily on aquatic resources for centuries after 1200 B.C. He is part of a new vanguard in Olmec household archaeology that is quietly reexamining such long-held assumptions. "Nobody has done any comprehensive and consistent analysis of plant remains," notes Amber VanDerwarker, a 32-year-old archaeologist at Muhlenberg College in Pennsylvania. "It has been almost completely neglected." Like Arnold, she's trying to fill that gap by examining not just what people ate, but how their diet shifted over time. "The old idea is that the rise to power was linked to maize—but nobody had really analyzed remains." She also believes that while maize production was important, it wasn't the be-all and end-all, and that even during San Lorenzo's heyday locals were busy hunting and fishing as well. "It was a fairly diverse and mixed economy." Given that societies in Mesopotamia and Egypt developed as they learned to store and redistribute dry crops, the research has interesting implications for understanding civilization's emergence.

Archaeologists also are reexamining how the Olmec and other groups interacted. Coe and other backers of the mother-culture approach argue that the Olmec had wide influence throughout Mesoamerica, exporting pottery and even religion to their contemporaries. That view has been fiercely opposed by those who work in other areas of Mesoamerica, such as Kent Flannery of the University of Michigan. He and his colleague Joyce Marcus have spent decades examining the urban evolution in Oaxaca. Though they declined to talk to ARCHAEOLOGY, Flannery and Marcus insist in many publications that trade was on a reciprocal basis and that San Lorenzo was not at the center of the network.

But to a younger generation, both points of view lack the subtlety necessary to understand life in ancient Mesoamerica. Decorative cubes of ilmenite (a black iron-titanium mineral) from Chiapas and polished gray-black magnetite mirrors possibly from Oaxaca are among the luxury imports found at San Lorenzo, indicating that its rulers imported as well as exported luxury goods. At the same time, the widespread presence of Olmec pottery—from the northern Mexican highlands to Guatemala—is solid evidence that San Lorenzo was more than just another stop on the trading path.

And a good deal of that pottery was not only in the Olmec style, it was actually made in San Lorenzo. That is the surprising conclusion of a 2005 study led by Jeffrey Blomster of George Washington University that pinpointed the origin of the clay used to make pottery found from the Basin of Mexico to the north to Chiapas to the south. "We're using robust statistical techniques to get compositional data," says the 40-year-old researcher. "Before there was very little data—all we had was theory." By bringing modern analytical methods into the mix, younger scientists such as Blomster hope to provide more data to resolve debates about the Olmec.

Recent finds by David Cheetham, a Ph.D. candidate at Arizona State University, at Cantón Corralito in distant Chiapas ("The Americas' First Colony?"

January/February 2006), where up to 20 percent of the pottery is Olmec in origin (including more than 4,000 pieces of San Lorenzo–style ware) underscore the extent of San Lorenzo's influence. Cantón, which covered 60 acres by the time of its demise in 1000 B.C., shows the presence of people who either were from the Olmec heartland, or had an unusually strong affinity to it. Whether they were colonists, merchants, or renegades is not known.

Both the Cantón excavations and Blomster's work, which included sherds from that site, draw fire from some researchers. Some insist that Cantón's percentage of Olmec ware is much lower, closer to five percent. And Flannery leads a group that questions Blomster's analysis of the sherds and criticizes the sampling as skewed to favor San Lorenzo wares. Flannery's group recently dismissed Blomster and his colleagues in a journal article for seeing "Meso-american civilization as the product of a kind of intelligent design." That reference to creationism—a bitter insult in the world of science—shows how vicious the debate among Mesoamerican archaeologists can be.

"There's a lot of hot air being blown over this," says Arnold. But he and other younger archaeologists are impressed by the quality and quantity of data, which could eventually clarify San Lorenzo's influence.

Another surprising piece of data published in 2006 also sets the Olmec apart from other societies of the time such as that in Oaxaca. Though the Olmec left behind the occasional intriguing symbol, it was not until after 500 B.C. that a writing system in Oaxaca and one near the Olmec heartland appear. But then a team of Mexican and U.S. scholars closely examined a 26-pound serpentine block found by locals in 1999 from a gravel quarry in a place called Cascajal, just a mile from San Lorenzo ("The Cascajal Block," January/February 2007). On one side of it are 62 carved signs. The meaning of these signs is unknown, though similar ones appear at an Olmec site in Chiapas. But given the organization of the symbols and their repetition in the inscription, the team concluded that the block conformed to all expectations of writing. Yet the script appears to have been a dead end; it bears no obvious resemblance to Isthmian, a later script found in the region, or Mayan.

Dating the block proved problematic because it was already out of context when archaeologists examined it. But given that the majority of potsherds associated with the block's original location—as stated by the locals who found it—are primarily from the end of the San Lorenzo phase, the team estimates that it was carved in 900 B.C., as the city began its decline. Some skeptics say that linking the potsherds with the block is guesswork, but even sister-culture backers such as David Grove, professor emeritus at the University of Illinois, acknowledge that the stone provides strong evidence for Olmec writing.

Stephen Houston, a Brown University anthropologist who was part of the team that studied the Cascajal block, says future excavations could at least provide more examples of Olmec writing. For Houston, Coe, and others on the team, the inscription is yet more proof that the Olmec achieved a complexity unrivaled in Mesoamerica.

Yet the Cascajal block, the Cantón excavations, and Blomster's study aren't the only parts of the emerging picture of ancient Mesoamerica. There are also new finds that hint at the sophistication of other regions even before the appearance of the Olmec. The oldest ballcourt known today predates Olmec prominence by several centuries and is found in faraway Chiapas. Flannery and Marcus have evidence that Oaxacans built ceremonial structures and defensive palisades in the century before San Lorenzo's rise. And to the south, along the Pacific, inhabitants traded up and down the coast while producing elaborate pottery long before the kilns of San Lorenzo were fired. And excavations by Grove at Chalcatzingo, a 100-acre site between the Basin of Mexico, Oaxaca, and the Gulf lowlands, hint at massive terraces built by local people that may predate those at Olmec sites.

If ballcourts, terraces, and ceremonial structures existed in other areas, the Olmec clearly didn't invent Mesoamerican civilization. In the vibrant trade among and within the northern highlands and the southern lowlands, more than just goods were exchanged. Religious ideas, building techniques, and political systems inevitably mixed as well. Yet many younger scholars believe something special took place in San Lorenzo. "Oaxaca is isolated, the Basin is cold, and you have metals and pottery coming up the coast from the south," says Pye. "The Olmec is where it all comes together for the first time." But Pye also acknowledges the extensive trade and societal complexity elsewhere. And she notes that some areas in Mesoamerica, particularly along the Pacific coast, remain largely unexplored.

What may emerge is a broader picture of a multicenter evolution in which all the pieces fall together in one place—but that one place did not "invent" civilization as the older mother-culture folks contend.

New world archaeologists might take a page from their Old World colleagues. The latter long assumed that the Sumerians of southern Mesopotamia were the first civilization, and that great cities like Uruk, home to the legendary King Gilgamesh, brought their new way of life to their uncouth neighbors around 3000 B.C. The presence of Uruk pottery from the Iranian plateau to the Mediterranean led researchers to imagine a colonial-style system administered from Uruk.

But now, excavators in Syria and Turkey are finding that the northern end of Mesopotamia was far more advanced than scholars once thought. Though there is little doubt the Sumerians first put together all the pieces of civilization, northerners in settlements like Syria's Tell Brak were living in impressive towns with large buildings surrounded by suburbs as early as 4000 B.C. Archaeologists now understand that Mesopotamia's vastly different northern and southern regions invariably traded ideas as well as goods, no doubt increasing the tempo of creativity in both areas.

Whether the northern highlands and southern lowlands of Mesoamerica competed and cooperated in a similar way in the push toward civilization remains unproven. But there are signs that even the older generation is coming around to a more complex view than the "is not—is too" debate of the past 50 years. Grove, a respected sister-culture supporter, acknowledges that the Olmec had a large and important influence on emerging civilization in the region. "And you can't explain it all as emanating from San Lorenzo," says Richard Diehl, a University of Alabama anthropologist who worked with Coe and has long backed the mother side.

"The burning question of this generation becomes the white noise of the next," says Houston. And the new generation is already too busy looking into the day-to-day life of your average Olmec to bother with the old family feud. "When you polarize a debate, you limit the opportunities to learn," says Arnold. Studying the plant and animal remains, patterns of settlement, and pottery origin, he says, ultimately will make the old argument seem two-dimensional and obsolete. "That debate obscures who the people were," adds VanDerwarker. "And I'm interested in the people." That's an approach that ultimately may give us greater insight into the Olmec than all their magnificent, but mute, stone heads.

ANDREW LAWLER is a staff writer for *Science* and lives in rural Maine.

UNIT 4

The Later Civilizations to 500 C.E.

Unit Selections

Key Points to Consider

- What role did the agora play in the life and times of the Greek city-states, especially Athens? What places in our cities today serve the purpose the agora served in ancient Greece?

- What factors made Alexander's greatness possible? Why does he continue to fascinate us today?

- What role did gladiatorial games play in Roman society? What do they tells us about Roman society?

- What can the Roman use of "graffiti" tell us about their lives? Can these be used as authentic historical sources?

- What did the excavation of the Maya city of Waka' reveal? How did this excavation differ from other Maya excavations?

- What proof exists to support the claim that Petra was a thriving desert metropolis? How have recent archaeological discoveries revealed this city's past as even more remarkable?

- What challenges were hurled against the Jews in the past? How have they risen to meet each challenge, and lived to see the next?

Student Web Site

www.mhcls.com

Internet References

Alexander the Great
http://1stmuse.com/frames/

Ancient City of Athens
http://www.stoa.org/athens

Cracking the Maya Code
www.pbs.org/wgbh/nova/mayacode

Illustrated History of the Roman Empire
http://www.roman-empire.net

Internet Ancient History Sourcebook
http://www.fordham/halsall/ancient/asbook9.html

Internet East Asian Sourcebook
http://www.fordham/halsall/eastasia/eastasiasbook.html

Reconstructing Petra
http://www.smithsonianmag.com/history-archaeology/petra.html

Life in the ancient world was likely to be short and brutal. Poor nutrition, disease, hazards of childbirth, warfare, and violence all took their toll. In the Roman Empire, for example, only one child in eight could expect to reach 40 years of age. Since value depended upon usefulness, long life was not necessarily a blessing. Women were typically subservient and mistreated, criminals and slaves were publicly slaughtered, and unwanted or imperfect children were abandoned to die. Yet, despite these harsh realities, humankind built splendid cities, formed empires, wrote history, invented sports, and created great art. Aspects of this growing diversity is explored in this section.

Athens inspired our modern ideas about government, philosophy, art, and sport. At the center of the *polis,* as these city-states were known, was the agora, a plaza ringed with civic and religious buildings. In Athens, the agora served as a meeting place for merchants and thinkers who were equally valued. Both goods and ideas were traded in this marketplace of products and ideas.

As historians continue the never-ending process of revision, peoples whose contributions have been unacknowledged can receive long overdue credit. Much of science, medicine, religion, music, finance, and philosophy has its roots in Jewish culture. Despite centuries of discrimination and persecution, the Jews have outlasted all the civilizations that were once their ancient contemporaries, and left a stunning heritage of accomplishments.

And well-known figures can have their legacies exalted by the ancient equivalents of entertainment and popular culture. As we are learning, Alexander became an almost godlike mythical figure. At the same time, the voice of the people could capture critical judgments, in the early equivalents of graffiti. Peeling back the layers of distortion is one of the chief tasks of the historian.

As the Greeks and Romans created heroes and debunked the high and mighty, we see the emergence of mass entertainment as a diversion from the pressures of ordinary life. Although the gladiators were the Western world's first superstars, their

© Pixtal/age Fotostock

lives were brutal and short. But, the cheering crowds identified for a moment with their strength and prowess, escaping for a few hours into the life of imagination. Do humans require some form of entertainment and escapism? Or is this merely a habit we began acquiring two thousand years ago?

In Classical Athens, a Market Trading in the Currency of Ideas

For 60 years, archaeologists have pursued secrets of the Agora, where Socrates' society trafficked in wares from figs to philosophy.

JOHN FLEISCHMAN

Athens on an August afternoon: the clear radiant light of Greece suffuses every stone and walkway. From my vantage point, I squint upward to the outcropping of the Acropolis, crowned by Athena's temple, the Parthenon; hordes of tourists lay constant siege to the site. Standing at the base of that fabled rampart, I begin to traverse a quiet, heat-baked square, crisscrossed by gravel paths, dotted with the stubs of ancient walls and scrubby pomegranate and plane trees.

This dusty archaeological park, a sanctuary amid the roar of overmotorized Athens, is in fact one of the most remarkable sites in Classical archaeology. I am crossing the Agora—or central marketplace—of ancient Athens. That this place still exists seems nothing short of miraculous. I am walking in Socrates' footsteps.

The gadfly philosopher frequented this very square—as did his compatriots in the extraordinary experiment that was Classical Athens. Shades of Pericles, Thucydides, Aristophanes, Plato. They all strolled in this place—the Agora, where philosophy and gossip were retailed along with olive oil. And where Classical Athenians actually lived, traded, voted and, of course, argued. The Agora was the city's living heart. Here, politics, democracy and philosophy (their names, after all, are Greek) were born.

For every ten tourists who climb to the Parthenon, only one discovers the precincts of the serene archaeological site at its base. Those visitors are in fact missing an excursion into history made palpable, as well as a glimpse into what must be acclaimed as one of this century's most triumphant urban archaeology undertakings.

Since 1931, the American School of Classical Studies has been digging here, unearthing a dazzling array of artifacts from the layers of history compacted under this earth: Neolithic, Mycenaean, Geometric, Classical, Hellenistic, Roman, Byzantine and more—all collected from this 30-acre site. Still, it is the objects from Classical Athens that seem to speak with greatest resonance.

And fortunately for those of us unable to make it to Athens anytime soon, we have a chance to see for ourselves some of the Agora's most celebrated artifacts. The occasion of this opportunity is a striking anniversary: 2,500 years ago, the Athenian reformer Cleisthenes renounced tyranny and proclaimed the birth of a radically new form of government, democracy. His genius was to offer a straightforward plan. To diffuse powerful political factions, Cleisthenes reshuffled the Athenian city-state into ten arbitrary tribes and called 50 representatives from each to a senate, or boule, of 500. This, then, was the beginning of democracy, however imperfect and subject to subversion and strife it might have been.

Hence the arrival of the exhibition "The Birth of Democracy," which opened recently in the rotunda of the National Archives in Washington, D.C. and continues there through January 2, 1994. A few steps from our own Declaration of Independence, Constitution and Bill of Rights lie the humble tools of Athenian self-government, nearly all of them unearthed in the Agora over the past 60 years by American excavators.

You can look upon actual fourth-century B.C. Athenian jurors' ballots, discovered still inside a terra-cotta ballot box. The ballots, stamped "official ballot," look like metal tops. Each juror was handed two; the spindle shafts designated the vote, solid for acquittal and hollow for guilty. Taking the spindle ends between thumb and forefinger, an Athenian juror was assured that no one could see which spindle he deposited in the ballot box.

For the Too Powerful, a Decree of Exile

Also on view are ostraca, pottery fragments on which Athenians inscribed the names of persons they felt too powerful for the good of the city and deserving of ostracism, or ten years' exile, a procedure formalized by Cleisthenes. More than 1,300 ostraca, condemning many famous figures—Pericles, for instance, and

Aristides and Themistocles—have been found in the Agora. Looking closely at the sherds, you can spell out the names straight from the history books and realize that these ostraca were written out by contemporaries who knew these men personally. And in some cases hated them.

Ostracism was not the worst punishment the democracy could decree. The National Archives also displays a set of distinctive pottery vials uncovered from the fifth-century B.C. Athenian state prison. These tiny vials were used to hold powerful drugs, such as lethal doses of hemlock. Socrates swallowed just such a dose, voted for him in 399 B.C. by his fearful fellow citizens. Archaeologists say the death scene of Socrates described in Plato's *Phaedo* fits the layout of a precise location in the Agora—a building near the southwest corner of the market square.

Plato recounts that after Socrates took the poison, he walked about, then lay down, telling his friends to stop weeping "for I have heard that one ought to die in peace." When the numbness spread from his legs upward to his abdomen, he covered his face. His last words were, as always, ironic. Socrates claimed he had a debt to the god of medicine. "I owe a cock to Asclepius," he informed a companion, "do not forget, but pay it."

The exhibition contains several other objects associated with Socrates, including part of a small marble statue, thought to be of the philosopher, that was also recovered from the prison. Visitors can find, as well, actual hobnails and bone eyelets from the Agora shop of one Simon the cobbler. Socrates is known to have met at such a shop with young students and prominent Athenians alike.

The boundaries of the Agora were clearly marked, and entrance was forbidden to Athenian citizens who had avoided military service, disgraced themselves in the field—or mistreated their parents. Around the open square, but outside its actual boundaries, lay the key civic buildings—courts, assembly halls, military headquarters, the mint, the keepers of the weights and measures, commercial buildings and shrines to the city gods. One such shrine, the Altar of the Twelve Gods, stood within the Agora and marked the city's center.

On business days, the square was filled with temporary wicker market stalls, grouped into rings where similar wares were offered. There was a ring for perfume, for money changing, for pickled fish, for slaves. The Agora was a constantly changing mix of the mundane and the momentous—pickled fish and the world's first democracy. The comic poet Eubulus described the scene: "You will find everything sold together in the same place at Athens: figs, witnesses to summonses, bunches of grapes, turnips, pears, apples, givers of evidence, roses, medlars, porridge, honeycombs, chickpeas, lawsuits, beestings-puddings, myrtle, allotment machines, irises, lambs, water clocks, laws, indictments."

"The Agora was a place for hanging out," according to archaeologist John M. Camp, who is my patient guide this afternoon. "You'd have men of affairs doing a little business, conducting a little politics and stirring up a little trouble." Camp has spent most of his adult life digging here, and he's tireless even in the heat. (He's also the author of *The Athenian Agora,* an erudite and delightful guide to the site, written for a general audience.) The real pleasure of studying this site, he says, is the shock of recognition. "Our own ideas, our own concepts originated right *here,*" he told me, gesturing toward the bright open square of the Agora. "It's not only democracy, it's virtually all of Western drama, law—you name it. Over and over again, you find the only thing that's really changed is the technology. Everything else, they thought of it before. They did it before, and it all happened *here.*"

In the Beginning, Archaeologists Banked on Hope

The open Agora at midday is suited only for mad tourists and foreign archaeologists, both on tight schedules. The tourists can see the Agora today because American archaeologists (funded in large part by American philanthropists—principally John D. Rockefeller Jr. and the David and Lucile Packard Foundation) saved the site from total obliteration. At the outset, the archaeologists who began nosing around here in the late 1920s were banking on educated hope. Although the memory of the Agora was preserved by sources such as Plato and the historian Xenophon, tantalizing description was all that remained. That celebrated site had vanished at least 1,400 years before, lost to waves of pillaging barbarians, buried under layers of settlement from medieval times on.

In short, no one knew for sure where the ancient Agora really was. (Greek and German archaeologists had made some tentative beginnings in the 19th century, but their efforts had shed little light on the actual location.) The most likely site, authorities agreed, was at the foot of the northwestern slopes of the Acropolis. That area, however, was buried beneath a dense neighborhood of 19th-century houses and shops.

The debate remained largely academic until 1929, when the Greek government offered to the American School of Classical Studies a dig-now-or-forever-hold-your-peace deal. The Americans would have to demolish 300 houses and relocate 5,000 occupants. The Greek government required that a permanent museum be built for any finds and that the Agora be landscaped as a park.

The American School finally commenced excavations in 1931. As archaeologists have labored here for more than 60 years, we can read the life and times of Classical Athens in the spaces they have cleared and excavated.

Take the Panathenaic Way, for example, a diagonal street running uphill to the Acropolis. The roadway is packed gravel today, as it was in the days of the Panathenaia, the city's great religious festival. The celebrations began with the Athenian cavalry leading a procession of priests, sacrificial animals, chariots, athletes and maidens across the Agora to the temples of the gods above. All of Athens would have gathered along this route to witness the splendid parade wending across the marketplace. One Panathenaic event, the *apobates* race, in which a contestant in full armor leapt on and off a moving chariot, continued in the Agora well into the second century B.C.

With or without armor, walking uphill is not a recommended Athenian summer-afternoon activity. But taking your time and picking your shade, you can cut across the square to the base of a sharply inclined hill and look upward at a large Doric temple just beyond the western limit of the Agora. This is the Hephaisteion—a temple dedicated to Hephaestus, the god of the forge, and to Athena, patron deity of the city and of arts and crafts. Excavations have shown that it was once surrounded by shops where bronze sculpture, armor and fine pottery were made. Today the world's best-preserved Classical temple, it is a marvel unto itself. Somehow it has survived from Pericles' time onward, a marble monument to the miracle of Athens.

The temple's friezes are carved with scenes that spoke to the imagination of every Athenian. Theseus battling the Minotaur, the labors of Hercules, the Battle of the Centaurs—all images from a world where gods and men resided in a kind of rarefied complicity.

Below the Hephaisteion stood the most important buildings of the Athenian city-state. Here was the Bouleuterion where the 500 representatives of the tribes met. (An older assembly hall stood next door.) Nearby was the round, beehive-shaped Tholos where the 50 members of the executive committee of the Boule served 35- or 36-day terms of continuous duty, living and dining in the Tholos at state expense. (Those early practitioners of democracy apparently subsisted on simple fare—cheese, olives, leeks, barley, bread and wine. No lavish state dinners yet.)

In front of the Bouleuterion stood the statues of the Eponymous Heroes, the ten tribal namesakes chosen by the Delphic Oracle (and the source of our word for a group or thing named after a real or mythical person). Athenians tended to throng before this monument—not out of piety but because this was the site of the city's public notice board, a kind of proto-daily-paper for ancient news junkies. Nearby lay the Strategeion where the ten military leaders of the tribes made their headquarters (and gave us a Greek word for military planning).

North of the Bouleuterion complex rose the Stoa, or covered colonnade, of Zeus, a religious shrine but apparently an excellent place to practice philosophy. Both Plato and Xenophon said that the Stoa of Zeus was a favorite teaching post of Socrates. No one is more closely associated with the Agora than Socrates. He lived his life here. He met his death here. Xenophon remembered his former teacher moving among the market tables and stoas: "he was always on public view; for early in the morning he used to go to the walkways and gymnasia, to appear in the agora as it filled up, and to be present wherever he would meet with the most people."

As much as Socrates enjoyed the public scene in the Agora, he made it clear, according to Plato, that he was not a "public" person, that is, he was not interested in politics. This was a scandalous opinion to hold in Athens, where the real work of every Athenian citizen was just that—being a citizen. In Plato's *Apology,* Socrates rounded on his critics: "Now do you really imagine that I could have survived all those years, if I had led a public life, supposing that . . . I had always supported the right and had made justice, as I ought, the first thing?"

He had learned the hard way. Allotted to a turn in the Bouleterion in 406–05 B.C., he was assigned to the Tholos as a member of the executive committee. And thus it fell to Socrates to preside over a wild meeting of the mass Athenian Assembly when word arrived of the sea battle at Arginusae. It was an Athenian win, but the victorious generals were accused of leaving their own dead and dying behind. The majority moved to condemn the generals to death as a group without individual trials. Socrates resisted. "Serving in the Boule and having sworn the bouleutic oath [to serve in accordance with the law], and being in charge of the Assembly, when the People wished to put all nine [actually eight of the ten] generals to death by a single vote, contrary to the laws, he refused to put the vote," according to Xenophon. "He considered it more important to keep his oath than to please the People by doing wrong."

That was the sort of behavior that could earn you a great many enemies. Eventually, three citizens brought charges against Socrates for mocking the gods and corrupting Athenian youth. The exact location of the courtroom where Socrates stood trial still eludes identification, but the place of his indictment, the Royal Stoa, has been excavated. As for the place of his death, if you hunt carefully on the rising slope beyond the Tholos, you can find the low precinct of exposed stones that archaeologists believe was the site of his demise.

The precise forces and circumstances that led to the jury's death sentence have never been elucidated completely. What is clear is that the questions raised by that trial so long ago are not dead letters. Dissent versus consent, public good versus private conscience, they still buzz about the ears of modern democracies. "I am the gadfly which the god has given the state," Socrates told his jury in the *Apology,* "and all day long and in all places am always fastening upon you, arousing and persuading and reproaching you."

The Athenian Agora still buzzes with surprises and mysteries. In 1981, on the northern edge of the Agora, Princeton archaeologist T. Leslie Shear Jr. hit the corner of one of the most famous buildings of ancient Athens, the Poikile, or Painted, Stoa. This discovery was stunning good news for Agora archaeology. The structure had been renowned throughout the ancient world for its spectacular wall paintings. The glowing images, covering enormous wooden panels, lionized Athenian victories both mythological (over the Amazons, for instance) and historical (over the Persians at Marathon).

The fabled paintings were removed by the Romans in the fourth century A.D. but survived long enough to have been described by the second-century A.D. chronicler Pausanias. "The last part of the painting," he recorded, "consists of those who fought at Marathon. . . . In the inner part of the fight the barbarians are fleeing and pushing one another into the marsh; at the extreme end of the painting are the Phoenician ships and the Greeks killing the barbarians who are tumbling into them."

For Athenians, the Painted Stoa was the arena of their triumphs made visible. It was also a hotbed of philosophical speculation, eventually turning up as the gathering place of the third-century B.C. followers of Zeno of Citium. Zeno preached that the wise man should remain indifferent to the vanities of the transient world. The people of Athens associated the school of thought with the building, calling Zeno's disciples Stoics and their philosophy Stoicism. And 2,300 years later, so do we.

Stoicism is a necessity in Agora archaeology. As Leslie Shear explains, his father had, in some ways, an easier time of it here. The elder Shear supervised the original excavations during the 1930s. He had a squad of colleagues and 200 paid workmen to take down a whole neighborhood at a time. This summer, Shear has John Camp, his coinvestigator and colleague of 25 years, a nine-week season, and 33 student volunteers (American, Canadian and British) in addition to a small crew of Greek workmen who handle the heavy machinery and earthmoving. And he has his wife, Ione, a highly trained archaeologist in her own right, who has also worked at the site for 25 years.

Pursuing the Agora in the present Athens real estate market is tedious and expensive. It is house-to-house archaeology—negotiation, demolition and then excavation. While he has been busy elsewhere on the site, Shear is still waiting patiently to acquire the five-story building that is standing on the rest of the Painted Stoa.

Meanwhile, every water jug, bone or loom weight excavated anywhere in the Agora must receive a numbered tag. Every number goes into the dig's records, meticulously kept in special 4-by-6-inch clothbound notebooks. When in use in the field, these notebooks reside in an old, cheap suitcase that sits on a rough wooden desk that looks even older and cheaper. With a folding umbrella for shade, this is the nerve center for the dig. The senior archaeologists sit here, drawing tiny diagrams of the strata and the find location for every tagged item.

May 28, 1931: "H. A. Thompson Commenced . . ."

It is, as Camp puts it, "dinosaur-age" archaeology in the era of field computers, but it works. Completed notebooks go into filing cabinets in offices inside the Stoa of Attalos. (This colonnade, originally a great commercial arcade in the second century B.C., was completely reconstructed in the 1950s to house the excavation's museum, laboratories, offices and storage vaults.) There the records march back in unbroken order through the decades to May 28, 1931, and the very first entry: "In the afternoon, H. A. Thompson commenced the supervision of Section A."

Looking back over more than 60 years, from the other side of the Atlantic, Homer Thompson smiled when he heard again that clipped description of the first day. He was a young, relatively inexperienced archaeologist then. Today he is a vigorous professor emeritus at the Institute for Advanced Study in Princeton, New Jersey. He oversaw the Agora excavations from 1947 to 1967.

Back in the '30s, he recalls, it took seven years to find the first boundary stone that used the word "Agora." It wasn't a thrill so much as a relief, says Thompson, who was in charge of the crew that uncovered the marker, wedged in by the wall of Simon the cobbler's shop. "We believed we were working in the Agora, but we had so little to show for it—in inscriptions—that some of our colleagues would come by and ask 'How do you know that you're in the Agora?' Well, this settled it."

Finding the second boundary stone took another 30 years. The marker lies on the southwest corner of the square. Ione Shear uncovered it one afternoon in 1967.

It is a very ordinary marble block. The faintly visible lettering runs across the top and then down one side. The important thing, says Leslie Shear, is that this block and the one found near Simon's shop have not been moved in 2,500 years. Other boundary stones have been found uprooted, buried in rubble fill. "But these two stand where they've stood since the sixth century B.C.," he observes. "They were set out at about the time the democracy was founded. In a very real sense, democracy as we understand it was invented in the Agora of Athens." He leaned down to trace the letters.

Stones can speak, although they rarely speak in the first person. This one spoke loud and clear: "I am the boundary of the Agora." There was no dispute after that. This was the word. This was the place.

Additional Readings

The Athenian Agora: Excavations in the Heart of Classical Athens by John M. Camp, Thames and Hudson (London), 1986.

The Birth of Democracy: An Exhibition Celebrating the 2500th Anniversary of Democracy, edited by Josiah Ober and Charles W. Hedrick, American School of Classical Studies at Athens (Princeton, New Jersey), 1993.

The Athenian Agora: A Guide to the Excavation and Museum, American School of Classical Studies at Athens, 1990.

The Agora of Athens, The Athenian Agora, Volume XIV by H. A. Thompson and R. E. Wycherley, American School of Classical Studies at Athens, 1972.

JOHN FLEISCHMAN, who wrote about the excavation of the legendary site of Troy in a past *Smithsonian,* braved Athens' summer heat on the trail of his story.

Alexander the Great: Hunting for a New Past?

Paul Cartledge goes in search of the elusive personality of the world's greatest hero.

PAUL CARTLEDGE

Once upon a time, in the public square of the ancient city of Corinth, Alexander—already king of the Macedonians, but not yet 'the Great'—encountered the notoriously unconventional Diogenes the Cynic. Before he could engage the sage in any sort of philosophic dialogue, however, Diogenes curtly told him to go away, as he was blocking out the sunlight. First blood to Diogenes. Alexander, by no means unintelligent, was later questioned about the encounter, and is supposed to have responded: 'Had I not been Alexander, I should have wished to be Diogenes'.

Ben trovato, no doubt, though Alexander (356BC to 323BC) could of course afford to say that. He was Alexander, after all. Or rather: before all, before all else, and before all others. For Alexander personally embodied to the utmost degree the Homeric injunction 'always to be the best and excel all others' (in the words of E.V. Rieu's translation). Paradoxically, though, that is one of the very few things we can know for certain about Alexander the man (as opposed to Alexander the world-conqueror). For the evidence for his personal life and inner motivation is not at all extensive or reliable. Nor are the available sources for his public career much better. Perhaps borrowing a leaf out of his tutor Aristotle's book, Alexander took unusual care to try to ensure that his deeds were reported and recorded. He also tried to make sure they were interpreted correctly among the various constituencies to which they were broadcast: Macedonians, Greeks, Persians, and the countless other subjects of his vast empire. Yet no contemporary narrative account of his career exists, and what is generally reckoned to be the most persuasive of those that do survive was written by Arrian, a Greek from Asia Minor, well over four centuries after Alexander's premature death, aged thirty-two, at Babylon in 323 BC. This situation makes the search for the 'real' Alexander almost impossibly difficult.

For this reason, and because Alexander soon passed from the territory of factual history proper to the plane of myth and legend (thanks, not least, to his own self-propagandising efforts), the search for him has been likened to that for the historical Jesus. Much was written about both men, but practically nothing contemporary has survived, and very little indeed without a severely prejudiced axe to grind.

The risk, therefore, as well as the opportunity, is that we tend to create the Alexander of our dreams—or nightmares. There have been as many Alexanders as there have been students of Alexander.

My own version of him seeks to do some sort of justice to the many facets of this multi-talented individual. In my search for what made him 'tick', I draw, both literally and metaphorically, on the semantic field of the chase. Hunting wild game was not just an optional pastime in ancient Macedonia. It was integrated organically into the education and elevation of the aristocratic elite. It was therefore a relatively short step, I argue, for Alexander to go from hunting lot game to hunting for undying glory, and to aim to achieve that goal by trekking to the very ends of the earth and hunting down many thousands of human beings and wild animals en route.

Alexander's mother Olympias (after whom a reconstructed trireme commissioned in 1987 into the Hellenic navy is named) was a Greek princess from Epirus, in the northwest of the Greek peninsula. Her marriage to the far-from-monogamous Philip of Macedon was reportedly a love-match, although in this marriage as in his other six Philip was no doubt fighting his wars by matrimony, as an ancient biographer put it: using marriage alliance as a diplomatic tool. Not the least of his wars, though, was fought within the tempestuous marriage to Olympias. In one of the more remarkable moves of their incessant marital combat, the hyper-religiose Olympias ventured to claim that Alexander had been fathered by a snake—not a reference to her human husband, but to the Egyptian god Ammon (Amun) in disguise. Whatever his true paternity, Alexander was born in 356 BC at the Macedonian capital, Pella, about the time of the Olympic Games at which one of his father's racehorses carried off an olive crown.

Philip was not alone in finding the fiery Olympias difficult. Alexander once allegedly remarked that through her antics she made him pay a high rent for the nine months she had housed him in her womb. Indeed, he tried to distance himself so far from his natural mother that he had himself adopted symbolically by Queen Ada, the non-Greek ruler of Carla, the area around Halicarnassus (modern Bodrum in Turkey), and later formed a close, possibly even intimate, relationship with the mother of his defeated enemy, Great King Darius III of Persia. Yet it can be argued that, but for Olympias, Alexander would not have become king when he did: in 336 BC at the relatively early age of twenty, following Philip's assassination during the wedding celebrations for his and Olympias' other child, Cleopatra. And to Olympias, probably, is to be traced the streak of passionate mysticism that led Alexander to claim to be more than merely mortal, thanks to his supernatural birth as well as his super-human achievements.

At a young age (perhaps even before his teens) Alexander is said to have singlehandedly tamed an unusually fiery and exorbitantly expensive Thessalian stallion called Bucephalas ('Ox-Head'—probably named for the shape of the white blaze on his muzzle). He rode Bucephalas both in war (for example, at the battle of Issus, 333 BC) and when indulging his insatiable passion for hunting wild animals in the rare intervals of rest between campaigning and marching.

Alexander was indeed almost inseparable from Bucephalas until the steed's death in Pakistan at the ripe age of around thirty. The Roman emperor Caligula later made one of his horses a consul of Rome; Shakespeare's Richard III would have given his kingdom for a horse; and Lt Col Rodolph de Salis of the Balaklava Light Brigade awarded a campaign medal to his charger Drummer Boy; but only Alexander founded a city in honour of his favourite mount and named it after him as a public memorial. The site of Bucephala has not, however, been identified.

Alexander was appointed regent of Macedon at the age of just sixteen, when father Philip was abroad on one of his many campaigns. The precocious Alexander seized—or created—the opportunity to wage war on a local non-Greek Thracian people and to establish a new city on the site of their former capital. That was not all. Philip had already founded two cities and named them after himself: Philippi (later celebrated for the Pauline epistle) and Philippopolis (modern Plovdiv in Bulgaria). Not to be outdone, Alexander named his new Thracian city after himself, Alexandroupolis—as it is still called. What the masterful Philip thought of his son's teenage presumption is not recorded.

In his formative years Alexander triumphantly passed two of the crucial tests of Macedonian manhood—hunting and killing a wild boar and a human enemy; 'being a man', in ancient Macedonia, had a more savage ring to it than the modern usage of the phrase might suggest. These feats of hunting prowess entitled Alexander to wear a distinctive kind of belt and to recline rather than sit during the symposia (drinking-parties) that were a prominent feature of Macedonian court life. In most of Greece the consumption of alcohol at symposia was normally quite carefully regulated. But Macedonians—at least so it seemed to Greeks—drank to get drunk. One

recent historian (J. Maxwell O'Brien) has followed the lead of Alexander's Greek critics and given this a modern 'scientific' spin, claiming that Alexander became a clinical alcoholic. This claim cannot be proven today, but there undoubtedly were episodes in which Alexander acted unfortunately when under the influence of alcohol—most disastrously in 328 BC, at Samarkand in central Asia, when in a drunken fit he killed 'Black' Cleitus, a senior cavalry commander who had been a personal companion since boyhood. His own early death, too, may well have been precipitated by unwisely immoderate consumption of alcohol.

From the age of thirteen to about sixteen Alexander was tutored at Mieza, away from the royal court, by Aristotle, the greatest intellectual of his day. But who influenced whom most, it would be hard to decide. Perhaps it was something of a dialogue of the deaf. Aristotle wrote at length about kingship in his treatise entitled *Politics*, and had some interesting things to say about a figure whom he called 'All-King', so wise and beneficent that his commands should unquestioningly be obeyed to the letter. But that figure, clearly, was a theoretical construct rather than an allusion to the living and breathing Alexander. On the other hand, Alexander shared his teacher's passion for Homer, treasuring a copy of the *Iliad* that Aristotle had personally annotated, and sending back botanical and other specimens from Asia to Aristotle's Lyceum institute for advanced study in Athens.

Aristotle is also said to have advised Alexander to treat all nonGreeks as slavish 'barbarians', advice which Alexander—to his credit—conspicuously did not follow. Indeed, he married, polygamously, three 'barbarians'—the daughter of a Sogdian warlord and two Persian royal women—and encouraged his closest companions to take foreign wives too. No doubt, as with Philip's marriages, these were predominantly motivated by realpolitik. It is notable that, unlike his father, Alexander married no Macedonian nor Greek woman. Moreover his marriages were designed to further a policy of orientalisation, the playing down of an exclusive Hellenism and the promotion of Graeco-oriental political and cultural mix.

The question of Alexander's sexuality—his predominant sexual orientation—has enlivened, or bedevilled, much Alexander scholarship. That he loved at least two men there can be little doubt. The first was the Macedonian noble Hephaestion, another friend from boyhood, whom he looked on—and may actually have referred to—as his alter ego. The Persian queen mother, it was said, once mistook the taller Hephaestion for Alexander, who graciously excused her blushes by murmuring that 'he too is Alexander'. Whether Alexander's relationship with the slightly older Hephaestion was ever of the sort that once dared not speak its name is not certain, but it is likely enough that it was. At any rate, Macedonian and Greek mores would have favoured an actively sexual component rather than inhibiting or censoring it. Like hunting, pederasty was thought to foster masculine, especially martial, bravery.

The other non-female beloved of Alexander's was named Bagoas. He was not just a 'barbarian' (Persian) but also a eunuch. There was a long Middle Eastern tradition of employing eunuchs as court officials, especially where a harem system was in place, as at the Achaemenid royal court (witness the Biblical book of Esther). Bagoas was not the first Persian court eunuch, either, to act as a power-broker between rival individuals and factions. A homonymous predecessor had done his murderous worst through the arts of poison, paving the way for Darius III's immediate predecessor to assume the Persian throne. The methods of Alexander's Bagoas were no less effective, if less violent, and Alexander's personal commitment to him seems to have attained levels of sexual intimacy that his Greek and Macedonian courtiers found embarrassing.

Yet in terms of his known activity, as opposed to his possible preferred orientation, Alexander was undoubtedly bisexual. He fathered at least one child, with his Sogdian wife Roxane. But perhaps sex as such did not hold as much attraction for him as other passions did (the Greek word eros could cover other strong desires too). Arrian, at least, thought that fighting and conquering gave him the same sort of thrills and satisfactions as sex did other men. By the age of twenty-six (in 330 BC) Alexander had conquered most of the known ancient world—that is, east of the Adriatic and as far east as modern Pakistan.

As a conqueror, Alexander is in a stratospheric league with Napoleon, Genghis Khan and few others. A combination of boldness of strategic invention, unshakeable personal courage, dashing leadership from the front, willingness to share the toughest rigours suffered by the ordinary soldiers, and a liberal dose of sheer good fortune ensured his stature as a great general. He was as magnificently successful in coping with the grim necessities and improvisatory diversions of sieges (as at Tyre in 332 BC) and guerrilla warfare as he was in executing theatrically staged set-piece pitched battles (the River Granicus in 334 BC, Gaugamela in 331 BC, and River Hydaspes in 326 BC, as well as Issus). In terms of his prowess in military command he truly earned his title 'the Great'.

Alexander made it clear from early on that he intended to go to the outermost edge of the inhabited world, to what he conceived to be the girdling Ocean. For him, as for his latterday fictional avatar James Bond, the world was not enough. But in 326 BC his mainly Macedonian troops, on reaching the river Hyphasis (modern Beas in Pakistan), declared 'Not a step more!', and in 324 BC at Opis (near modern Baghdad) they again rejected his plans for permanent conquest, first of the Arabs and then, perhaps, the Carthaginians, and then . . . who knows? Those two mutinies prompted the adage that the only defeats Alexander suffered were at the hands of his own men, most of whom were most of the time fanatically loyal.

This is not to say that Alexander did not experience opposition to his person, his status, or his inferred programmes and plans. On the contrary, his career as king opened in a flurry of accusation and counter-accusation (whole books have been written to exonerate him from the charge of patricide-regicide). And it continued as it had begun, punctuated at regular intervals by plots, real or alleged, followed by exemplary treason trials and executions, or even straightforward assassinations of perceived rivals and enemies. His drunken manslaughter of 'Black' Cleitus was occasioned by taunts of tyrannical rule and excessive orientalism. The judicial murder of the cavalry commander Philotas and the consequent assassination of the latter's father Parmenion (Alexander's—and

Philip's—premier general) were due more to concern for his personal authority and standing than to the need to extirpate genuine treachery. The execution of his official historian, the Callisthenes (a younger relative of Aristotle), followed a highly controversial attempt by Alexander to have himself kowtowed to in public in the Persian manner, to which Callisthenes had led the—all-too—successful Greek and Macedonian court opposition.

Not the least of the many extraordinary facts about Alexander is that both in his lifetime and after his death he was worshipped as a god, by Greeks and Macedonians as well as, for example, Egyptians (to whom he was Pharaoh). The episode that led to Callisthenes' death in 327 BC was connected to this fact. Greeks and Macedonians believed that formal obeisance should be paid only to gods. So the refusal of his Greek and Macedonian courtiers to pay it to Alexander implied that they, at any rate, did not believe he genuinely was a living god, at least not in the same sense as Zeus or Dionysus were. Alexander, regardless, did nothing to discourage the view that he really was divine. His claim to divine birth, not merely divine descent, was part of a total self-promotional package, which included the striking of silver medallions in India depicting him with the attributes of Zeus. Through sheer force of personality and magnitude of achievement he won over large numbers of ordinary Greeks and Macedonians to share this view of himself, and to act on it by devoting shrines to his cult.

The divine worship of a living ruler was one of his few unambiguous legacies. Another is his fame. That his legend has spread so far and so wide—from Iceland to China—since his death in 323 BC is due very largely to the Alexander Romance. This fabulous fiction took shape in Egypt, mostly some three or more centuries after Alexander's death. The text, originally in Greek, was disseminated in several languages, both Indo-European and Semitic, throughout the old Greco-Roman world and the newer Muslim-Arabic Middle East. Partly thanks to this work, Alexander became in various countries and times a hero, a quasi-holy man, a Christian saint, a new Achilles, a philosopher, a scientist, a prophet, and a visionary. He has featured prominently in both the secular and the sacred visual art of numerous cultures.

Through his conquests Alexander ended the Achaemenid Persian empire that had been founded by Cyrus the Great more than two hundred years previously, in the mid-sixth century. He created the conditions for the development of new Graeco-Macedonian territorial kingdoms based on Macedonia, Syria and, most famously, Egypt—the Pharaoh Cleopatra, who committed suicide in 30 BC, was the last ruler of the Egyptian dynasty established by Alexander's boyhood companion and posthumous historian, Ptolemy son of Lagos (the Greek for 'hare'). Alexander is thus one of the few individuals in history who literally changed the world and was epoch-making.

But his achievement was also inchoate. Part of Alexander's enduring fascination, indeed, is that he died at the age of just thirty-two, at the height of his power and glory, with the world at his feet, full of plans, alleged or genuine. The new empire he had created was unlikely to have proved very lasting in any event.

But it crumbled all the sooner once his centripetal force was removed. Perhaps the brute imperialism that was involved in its creation is not something to be mourned, but Alexander's apparently sincere notion of ethnic fusion, or at least co-operation, at the top of the administrative pyramid across cultural and political divides, is one surely to be welcomed—and maybe even imitated.

Alexander the Great remains, for many, an iconic figure in everyday life, prayed to by Greek fishermen, hymned by Turkish storytellers, and anathematised by Zoroastrian followers. If the modern secular equivalent of ancient divinity is to be featured as a brilliantly glowing star of the silver screen, it is apt that at least one more Alexander movie is in active production as I write. And this is to say nothing of the number of books about him, including novels and how-to business primers as well as ideally more reliable histories . . . The Alexander legend lives on. The hunt for a new Alexander is a vital part of living history today.

Sudden Death

Gladiators Were Sport's First Superstars, Providing Thrills, Chills and Occasional Kills

FRANZ LIDZ

The ruins of Carthage, that great city-state crushed by the Romans in 146 B.C., rise from the Tunisian steppes like a mouthful of bad teeth. It was from here that North Africa's Three-H Club—Hamilcar, Hasdrubal and Hannibal—invaded Europe and challenged the Roman Empire in the Punic Wars. Hulking over the few bleak tombs that still stand is E1 Djem, a coliseum almost as massive as the one in Rome. Few monuments better embody humanity's inhumanity. Over two centuries, E1 Djem provided an enormous venue for satisfying the Roman appetite for gory spectacle. From dawn until after nightfall, fatal encounters between men and men, men and beasts, and beasts and beasts were staged in this arena, whose wooden floor was covered with sand that soaked up the blood spilled in combat.

That floor is now collapsed, exposing the narrow corridors below, where an intricate rope-and-pulley system hoisted gladiators, condemned prisoners and wild animals to the surface. You can stand down there and gaze upward, much like the poor souls funneled through there once did, awaiting their fate. The extravagant butchery that was the gladiatorial games—snuff theater, if you will—seems like something out of Monty Python, a point not lost on Flying Circus alumnus Terry Jones, an Oxford don in history who cowrote and narrated a four-part series on the Crusades for the BBC and also did a documentary for the network on gladiators. While scouting locations for *Monty Python's Life of Brian* in 1978, Jones padded though E1 Djem's underground passageways in awed silence. "I shuddered with gleeful disgust," he recalls, "and tried to imagine how the fighters must have felt sprinting into the sunlight, surrounded by mobs baying for blood."

For seven centuries the Romans celebrated murder as public sport. "A gladiator fight was something between a modem bullfight and a prizefight," says Jones. "It was like bullfighting in that the spectators appreciated the competitors' technique and applauded their skill and courage. It was like boxing in that you went to see people mashing each other into the ground. The games weren't decadent; they were an antidote to decadence. The Romans believed it was beneficial to watch people being slain—you learned how to meet death bravely. In the ancient city, where compassion was regarded as a moral defect, the savage killings weren't just good entertainment, but morally valuable."

The origins of the sport may lie in Etruscan slave fights, which were fought to the death to please the gods and to enhance the reputations of the slaves' owners. The Romans incorporated the tradition into their funeral ceremonies, beginning in 264 B.C. with that of Junius Brutus Pera's. Gradually, the spectacles became more lurid and more frequent—and more necessary for each ruler to provide in order to retain power and sustain the goodwill of a mostly unemployed populace. Before long, just about every Roman city had its own amphitheater. The most majestic, the Colosseum, held 50,000 spectators and offered every sort of diversion from circus acts to reenactments of historic naval battles on the flooded arena floor. Roman emperors spent vast sums on bread and circuses, entertaining the urban masses. Much like the dictators of today, emperors well understood the benefits of athletic triumphs, in propaganda and as a distraction from misery at home. The games that commemorated the emperor Trajan's victories on the Dacian frontier in 107 A.D. featured 10,000 gladiators and lasted 123 days.

Being a gladiator was a job first thought fit only for slaves, convicts or prisoners of war. But under the Republic, many freeborn citizens became gladiators, seeking a kind of macabre glamour. Under the Empire, noblemen, emperors and even women fought. As the games became more popular, criminals were sometimes remanded to gladiator schools. "In general, a sentence to the schools meant three years of training and combat in the arena followed by two years teaching in the schools," wrote Richard Watkins in *Gladiator*. Among the earliest training schools was the one near Capua from which Spartacus and 78 other gladiators made their historic escape in 73 B.C. Eluding the Roman garrison, they stole weapons, pillaged estates and freed thousands of slaves. Within a year, the bandit and his guerrilla band of 90,000 engaged the Roman legions in the Revolt of Spartacus, one of history's more forlorn campaigns. Emboldened by victories all over Southern Italy, the gladiators took on the main body of the Roman army. Its commander, Marcus Licinius Crassus, routed the rebels and cut Spartacus to pieces, celebrating his triumphal return by crucifying 6,000 of his captives along the Appian Way.

Most of the schools were run by "stable masters" who either bought and maintained gladiators for rental, or trained them for other owners. These overseers were called lanistae, which derives from the Etruscan word for butcher. Ranked and housed on the basis of experience, the four grades of trainees honed their swordmanship on straw men or fencing posts. Instructors taught them conditioning, toughness and the proper postures to assume when falling and dying. They were well-fed (barley porridge was the andro of its day) and pampered with massages and baths. In Rome, however, gladiator schools were in imperial hands. Gladiators owned by Caligula, the Empire's quintessential mad despot, supposedly trained themselves not to blink. The emperor sometimes sparred with them. "To be his partner might prove a dubious honour," wrote Anthony Barrett in *Caligula*. "It is said that when practising with a gladiator from the training school [who was armed] with [a] wooden sword, Caligula ran his partner through with a real one." (Caligula lived out every modern team owner's dream: He once ordered an entire section of gladiator fans thrown to the beasts for laughing at him.)

Every gladiator was a specialist: Spartacus was a Thracian, a class named for and outfitted in the equipment of one of Rome's vanquished enemies. Armored in shin guards and a crested helmet, and armed with a small, round shield and a dagger curved like a scythe, Thracians were generally matched against the mirmillones, who protected themselves with short Gallic swords, large oblong shields and fish-crowned helmets. The heavily armored secutor was often pitted against the practically bare-skinned retiarius, whose strategy was to entangle his opponent in a net and spear his legs with a trident. Then there were the lance-brandishing andabatae, believed to have fought on horseback in closed visors that left them more or less blind; the two-knife wielding dimachaeri; the lasso-twirling laqueari; the chariot-riding essedarii; and the befeathered Samnites, who lugged large, rectangular shields and a straight sword called a gladius, from which the word gladiator comes.

Not all gladiators were eager participants. "In Caligula's day," says Jones, "a dozen gladiators decided not to fight. They laid down their arms, figuring the emperor wouldn't want to waste 12 gladiators. It didn't work. Caligula was so infuriated by this early trade union thing that he ordered them all to be killed. Whereupon one of them jumped up, grabbed a weapon and slew all his unarmed ex-colleagues. Then Caligula stood up and said a very strange thing: 'I've never seen anything so cruel.'"

Cruelty, of course, was the sine qua non of the gladiatorial games. During a typical day out at the amphitheater, you could expect men stalking and killing beasts in the morning, execution of convicts at midday, gladiator bouts in the afternoon. The brutal truths: Mankind trumps the wild, law punishes criminality, valor vanquishes death. "The arena was ... a symbol of the ordered world, the cosmos," Thomas Wiedemann wrote in *Emperors and Gladiators*. "It was a place where the civilized world confronted lawless nature."

Morning sessions at the Colosseum were devoted to antisocial Darwinism. In venationes, wild game was hunted amid elaborate scenery depicting, say, mountains or glades; in bestiarii, ferocious predators faced off in bizarre combinations: bears against lions, lions against leopards, leopards against crocodiles. The scale of the slaughter could be staggering. A venatio put on by Pompey in 55 B.C. included the slaughter of 20 elephants, 600 lions, 410 leopards, numerous apes and Rome's first rhinoceros. At a hunt held by Augustus, the score was 49.0 leopards, dozens of elephants, and as many as 400 bears and 300 lions—a total later matched by Nero. Roughly nine thousand animal carcasses were dragged out of the Colosseum during the opening ceremonies in 80 A.D.; 11,000 more over Trajan's four-month shindig. The Romans were so efficient at keeping their arenas stocked that entire animal populations were wiped out: Elephants disappeared from Libya, lions from Mesopotamia and hippos from Nubia. "All sorts of exotic animals were trapped in African deserts and the forests of India," Jones says. "Fans must have sat in the stands thinking, 'Ooh, what's that? I've never seen one of them before.' A lot of ostriches would come out and the hunters would chase them around a bit, and then you'd get some tigers. 'Ooh, tigers! They're interesting!' Then the tigers would be set on the ostriches. It was kind of a zoo in action."

Around noon, in an Empirical version of a halftime show, it was mankind's turn to be massacred. While spectators snacked on fried chickpeas and were misted with perfume to mask the stench of carnage, pairs of meridiani—arsonists, murderers, Christians—were sometimes subjected to what the philosopher Seneca called "sheer murder . . . , a round-robin of death." One prisoner was handed a sword and ordered to kill the other. His job complete, he was disarmed and killed by the next armed captive. This went on until the last prisoner was whacked by an arena guard. Chariots were then wheeled out beating men and women chained to posts. At a signal, trapdoors opened and leopards sprang out. In Rome, Christians really were fed to the lions. And leopards.

Still, the highlight of most games was professional gladiatorial combat. The show opened with a procession heralded by trumpets. Dressed in purple and gold cloaks, gladiators circled the arena on foot, shadowed by slaves bearing their weapons. When the combatants reached the royal box, they supposedly thrust their right arms forward and shouted, "Ave, Imperator, morituri te salutant!" (Hail, Emperor, those who are about to die salute thee!)

Supposedly, because much of what we think we know about the games is in dispute, or evolved from Hollywood sword 'n' sandal sagas. No one is quite sure if "thumbs down" meant death and "thumbs up" a reprieve. Some scholars believe spectators would turn their thumbs toward their chests as a sign for the winner to stab the loser and that those in favor of mercy turned their thumbs down as a sign for the winner to drop his sword. Which would mean the best review a fallen fighter could hope for was "one enthusiastic thumb down."

After the procession and their salutation to the emperor, weapons were tested for sharpness and combatants paired off by lot. A typical show featured between 10 and 20 bouts, each lasting about 15 minutes. A horn was blown and timid fighters were prodded into the arena with whips and red-hot brands. Each fight was supervised by two referees. Coaches stood nearby, lashing reluctant fighters with leather straps. Just like at the ballpark, the house organist would rally the betting crowd. Cries of "Verbera!" (Strike!), "Iugula!" (Slay!) and "Habet!" (That's got him!) swept the stadium. If a Roman fan yelled "Kill the umpire!" he really meant it. The first gladiator to draw blood or knock his opponent down was the victor. A beaten gladiator could appeal for clemency by casting aside his weapon and raising his left hand. His fate was left to the spectators, those early Roger Eberts. The prevailing notion that most gladiators dueled to the death is no more likely than the idea that most died in the arena. Only about one in 10 bouts were lethal, and many of those fatalities can be blamed on overzealousness. "Gladiators were very, very expensive characters," says Jones. "It cost a great deal to keep them fed and exercised and comfortable. Unless you were Caesar and wanted to impress somebody, you tended not to squander them."

When a gladiator was mortally wounded, an attendant costumed as Charon, the mythical ferryman of the River Styx, finished the job (in a pure Pythonian moment) by smashing his skull with a mallet. After the body was carried off on a stretcher, sand was raked over the bloodstained ground to ready it for the next bout. The festivities ended at sunset, although sometimes, as under Emperor Domitian (81–96A.D.), contests were held by torchlight—night games.

Victors became instant heroes. They were crowned with a laurel wreath and given gold. Those who survived their term of service were awarded a rudis, the wooden sword signifying honorable discharge. Some so liked the gladiator life that they signed on for another tour. The Pompeiian fighter Flamma had four rudii in his trophy ease.

Gladiator sweat was considered such an aphrodisiac that it was used in the facial creams of Roman women, and top gladiators were folk heroes with nicknames, fan clubs and adoring groupies. "We think they were sex symbols," says Jones. "A piece of ancient graffito was found at the gladiatorial barracks in Rome that read SO-AND-SO MAKES THE GIRLS PANT." Gladiators were making Roman girls weak-kneed until the early fourth century A.D. Christian emperor Constantine abolished the games in 325, but without much conviction, or success. In 404, the emperor Honorius banned them again after a Christian monk tried to separate two gladiators and was torn limb from limb by the angry crowd. Despite Honorius' decree, the combat may have continued for another 100 years. "The sad truth is that the Christians of Rome became good Romans and staged their own gladiatorial contests," says Jones. "Popes even hired gladiators as bodyguards. The Christians are given far too much credit—they have a lot to answer for, like being responsible for the Dark Ages."

It was the barbarian invaders who shut down the sport for good. "Whenever Goths and Vandals moved into a Roman city, the games stopped," Jones says. "The barbarians disapproved of them and found them too disgusting." And, we assume, too barbaric.

Vox Populi
Sex, Lies, and Blood Sport

Gossip in the glory days of Rome was just like ours—but written in stone.

HEATHER PRINGLE

Pliny the Elder, the Roman savant who compiled the eclectic 37-book encyclopedia *Historia Naturalis* nearly 2,000 years ago, was obsessed with the written word. He pored over countless Greek and Latin texts, instructing his personal secretary to read aloud to him even while he was dining or soaking in the bath. And when he traveled the streets of Rome, he insisted upon being carried everywhere by slaves so he could continue reading. To Pliny, books were the ultimate repository of knowledge. "Our civilization—or at any rate our written records—depends especially on the use of paper," he wrote in *Historia Naturalis.*

Pliny was largely blind, however, to another vast treasury of knowledge, much of it literally written in stone by ordinary Romans. Employing sharp styli generally reserved for writing on wax tablets, some Romans scratched graffiti into the plastered walls of private residences. Others hired professional stonecutters to engrave their ramblings on tombs and city walls. Collectively, they left behind an astonishing trove of pop culture—advertisements, gambling forms, official proclamations, birth announcements, magical spells, declarations of love, dedications to gods, obituaries, playbills, complaints, and epigrams. "Oh, wall," noted one citizen of Pompeii, "I am surprised that you have not collapsed and fallen, seeing that you support the loathsome scribblings of so many writers."

More than 180,000 of these inscriptions are now cataloged in the *Corpus Inscriptionum Latinarum,* a mammoth scientific database maintained by the Berlin-Brandenburg Academy of Sciences and Humanities. The *Corpus* throws open a large window on Roman society and reveals the ragged edges of ordinary life—from the grief of parents over the loss of a child to the prices prostitutes charged clients. Moreover, the inscriptions span the length and breadth of the empire, from the Atlantic coast of Spain to the desert towns of Iraq, from the garrisons of Britain to the temples of Egypt. "It would be impossible to do most of Roman history without them," says Michael Crawford, a classicist at University College London.

The *Corpus* was conceived in 1853 by Theodor Mommsen, a German historian who dispatched a small army of epigraphists to peruse Roman ruins, inspect museum collections, and ferret out inscribed slabs of marble or limestone wherever they had been recycled, including the tops of medieval bell towers and the undersides of toilet seats. Working largely in obscurity, Mommsen's legions and their successors measured, sketched, and squeezed wet paper into crevices (see "Graffito Preservation,"). Currently, Corpus researchers add as many as 500 inscriptions each year to the collection, mostly from Spain and other popular tourist destinations in the Mediterranean where excavations for hotel and restaurant foundations reveal new epigraphic treasures.

Packed with surprising details, the *Corpus* offers scholars a remarkable picture of everyday life: the tumult of the teeming streets in Rome, the clamor of commerce in the provinces, and the hopes and dreams of thousands of ordinary Romans—innkeepers, ointment sellers, pastrycooks, prostitutes, weavers, and wine sellers. The world revealed is at once tantalizingly, achingly familiar, yet strangely alien, a society that both closely parallels our own in its heedless pursuit of pleasure and yet remains starkly at odds with our cherished values of human rights and dignity.

The Gift of Bacchus

To most Romans, civilization was simply untenable without the pleasures of the grape. Inscriptions confirm that wine was quaffed by everyone from the wealthy patrician in his painted villa to soldiers and sailors in the roughest provincial inns. And although overconsumption no doubt took a toll, wine was far safer than water: The acid and alcohol in wine curbed the growth of dangerous pathogens.

Epicures took particular delight in a costly white wine known as Falernian, produced from Aminean grapes grown on mountain slopes south of modern-day Naples. To improve the flavor, Roman vintners aged the wine in large clay amphorae for at least a decade until it turned a delicate amber. Premium vintages—some as much as 160 years old—were reserved for the emperor and were served in fine crystal goblets. Roman oenophiles, however, could purchase younger vintages of Falernian, and they clearly

Graffito Preservation

A paper replica called a squeeze is the primary medium Manfred Schmidt, director of the Berlin-based *Corpus Inscriptionum Latinarum* project, and his colleagues use to document Roman inscriptions. Schmidt cleans the stone with water. Then he lays a wet sheet of paper over the carved lettering and begins beating the surface of the paper with a brush in order to push the paper fibers evenly into all the indentations and contours. The paper is then left to dry and later peeled off the stone face as a mirror image of the original carving. Squeezes require less technical expertise to make than archival photographs and often reveal more detail, especially with weathered and hard-to-read inscriptions. "Photos can sometimes be misleading," says Schmidt. "But with the squeezes you can always put them out in the sun and look for the right light."

delighted in bragging of its expense. "In the grave I lie," notes the tombstone of one wine lover, "who was once well known as Primus. I lived on Lucrine oysters, often drank Falernian wine. The pleasures of bathing, wine, and love aged with me over the years."

Estate owners coveted their own vineyards and inscribed heartfelt praises for "nectar-sweet juices" and "the gift of Bacchus" on their winepresses. Innkeepers marked their walls with wine lists and prices. Most Romans preferred their wine diluted with water, perhaps because they drank so much of it, but they complained bitterly when servers tried to give them less than they bargained for. "May cheating like this trip you up, bartender," noted the graffito of one disgruntled customer. "You sell water and yourself drink undiluted wine."

So steeped was Roman culture in wine that its citizens often rated its pleasures above nearly all else. In the fashionable resort town of Tibur, just outside Rome, the tomb inscription of one bon vivant counseled others to follow his own example. "Flavius Agricola [was] my name. . . . Friends who read this listen to my advice: Mix wine, tie the garlands around your head, drink deep. And do not deny pretty girls the sweets of love."

Pleasures of Venus

Literary scholars such as C. S. Lewis (who wrote, among many other things, *The Chronicles of Narnia*) have often suggested that romantic love is a relatively recent invention, first surfacing in the poems of wandering French and Italian troubadours in the 11th and 12th centuries. Before then, goes the argument, couples did not know or express to one another a passionate attachment, and therefore left no oral or written record of such relationships. Surviving inscriptions from the Roman Empire paint a very different portrait, revealing just how much Romans delighted in matters of the heart and how tolerant they were of the love struck. As one nameless writer observed, "Lovers, like bees, lead a honeyed life."

Many of the infatuated sound remarkably like their counterparts today. "Girl," reads an inscription found in a Pompeian bedroom, "you're beautiful! I've been sent to you by one who is yours." Other graffiti are infused with yearning that transcends time and place. "Vibius Restitutus slept here alone, longing for his Urbana," wrote a traveler in a Roman inn. Some capture impatience. "Driver," confides one, "if you could only feel the fires of love, you would hurry more to enjoy the pleasures of Venus. I love a young charmer, please spur on the horses, let's get on."

Often, men boasted publicly about their amorous adventures. In bathhouses and other public buildings, they carved frank descriptions of their encounters, sometimes scrawling them near the very spot where the acts took place. The language is graphic and bawdy, and the messages brim with detail about Roman sexual attitudes and practices. Many authors, for example, name both themselves and their partners. In Rome, men who preferred other men instead of women felt no pressure to hide it.

A large and lucrative sex trade flourished in Roman cities, and prostitutes often advertised their services in short inscriptions. One of the stranger aspects of Roman life is that many wealthy families rented out small rooms in their homes as miniature brothels, known as *cellae meretriciae*. Such businesses subsidized the lavish lifestyles of the owners. At the other end of the sex trade were elegant Roman courtesans. In Nuceria, near present-day Naples, at least two inscriptions describe Novelli Primigenia, who lived and worked in the "Venus Quarter." So besotted was one of her clients that he carved: "Greetings to you, Primigenia of Nuceria. Would that I were the gemstone (of the signet ring I gave you), if only for one single hour, so that, when you moisten it with your lips to seal a letter, I can give you all the kisses that I have pressed on it."

Most Roman citizens married, and some clearly enjoyed remarkably happy unions. One inscription unearthed just outside Rome records an epitaph for a particularly impressive woman, composed by her adoring husband. Classicists have fervently debated the identity of this matron, for the epitaph recalls the story of Turia, who helped her husband escape execution during civil unrest in the first century B.C. The inscription has crumbled into fragments, however, and the section containing the name of the woman has been lost, but it is clear her cleverness and audacity saved the day for her spouse. "You furnished most ample means for my escape," reads the inscription, elegantly carved by a stonecutter. "With your jewels you aided me when you took off all the gold and pearls from your person, and handed them over to me, and promptly, with slaves, money, and provisions, having cleverly deceived the enemies' guards, you enriched my absence."

Little Darlings

A prominent French historian, Philippe Ariès, has theorized that it was not until the beginning of industrialization—which boosted the standard of living in Europe during the 18th and 19th centuries—that parents began bonding deeply with their babies. In earlier times, infant mortality rates were staggering, leading parents to distance themselves emotionally from babies who might perish from malnutrition or infection before learning to walk.

Intriguingly, studies of Roman tomb inscriptions lend credence to Ariès's idea. The British classicist Keith Hopkins has estimated, based on comparative demographic data, that 28 percent of all Roman children died before reaching 12 months of age. Yet epigraphists have found relatively few inscribed tombs for Roman infants in Italy: Just 1.3 percent of all funerary stones mark such burials. The statistical discrepancy suggests to many classicists that parents in ancient Rome refrained from raising an expensive marble monument for a child, unwilling to mourn publicly or privately.

Some Romans, however, could not and did not repress the love they felt for their infants. As many graffiti reveal, they celebrated a baby's birth in an openly sentimental manner recognizable to parents today. "Cornelius Sabinus has been born," announced a family in a message carved in a residential entranceway, a spot where neighbors and passersby could easily see it. Others went further, jubilantly inscribing the equivalent of baby pictures. "Iuvenilla is born on Saturday the 2nd of August, in the second hour of the evening," reads one such announcement; nearby, someone sketched in charcoal a picture of a newborn.

The epitaphs composed for infant tombs also disclose a great deal about the intense grief some parents suffered. One inscription describes a baby whose brief life consisted of just "nine sighs," as if the parents had tenderly counted each breath their newborn had taken. Another funerary inscription describes in poignant detail a father's grief. "My baby Acerva," he wrote, "was snatched away to live in Hades before she had her fill of the sweet light of life. She was beautiful and charming, a little darling as if from heaven. Her father weeps for her and, because he is her father, asks that the earth may rest lightly on her forever."

Other carved messages supply details about schooling. As children learned to write, local walls served as giant exercise books where they could practice their alphabets. On one, a young student scrawled what seems to be a language arts drill, interlacing the opening letters of the Roman alphabet with its final ones—A X B V C T. In another inscription, a Roman couple marveled at the eloquence of their 11-year-old son, who had entered a major adult competition for Greek poetry. The boy took his place, they noted, "among 52 Greek poets in the third lustrum of the contest, [and] by his talent brought to admiration the sympathy that he had roused because of his tender age, and he came away with honor." The young poet died shortly after his performance.

not trouble most Romans: They believed that a demonstration of bravery in the arena brought nobility to even the lowliest slave and that the price—death—was worth it.

So ingrained were gladiatorial games in Roman culture that senior government officials dug into their own pockets and emptied public purses to stage them. To pack an arena, the sponsor often advertised the games with an *edicta munerum*, an inscription painted by teams of professional artists on walls near the local amphitheater. One surviving poster describes how Decimus Lucretius Satrius Valeris, a priest of Nero, and another prominent Roman sponsored a major event in Pompeii spanning five consecutive days before the ides of April. The expensive attractions included 20 pairs of gladiators, the "customary [wild] beast hunt," and "awnings" to shade spectators against the summer sun.

The gladiators steeled themselves for the battle ahead, practicing their deadly swordplay. The devout among them prayed to gods for a victory. In a North African barrack, Manuetus the Provocator, a gladiator who fought with a short, straight sword, made a last vow, promising to "bring Venus the gift of a shield if victorious." Outside the gladiators' barracks, scribes painted walls with announcements and programs for the upcoming event, listing the combatants' names and career records.

On the day of the games, raucous and bloodthirsty crowds flooded the arena. At Rome's Colosseum, each spectator held a tessera, a ticket corresponding to a number inscribed on one of the building's 80 arcades. Each arcade then led ticket holders to a staircase and a specific section of seating. As spectators waited for the bloody combat matches to begin, they snacked on bread or cakes purchased from stalls outside the arena. Local chefs baked breads especially for the games, employing molds bearing designs of dueling gladiators and the name of the baker.

At the end of each fatal match, stretcher bearers hustled out on the floor of the arena to collect the fallen gladiator and carry his body to a nearby morgue, or *spoliarium*. There officials slit the man's throat to ensure that he was truly dead: Roman bettors despised fixed matches. Friends and family members then claimed the body and, if they possessed sufficient funds, raised a tomb in his memory. "To the reverend spirits of the Dead," inscribed one grieving widow. "Glauca was born at Mutina, fought seven times, died in the eighth. He lived 23 years, 5 days. Aurelia set this up to her well-deserving husband, together with those who loved him. My advice to you is to find your own star. Don't trust Nemesis [patroness of gladiators]; that is how I was deceived. Hail and Farewell."

As studies of epitaphs show, skilled gladiators rarely survived more than 10 matches, dying on average at the age of 27.

The Sporting Life

The Romans loved to be entertained, and few things riveted them more than the spectacle of gladiatorial combat. Sports fans fervently tracked the career records of the most skilled gladiators and laid wagers on their survival, while well-to-do female admirers stole into gladiator barracks by night, prompting one combatant, Celadus, to boast in an inscription that he was "the girls' desire." That most gladiators were slaves forced to fight to the death for an afternoon's entertainment of the public did

Ancient Pipe Dreams

Some of the humblest inscriptions shed surprising light on one of the glories of Roman technology, revealing just how close ancient metalworkers came to a major coup—the invention of printing. In the Roman waterworks, messages were raised in relief on the lead pipes that fed fountains, baths, and private homes. As a rule, these short texts recorded the name of the emperor or the municipal official who had ordered and paid for the expansion of the water system.

To form these inscriptions, workers first created small individual molds for each letter in the Latin alphabet. They then spelled out the name of the emperor or official by selecting the appropriate letter molds, placing them into a carved slot in a stone slab. Ensuring that the molds lay flush with the surface of the stone, they locked the type into place and laid the stone slab on a large flat tray. Then they poured molten lead across slab and tray, forming a large metal sheet. Once cooled, the sheet could be rolled into a cylinder and soldered at the seam. On the pipe's contour, the emperor's name appeared in elevated letters.

The pipemakers' ingenuity in using movable type to form a line of text is eerily similar to the method used by Johannes Gutenberg and other European printers more than 1,000 years later. As Canadian classicist A. Trevor Hodge has noted, this overlooked Roman technology "tempts one into speculating how close the ancient world was to making the full-scale breakthrough into printing." But the Romans failed to capitalize on this remarkable invention.

Perhaps they were simply too immersed in the culture of carved and painted words to see the future of print—the real writing on the wall.

Woman Power in the Maya World

CHRIS HARDMAN

In Guatemala's Laguna del Tigre National Park, the dense forest hides many treasures: endangered scarlet macaws flit among the treetops, while rare jaguars hunt on the forest floor. Only recently has the world learned about one of Laguna del Tigre's greatest treasures, a 2,500-year-old city that once stood at the crossroads of the ancient Maya world. The archaeologists working on the site believe this city can answer many of the lingering questions about political events in the Petén region during the Classic Period of Maya history.

The ancient city of Waka'—known today as El Perú—first came to the attention of the modern world after oil prospectors stumbled upon it in the 1960s. Ten years later, Harvard researcher Ian Graham recorded the site's monuments, and then in 2003 two veteran archaeologists, David Freidel of Southern Methodist University (SMU) in Texas and Héctor Escobedo of the University of San Carlos in Guatemala, launched a full-scale excavation of the site.

According to the historical record, Waka' was inhabited as early as 500 BC. The city reached its political peak around 400 AD and was abandoned some four centuries later. In its heyday, Waka' was an economically and strategically important place with tens of thousands of inhabitants, four main plazas, hundreds of buildings, and impressive ceremonial centers. Researchers say the key to the city's importance was its location between two of the most powerful Maya capitals—Calakmul to the north and Tikal to the east—and that in its history Waka' switched its alliance back and forth between the two rivals. They suggest that the final choice of Calakmul may have led to the eventual demise of Waka' at the hands of a Tikal king.

"We know a great deal about the ancient inhabitants of this site from their monuments," Freidel writes in an article for *SMU Research*. "The more than 40 carved monuments, or stelae, at the site chronicle the activities of Waká's rulers, including their rise to power, their conquests in war, and their deaths." The location of Waka' right by the San Pedro Mártir River, which was navigable for 50 miles in both directions, gave it great power as a trading center. In addition to the waterway, Freidel suggests that Waka' controlled a strategic north-south overland route that linked southern Campeche to central Petán. Freidel calls Waka' a "crossroads of conquerors in the pre-Columbian era."

One of the most intriguing people who inhabited Waka' was a woman of uncommon power and status. The discovery and excavation of her tomb in 2004 by team member José Ambrosio Díaz drew a lot of attention to the site. "We knew that we were dealing with a royal tomb right away because you could see greenstone everywhere," says David Lee, a PhD candidate at SMU who is investigating the Waka' palace complex. Greenstone is archaeologists' term for the sacred jade the ancient Maya used to signify royalty. The team found hundreds of artifacts in the tomb, which dates to sometime between 650 and 750 AD.

There were several indicators that this woman was important and powerful. Her tomb lay underneath a building on the main courtyard of the city's main palace. Her stone bed was surrounded by 23 offering vessels and hundreds of jade pieces, beads, and shell artifacts. Among the rubble, the researchers discovered a four- by two-inch jewel called a *huunal* that was worn only by kings and queens of the highest status. Typically a *huunal* was affixed to a wooden helmet called a *ko'haw* that was covered in jade plaques. Carved depictions suggest that only powerful war leaders wore these helmets. On the floor of the queen's tomb near her head, researchers found 44 square and rectangular jade plaques they believe were glued onto the wooden part of the *ko'haw*. The presence of this helmet in her tomb has led the researchers to the conclusion that this queen held a position of power not typically afforded women of the time. "She may have been more powerful than her husband, who was actually the king of El Peru," Lee concludes.

Although the presence of the helmet identifies her as a warlord, archaeologists have found no evidence of Maya women physically fighting in battles. What they have discovered are images of women as guardians of the tools of war. "The curation of the war helmet is one of the roles of royal women," says the excavation's bone expert, Jennifer Piehl. She explains that Maya iconography describes how royal women safeguarded these helmets and then presented them to their kings when they prepared for war. David Freidel says that to the Maya, war was more than just a physical act; it was also an encounter between supernaturally charged beings. Women had an active role in battle by conjuring up war gods and instilling sacred magical power in battle gear.

Other symbols of royalty were the stingray spines found in the pelvic regions of the queen's remains. Stingray spines are bloodletting implements that were used in ceremonies by Maya kings to drain blood from their genitalia. "The association between gender and power becomes blended because this person represents both kinds of power," explains Lee. "As we learn more, we are discovering that what our culture considers traditional ideas of male-female roles don't hold true for Maya royalty."

Researchers could also determine the importance of the woman by what was missing from her tomb. Some time after her burial, the tomb was opened up to remove her skull and femurs. "The cranium and crossed femurs is a very salient symbol in Maya ritual. It is the ancestor," says Piehl. The Maya would take the skull and femurs from an important ancestor and preserve them in bundles. Maya images show how these bundles were used during ceremonies or were worn on the back of the ruler's regalia. "They are literally carrying their ancestor around with them," says Lee. Researchers surmise that possession of a bundle gave legitimacy and power to the owners.

Once her status as a queen was confirmed, the question became, which queen was she? A good candidate is a woman named Lady K'abel who lived during the Late Classic period and was the daughter of the King Yuknoom Yich'aak K'ak' of Calakmul. Researchers interpret her marriage to King K'inich B'ahlan II of Waka' as a savvy political move for Calakmul, because a royal marriage could forge a permanent political bond between the two cities. Unfortunately the union would not prove to be a good political move for Waka'. Researchers suggest that it was considered an act of betrayal by Tikal, which eventually defeated Waka' in 743 AD.

A detailed portrait of Lady K'abel comes from a stela dated to 692 AD that was looted from Waka' in the late 1960s. According to Maya expert and project epigrapher Stanley Guenter, inscriptions on the front face of the stela—curated by the Cleveland Museum of Art in Ohio—clearly identify the woman as Ix Kaloomte' (lady warlord) or Lady K'abel, princess of Calakmul. "Mosaic mask pectorals formed of greenstone, shell teeth and eye whites, and obsidian pupils found in the interment are consistent with the image of Lady K'abel on Stela 34," Lee and Piehl posit in a recent paper. "These attributes clearly demonstrate the royal status of the woman and an identification with Lady K'abel." Radiocarbon dating of the queen's remains will confirm whether the woman in the tomb lived during the same time period as Lady K'abel.

Another tomb, discovered by archaeologists Michelle Rich and Jennifer Piehl in 2005, tells the story of two women from an earlier part of Waka's history, dating back to between 350 and 400 AD. The tomb contains the remains of two women between 25 and 35 years old, placed back to back, one on top of the other, with stingray spines near their groins. The bottom woman, who was pregnant, lay face down and the top woman face up. Although the tomb is tiny by royal standards—some 3 feet wide, 4 feet high and 6.5 feet long—Rich and Piehl believe that these women were high-ranking members of a royal family.

By analyzing their skeletal remains, archaeologist and osteologist Jennifer Piehl can tell a great deal about the status of these women in life. "What we can say of the bones of the two Waka' women is they were in excellent health—better than the majority of the Waka' population—which fits with them being royal," she says. In addition, the lack of dental cavities suggests that unlike ordinary Maya, these women were treated to special foods, including meat, fish, and fruit.

Further evidence of the elite status of these women comes from the seven ceramic vessels that accompanied them in death. "The first thing we saw was the cluster at [their] feet of three gorgeous, museum quality polychrome vessels," Piehl recalls.

The quality of the vessels and the symbols of royalty on them indicate that the women came from a royal bloodline. Vessels of the exact stone style were also found at Tikal in a similar set of tombs containing members of a royal dynasty who were probably killed by the great fourth-century conqueror Siyaj K'ak' from Teotihuacan. According to the stone stelae from the main plazas of Waka', Siyaj K'ak' also visited that city in 378 AD on his way to conquer Tikal. "My conclusion is that these are members of the royal family that was in power before the arrival of Siyaj K'ak'," Piehl says. Freidel calls Siyaj K'ak's visit to Waka' the city's "first great experience as a crossroads of conquerors."

Rich suggests that the women were sacrificed as part of a lineage replacement, whereby one invading ruler comes in and kills the current royal family to establish his family as the only royal blood in the kingdom. "The king would have been the primary focus of sacrifice, but then the rest of the family would have to be exterminated in order to wipe out the entire ruling line," Rich says. To prove that hypothesis, the team is searching for a king from the same time period. In 2006, Héctor Escobedo and Juan Carlos Meléndez uncovered the tomb of a king under the site's main pyramid, but more research needs to be done to fully understand who that man was. Also in 2006, Rich and Varinia Mature found another ruler, but he dates to approximately 550–650, a couple of hundred years later than the women. "At this point we have two rulers and no connection to the sacrificed women," Rich says. "El Perú is a huge site, and there is so much we can learn."

Although the archaeologists involved with this project agree that further excavations of Waka' have the potential to fill in some of the gaps in the political history of the region, the future of the Waka' Archaeological Project is uncertain. Laguna del Tigre, where the Waka' archaeological site is located, is the largest nature reserve in Central America, covering some 118,600 acres of such biologically significant habitat that in 1990 it was the first site in Guatemala named to the List of Wetlands of International Importance under the Ramsar Convention on Wetlands. Despite its protected status, the forest of Laguna del Tigre is in danger due to illegal logging, slash-and-burn agriculture, and drug smuggling. Just as the forest is in peril, so is the city of Waka' and any other archaeological treasures hidden in the forest.

To ensure the protection of Waka' and the rainforest that surrounds it, Freidel developed partnerships with the government of Guatemala, the Wildlife Conservation Society, and the nongovernmental organization ProPetén to try and safeguard 230,000 acres of the forest. The group formed the K'ante'el Alliance, which means "precious forest" in Maya and refers to the mystical place where the Maya Maize God was said to be reborn and where the Maya believe their civilization began. The K'ante'el Alliance plans to protect the park by developing environmentally friendly sources of income for local communities that will celebrate the forest's resources instead of destroy them. The hope is that Waka' and Laguna del Tigre will continue to share their hidden treasures for years to come.

CHRIS HARDMAN contributes regularly to *Américas* on archaeology, science, and conservation news.

Secrets of a Desert Metropolis
The Hidden Wonders of Petra's Ancient Engineers

Evan Hadingham

Today, Petra is a vast empty canyon encircled by astoishing tombs. Their magnificent facades, carved into sandstone cliffs, overlook a chaos of eroded ruins on the valley floor. Until recently, so little of the 2,000-year-old city had been explored that some scholars had branded Petra a "city of the dead" or a "tent city"—an occasional metropolis settled only seasonally by wandering peddlers and pilgrims.

Recent excavations reveal a very different city. The archaeological jewel of Jordan was, in fact, a fabulously wealthy hub of merchants and traders known from Rome to China. Surrounded by a brutal desert, some 30,000 people thrived in a city that for centuries lavished precious water on public pools, baths, and fountains. Petra in its prime virtually ruled the incense trade.

The city's rulers enjoyed a reputation as canny diplomats and generals skilled in outwitting more powerful neighbors. By the first century A.D., the city boasted graceful temples, a broad avenue lined with shops, public gardens, and water brought through more than six kilometers (3.7 miles) of ceramic pipes. The canyon walls that encircled the city were crowded with more than 800 tombs that awe today's visitors as completely as they must have amazed travelers two millennia ago.

Archaeologists finally are discovering and fitting critical pieces into the abiding puzzles of Petra: How could scattered desert nomads have created so mighty a citadel? And what finally caused their prosperity to falter and their wondrous city to fade?

Investigations built on satellite imagery, aerial photography, and extensive ground surveys have banished old theories of Petra and its founders, who were known to the ancient world as Nabataeans.

Once visualized as little more than wandering, camel-borne traders, the Nabataeans are now known to have deliberately planted year-round settlements throughout the arid wilderness of southern Jordan and northern Saudi Arabia. In a region that tastes barely 10 centimeters (3.9 inches) of rain annually, these outposts were succored with the same ingeniously engineered water systems recently revealed at Petra.

And while the city's demise has been blamed on everything from the Romans to a series of devastating earthquakes, new evidence suggests a completely unexpected scenario for Petra's final centuries.

Nomadic Origins

History's first notice of the Nabataeans is in a fourth-century B.C. account by the Greek historian Hieronymus. He describes nomadic bands—wandering traders and herders of sheep and camels—who forbade the growing of grain or the construction of houses on pain of death. The archaeological picture of Nabataean origins remains obscure, although some argue their ancestors were pastoralists in the deserts of northeast Arabia.

The first Nabataean sites appear abruptly during the first century B.C. Within 100 years, they had exploded all over what is now southern Jordan and northern Saudi Arabia, including such hostile environments as the Negev and Hisma deserts.

Four centuries after Hieronymus, another Greek historian, Strabo, describes a radically different Nabataean culture. Strabo discovered a pleasure-loving people who lived in fine, stone houses and cultivated fruit and vines. The king, the historian contended, presided over lavish banquets with female singers and poured wine into his guests' golden cups. Strabo also reported that the king answered to a popular assembly.

This image of a fun-loving, populist monarchy may well be as mythical as Hieronymus' hardy, nomadic shepherds. Nonetheless, Nabataean society doubtless underwent extraordinary changes that drove its explosive growth during the first century B.C.

By that time, Nabataeans were the primary transporters of frankincense and myrrh from their sources in the southern Arabian desert. These aromatic resins were prized throughout the known world for cosmetic, medicinal, and spiritual uses, as their prominence in the Christian Nativity story implies. (Some early Christian sources suggest the Three Magi may have been Nabataean merchants.)

Camels and Caravans

The precious gums were harvested from spindly trees grown mainly in a narrow coastal region of Oman and Yemen. Petra's position at the crossroads of the incense trade produced the city's extraordinary wealth. Strabo describes caravans of as many as 2,000 camels that crossed the desert from southern Arabia to Petra and then on to Mediterranean ports or Egypt.

"These vast caravans must have needed protection from thieves and numerous stops for refreshment as they crossed the desert. There were probably lots of opportunities for Nabataean camel guides and merchants to line their pockets along the way," says University of Miami historian David Graf.

An eloquent relic of the camel-borne trade was unearthed in 1997, when archaeologists with the Petra National Trust began removing tons of sand and debris from the bottom of the Siq—a narrow gorge that provided a winding, kilometer-long (.6-mile) route into the city. There, alongside ancient paving stones that once floored the Siq, archaeologists found the stumps of larger-than-life relief sculptures carved into the cliff wall. They depict a pair of robed men, each leading a camel. One appears to be facing toward the city, while the other seems to be departing—symbols, perhaps, of the camel traffic that once echoed through this towering ravine.

If camel caravans were the bedrock of Nabataean wealth, did Petra's population live like desert nomads in roomy tents of woven camel hair, as traditional Bedouin families still do today? Little more than a decade ago, some scholars still visualized Petra as a seasonal tent city, occupied only for rituals connected with the great tombs. Such notions held as long as archaeologists mostly confined their attention to imposing tombs and temple ruins.

'Stone Tents'

Then in 1988, a joint team from Switzerland and Liechtenstein led by Rolf Stucky launched the first systematic effort to explore the urban heart of Petra. In the years since, they have discovered what Stucky describes as "a city of stone tents." The tent platforms that marked Petra's early days were replaced by substantial stone houses that were scattered informally (as tents might be) across the landscape.

In one house, excavations revealed a bowl still bearing traces of fish sauce. Another yielded a bear paw that probably came from an imported fur rug. One house even preserved traces of a multicolored wall painting from the first century A.D. It depicts architectural motifs similar to the elaborately carved tomb entrances that line the surrounding canyon.

The style of Petra was heavily influenced by the classic Greek architecture that Nabataean merchants encountered on trading visits around the Mediterranean. Local craftsmen freely adapted the Hellenistic designs to their own tastes to produce a unique blend. Both on their massive tombs and inside their homes, the people of Petra invoked the urban sophistication of the Greek and Roman world as evidence of their wealth.

High above the ruins of these prosperous homes are mountain shrines that crown the peaks around Petra. They are connected to the valley floor by broad stairways, carved in the cliff face at enormous labor by the Nabataeans. It is easy to visualize them, robed and in solemn procession, toiling slowly up these stairways to the rock-carved altars and receptacles for sacrificial blood—which at least one Nabataean inscription implies was sometimes human.

Other inscriptions—written in a precursor of today's Arabic script—identify the chief Nabataean deities as Dushara (a male god of fertility, vegetation, and everlasting life) and Al-'Uzza (a mother goddess often identified with Aphrodite of the Greeks or Isis of the Egyptians.).

Ceremonies invoking these deities occurred not only on mountaintops but also in at least four freestanding temples on either side of Petra's main street. One temple, excavated for nearly three decades by Phillip C. Hammond, was probably dedicated to Al-'Uzza or another female deity. A small, carved idol bears the tantalizing, but fragmentary inscription: "Goddess of . . ."

An Amazing Temple

One of the biggest surprises from recent work at Petra came in 1997, when Brown University archaeologists unearthed an amphitheater at the heart of a sprawling ruin dubbed the "Great Temple." The entrance to this building, erected in the first century B.C., was framed by a massive portico some 18 meters (60 feet) high, supported by four huge columns, and vividly decorated with red and white stucco and delicate floral sculptures.

The purpose of this structure in the center of the temple is a mystery. Could it be that the great temple was not really a temple at all, but the "popular assembly" mentioned by Strabo, the Greek historian?

"There are quite a few possibilities," says Martha Sharp Joukowsky, leader of the Brown team. "It could be that we're looking at a kind of temple/theater, or a law court, or a *curia*—a Roman [style] political meeting place. In future seasons, we'll search for evidence to test these various possibilities."

Barely a year after the amphitheater was found, an even more startling discovery—a true measure of Petra's extravagance—came from the area long assumed to be a marketplace. This area was, in fact, a public garden with a promenade surrounding an open-air pool, says Pennsylvania University archaeologist Leigh-Ann Bedal. A little island at the center of the pool supported a lavishly decorated structure interpreted by Bedal as a recreational pavilion.

The pool was nearly identical in size to a modern Olympic pool—50 meters (165 feet) across. An elaborate network of ceramic pipes channeled water to it from the Ain Musa gorge over six kilometers (nearly four miles) away. The pipeline carried water through the Siq to the city center, then branched off to supply the pool, the Great Temple, public baths, fountains, and other luxurious amenities.

In the middle of a blazing, barren desert, what better symbol of Petra's opulence could there be than such an extravagant use of water?

Remote Outposts

The great city was unique only in scale. Much smaller Nabataean settlements reveal traces of elaborate waterworks, temples, and bathhouses. University of Victoria archaeologist John P. Oleson, excavating a remote outpost called Humeima in southern Jordan, found a roofed, stone aqueduct 27 kilometers (17 miles) long—a remarkable feat of planning and construction.

Oleson believes that Petra's first-century monarchs actively encouraged the spread of a more settled way of life throughout their realm, building water channels and bath-houses even in the parched canyons of the Hisma desert. "We're not sure what lay behind this wide-scale settlement planning," Oleson says, "but one idea is that new villages and towns helped discourage attacks by desert nomads on the caravan routes. Also, the Nabataean kings probably wanted to encourage the growth of a new economy in case the incense trade faltered."

The classic tale of Petra's demise begins with the city's annexation by the Romans in A.D. 106. The Romans, in this telling, gradually drained Petra's wealth by diverting caravans northward to new centers, notably Palmyra in Syria. Then, in A.D. 363, a devastating earthquake supposedly finished off the impoverished Nabataeans.

New work by David Graf and others, however, indicates that Nabataean sites and the old caravan routes still prospered well into the Roman era. Petra, in fact, was given the Roman title *metropolis,* while the governor of Rome's Arabian province chose to be buried in one of Petra's fanciest tombs.

Petra's Demise

The spectacular discovery in 1993 of the Petra scrolls proves that as late as the sixth century A.D., when these papyrus records were compiled, Petra's traditional systems of land ownership and irrigation were still in place. Indeed, fragments of old Nabataean beliefs and values may well have lingered until the coming of Islam in A.D. 631.

Skillfully exploiting their position as middlemen on the fringes of the classical world, the Nabataeans blended the comforts and style of Greece and Rome with their Arabian roots. This exotic cultural mixture captivates both researchers and visitors to Petra. Yet even more remarkable was the Nabataeans' command of water, a mastery that enabled them to colonize the desert and protect the caravans that had brought them so much wealth and greatness.

EVAN HADINGHAM is Science Editor of NOVA, the PBS science series, and author of *Lines to the Mountain Gods* and other books on prehistory.

From *Scientific American Discovering Archaeology,* September/October 2000, pp. 70–77. Copyright © 2000 by Evan Hadingham. Reprinted by permission of the author.

It Happened Only Once in History!

MAX I. DIMONT

There are approximately three billion people on this earth, of whom twelve million—less than one half of one percent—are classified as Jews. Statistically, they should hardly be heard of, like the Ainu tucked away in a corner of Asia, bystanders of history. But the Jews are heard of totally out of proportion to their small numbers. No less than 12 percent of all the Nobel prizes in physics, chemistry, and medicine have gone to Jews. The Jewish contribution to the world's list of great names in religion, science, literature, music, finance, and philosophy is staggering.

The period of greatness of ancient Greece lasted five hundred years. Then that nation lapsed into a former glory. Not so with the Jews. Their creative period extends through their entire four-thousand-year history. Their contributions have been absorbed by both East and West, though neither is always aware of it nor willing to admit the debt if made aware of it.

From this people sprang Jesus Christ, acclaimed Son of God by more than 850 million Christians, the largest religious body in the world. From this people came Paul, organizer of the Christian Church. The religion of the Jews influenced the Mohammedan faith, second-largest religious organization in the world, with over 400 million adherents claiming descent from Abraham and Ishmael. The Mormons say they are the descendants of the tribes of Israel.

Another Jew is venerated by more than one billion people. He is Karl Marx, whose book *Das Kapital* is the secular gospel of Communists the world over, with Marx himself enshrined in Russia and China. Albert Einstein, the Jewish mathematician, ushered in the atomic age and opened a path to the moon with his theoretical physics. A Jewish psychiatrist, Sigmund Freud, lifted the lid of man's mind. His discovery of psychoanalysis revolutionized man's concept of himself and the relation of mind to matter. Three hundred years earlier, a Jewish philosopher, Baruch Spinoza, pried philosophy loose from mysticism, opening a path to rationalism and modern science.

Through the ages, the Jews successively introduced such concepts as prayer, church, redemption, universal education, charity—and did so hundreds of years before the rest of the world was ready to accept them. And yet, up until 1948, for close to three thousand years, the Jews did not even have a country of their own. They dwelt among the Babylonians, lived in the Hellenic world, stood at the bier of the Roman Empire, flourished in the Mohammedan civilization, emerged from a twelve-hundred-year darkness known as the Middle Ages, and rose to new intellectual heights in modern times.

Great nations of the pagan era which appeared at the same time the Jews did have totally disappeared. The Babylonians, the Persians, the Phoenicians, the Hittites, the Philistines—all have vanished from the face of the earth, after once having been great and mighty powers. The Chinese, Hindu, and Egyptian peoples are the only ones living today who are as old as the Jewish people. But these three civilizations had only *one* main cultural period and their impact on succeeding civilizations has not been great. They contained neither the seeds for their own rebirth nor the seeds for the birth of other civilizations. Unlike the Jews, they were not driven out of their countries, nor did they face the problem of survival in alien lands. The Greeks and the Romans are the only other nations which have influenced the history of Western man as profoundly as the Jews. But the people who now dwell in Greece and Italy are not the same as those who dwelt in ancient Hellas and Rome.

Thus, there are three elements in Jewish survival which make the history of this people different from that of all other people. They have had a continuous living history for four thousand years. They survived three thousand years without a country of their own, yet preserved their ethnic identity among alien cultures. They have expressed their ideas not only in their own language, but in practically all the major languages of the world.

Little is generally known of the extent of Jewish writings in every field of human thought. The reason for this in not hard to find. To read French, German, or English literature of science one needs only to know French, German, or English. To read Jewish literature and science one has to know not only Hebrew and Yiddish, but also Aramaic, Arabic, Latin, Greek, and virtually every modern European language.

All civilizations we know about have left a record of their history in material things. We know them through tablets or ruins dug up by archaeologists. But we know of the Jews in ancient times mostly from the ideas they taught and the impact which these ideas had upon other people and other civilizations. There are few Jewish tablets to tell of battles and few Jewish ruins to tell of former splendor. The paradox is that those people who left only monuments behind as a record of their existence have vanished with time, whereas the Jews, who left ideas, have survived.

World history has hurled six challenges at the Jews, each a threat to their very survival. The Jews rose to each challenge and lived to meet the next.

The pagan world was the first challenge to Jewish survival. The Jews were a small band of nomads, stage extras among such mighty nations as Babylonia, Assyria, Phoenicia, Egypt, Persia. How did they manage to survive as a cultural group during this seventeen-hundred-year span of their history, when all these great nations clashed and annihilated one another? During this period the Jews came perilously close to disappearing. What saved them were the ideas with which they responded to each of the dangers encountered.

Having survived seventeen hundred years of wandering, enslavement, decimation in battle, and exile, the Jews returned to their homeland only to run into the Greco-Roman period of their history. This was their second challenge, and it was a miracle that the Jews emerged from it at all. Everything Hellas touched during those magic years of her greatness became Hellenized, including her conquerors, the Romans. Greek religion, art, and literature; Roman legions, law, and government—all left an indelible stamp on the entire civilized world. But when the Roman legions were defeated, this culture collapsed and died. The nations which were subjugated first by Greece and then by Rome disappeared. New nations took their place by force of arms. The Jews however remained, not by the might of their arms but by the might of their cohesive ideas.

The third challenge to the Jews came about through a phenomenon which is unique and unparalleled in history. Two Judaisms had been created, one in Palestine, the other in *Diaspora*, a word from the Greek meaning a scattering, or scatter about, and signifying that body of Jews scattered about in the gentile world outside Palestine. From the time of the expulsion of the Jews from Jerusalem by the Babylonians in the sixth century B.C. to the time of the liberation of the Jews from the ghettos in the nineteenth century A.D. was the era of the fragmentation of the Jewish people into small groupings, dispersed over tremendous land areas and among the most divergent cultures. How could the Jews be kept from assimilation and absorption into the sea of alien people around them?

The Jews met this challenge with the creations of a religious-legal code—the Talmud—which served as a unifying force and a spiritual rallying point. This was the Talmudic Age in Jewish history, when the Talmud almost invisibly ruled the Jews for close to fifteen hundred years.

In the seventh century, Judaism gave birth to yet another religion—Islam, founded by Mohammed—and this was its fourth challenge. Within a hundred years the Mohammedan Empire rose to challenge Western civilization. Yet, within this religion, whose adherents hated Christianity with an unrelenting hatred, the Jews not only survived but rose to one of their greatest literary, scientific, and intellectual peaks. The Jew in this age became statesman, philosopher, physician, scientist, tradesman, and cosmopolitan capitalist. Arabic became his mother tongue. This era also saw the philandering Jew. He wrote not only on religion and philosophy, but also rhapsodized about love. Seven hundred years passed and the pendulum swung. The Islamic world crumbled and the Jewish culture in the Islamic world crumbled with it.

The fifth challenge was the Middle Ages, and this period was a dark one for both Jew and Western man. It was a twelve-hundred-year fight by the Jews against extinction. All non-Christian nations which were defeated in the name of the Cross were converted to the Cross, except the Jews. Yet the Jews emerged from this twelve-hundred-year dark age spiritually and culturally alive. The ideas their great men had given them had been tested and found workable. When the walls of the ghetto fell, it did not take the Jews more than one generation to become part of the warp and woof of Western civilization. Within one generation, and within the shadow of the ghetto, they became prime ministers, captains of industry, military leaders, and charter members in an intellectual avant-garde which was to reshape the thinking of Europe.

The sixth challenge is the Modern Age itself. The appearance of nationalism, industrialism, communism, and fascism in the nineteenth and twentieth centuries has held special challenges for Jews, in addition to a new, virulent disease of the Western mind—anti-Semitism. New responses for survival have had to be forged to meet these new challenges. Whether these responses will be adequate, only the future will tell.

We see, then, that Jewish history unfolds not within one but within six civilizations. This contradicts many schools of history, which hold that this is an impossibility since, like a human being, a civilization has only one life span, usually lasting five hundred years, but no longer than a thousand years. Yet, as we have seen, the Jews have lasted four thousand years, have had six cultures in six alien civilizations, and most likely will have a seventh. How can we reconcile fact and theory?

There are eight basic ways of viewing history, each from a different vantage point. Generally, a historian selects a face of history to his liking, thus stressing the viewpoint which seems best to him. We will make use of all of these faces of history except the first one, the "unhistoric" or "Henry Ford" way. It was Ford who once declared that "history is bunk," and that if he wanted to know anything he could always hire a professor who would tell him. This view sees all events as unrelated occurrences, a mishmash of dates, names, and battles, from which nothing can be learned or divined.

The second way of looking at history might be termed the "political interpretation." Here, history is looked upon as a succession of dynasties, laws, battles. Kings are strong or weak, wars won or lost, laws good or bad, and all events are presented in neat order from A to Z, from 2000 B.C. to 2000 A.D. This, as a rule, is the type of history taught in schools.

A third face is the geographic one. According to this school, climate and soil determine formation of character. This idea originated with the Greeks. Even today there are many who contend that the only scientific way to explain man's social institutions is to study his physical environment, such as topography, soil, climate. This is a rather difficult theory to apply to the Jews. They have lived in practically every climate, yet managed to retain a common ethnic identity and culture. This is evident in Israel today, where Jewish exiles from all over the world—Arabia, North Africa, Europe, America—within a short time were fused into one people. It cannot be denied, though, that geographic factors have changed or modified many traits and behavior patterns of the Jews.

The fourth way to interpret history is an economic one. This is the Marxian school. This says that history is determined by the way goods are produced. Let us suppose, says the Marxist, that the economy of a feudal system is being changed to capitalism. This new capitalistic mode of production, says the Marxist, will change that country's social institutions—its religion, ethics, morals, and values, in order to justify and sanctify and institutionalize the new way of economic life. In the same way, if a capitalist country were transformed into a communist society, it would automatically begin to change its cultural and social institutions to conform with the new way of producing things until the new way of life became part of everyday behavior.

The fifth is an even newer concept than the economic interpretation of history. Founded by Professor Sigmund Freud at the beginning of the twentieth century, this school holds that social institutions and human history are the result of a process of repressing unconscious hostilities. Civilization, says the psychoanalytic historian, can be obtained only at the price of giving up the lusts that lurk in our unconscious—unbridled sexual gratification, murder, incest, sadism, violence. Only when man has mastered his impulses can he turn his energies into creative, civilizing channels. Which impulses man represses, how severely he represses them, and what methods he uses for this repression will determine his culture and his art forms, says the psychoanalyst.

The sixth face is the philosophical one. Its three most famous followers are the German philosopher Georg Wilhelm Friedrich Hegel, the Prussian philosopher-historian Oswald Spengler, and the British historian Arnold Toynbee. Though these three philosophical interpreters of history differ widely, they have this in common. They see history not as a series of isolated happenings, but as a flow of events having continuity. Each civilization, they hold, follows a more or less predictable pattern. They think of each civilization as a living thing, which, like a human being, has an infancy, childhood, adolescence, maturity, old age, and finally death. How long a civilization lasts, they say, depends upon the ideas and ideals by which that civilization lives. The philosophical interpreters of history try to discover these forces within all civilizations in order to find their common element.

In Spengler's view, civilizations are foredoomed to death. Civilizations go through the Spring of their early origins, mature into the Summer of their greatest physical achievement, grow into the Autumn of great intellectual heights, decline into the Winter of their civilization, and finally die. Writing in 1918, when England was at the height of her prestige, and Russia and China but fifth-rate powers, Spengler predicted in his book *The Decline of the West* that Western civilization was in the Winter of its cycle and would die by the twenty-third century, to be superseded either by a Slavic civilization (Russia) or by a Sinic one (China), which were in the Spring of their development. This way of viewing history is known as "cyclic," because each civilization has its own beginning, middle, and end.

In contrast to the cyclic view, we have Toynbee's linear concept, as expressed in his *A Study of History.* Toynbee holds that a civilization is not an independent totality but a progression—an evolution—from lower to higher forms. So, for instance, in his view the Islamic civilization was derived from lower Iranic and Arabic cultures, which in turn were given birth by something he calls "Syriac society." Thus, the Islamic civilization need not have died, Toynbee holds, but could have evolved into an even higher culture had it responded properly to the challenges hurled at it in the thirteenth and fourteenth centuries. In the Toynbee philosophy, civilizations can go on eternally if they continue to meet new challenges with the right responses.

Since the history of the Jews did not fit into either Spengler's or Toynbee's systems, Spengler ignored them and Toynbee reduced them to an occasional footnote, describing the Jews as fossils of history. Yet, if both Spengler and Toynbee had been less blinded by prejudice and misconceptions about Jewish history, they could well have fitted it within the framework of their philosophies. In this book, we shall use their theories to explain this seemingly "impossible" Jewish survival.

The "cult of personality" is the seventh face of history. Proponents of this school hold that events are motivated by the dynamic force of great men. If not for Washington, they say, there would have been no American Revolution; if not for Robespierre, there would have been no French Revolution; if not for Lenin, there would have been no Russian Revolution. Men create the events, claim these historians, in contrast to the economic interpreters who insist on the exact opposite, that events create the men.

The eighth face of history, the religious, is both the oldest and newest concept. The Bible is the best example of this type of historical writing in the past. This way of viewing history looks upon events as a struggle between good and evil, between morality and immorality. Most Jewish history, until recent times, has been written from this viewpoint.

The religious way of writing history has become discredited in modern times. But it has been resurrected by a new *genre* of writers known as "existential theologians," such as the Roman Catholic Jacques Maritain, the Russian Orthodox Catholic Nikolai Berdyaev, the Protestant Paul Tillich, and the Jewish Martin Buber. In essence, these existential theologians hold that though God may not interfere directly in the shaping of history, it is the relationship which man thinks exists between him and God that does shape history. We are so obsessed today by the notion that only "scientific facts" have validity, we are inclined to forget that people holding "unscientific," unprovable ideas may determine the course of history more often than do rational facts.

This is especially true in the case of the Jews. Martin Buber holds that the central theme running through their history is the relation between the Jew and his God, Jehovah. In the Jewish religious view of history, God has given man freedom of action. Man, as conceived by the Jewish existentialists, has the power to turn to God or away from God. He can act either for God or against God. What happens between God and man is history. In the Jewish way of looking at things, success in an undertaking, for instance, is not viewed as blessed by God. A man may arrive at power because he was unscrupulous, not because God aided him. This leaves God free to hold man accountable for his actions—both successes and failures.

This man-God relationship was responsible for the great gulf in thinking which began to separate the Jews from the rest of the pagan world four thousand years ago. The pagan idea of god tied man to his gods. The Jewish concept of man's relation to God freed the Jews for independent action. Western man, in fact, did not arrive at this idea of religious freedom until the Reformation, when Martin Luther rejected the Papacy and changed the man-God relationship to one approximating that of the Jews. Luther then invited the Jews to join Protestantism, because he believed there now was no gulf between Judaism and Christianity. There is not a single "concrete fact" in this series of events, only men holding "unscientific ideas"; yet we can see how decisive were these unprovable ideas for the course of world history.

The circle is complete. Beginning with God as the Creator of history, man invented other explanations—an anarchic one viewing history as a series of blind events, a philosophic one looking at history as a series of purposive events, an economic one holding productive methods as a determinant force, a psychological one giving priority to unconscious drives, a "great man" theory hewing to the idea of man himself as the creator of his historic destiny, and, finally, back to God at the helm.

In this book we shall view Jewish history from all vantage points, without stopping to debate the merits or demerits of theological disputes. Whether true or not, men have always believed in "unscientific concepts," and these beliefs often are the real "facts" which shape their destiny. This author holds with the psychoanalytic, philosophical, and existentialist interpreters of history, that ideas motivate man and that it is these ideas which create history. A society without ideas has no history. It merely exists.

From *Jews, God, and History* by Max I. Dimont, (1994). Copyright © 1994 by Penguin Group (USA) Inc. Reprinted by permission.

UNIT 5
The Great Religions

Unit Selections

Key Points to Consider

- What contributions has ancient India made to the history of world religions? How are these contributions still relevant today?

- Why is it difficult to place the Koran in a historical context without arousing controversy among its adherents? Yet, why is this historicization necessary?

- Why is Jerusalem so central to the monotheistic religions of the Middle East? How and why does the Dome of the Rock reflect this centrality?

- Describe the contents of recently excavated, ancient Christian churches. What can they tell us about the earliest days of this religion and how well it was tolerated by its neighbors?

- What evidence is offered to prove that women actively participated in the life of the early Christian faith? What relevance does this have for our contemporary world?

Student Web Site
www.mhcls.com

Internet References

Cultural India
   www.culturalindia.net
Major World Religions
   http://www.omsakthi.org/religions.html
Religion Search Engines: Christianity and Judaism
   http://www.suite101.com/article.cfm/search_engines/13501
Religion Search Engines: Islam, Hinduism, Buddhism and Baha'i
   http://www.suite101.com/article.cfm/search_engines/14603

According to the World Almanac, there are approximately 2.1 billion Christians, 1.4 billion Muslims, 900 million Hindus, 375 million Buddhists, and 14 million Jews in the world. More than two thirds of the world's population affirms a religious affiliation. As shapers of values, history, loyalties, and daily life, the world's religions have played a powerful role in world history. Sometimes, religion is a source of conflict, as it currently is between Jews and Muslims in the Middle East, or between Hindus and Muslims in Kashmir. At the same time, religion is a potent force for binding people together and creating a shared identity.

Religion and culture have a reciprocal relationship—each shapes and is shaped by the other. Since religions tell a story, that narrative is often bound up with the history of a civilization. Because the great world religions have their origins in premodern times, understanding the stories they tell can shed light on the development and evolution of world cultures. Common themes in world religions include the moral codes that determine the relationship between one person and another, and the larger question of the relationship between humans and a greater entity—either a personal deity or an impersonal force.

Indian civilization, the world's oldest, produced Hinduism, Buddhism, Jainism, and Sikhism. The Buddha grew up as a Hindu, but centuries after his enlightenment Buddhism crossed the Himalayas into China and, ultimately, into the wider world. Globalization has carried all these faiths around the world through immigration, and many in the United States have become attracted to Buddhism as converts.

Since the 1949 Communist Revolution, China has been officially atheistic. So, the number of Confucians and Taoists is vastly underrepresented. Confucianism, however, has spread throughout the Pacific Rim, shaping the conduct of business and government, and Taoism has offered a quiet way of living for millions who feel pressured by the stresses of modern life. The translation of ancient texts, begun in earnest in the West during the nineteenth century, has made the wisdom of ancient faiths accessible to a worldwide audience.

The monotheisms of Judaism, Christianity, and Islam rest on revealed truth. For followers of these faiths, sacred texts often have enormous authority. Although there is a shared heritage among these religions through the spiritual "fatherhood" of Abraham, there are also substantive differences. In Jerusalem, sites sacred to all three traditions stand within yards of one another—the Wailing Wall, what remains of the now-destroyed Jewish Temple; the site of Jesus' crucifixion and burial, sacred to Christians; and the Dome of the Rock, from which Muslims believe the Prophet Muhammad rose into heaven to converse with God. Little wonder, then, that disputes over control of these holy places can lead to war.

Scholarly analysis of sacred texts can be threatening to orthodox believers. Muslims hold the Qur'an/Koran unchanged from God's original speaking through the Prophet; yet, textual

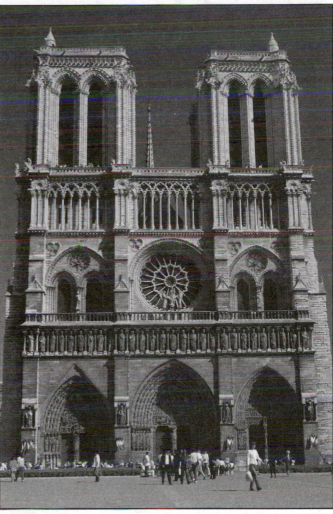

Royalty-Free/CORBIS

comparisons reveal subtleties of interpretation and context. In Christianity, the discovery of ancient Gospels, once honored but excluded from the New Testament canon, has revealed the active participation of women in early Christianity—as disciples, prophets, preachers, and teachers. Suppressed for centuries, these texts allow us to recover a lost heritage of equality between women and men. Recent attempts on the parts of Jews, Christians, and Muslims to rediscover their common inheritance as the children of Abraham offer some hope for expanded interfaith dialogue.

Even in officially secular nations, such as France and the United States, where religious freedom and the separation of church and state prevail, religion remains a permeating influence. Immigrant populations have sometimes brought fervent belief systems that clash with a more secular dominant culture.

There is often tension over how law ought to operate. As we evaluate human history, the role of religion in human culture has been and continues to be a vital one.

Ancient Jewel

From early Greece to the modern civil rights movement, Indian thought and philosophy have had a wide-ranging influence on Western culture.

T. R. (Joe) Sundaram

The very word *India* conjures up exotic images in one's mind. Yet this name for the south Asian subcontinent is of Western making, mediated by the Persians and the Arabs. The name used in ancient Sanskrit texts is *Bharat* (for the land of Bharatha, a legendary king), which is also the official name of the modern republic. Other familiar Western words such as *Hindu, caste,* and *curry* are also totally foreign to India. The general knowledge that exists in the West about India, its early history, philosophy, and culture is, at best, superficial. Nevertheless, since it would be impossible in a brief article to do justice to even one of these topics, I shall provide a brief, accurate glimpse into each.

India covers about 1.2 million square miles and is home to a population of 895 million; in comparison, the United States covers 3.6 million square miles and has 258 million residents. Thus, the population density of India is nearly 10 times that of the United States. (The size of classical India—which includes modern-day India, Pakistan, Bangladesh, and parts of Afghanistan—is about two-thirds that of the continental United States.)

But statistics about India can be misleading. For example, while only about one-quarter of the population is "literate," able to read and write, this has to be viewed in light of the strong oral traditions present in India since antiquity. Therefore, while a "literate" American may often be unaware of the collective name of the first 10 amendments to the U.S. Constitution, an "illiterate" Indian peasant would be aware of the history of his ancestors from antiquity to the present day.

Not only is India one of the oldest civilizations in the world, being more than 6,000 years old, but also it may be the oldest continuing civilization in existence; that is, one without any major "gaps" in its history. As the renowned historian A. L. Basham has pointed out,

> Until the advent of archeologists, the peasant of Egypt or Iraq had no knowledge of the culture of his forefathers, and it is doubtful whether his Greek counterpart had any but the vaguest ideas about the glory of Periclean Athens. In each case there had been an almost complete break with the past. On the other hand, the earliest Europeans to visit India found a culture fully conscious of its own antiquity.

Crucible of Learning

- India's may be the oldest continuing civilization in existence.
- To avoid misunderstanding India, it is essential to appreciate three central tenets of Indian thinking: assimilating ideas and experiences, a belief in cycles, and the coexistence of opposites.
- India has made numerous contributions to contemporary Western understanding of mathematics, science, and philosophy.

India is a land of many ancient "living" cities, such as, for example, Varanasi. Even at sites like Delhi, many successive cities have been built over thousands of years. Among old buried cities that have been unearthed in modern times by archaeologists are Mohenjo-Daro and Harappa.

Of these cities, the renowned archaeologist Sir John Marshall writes that they establish the existence

> in the fourth and third millennium B.C., of a highly developed city life; and the presence in many houses, of wells and bathrooms as well as an elaborate drainage system, betoken a social condition of the citizens at least equal to that found in Sumer, and superior to that prevailing in contemporary Babylonia and Egypt.

Thus, India was the "jewel of the world" long before the Greek and Roman civilizations.

Nor was classical India isolated from developing civilizations in other parts of the world. Clay seals from Mohenjo-Daro have been found in Babylonia and vice versa. Ancient Indian artifacts such as beads and bangles have been found in many parts of the Middle East and Africa. India and Indian culture were known to the Greeks even before the time of Alexander the Great. The Greek historian Herodotus wrote extensively about India during the sixth century B.C. Also, during this period many Greeks, including Pythagoras, are known to have traveled to India.

Figure 1 Continuous civilization: Excavations at Mohenjo-Daro and Harappa reveal well-planned towns and a sophisticated urban culture dating back to 2500 B.C.
Note: Embassy of India.

Sixth century B.C. was a period of great religious and philosophical upheaval in India. Hinduism was already an established, "old" religion, and reform movements were beginning to appear, such as one by a prince known as Siddhartha Gautama, who later came to be known as the Buddha. The religion that was founded based on his teachings spread not only throughout Asia but also to many parts of the world, including Greece, and it helped spread Indian culture in the process.

In Alexander the Great's campaign to conquer the world, his ultimate goal was India; he died without achieving that objective. When Seleucus Nicator, Alexander's successor, tried to follow in Alexander's footsteps, he was soundly defeated by Indian emperor Chandragupta Maurya. A peace treaty was signed between the two, and Seleucus sent an ambassador, Megasthenes, to the court of Chandragupta. Megasthenes sent glowing reports back to Greece about India, and he pronounced Indian culture to be equal or superior to his own, a high compliment indeed, since Greece was then near its zenith.

For the next 1,500 years or so, India—rich in material wealth, scientific knowledge, and spiritual wisdom—enjoyed the reputation of being at the pinnacle of world civilizations. Arab writers of the Middle Ages routinely referred to mathematics as *hindsat*, the "Indian science."

And as is well known now, it was Columbus' desire to reach India that led to the discovery of America. Indeed, the explorer died thinking that he had discovered a new sea route to India, while he had merely landed on a Caribbean island. Columbus' mistake also led to the mislabeling of the natives of the land as "Indians," a label that survived even after the mistake had been discovered.

The Upanishads

Indian philosophy is almost as old as Indian civilization, and its zenith was reached nearly 3,000 years ago with the compilation, by unknown sages, of 108 ancient philosophical texts known as the Upanishads. These texts reflect even older wisdom, which was passed down from generation to generation through oral transmission. A Western commentator has remarked that in the Upanishads the Indian mind moved from cosmology to psychology, and that while most other contemporary civilizations were still asking the question "What am I?" the Indian mind was already asking, "Who am I?"

When translations of the Upanishads first became available in the West in the nineteenth century, the impact on European philosophers such as Goethe and Schopenhauer and on American writers such as Emerson and Whitman was profound. "In the whole world," wrote Schopenhauer emotionally, "there is no study as beneficial and as elevating as the Upanishads." Emerson wrote poems based on the texts.

One of the principal underlying themes in the Upanishads is the quest for a "personal reality." This quest began with the conviction that the limitations of our sensory perceptions give us an imperfect model to comprehend the real world around us; this is known as the concept of *maya*. Since individual

Figure 2 A terra-cotta toy cow: Ancient Indian civilizations featured highly talented artisans and craftsmen.

Note: Embassy of India.

Figure 3 Indian music has influenced Western artists, particularly in modern times. The beat of the tabla can be heard in pop music ranging from the Beatles to Michael Jackson.

Note: Khorrum Omer/The World & I.

perceptions can be different, different people can also have different "realities."

For example, a happy event for one individual may be an unhappy one for another. Recognition and perfection of our personal reality is the quintessential goal of Indian philosophy and is also the basic principle behind yoga. Indeed, the literal meaning of the Sanskrit word *yoga* is "union," and the union that is sought is not with any external entity but with one's self. This is, of course, also the principal tenet of modern psychoanalysis.

From a Western perspective, to avoid misunderstanding India in general, and Indian philosophy in particular, it is essential to appreciate three central tenets of the Indian way of thinking. These are:

Assimilation. In the Indian way of thinking, new experiences and ideas never replace old ones but are simply absorbed into, and made a part of, old experiences. Although some have characterized such thinking as static, in reality such thinking is both dynamic and conservative, since old experiences are preserved and new experiences are continually accumulated.

Belief in cycles. Another central tenet of the Indian character is the belief that all changes in the world take place through cycles, there being cycles superimposed on other cycles, cycles within cycles, and so on. Inherent in the concept of cycles is alternation, and the Upanishads speak of the two alternating states of all things being "potentiality" and "expression."

Acceptance of the coexistence of opposites. Early Western readers of the Upanishads were puzzled by the apparent inherent ability of the Indian mind to accept the coexistence of seemingly diametrically opposite concepts. Belief in, and acceptance of, contradictory ideas is a natural part of the Indian way of life, and the logical complement to the tenets already mentioned. It is an indisputable fact that birth (creation) must necessarily be eventually followed by death (destruction). Creation and destruction are inseparable alternations. Even concepts such as "good" and "evil" are complementary, as each of us may have within us the most lofty and divine qualities and at the same time the basest qualities. We ourselves and the whole world can be whatever we want to make of them.

These three tenets are responsible for the amazing continuity of the Indian civilization, its reverence for the elderly, and the acceptance of the aging process without a morbid fear of death.

Ironically, the culture that taught of the need to renounce materialistic desires also produced some of the most pleasurable things in life. The intricacies and highly developed nature of Indian art, music, dance, and cuisine are examples. And the *Kama Sutra* is perhaps the oldest, and best known, manual on the pleasures of love and sex.

From Pythagoras to King

Throughout history, India's contributions to the Western world have been considerable, albeit during the Middle Ages they were often felt only indirectly, having been mediated by the Middle Eastern cultures.

After the early contacts between Greece and India in the sixth and fifth centuries B.C., many concepts that had been in use in India centuries earlier made their appearance in Greek literature,

Figure 4 Melodic inspiration: Performing traditional dance and music in Orissa.
Note: Khorrum Omer/The World & I.

although no source was ever acknowledged. For example, consider the so-called Pythagorean theorem of a right triangle and the Pythagorean school's theory of the "transmigration of souls"; the former was in use in India (for temple construction) centuries earlier, and the latter is merely "reincarnation," a concept of Vedic antiquity. There was also a flourishing trade between the Roman Empire and the kingdoms in southern India, through which not only Indian goods but also ideas made their journey westward.

During the Middle Ages, the Arabs translated many classical Indian works into Arabic, and the ideas contained in them eventually made their way to Europe. A principal mission of the "House of Wisdom" that was established by the caliph in Baghdad in the eighth century was the translation of Indian works.

Among the major Indian ideas that entered Europe through the Arabs are the mathematical concept of zero (for which there was no equivalent in Greek or Roman mathematics) and the modern numerical system we use today. Until the twelfth century, Europe was shackled by the unwieldy Roman numerals. The famous French mathematician Laplace has written: "It is India that gave us the ingenious method of expressing all numbers by ten symbols, each receiving a value of position as well as an absolute value, a profound and important idea which appears so simple to us now that we ignore its true merit."

India's contributions to other areas of science and mathematics were equally important. The seventh-century Syrian astronomer Severus Sebokht wrote that "the subtle theories" of Indian astronomers were "even more ingenious than those of the Greeks and the Babylonians."

The scientific approach permeated other aspects of Indian life as well. For example, classical Indian music has a highly mathematical structure, based on divisions of musical scales into tones and microtones.

In modern times, Indian music has had a considerable influence on Western music. Starting in the 1960s, the famous Indian sitar virtuoso Ravi Shankar popularized sitar music in the West, and now the melodic strains of the sitar, as well as the beat of the Indian drum known as tabla, can be heard in the works of many pop-music artists, ranging from the Beatles to Michael Jackson. The movies of the Indian filmmaker Satyajit Ray have also made a significant impact on the West.

The contributions of many modern Indian scientists have been important to the overall development of Western science. The mathematical genius Srinivasa Ramanujan, who died in 1920, has been called "the greatest mathematician of the century" and "the man who knew infinity." The discovery by the Nobel Prize–winning Indian physicist Chandrasekhara Venkata Raman of the effect (which bears his name) by which light diffusing through a transparent material changes in wavelength has revolutionized laser technology. The theoretical predictions by the Nobel Prize–winning astrophysicist Subrahmanyan Chandrasekhar on the life and death of white-dwarf stars led to the concept of "black holes."

In the literary area, the poetry of Nobel laureate Rabindranath Tagore and the philosophical interpretations of the scholar (and a former president of India) Sarvepalli Radhakrishnan have inspired the West. Albert Einstein was one of the admirers of the former and corresponded with him on the meaning of "truth."

In terms of our daily dietary habits, many vegetables such as cucumber, eggplant, okra, squash, carrots, many types of beans, and lentils were first domesticated in India. Rice, sugarcane, and tea, as well as fruits such as bananas and oranges, are of Indian origin. The name *orange* is derived from the Sanskrit word *narangi*. Chicken and cattle were also first domesticated in India, albeit the latter for milk production and not for meat consumption. Cotton was first domesticated in India. The process of dying fabrics also was invented in India. Indian fabrics (both cotton and silk) have been world renowned for their quality since antiquity. The game of chess was invented in India, and the name itself derives from the Sanskrit name Chaturanga.

India's most popular modern exports have been yoga and meditation. Hatha yoga, the exercise system that is a part of yoga, is now taught widely in America, in institutions ranging from colleges to hospitals. Many scientific studies on the beneficial effects of yoga practice are now under way. A similar state of affairs is true of Indian meditation techniques, which people under stress use for mental relaxation.

Finally the Rev. Martin Luther King, Jr., repeatedly acknowledged his debt to Mahatma Gandhi for the technique of nonviolent civil disobedience, which he used in the civil rights movement. For all India's material contributions to the world, it is its spiritual legacy that has had the widest impact. The ancient sages who wrote the Upanishads would have been pleased.

Additional Reading

A. L. Basham, *The Wonder That Was India,* Grove Press, New York, 1959.

———, *Ancient India: Land of Mystery,* Time-Life Books, Alexandria, Virginia, 1994.

Will Durant, *The Story of Civilization: Part I, Our Oriental Heritage,* Simon and Schuster, New York, 1954.

T. R. (JOE) SUNDARAM is the owner of an engineering research firm in Columbia, Maryland, and has written extensively on Indian history, culture, and science.

What Is the Koran?

Researchers with a variety of academic and theological interests are proposing controversial theories about the Koran and Islamic history, and are striving to reinterpret Islam for the modern world. This is, as one scholar puts it, a "sensitive business."

TOBY LESTER

In 1972, during the restoration of the Great Mosque of Sana'a, in Yemen, laborers working in a loft between the structure's inner and outer roofs stumbled across a remarkable gravesite, although they did not realize it at the time. Their ignorance was excusable: mosques do not normally house graves, and this site contained no tombstones, no human remains, no funereal jewelry. It contained nothing more, in fact, than an unappealing mash of old parchment and paper documents—damaged books and individual pages of Arabic text, fused together by centuries of rain and dampness, gnawed into over the years by rats and insects. Intent on completing the task at hand, the laborers gathered up the manuscripts, pressed them into some twenty potato sacks, and set them aside on the staircase of one of the mosque's minarets, where they were locked away—and where they would probably have been forgotten once again, were it not for Qadhi Isma'il al-Akwa', then the president of the Yemeni Antiquities Authority, who realized the potential importance of the find.

Al-Akwa' sought international assistance in examining and preserving the fragments, and in 1979 managed to interest a visiting German scholar, who in turn persuaded the German government to organize and fund a restoration project. Soon after the project began, it became clear that the hoard was a fabulous example of what is sometimes referred to as a "paper grave"—in this case the resting place for, among other things, tens of thousands of fragments from close to a thousand different parchment codices of the Koran, the Muslim holy scripture. In some pious Muslim circles it is held that worn-out or damaged copies of the Koran must be removed from circulation; hence the idea of a grave, which both preserves the sanctity of the texts being laid to rest and ensures that only complete and unblemished editions of the scripture will be read.

Some of the parchment pages in the Yemeni hoard seemed to date back to the seventh and eighth centuries A.D., or Islam's first two centuries—they were fragments, in other words, of perhaps the oldest Korans in existence. What's more, some of these fragments revealed small but intriguing aberrations from the standard Koranic text. Such aberrations, though not surprising to textual historians, are troublingly at odds with the orthodox Muslim belief that the Koran as it has reached us today is quite simply the perfect, timeless, and unchanging Word of God.

The effort to reinterpret the Koran, thus far confined to scholarly argument, could lead to major social change. The Koran, after all, is currently the world's most ideologically influential text.

The mainly secular effort to reinterpret the Koran—in part based on textual evidence such as that provided by the Yemeni fragments—is disturbing and offensive to many Muslims, just as attempts to reinterpret the Bible and the life of Jesus are disturbing and offensive to many conservative Christians. Nevertheless, there are scholars, Muslims among them, who feel that such an effort, which amounts essentially to placing the Koran in history, will provide fuel for an Islamic revival of sorts—a reappropriation of tradition, a going forward by looking back. Thus far confined to scholarly argument, this sort of thinking can be nonetheless very powerful and—as the histories of the Renaissance and the Reformation demonstrate—can lead to major social change. The Koran, after all, is currently the world's most ideologically influential text.

Looking at the Fragments

The first person to spend a significant amount of time examining the Yemeni fragments, in 1981, was Gerd-R. Puin, a specialist in Arabic calligraphy and Koranic paleography based at Saarland University, in Saarbrücken, Germany. Puin, who had been sent by the German government to organize and oversee the restoration project, recognized the antiquity of some of the parchment fragments, and his preliminary inspection also revealed unconventional verse orderings, minor textual variations, and rare styles of orthography and artistic embellishment. Enticing, too, were the sheets of the scripture written in the rare and early Hijazi Arabic script: pieces of the earliest Korans known to exist, they were also palimpsests—versions very clearly written over even earlier, washed-off versions. What the Yemeni Korans seemed to suggest, Puin began to feel, was an *evolving* text rather than simply the Word of God as revealed in its entirety to the Prophet Muhammad in the seventh century A.D.

Since the early 1980s more than 15,000 sheets of the Yemeni Korans have painstakingly been flattened, cleaned, treated, sorted, and assembled; they now sit ("preserved for another thousand years," Puin says) in Yemen's House of Manuscripts, awaiting detailed examination. That is something the Yemeni authorities have seemed reluctant to allow, however. "They want to keep this thing low-profile, as we do too, although for different reasons," Puin explains. "They don't want attention drawn to the fact that there are Germans and others working on the Korans. They don't want it made public that there is work being done *at all*, since the Muslim position is that everything that needs to be said about the Koran's history was said a thousand years ago."

To date just two scholars have been granted extensive access to the Yemeni fragments: Puin and his colleague H.-C. Graf von Bothmer, an Islamic-art historian also based at Saarland University. Puin and von Bothmer have published only a few tantalizingly brief articles in scholarly publications on what they have discovered in the Yemani fragments. They have been reluctant to publish partly because until recently they were more concerned with sorting and classifying the fragments than with systematically examining them, and partly because they felt that the Yemeni authorities, if they realized the possible implications of the discovery, might refuse them further access. Von Bothmer, however, in 1997 finished taking more than 35,000 microfilm pictures of the fragments, and has recently brought the pictures back to Germany. This means that soon von Bothmer, Puin, and other scholars will finally have a chance to scrutinize the texts and to publish their findings freely—a prospect that thrills Puin. "So many Muslims have this belief that everything between the two covers of the Koran is just God's unaltered word," he says. "They like to quote the textual work that shows that the Bible has a history and did not fall straight out of the sky, but until now the Koran has been out of this discussion. The only way to break through this wall is to prove that the Koran has a history too. The Sana'a fragments will help us to do this."

Puin is not alone in his enthusiasm. "The impact of the Yemeni manuscripts is still to be felt," says Andrew Rippin, a professor of religious studies at the University of Calgary, who is at the forefront of Koranic studies today. "Their variant readings and verse orders are all very significant. Everybody agrees on that. These manuscripts say that the early history of the Koranic text is much more of an open question than many have suspected: the text was less stable, and therefore had less authority, than has always been claimed."

Copyediting God

By the standards of contemporary biblical scholarship, most of the questions being posed by scholars like Puin and Rippin are rather modest; outside an Islamic context, proposing that the Koran has a history and suggesting that it can be interpreted metaphorically are not radical steps. But the Islamic context—and Muslim sensibilities—cannot be ignored. "To historicize the Koran would in effect delegitimize the whole historical experience of the Muslim community," says R. Stephen Humphreys, a professor of Islamic studies at the University of California at Santa Barbara. "The Koran is the charter for the community, the document that called it into existence. And ideally—though obviously not always in reality—Islamic history has been the effort to pursue and work out the commandments of the Koran in human life. If the Koran is a historical document, then the whole Islamic struggle of fourteen centuries is effectively meaningless."

The orthodox Muslim view of the Koran as self-evidently the Word of God, perfect and inimitable in message, language, style, and form, is strikingly similar to the fundamentalist Christian notion of the Bible's "inerrancy" and "verbal inspiration" that is still common in many places today. The notion was given classic expression only a little more than a century ago by the biblical scholar John William Burgon.

> The Bible is none other than *the voice of Him that sitteth upon the Throne!* Every Book of it, every Chapter of it, every Verse of it, every word of it, every syllable of it . . . every letter of it, is the direct utterance of the Most High!

Not all the Christians think this way about the Bible, however, and in fact, as the *Encyclopaedia of Islam* (1981) points out, "the closest analogue in Christian belief to the role of the Kur'an in Muslim belief is not the Bible, but Christ." If Christ is the Word of God made flesh, the Koran is the Word of God made text, and questioning its sanctity or authority is thus considered an outright attack on Islam—as Salman Rushdie knows all too well.

The prospect of a Muslim backlash has not deterred the critical-historical study of the Koran, as the existence of the essays in *The Origins of the Koran* (1998) demonstrate. Even in the aftermath of the Rushdie affair the work continues: In 1996 the Koranic scholar Günter Lüling wrote in *The Journal of Higher Criticism* about "the wide extent to which both the text of the Koran and the learned Islamic account of Islamic origins have been distorted, a deformation unsuspectingly accepted by Western Islamicists until now." In 1994 the journal *Jerusalem Studies in Arabic and Islam* published a posthumous study by Yehuda D. Nevo, of the Hebrew University in Jerusalem, detailing seventh- and eighth-century religious inscriptions on stones in the Negev Desert which, Nevo suggested, pose "considerable problems for the traditional Muslim account of the history of Islam." That same year, and in the same journal, Patricia Crone, a historian of early Islam currently based at the Institute for Advanced Study, in Princeton, New Jersey, published an article in which she argued that elucidating problematic passages in the Koranic text is likely to be made possible only by "abandoning the conventional account of how the Qur'an was born." And since 1991 James Bellamy, of the University of Michigan, has proposed in the *Journal of the American Oriental Society* a series of "emendations to the text of the Koran"—changes that from the orthodox Muslim perspective amount to copyediting God.

Crone is one of the most iconoclastic of these scholars. During the 1970s and 1980s she wrote and collaborated on several books—most notoriously, with Michael Cook, *Hagarism: The Making of the Islamic World* (1977)—that made radical arguments about the origins of Islam and the writing of Islamic history. Among *Hagarism*'s controversial claims were suggestions that the text of the Koran came into being later than is now believed ("There is no hard evidence for the existence of the Koran in any form before the last decade of the seventh century"); that Mecca was not the initial Islamic sanctuary ("[the evidence] points unambiguously to a sanctuary in northwest Arabia . . . Mecca was secondary"); that the Arab conquests preceded the institutionalization of Islam ("the Jewish messianic fantasy was enacted in the form of an Arab conquest of the Holy Land"); that the idea of the *hijra*, or the migration of Muhammad and his followers from Mecca to Medina in 622, may have evolved long after Muhammad died ("No seventh-century source identifies the Arab era as that of the *hijra*"); and that the term "Muslim" was not commonly used in early Islam ("There is no good reason to suppose that the bearers of this primitive identity called themselves 'Muslims' [but] sources do . . . reveal an earlier designation of the community [which] appears in Greek as 'Magaritai' in a papyrus of 642, and in Syriac as 'Mahgre' or 'Mahgraye' from as early as the 640s").

Hagarism came under immediate attack, from Muslim and non-Muslim scholars alike, for its heavy reliance on hostile sources. ("This is a book," the authors wrote, "based on what from any Muslim perspective must appear an inordinate regard for the testimony of infidel sources.") Crone and Cook have since backed away from some of its most radical propositions—such as, for example, that the Prophet Muhammad lived two years longer than the Muslim tradition claims he did, and that the historicity of his migration to Medina is questionable. But Crone has continued to challenge both Muslim and Western orthodox views of Islamic history. In *Meccan Trade and the Rise of Islam* (1987) she made a detailed argument challenging the prevailing view among Western (and some Muslim) scholars that Islam arose in response to the Arabian spice trade.

Gerd-R. Puin's current thinking about the Koran's history partakes of this contemporary revisionism. "My idea is that the Koran is a kind of cocktail of texts that were not all understood even at the time of Muhammad," he says. "Many of them may even be a hundred years older than Islam itself. Even within the Islamic traditions there is a huge body of contradictory information, including a significant Christian substrate; one can derive a whole Islamic *anti-history* from them if one wants."

The Koran is a scripture with a history like any other," one scholar says, "except that we tend to provoke howls of protest when we study it. But we are not trying to destroy anyone's faith.

Patricia Crone defends the goals of this sort of thinking. "The Koran is a scripture with a history like any other—except that we don't know this history and tend to provoke howls of protest when we study it. Nobody would mind the howls if they came from Westerners, but Westerners feel deferential when the howls come from other people: who are you to tamper with *their* legacy? But we Islamicists are not trying to destroy anyone's faith."

Not everyone agrees with that assessment—especially since Western Koranic scholarship has traditionally taken place in the context of an openly declared hostility between Christianity and Islam. (Indeed, the broad movement in the West over the past two centuries to "explain" the East, often referred to as Orientalism, has in recent years come under fire for exhibiting similar religious and cultural biases). The Koran has seemed, for Christian and Jewish scholars particularly, to possess an aura of heresy; the nineteenth-century Orientalist William Muir, for example, contended that the Koran was one of "the most stubborn enemies of Civilisation, Liberty, and the Truth which the world has yet known." Early Soviet scholars, too, undertook an ideologically motivated study of Islam's origins, with almost missionary zeal: in the 1920s and in 1930 a Soviet publication titled *Ateist* ran a series of articles explaining the rise of Islam in Marxist-Leninist terms. In *Islam and Russia* (1956), Ann K. S. Lambton summarized much of this work, and wrote that several Soviet scholars had theorized that "the motive force of the nascent religion was supplied by the mercantile bourgeoisie of Mecca and Medina"; that a certain S. P. Tolstov had held that "Islam was a social-religious movement originating in the slave-owning, not feudal, form of Arab society"; and that N. A. Morozov had argued that "until the Crusades Islam was indistinguishable from Judaism and . . . only then did it receive its independent character, while Muhammad and the first Caliphs are mythical figures." Morozov appears to have been a particularly flamboyant theorist: Lambton wrote that he also argued, in his book *Christ* (1930), that "in the Middle Ages Islam was merely an off-shoot of Arianism evoked by a meteorological event in the Red Sea area near Mecca."

Not surprisingly, then, given the biases of much non-Islamic critical study of the Koran, Muslims are inclined to dismiss it outright. A particularly eloquent protest came in 1987, in the *Muslim World Book Review*, in a paper titled "Method Against Truth: Orientalism and Qur'anic Studies," by the Muslim critic S. Parvez Manzoor. Placing the origins of Western Koranic scholarship in "the polemical marshes of medieval Christianity" and describing its contemporary state as a "cul-de-sac of its own making," Manzoor orchestrated a complex and layered assault on the entire Western approach to Islam. He opened his essay in a rage.

The Orientalist enterprise of Qur'anic studies, whatever its other merits and services, was a project born of spite, bred in frustration and nourished by vengeance: the spite of the powerful for the powerless, the frustration of the "rational" towards the "superstitious" and the vengeance of the "ortho-dox" against the "non-conformist." At the greatest hour of his worldly-triumph, the Western man, coordinating the powers of the State, Church and Academia, launched his most determined assault on the citadel of Muslim faith. All the aberrant streaks of his arrogant personality—its reckless rationalism, its world-domineering phantasy and its sectar-ian fanaticism—joined in an unholy conspiracy to dislodge the Muslim Scripture from its firmly entrenched position as the epitome of historic authenticity and moral unassail-ability. The ultimate trophy that the Western man sought by his dare-devil venture was the Muslim mind itself. In order to rid the West forever of the "problem" of Islam, he reasoned, Muslim consciousness must be made to despair of the cognitive certainty of the Divine message revealed to the Prophet. Only a Muslim confounded of the historical authenticity or doctrinal autonomy of the Qur'anic revela-tion would abdicate his universal mission and hence pose no challenge to the global domination of the West. Such, at least, seems to have been the tacit, if not the explicit, rationale of the Orientalist assault on the Qur'an.

Despite such resistance, Western researchers with a variety of academic and theological interests press on, applying mod-ern techniques of textual and historical criticism to the study of the Koran. That a substantial body of this scholarship now exists is indicated by the recent decision of the European firm Brill Publishers—a long-established publisher of such major works as *The Encyclopaedia of Islam* and *The Dead Sea Scrolls Study Edition*—to commission the first-ever *Encyclopaedia of the Qur'an.* Jane McAuliffe, a professor of Islamic studies at the University of Toronto, and the general editor of the ency-clopedia, hopes that it will function as a "rough analogue" to biblical encyclopedias and will be "a turn-of-the-millennium summative work for the state of Koranic scholarship." Articles for the first part of the encyclopedia are currently being edited and prepared for publication later this year.

The *Encyclopaedia of the Qur'an* will be a truly collabora-tive enterprise, carried out by Muslims and non-Muslims, and its articles will present multiple approaches to the interpretation of the Koran, some of which are likely to challenge traditional Islamic views—thus disturbing many in the Islamic world, where the time is decidedly less ripe for a revisionist study of the Koran. The plight of Nasr Abu Zaid, an unassuming Egyp-tian professor of Arabic who sits on the encyclopedia's advisory board, illustrates the difficulties facing Muslim scholars trying to reinterpret their tradition.

"A Macabre Farce"

"The Koran is a text, a *literary* text, and the only way to under-stand, explain, and analyze it is through a literary approach," Abu Zaid says. "This is an essential theological issue." For expressing views like this in print—in essence, for challenging the idea that the Koran must be read literally as the absolute and unchanging Word of God—Abu Zaid was in 1995 officially branded an apostate, a ruling that in 1996 was upheld by Egypt's highest court. The court then proceeded, on the grounds of an Islamic law forbidding the marriage of an apostate to a Muslim, to order Abu Zaid to divorce his wife, Ibtihal Yunis (a ruling that the shocked and happily married Yunis described at the time as coming "like a blow to the head with a brick").

Abu Zaid steadfastly maintains that he is a pious Muslim, but contends that the Koran's manifest content—for example, the often archaic laws about the treatment of women for which Islam is infamous—is much less important than its complex, regen-erative, and spiritually nourishing latent content. The orthodox Islamic view, Abu Zaid claims, is stultifying; it reduces a divine, eternal, and dynamic text to a fixed human interpretation with no more life and meaning than "a trinket . . . a talisman . . . or an ornament."

For a while Abu Zaid remained in Egypt and sought to refute the charges of apostasy, but in the face of death threats and relentless public harassment he fled with his wife from Cairo to Holland, calling the whole affair "a macabre farce." Sheikh Youssef al-Badri, the cleric whose preachings inspired much of the opposition to Abu Zaid, was exultant. "We are not terrorists; we have not used bullets or machine guns, but we have stopped an enemy of Islam from poking fun at our religion. . . . No one will even dare to think about harming Islam again."

Abu Zaid seems to have been justified in fearing for his life and fleeing: in 1992 the Egyptian journalist Farag Foda was assassinated by Islamists for his critical writings about Egypt's Muslim Brotherhood, and in 1994 the Nobel Prize–winning novelist Naguib Mahfouz was stabbed for writing, among other works, the allegorical *Children of Gabalawi* (1959)—a novel, structured like the Koran, that presents "heretical" conceptions of God and the Prophet Muhammad.

Deviating from the orthodox interpretation of the Koran, says the Algerian Mohammed Arkoun, a professor emeritus of Islamic thought at the University of Paris, is "a *very* sensitive business" with major implications. "Millions and millions of people refer to the Koran daily to explain their actions and to justify their aspirations," Arkoun says. "This scale of reference is much larger than it has ever been before."

Muhammad in the Cave

Mecca sits in a barren hollow between two ranges of steep hills in the west of present-day Saudi Arabia. To its immediate west lies the flat and sweltering Red Sea coast; to the east stretches the great Rub'al-Khali, or Empty Quarter—the largest continuous body of sand on the planet. The town's setting is uninviting: the earth is dry and dusty, and smolders under a relentless sun; the whole region is scoured by hot, throbbing desert winds. Although sometimes rain does not fall for years, when it does come it can be heavy, creating torrents of water that rush out of the hills and flood the basin in which the city lies. As a backdrop for divine revelation, the area is every bit as fitting as the mountains of Sinai or the wilderness of Judea.

The only real source of historical information about pre-Islamic Mecca and the circumstances of the Koran's revelation is the classical Islamic story about the religion's founding, a distillation of which follows.

In the centuries leading up to the arrival of Islam, Mecca was a local pagan sanctuary of considerable antiquity. Religious rituals revolved around the Ka'ba—a shrine, still central in Islam today, that Muslims believe was originally built by Ibrahim (known to Christians and Jews as Abraham) and his son Isma'il (Ishmael). As Mecca became increasingly prosperous in the sixth century A.D., pagan idols of varying sizes and shapes proliferated. The traditional story has it that by the early seventh century a pantheon of some 360 statues and icons surrounded the Ka'ba (inside which were found renderings of Jesus and the Virgin Mary, among other idols).

Such was the background against which the first installments of the Koran are said to have been revealed, in 610, to an affluent but disaffected merchant named Muhammad bin Abdullah. Muhammad had developed the habit of periodically withdrawing from Mecca's pagan squalor to a nearby mountain cave, where he would reflect in solitude. During one of these retreats he was visited by the Angel Gabriel—the very same angel who had announced the coming of Jesus to the Virgin Mary in Nazareth some 600 years earlier. Opening with the command "Recite!," Gabriel made it known to Muhammad that he was to serve as the Messenger of God. Subsequently, until his death, the supposedly illiterate Muhammad received through Gabriel divine revelations in Arabic that were known as qur'an ("recitation") and that announced, initially in a highly poetic and rhetorical style, a new and uncompromising brand of monotheism known as Islam, or "submission" (to God's will). Muhammad reported these revelations verbatim to sympathetic family members and friends, who either memorized them or wrote them down.

Powerful Meccans soon began to persecute Muhammad and his small band of devoted followers, whose new faith rejected the pagan core of Meccan cultural and economic life, and as a result in 622 the group migrated some 200 miles north, to the town of Yathrib, which subsequently became known as Medina (short for Medinat al-Nabi, or City of the Prophet). (This migration, known in Islam as the hijra, is considered to mark the birth of an independent Islamic community, and 622 is thus the first year of the Islamic calendar.) In Medina, Muhammad continued to receive divine revelations, of an increasingly pragmatic and prosaic nature, and by 630 he had developed enough support in the Medinan community to attack and conquer Mecca. He spent the last two years of his life proselytizing, consolidating political power, and continuing to receive revelations.

The Islamic tradition has it that when Muhammad died, in 632, the Koranic revelations had not been gathered into a single book; they were recorded only "on palm leaves and flat stones and in the hearts of men." (This is not surprising: the oral tradition was strong and well established, and the Arabic script, which was written without the vowel markings and consonantal

dots used today, served mainly as an aid to memorization.) Nor was the establishment of such a text of primary concern: the Medinan Arabs—an unlikely coalition of ex-merchants, desert nomads, and agriculturalists united in a potent new faith and inspired by the life and sayings of Prophet Muhammad—were at the time pursuing a fantastically successful series of international conquests in the name of Islam. By the 640s the Arabs possessed most of Syria, Iraq, Persia, and Egypt, and thirty years later they were busy taking over parts of Europe, North Africa, and Central Asia.

In the early decades of the Arab conquests many members of Muhammad's coterie were killed, and with them died valuable knowledge of the Koranic revelations. Muslims at the edges of the empire began arguing over what was Koranic scripture and what was not. An army general returning from Azerbaijan expressed his fears about sectarian controversy to the Caliph 'Uthman (644–656)—the third Islamic ruler to succeed Muhammad—and is said to have entreated him to "overtake this people before they differ over the Koran the way the Jews and Christians differ over their Scripture." 'Uthman convened an editorial committee of sorts that carefully gathered the various pieces of scripture that had been memorized or written down by Muhammad's companions. The result was a standard written version of the Koran. 'Uthman ordered all incomplete and "imperfect" collections of the Koranic scripture destroyed, and the new version was quickly distributed to the major centers of the rapidly burgeoning empire.

During the next few centuries, while Islam solidified as a religious and political entity, a vast body of exegetical and historical literature evolved to explain the Koran and the rise of Islam, the most important elements of which are hadith, or the collected sayings and deeds of the Prophet Muhammad; sunna, or the body of Islamic social and legal custom; sira, or biographies of the Prophet; and tafsir, or Koranic commentary and explication. It is from these traditional sources—compiled in written form mostly from the mid eighth to the mid tenth century—that all accounts of the revelation of the Koran and the early years of Islam are ultimately derived.

"For People Who Understand"

Roughly equivalent in length to the New Testament, the Koran is divided into 114 sections, known as suras, that vary dramatically in length and form. The book's organizing principle is neither chronological nor thematic—for the most part the suras are arranged from beginning to end in descending order of length. Despite the unusual structure, however, what generally surprises newcomers to the Koran is the degree to which it draws on the same beliefs and stories that appear in the Bible. God (Allah in Arabic) rules supreme: he is the all-powerful, all-knowing, and all-merciful Being who has created the world and its creatures; he sends messages and laws through prophets to help guide human existence; and, at a time in the future known only to him, he will bring about the end of the world and the Day of Judgement. Adam, the first man, is expelled from Paradise for eating from the forbidden tree. Noah builds an ark to save a select few from a flood brought on by the wrath of God.

Abraham prepares himself to sacrifice his son at God's bidding. Moses leads the Israelites out of Egypt and receives a revelation on Mount Sinai. Jesus—born of the Virgin Mary and referred to as the Messiah—works miracles, has disciples, and rises to heaven.

The Koran takes great care to stress this common monotheistic heritage, but it works equally hard to distinguish Islam from Judaism and Christianity. For example, it mentions prophets—Hud, Salih, Shu'ayb, Luqman, and others—whose origins seem exclusively Arabian, and it reminds readers that it is "A Koran in Arabic/For people who understand." Despite its repeated assertions to the contrary, however, the Koran is often extremely difficult for contemporary readers—even highly educated speakers of Arabic—to understand. It sometimes makes dramatic shifts in style, voice, and subject matter from verse to verse, and it assumes a familiarity with language, stories, and events that seem to have been lost even to the earliest of Muslim exegetes (typical of a text that initially evolved in an oral tradition). Its apparent inconsistencies are easy to find: God may be referred to in the first and third person in the same sentence; divergent versions of the same story are repeated at different points in the text; divine rulings occasionally contradict one another. In this last case the Koran anticipates criticism and defends itself by asserting the right to abrogate its own message ("God doth blot out/Or confirm what He pleaseth").

Criticism did come. As Muslims increasingly came into contact with Christians during the eighth century, the wars of conquest were accompanied by theological polemics, in which Christians and others latched on to the confusing literary state of the Koran as proof of its human origins. Muslim scholars themselves were fastidiously cataloguing the problematic aspects of the Koran—unfamiliar vocabulary, seeming omissions of text, grammatical incongruities, deviant readings, and so on. A major theological debate in fact arose within Islam in the late eighth century, pitting those who believed in the Koran as the "uncreated" and eternal Word of God against those who believed in it as created in time, like anything that isn't God himself. Under the Caliph al-Ma'mum (813–833) this latter view briefly became orthodox doctrine. It was supported by several schools of thought, including an influential one known as Mu'tazilism, that developed a complex theology based partly on a metaphorical rather than simply literal understanding of the Koran.

By the end of the tenth century the influence of Mu'utazili school had waned, for complicated political reasons, and the official doctrine had become that of i'jaz or the "inimitability" of the Koran. (As a result, the Koran has traditionally not been translated by Muslims for non-Arabic-speaking Muslims. Instead it is read and recited in the original by Muslims worldwide, the majority of whom do not speak Arabic. The translations that do exist are considered to be nothing more than scriptural aids and paraphrases.) The adoption of the doctrine of inimitability was a major turning point in Islamic history, and from the tenth century to this day the mainstream Muslim understanding of the Koran as the literal and uncreated Word of God has remained constant.

Psychopathic Vandalism?

Gerd-R. Puin speaks with disdain about the traditional willingness, on the part of Muslim and Western scholars, to accept the conventional understanding of the Koran. "The Koran claims for itself that it is 'mubeen,' or 'clear.'" he says. "But if you look at it, you will notice that every fifth sentence or so simply doesn't make sense. Many Muslims—and Orientalists—will tell you otherwise, of course, but the fact is that a fifth of the Koranic text is just incomprehensible. This is what has caused the traditional anxiety regarding translation. If the Koran is not comprehensible—if it can't even be understood in Arabic—then it's not translatable. People fear that. And since the Koran claims repeatedly to be clear but obviously is not—as even speakers of Arabic will tell you—there is a contradiction. Something else must be going on."

Trying to figure out that "something else" really began only in this century. "Until quite recently," Patricia Crone, the historian of early Islam, says, "everyone took it for granted that everything the Muslims claim to remember about the origin and meaning of the Koran is correct. If you drop that assumption, you have to start afresh." This is no mean feat, of course; the Koran has come down to us tightly swathed in a historical tradition that is extremely resistant to criticism and analysis. As Crone put it in Slaves on Horses,

> The Biblical redactors offer us sections of the Israelite tradition at different stages of crystallization, and their testimonies can accordingly be profitably compared and weighed against each other. But the Muslim tradition was the outcome, not of a slow crystallization, but of an explosion; the first compilers were not redactors, but collectors of debris whose works are strikingly devoid of overall unity; and no particular illuminations ensue from their comparison.

Not surprisingly, given the explosive expansion of early Islam and the passage of time between the religion's birth and the first systematic documenting of his history, Muhammad's world and the worlds of the historians who subsequently wrote about him were dramatically different. During Islam's first century alone a provincial band of pagan desert tribesmen became the guardians of a vast international empire of institutional monotheism that teemed with unprecedented literary and scientific activity. Many contemporary historians argue that one cannot expect Islam's stories about its own origins—particularly given the oral tradition of the early centuries—to have survived this tremendous social transformation intact. Nor can one expect a Muslim historian writing in ninth- or tenth-century Iraq to have discarded his social and intellectual background (and theological convictions) in order accurately to describe a deeply unfamiliar seventh-century Arabian context. R. Stephen Humphreys, writing in Islamic History: A Framework for Inquiry (1988), concisely summed up the issue that historians confront in studying early Islam.

> If our goal is to comprehend the way in which Muslims of the late 2nd/8th and 3rd/9th centuries [Islamic calendar/Christian calendar] understood the origins of their

society, then we are very well off indeed. But if our aim is to find out "what really happened" in terms of reliably documented answers to modern questions about the earliest decades of Islamic society, then we are in trouble.

The person who more than anyone else has shaken up Koranic studies in the past few decades is John Wansbrough, formerly of the University of London's School of Oriental and African studies. Puin is "re-reading him now" as he prepares to analyze the Yemeni fragments. Patricia Crone says that she and Michael Cook "did not say much about the Koran in *Hagarism* that was not based on Wansbrough." Other scholars are less admiring, referring to Wansbrough's work as "drastically wrongheaded," "ferociously opaque," and a "colossal self-deception." But like it or not, anybody engaged in the critical study of the Koran today must contend with Wansbrough's two main works—*Quranic Studies: Sources and Methods of Scriptural Interpretation* (1977) and *The Sectarian Milieu: Content and Composition of Islamic Salvation History* (1978).

Wansbrough applied an entire arsenal of what he called the "instruments and techniques" of biblical criticism—form criticism, source criticism, redaction criticism, and much more—to the Koranic text. He concluded that the Koran evolved only gradually in the seventh and eighth centuries, during a long period of oral transmission when Jewish and Christian sects were arguing volubly with one another to the north of Mecca and Medina, in which are now parts of Syria, Jordan, Israel and Iraq. The reason that no Islamic source material from the first century or so of Islam has survived, Wansbrough concluded, is that it never existed.

To Wansbrough, the Islamic tradition is an example of what is known to biblical scholars as a "salvation history": a theologically and evangelically motivated story of a religion's origins invented late in the day and projected back in time. In other words, as Wansbrough put it in *Quranic Studies,* the canonization of the Koran—and the Islamic traditions that arose to explain it—involved the

> attribution of several, partially overlapping, collections of *logia* (exhibiting a distinctly Mosiac imprint) to the image of a Biblical prophet (modified by the material of the Muhammadan *evangelium* into an Arabian man of God) with a traditional message of salvation (modified by the influence of Rabbanic Judaism into the unmediated and finally immutable word of God).

Wansbrough's arcane theories have been contagious in certain scholarly circles, but many Muslims understandably have found them deeply offensive. S. Parvez Manzoor, for example, has described the Koranic studies of Wansbrough and others as "a naked discourse of power" and "an outburst of psychopathic vandalism" But not even Manzoor argues for a retreat from the critical enterprise of Koranic studies; instead he urges Muslims to defeat the Western revisionists on the "epistemological battlefield," admitting that "sooner or later [we Muslims] will have to approach the Koran from methodological assumptions and parameters that are radically at odds with the ones consecrated by our tradition."

Revisionism Inside the Islamic World

Indeed, for more than a century there have been public figures in the Islamic world who have attempted the revisionist study of the Koran and Islamic history—the exiled Egyptian professor Nasr Abu Zaid is not unique. Perhaps Abu Zaid's most famous predecessor was the prominent Egyptian government minister, university professor, and writer Taha Hussein. A determined modernist, Hussein in the early 1920s devoted himself to the study of pre-Islamic Arabian poetry and ended up concluding that much of that body of work had been fabricated well after the establishment of Islam in order to lend outside support to Koranic mythology. A more recent example is the Iranian journalist and diplomat Ali Dashti, who in his *Twenty Three Years: A Study of the Prophetic Career of Mohammed* (1985) repeatedly took his fellow Muslims to task for not questioning the traditional accounts of Muhammad's life, much of which he called "myth-making and miracle-mongering."

Abu Zaid also cites the enormously influential Muhammad 'Abduh as a precursor. The nineteenth-century father of Egyptian modernism, 'Abduh saw the potential for a new Islamic theology in the theories of the ninth-century Mu'tazilis. The ideas of the Mu'tazilis gained popularity in some Muslim circles early in this century (leading the important Egyptian writer and intellectual Ahmad Amin to remark in 1936 that "the demise of Mu'tazilism was the greatest misfortune to have afflicted Muslims; they have committed a crime against themselves"). The late Pakistani scholar Fazlur Rahman carried the Mu'tazilite torch well into the present era: he spend the later years of his life, from the 1960s until his death in 1988, living and teaching in the United States, where he trained many students of Islam—both Muslims and non-Muslims—in the Mu'tazilite tradition.

Such work has not come without cost, however: Taha Hussein, like Nasr Abu Zaid, was declared an apostate in Egypt: Ali Dashti died mysteriously just after the 1979 Iranian revolution; and Fazlur Rahman was forced to leave Pakistan in the 1960s. Muslims interested in challenging orthodox doctrine must tread carefully. "I would like to get the Koran out of this prison," Abu Zaid has said of the prevailing Islamic hostility to reinterpreting the Koran for the modern age, "so that once more it becomes productive for the essence of our culture and the arts, which are being strangled in our society." Despite his many enemies in Egypt, Abu Zaid may well be making progress toward this goal: there are indications that his work is being widely, if quietly, read with interest in the Arab world. Abu Zaid says, for example, that his *The Concept of the Text* (1990)—the book largely responsible for his exile from Egypt—has gone through at least eight underground printings in Cairo and Beirut.

Another scholar with a wide readership who is committed to re-examining the Koran is Mohammed Arkoun, the Algerian professor at the University of Paris. Arkoun argued in *Lectures du Coran* (1982), for example, that "it is time [for Islam] to assume, along with all of the great cultural traditions, the modern risks of scientific knowledge," and suggested that "the problem of the divine authenticity of the Koran can serve to reactivate Islamic thought and engage it in the major debates of our age." Arkoun regrets the fact that most Muslims are unaware that a different conception of the Koran exists within their own historical tradition. What a re-examination of Islamic history offers Muslims, Arkoun and others argue, is an opportunity to challenge the Muslim orthodoxy from within, rather than having to rely on "hostile" outside sources. Arkoun, Abu Zaid, and others hope that this challenge might ultimately lead to nothing less than an Islamic renaissance.

The gulf between such academic theories and the daily practice of Islam around the world is huge, of course—the majority of Muslims today are unlikely to question the orthodox understanding of the Koran and Islamic history. Yet Islam became one of the world's great religions in part because of its openness to social change and new ideas. (Centuries ago, when Europe was mired in its feudal Dark Ages, the sages of a flourishing Islamic civilization opened an era of great scientific and philosophical discovery. The ideas of the ancient Greeks and Romans might never have been introduced to Europe were it not for the Islamic historians and philosophers who rediscovered and revived them.) Islam's own history shows that the prevailing conception of the Koran is not the only one ever to have existed, and the recent history of biblical scholarship shows that not all critical-historical studies of a holy scripture are antagonistic. They can instead be carried out with the aim of spiritual and cultural regeneration. They can, as Mohammed Arkoun puts it, demystify the text while reaffirming "the relevance of its larger intuitions."

Increasingly diverse interpretations of the Koran and Islamic history will inevitably be proposed in the coming decades, as traditional cultural distinctions between East, West, North and South continue to dissolve, as the population of the Muslim world continues to grow, as early historical sources continue to be scrutinized, and as feminism meets the Koran. With the diversity of interpretations will surely come increased fractiousness, perhaps intensified by the fact that Islam now exists in such a great variety of social and intellectual settings—Bosnia, Iran, Malaysia, Nigeria, Saudi Arabia, South Africa, the United States, and so on. More than ever before, anybody wishing to understand global affairs will need to understand Islamic civilization, in all its permutations. Surely the best way to start is with the study of the Koran—which promises in the years ahead to be at least as contentious, fascinating, and important as the study of the Bible has been in this century.

TOBY LESTER is the executive editor of Atlantic Unbound, the *Atlantic Monthly* Web site.

From *The Atlantic,* January 1999, pp. 43–46, 48–51, 54–56. Copyright © 1999 by Toby Lester. Reprinted by permission of the author.

The Dome of the Rock: Jerusalem's Epicenter

WALID KHALIDI

Islam is the third great monotheistic religion of the world. Its followers, about a billion people, constitute the majority of the population in some 50 countries. Like Judaism and Christianity, Islam has rich and deep associations with the city of Jerusalem.

Islam is an Arabic word which means "submission"; in its religious context it means submission to the will of God alone. The message of Islam was delivered by the Prophet Muhammad, who was born in Makkah, in present-day Saudi Arabia, in the year 570 and died in 632. Such was the power of the divine message he preached that, within 100 years of his death in Madinah, Islam had spread across North Africa, into Spain and across the borders of France in the West, and to the borders of India and China in the East. (See *Aramco World,* November/December 1991.)

Very early in this period—in 637—the forces of Islam won Jerusalem from the Byzantine Empire, whose capital was in Constantinople, signing a treaty by which the holy city was surrendered to 'Umar ibn al-Khattab, the second caliph, or successor, of Muhammad. For the following 1280 years, except for the period between 1109 and 1187, during the Crusades, Jerusalem remained in Muslim hands: In 1917, during World War I, the British took control of the city Muslims call al-Quds, "The Holy."

To understand Jerusalem's position in Islam, we need to look at how Islam sees itself in relation to Judaism and Christianity, to which of course Jerusalem is also sacred.

Islamic doctrine states that God has, since creation, revealed His teachings repeatedly to humankind through a succession of prophets and scriptures. The first of this line was the prophet Noah, according to many Muslim scholars; others believe Adam must be considered the first. But in this line of succession, Muhammad is the last, or "seal" of the prophets, and the teachings revealed to him are the culmination of all the previous messages. Muslims believe that the Qur'an, the literal word of God revealed to Muhammad, follows the Torah and the Gospels as God's final revelation. Thus the Qur'an accords great reverence to the Hebrew prophets, patriarchs and kings who received revelations from God and are associated with Jerusalem. Similarly, Jesus Christ is revered as one of God's most dedicated messengers, and Jerusalem, as the locus of much of his teaching, is further blessed by that association.

To Islam, then, Jerusalem is sacred for many of the reasons it is sacred to Judaism and Christianity, but in addition, it is sacred for specifically Muslim reasons. The most important of these is the Prophet Muhammad's miraculous nocturnal journey, or *isra',* to *Bayt al-Maqdis,* "the house of holiness," in Jerusalem and his ascent from there to heaven—the *mi'raj.* These events are mentioned in a number of verses of the Qur'an, most clearly in the first verse of Chapter 17, titled *Al-Isra'.* Accounts of the Prophet's life supply the details. Led by the angel Gabriel, Muhammad traveled in one night from Makkah to the site of *al-masjid al-aqsa,* "the furthest mosque," on Mount Moriah, called the Temple Mount, in Jerusalem. The site derives its name from the temples and houses of worship built there over the millennia, including the temple of the prophet Solomon, the temple of Jupiter, the Herodian temple and the al-Aqsa Mosque.

There, Muhammad led Abraham, Moses, Jesus and other prophets in prayer. Then, from a rock on the Temple Mount, Muhammad was taken by Gabriel to heaven itself, to "within two bowlengths" of the very throne of God.

The spot from which the Prophet's ascent began was sanctified in the eyes of Muslims by the *mi'raj;* the Qur'an refers to the prayer site as *al-masjid al-aqsa.* From Muhammad's journey evolved a vast body of Muslim devotional literature, some authentic and some uncanonical, that places Jerusalem at the center of Muslim beliefs concerning life beyond the grave. This literature is in circulation in all the diverse languages spoken by the world's one billion Muslims, most of whom to this day celebrate the anniversary of the *mi'raj.*

Jerusalem is also uniquely linked to one of the "pillars" of the Muslim faith, the five daily prayers. The earliest Muslims, for a time, turned toward Jerusalem to pray. A later revelation transferred the *qibla,* the direction of prayer, to Makkah, but to this day Jerusalem is known as "the first of the two *qiblas.*" And according to Muhammad's teachings, it was during the *mi'raj* that Muslims were ordered by God to pray, and that the number of the daily prayers was fixed at five.

The center of Muslim power shifted, through the centuries, from one great capital to the next: from Madinah to Umayyad Damascus to Abbasid Baghdad to Mamluk Cairo and to Ottoman Constantinople. But after Jerusalem became part of the Muslim state in 637, whichever dynasty was in control of that city lavished it with care and attention in the form of public

Figure 1 The noble sanctuary. The editors are grateful for the valuable help they received in compiling this map and checking it for accuracy. Thanks to architectural photographer Saïd Nuseibeh, whose book *The Dome of the Rock,* was published by Rizzoli (1996); to Jeff Spurr of the Aga Khan Program for Islamic Architecture and the Visual Collections of the Fine Arts Library at Harvard University; to Ahmad Nabal of the Aga Khan Visual Archives, Rotch Visual Collection, Massachusetts Institute of Technology; and to Dr. Walid Khalidi.

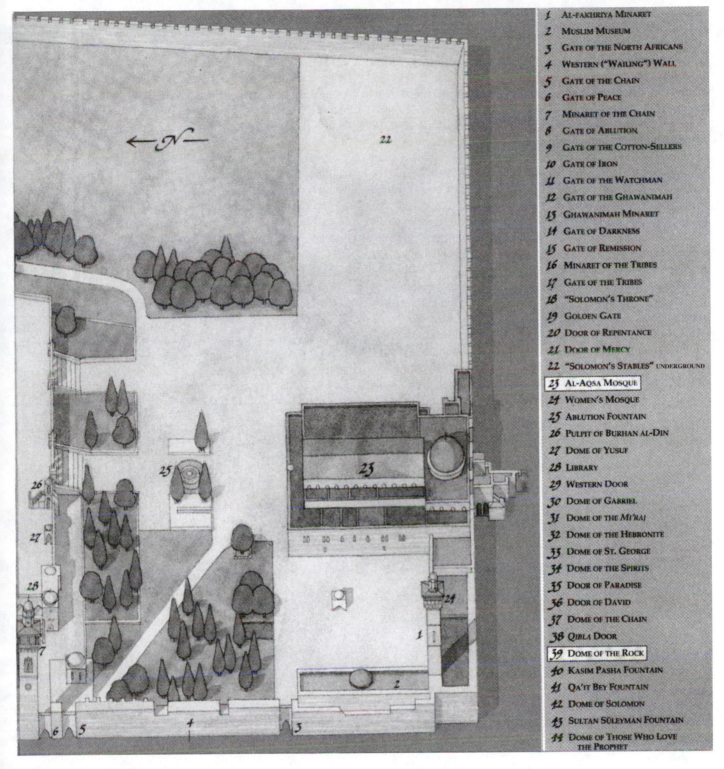

1 AL-FAKHRIYA MINARET
2 MUSLIM MUSEUM
3 GATE OF THE NORTH AFRICANS
4 WESTERN ("WAILING") WALL
5 GATE OF THE CHAIN
6 GATE OF PEACE
7 MINARET OF THE CHAIN
8 GATE OF ABLUTION
9 GATE OF THE COTTON-SELLERS
10 GATE OF IRON
11 GATE OF THE WATCHMAN
12 GATE OF THE GHAWANIMAH
13 GHAWANIMAH MINARET
14 GATE OF DARKNESS
15 GATE OF REMISSION
16 MINARET OF THE TRIBES
17 GATE OF THE TRIBES
18 "SOLOMON'S THRONE"
19 GOLDEN GATE
20 DOOR OF REPENTANCE
21 DOOR OF MERCY
22 "SOLOMON'S STABLES" UNDERGROUND
23 AL-AQSA MOSQUE
24 WOMEN'S MOSQUE
25 ABLUTION FOUNTAIN
26 PULPIT OF BURHAN AL-DIN
27 DOME OF YUSUF
28 LIBRARY
29 WESTERN DOOR
30 DOME OF GABRIEL
31 DOME OF THE MI'RAJ
32 DOME OF THE HEBRONITE
33 DOME OF ST. GEORGE
34 DOME OF THE SPIRITS
35 DOOR OF PARADISE
36 DOOR OF DAVID
37 DOME OF THE CHAIN
38 QIBLA DOOR
39 DOME OF THE ROCK
40 KASIM PASHA FOUNTAIN
41 QA'IT BEY FOUNTAIN
42 DOME OF SOLOMON
43 SULTAN SÜLEYMAN FOUNTAIN
44 DOME OF THOSE WHO LOVE THE PROPHET

Figure 1 *(continued)*

monuments: mosques, colleges for the study of the Qur'an and the traditions of the Prophet, hospitals, hospices, fountains, orphanages, caravansarais, baths, convents for mystics, pools and mausolea. This is why Jerusalem's Old City, within the 16th-century walls built by the Ottoman sultan Süleyman, strikes the modern-day visitor with its predominantly Muslim character.

Caliph 'Umar personally came to Jerusalem to accept the city's surrender from the Byzantines, and visited the site of *al-Masjid al-aqsa*, known to some Muslims today as *al-Haram al-Maqdisi al-Sharif*, "the Noble Sanctuary of Jerusalem," or simply *al-Haram al-Sharif*. The site lay vacant and in ruins; 'Umar ordered it cleaned, and, tradition says, took part in the work himself, carrying dirt in his own robe. When the site had been cleansed and sprinkled with scent, 'Umar and his followers prayed there, near the rough rock from which Muhammad had ascended to heaven.

Two generations later, about 691, the Umayyad caliph 'Abd al-Malik ibn Marwan's Syrian craftsmen built in the same location the earliest masterpiece of Islamic architecture, the Dome of the Rock *(Qubbat al Sakhra)*—the octagonal sanctuary, centered on the rock, whose golden dome still dominates the skyline of Old Jerusalem. 'Abd al-Malik's son al-Walid, who ruled from 705 to 715, built the second major monument, the al-Aqsa Mosque, also on the Temple Mount.

The octagonal plan of the Dome of the Rock may not have been accidental. Cyril Glassé, in his *Concise Encyclopedia of Islam,* points out that "the octagon is a step in the mathematical series going from square, symbolizing the fixity of earthly manifestation, to circle, the natural symbol for the perfection of heaven. . . . In traditional Islamic architecture this configuration symbolizes the link between earth . . . and heaven. . . ." Nor is it coincidence that the elegant calligraphy that encircles the structure inside and out—240 meters, or 785 feet, of it—includes all the Qur'anic verses about the prophet Jesus. "The calligraphic inscriptions," writes Glassé, "recall the relationship between Jerusalem and Jesus . . . and the architecture, above all the octagonal form supporting a dome, is symbolic of the . . . ascent to heaven by the Prophet, and thus by man." Mount Moriah, with the Dome of the Rock at its center, is thus "the place where man, as man, is joined once more to God. . . ."

History, tradition and symbolism intersect in this building, whose presence suffuses Jerusalem.

DR. WALID KHALIDI was educated in London and Oxford and has taught at Oxford University, the American University of Beirut and Harvard University. Since 1982, he has been a senior research fellow at Harvard's Center for Middle Eastern Studies. Members of his family have served Jerusalem as scholars, judges, diplomats and members of parliament since the late 12th century.

From *Aramco World,* September/October 1996, pp. 20–35. Copyright © 1996 by SaudiAramco World. Reprinted by permission.

First Churches of the Jesus Cult

ANDREW LAWLER

As dusk approaches, Korean pilgrims in white baseball caps blow horns and sing hymns atop Tel Megiddo. This crossroads in northern Israel—also known as Armageddon—is where the New Testament says the final battle pitting good against evil will begin. Below the huge mound, tour buses idle, throngs of visitors buy postcards, and a nearby McDonalds does a thriving business at its drive-through window.

On the opposite side of the busy highway are the grim brick walls and coiled barbed wire of a high-security prison. It is an awkward place for an important archaeological site. Unlike at the mound, visitors are not welcome here. Even archaeologists must apply well in advance for access—something I wasn't granted—so I am left standing outside the gates with Yotam Tepper of the Israel Antiquities Authority. The mosaic floor that he and a team of inmates discovered under the prison yard may mark one of the earliest known places of Christian worship.

Although the site may date to a full century before the Roman emperor Constantine issued the Edict of Milan transforming Christianity from a disparate group of Jesus-worshipping cults to a powerful state religion in A.D. 313, these early followers of the controversial faith weren't hiding their beliefs. "There were Samaritans and Jews and Romans and Christians all living together in just this small place," says Tepper. A Roman soldier paid for the mosaics, and members of the congregation may even have baked bread for Rome's sixth legion, stationed nearby.

The find at Megiddo is a key piece of evidence in a radical rethinking of how Christianity evolved during its first three centuries, before it was backed by the might of empire. Until recently, scholars had to rely on ancient texts that emphasize the vicious persecution of the church—think lions dining on martyrs in Rome's Colosseum. A growing body of archaeological data, however, paints a more diverse and surprising picture in which Christians thrived alongside Jews and the Roman military. These finds make this "a definitive time in our field" since they appear to contradict the literary sources on which historians have long depended, says Eric Meyers, a biblical archaeologist at Duke University.

Megiddo is only the latest in a series of recent digs in the Near East revealing a more complex history of the early Christian era. Near the Red Sea in the Jordanian city of Aqaba, archaeologists have uncovered what the dig director, Thomas Parker of North Carolina State University, argues is a pre-Constantinian prayer hall. At Capernaum, just an hour's drive from Megiddo, Franciscan monks believe they have excavated a pilgrimage site dating to as early as the first century A.D. on the shores of the Sea of Galilee. Such discoveries are unusual; the only undisputed early Christian worship site is at Dura Europas, on the Euphrates River in modern Syria, which was excavated in the 1920s and '30s by French and American teams. How the most recently discovered sites were used and dated, however, is hotly contested.

Formal churches were rare before A.D. 325, when Constantine convened the Council of Nicea formalizing many church practices, and embarked on a building campaign that used the Roman basilica—a spacious rectangular enclosed space, typically with an apse and an altar on one end—as the model for Christian places of worship. The basilica became the standard still used for churches around the world.

Before that innovation, however, Christians gathered in *domus ecclesiae,* or house churches. Eager to keep a low profile during uncertain times, many Christian communities met in homes throughout the first centuries to celebrate rituals such as the Eucharist, which used wine and bread to recall Christ's sacrifice and to bind the community of believers together. In a letter to the Romans, St. Paul mentions "the church that is in their house," and numerous other early writers cite homes where congregations met. "This type of architecture was quite private, so it was not visibly a Christian building," says Joan Taylor, a historian at University College in London. "Otherwise, it might get smashed and you might get killed."

That was a legitimate fear. The Jewish high council, according to the New Testament, ordered the death of the first Christian martyr, Stephen. Christians—who still were seen as a Jewish sect—refused to join Jews in the Bar Kokhba revolt against the Romans in A.D. 132–135. Judged as traitors by the Jewish community, they were killed in retribution. After the revolt, however, the decimated Jewish population posed far less of a threat than the Romans. Nero had already scapegoated Christians for burning Rome in A.D. 64; Emperor Decius (A.D. 249–251) had pursued lay Christians as well as clergy; and Diocletian and Galerius had infamously persecuted Christians at the end of the third and beginning of the fourth centuries A.D. There is little doubt Christians suffered terribly during the religions early days. But the evidence from Near Eastern digs, combined with new thinking about the Roman Empire, demonstrates that there were substantial periods when Christians were tolerated, accepted, and even embraced by their tormentors.

This is indisputably the case at Dura Europas, a formidable city and Roman garrison that guarded the eastern frontier of the empire. Excavations in the 1930s revealed a domus ecclesia that includes an inscription dating it to A.D. 231—the only Christian house church which scholars agree predates Constantine. The house church was located near the city gate where Roman soldiers would have been stationed. "There's no way the Romans didn't know about the Christians," says Simon James, an archaeologist at the University of Leicester.

For decades the house church has remained an archaeological oddity. New clues, however, have been emerging far to the south, at Capernaum along the Sea of Galilee in Israel, where Franciscan scholars have been excavating a site for the past century. They believe it was the house of Peter and other apostles; Jesus is said to have lived here and taught at the local synagogue. Today, a squat and ugly modern concrete church hovers above the house. Visiting Italian nuns and Nigerian pilgrims peer down through the church's glass floor at the foundations of the octagonal shrine built a century or so after Constantine legalized Christianity. The octagon was a typical shape for shrines and places of importance, from Roman tombs to the Dome of the Rock. Below the Capernaum structure, the excavators found 11 floors, layered one on top of the other, dating from the second century B.C. through the fourth century A.D., says Michele Piccirillo, a Franciscan archaeologist.

Piccirillo's office is a high-ceilinged room just off the Via Dolorosa in Jerusalem, with a bare bulb illuminating religious paintings and stacks of books. He makes strong and bitter coffee as he lays out the case for Capernaum as one of Christianity's most ancient places of worship. Digging through his papers, he points out the evolution of the house. He notes that the early layers include lamps and cooking pots, while from the second century A.D. on, they have only found lamps—circumstantial evidence that the site may have been transformed from a private home into a place of pilgrimage or worship. And some bits of plaster in the central room show graffiti by Christians, including the name Peter and references to "Christ" and "Lord" in Aramaic, Greek, Latin, and Syriac. "There is continuity—this house eventually was used as a church," he says. He believes the domus ecclesia dates from at least the third century.

> "There is no doubt that the graffiti suggests early Christian pilgrims venerated the site," Meyers says. "The excavators have been very, very responsible—they're not making this up."

Other archaeologists disagree with this interpretation. Taylor, who closely examined the data, believes the site was not used for worship until the fourth century. But Meyers is impressed with the evidence. "There is no doubt that the graffiti suggests early Christian pilgrims venerated the site," he says. "The excavators have been very, very responsible—they're not making this up." But he adds that Franciscans like Piccirillo "have a vested interest in proving the antiquity of holy sites." What is not in dispute, however, is the existence of an elaborate synagogue across the street, dating to the same time as the octagonal building. The Franciscans believe it was built on the foundation of an earlier Jewish house of worship dating to the first century A.D.—and

possibly the same one in which Jesus is said to have preached. Whether or not the monks have found Peter's house, it is clear that Jews and Christians coexisted peacefully here.

Further to the south, in Jordan, the team led by Parker uncovered another candidate for a pre-Constantinian church in the late 1990s. Located just a short walk from the Red Sea in the port of Aqaba, the small site is today surrounded by busy streets and hotels in this popular seaside resort. Like Dura Europas, the city in Roman times was a thriving center of trade at the edge of the empire—and an important military post. Unlike a scattering of other archaeological sites in this city, there are no signs yet explaining the potential significance of the mud-brick structure that lies crumbling in the sun, protected by a short wire fence. More than 100 coins, the latest dating to the last decade in the reign of Constantinius II (A.D. 337–361), were found in the building, which measures 85 by 53 feet. Based on the coins and pottery, Parker estimates that the building was constructed in the late third or early fourth century A.D.—though he says a post-325 date is not out of the question.

Given the east-west orientation, basilica-like plan, glass oil-lamp fragments, and a cross found in a grave in a nearby cemetery, he argues that the building was a formal church rather than a domus ecclesia. The theory has yet to win many supporters, but scholars are eager to see his final publication of the find, which should be out this year. "I am skeptical," says Jodi Magness, an archaeologist at the University of North Carolina at Chapel Hill who specializes in the period and is digging just across the border in Israel," I haven't seen anything yet that persuades me."

Magness has her own potential candidate for a pre-Constantine church in southern Israel at a site called Yotvata, a Roman fort that was built around A.D. 300. In 2006, her team found a semicircular niche cut into the fort's wall flanked by two pilasters and an inscription that may be a Christian prayer. The niche was likely built in the early fourth century but a more precise date will require further excavation—including the removal of a British police station that was built over it in the 1930s.

The controversy surrounding the church at Megiddo began in 2003, when prisoners were assigned to expand the buildings housing Christian and Muslim Palestinian prisoners. When the crew working in the interior yard hit archaeological remains, prison officials alerted the Israel Antiquities Authority, which put Tepper, a graduate student at Tel Aviv University, in charge of the salvage effort. He conducted the work primarily with a team made up of 70 prisoners.

Like Dura Europas and Aqaba, Megiddo was full of Roman soldiers. And like Capernaum, it was primarily a Jewish town. Situated on a strategic spot between the Mediterranean coast and the Sea of Galilee, its bloody future as the site of the last battle between good and evil forecast by the New Testament's Book of Revelation reflects its past: here, battles raged involving Egyptians, Canaanites, Assyrians, Greeks, Romans, Turks, and British. But during Roman times, it was the site of a Jewish village called Kefar 'Othnay, a Roman legion camp, and eventually a Byzantine city called Maximianopolis.

"It was a small village with nothing special," says Tepper. The settlement, likely founded by Jews or Samaritans in the second half of the first century, covered about 15 acres and was located next to a Roman legion base. In late 2005, as he was wrapping up the dig, Tepper came across the remains of a building on the edge of the village closest to the Roman camp. The building had four wings, an exterior courtyard with bread ovens, and a series of rooms opening onto an interior courtyard. In the western wing Tepper's team uncovered a hall measuring 5 by 10 yards and oriented north to south. In the middle of the hall, they found four mosaic panels with inscriptions surrounding a podium. Two panels are decorated with simple geometric patterns; a third is slightly larger with Greek inscriptions on each end. The fourth shows two flopping fish—a tuna and a sea bass—circled by squares, triangles, and diamonds with a large inscription on one end.

Tepper faxed images of the mosaics to Leah di Segni, an epigrapher at Hebrew University who was working from her third-floor walk-up apartment in West Jerusalem. At first she says she assumed the mosaics were part of a temple to Mithras, a Persian god popular with Roman troops from the empire's eastern frontier to Scotland. Di Segni translated one inscription as "Gaianus, also called Porphyrius, centurion, our brother, has made the pavement at his own expense as an act of liberality. Brutius has carried out the work." A second inscription is a memorial to four women with common Greek names. But the third inscription was the stunner: "The god-loving Akeptous has offered the table to God Jesus Christ as a memorial."

She immediately phoned Tepper and told him to look for Roman pottery. He promptly found sherds and coins that he says date the site to the early third century. They found more than 100 coins in the complex, one-third of which date to the second and third centuries A.D. and the remaining two-thirds to the fourth century. Almost all of the early coins come from the hall, including several in pristine condition from the reigns of emperors Elagabalus (A.D. 218–222) and Severus Alexander (A.D. 222–235). "These coins," Tepper says, "should probably be associated with the founding of the building." The latest one, he notes, is dated to Diocletian's reign in the late third century. The absence of any post-Diocletian coins may mean that the building was abandoned in the fourth century, says Tepper. He also says he has Roman pottery that confirms his conclusion.

Most of the jar fragments in the complex appear to be from the third century A.D., with the latest dating to the early fourth century. Pottery fragments found alongside and below the mosaic floor are no later than the third century, he adds. Two stone stamps that were used by the bakers of the Roman legions to mark the bread they made were found in the complex, another sign that soldiers may have been Christians at a time when the faith was officially outlawed.

Tepper's conclusions have been greeted skeptically by senior archaeologists, such as Magness and Piccirillo. "There are a lot of early coins—so what?" says Magness, who notes that the area under the mosaic floor, which might yield critical dating material, has yet to be excavated. "I don't think they have convincing evidence," she adds. Piccirillo agrees. An expert in Byzantine mosaics, he believes their style indicates they could be as late as the fifth century.

Others are more intrigued. "I'm open to Megiddo as a third-century site," says Taylor. "It's idiosyncratic," she adds, since it does not fit the model of Christian churches during and after the time of Constantine. Those structures are easily recognizable by their basilica shape with an altar on the east end and main entrance to the west. "This is a time before all the dictates come from above," says Taylor. And Meyers, a pottery expert, says that while everyone is awaiting a final publication, he is convinced that the sherds are distinctively mid-Roman rather than from a later era.

If Megiddo does prove to be an early prayer hall, then it will lend strength to the growing view among scholars that the early Church in the Holy Land was highly diverse during the two centuries between the death of Jesus and Constantine's edict. "The traditional view was that early Christianity was not licensed, that it had to hide," says Taylor. "That's shifting to a recognition that there were periods of persecution followed by periods of peace." And those well-documented periods of persecution might have had spotty results. Decrees issued from Rome, Taylor says, might have little impact at the fringes of a vast empire, at places like Megiddo and Dura Europas.

Meyers agrees. He also believes the Megiddo site is evidence that scholars need to rethink the idea that the Holy Land was largely devoid of Christians after the Roman destruction of Jerusalem and subsequent Jewish revolts. According to Meyers, the archaeological evidence points to a complex and closer relationship between early Christians and Jews. Despite Byzantine decrees persecuting Jews, he notes that impressive synagogues sprang up around the empire at places like Capernaum. "The two sister religions have an often robust and positive" relationship, says Meyers. He believes the excavations show that it goes back to Christianity's early days.

How Roman soldiers influenced the evolution of early Christianity remains an open question. Though the Roman army was often the weapon used to smash Christian places of worship, soldiers were also drawn to a host of eastern cults such as Mithraism and Christianity. "A lot of soldiers regarded it as sensible to get on the right side of the local deities," says James.

Meanwhile, work at the Megiddo site has stopped. Israeli officials would like to move the prison, but there is no budget to do so. There are not even funds to finish the excavations and conserve the site. The idea of turning the area into a major tourist destination—the nearby Tel Megiddo already draws hundreds of pilgrims each day—appears to be on indefinite hold. Standing outside the prison gate, Tepper says that the money and jobs involved make moving the prison difficult. He is currently busy with other salvage excavations around the Sea of Galilee. By now the sun is setting and the tourist buses have all left Tel Megiddo. Tepper gives the prison walls one last glance and climbs in his battered jeep as the gate opens briefly—but only to let in a new batch of prisoners.

ANDREW LAWLER is a staff writer for *Science* magazine.

Women in Ancient Christianity
The New Discoveries

Karen L. King

In the last twenty years, the history of women in ancient Christianity has been almost completely revised. As women historians entered the field in record numbers, they brought with them new questions, developed new methods, and sought for evidence of women's presence in neglected texts and exciting new findings. For example, only a few names of women were widely known: Mary, the mother of Jesus; Mary Magdalene, his disciple and the first witness to the resurrection; Mary and Martha, the sisters who offered him hospitality in Bethany. Now we are learning more of the many women who contributed to the formation of Christianity in its earliest years.

Perhaps most surprising, however, is that the stories of women we thought we knew well are changing in dramatic ways. Chief among these is Mary Magdalene, a woman infamous in Western Christianity as an adulteress and repentant whore. Discoveries of new texts from the dry sands of Egypt, along with sharpened critical insight, have now proven that this portrait of Mary is entirely inaccurate. She was indeed an influential figure, but as a prominent disciple and leader of one wing of the early Christian movement that promoted women's leadership.

Certainly, the New Testament Gospels, written toward the last quarter of the first century CE [Christian Era], acknowledge that women were among Jesus' earliest followers. From the beginning, Jewish women disciples, including Mary Magdalene, Joanna, and Susanna, had accompanied Jesus during his ministry and supported him out of their private means (Luke 8:1–3). He spoke to women both in public and private, and indeed he learned from them. According to one story, an unnamed Gentile woman taught Jesus that the ministry of God is not limited to particular groups and persons, but belongs to all who have faith (Mark 7:24–30; Matthew 15:21–28). A Jewish woman honored him with the extraordinary hospitality of washing his feet with perfume. Jesus was a frequent visitor at the home of Mary and Martha, and was in the habit of teaching and eating meals with women as well as men. When Jesus was arrested, women remained firm, even when his male disciples are said to have fled, and they accompanied him to the foot of the cross. It was women who were reported as the first witnesses to the resurrection, chief among them again Mary Magdalene.

Although the details of these gospel stories may be questioned, in general they reflect the prominent historical roles women played in Jesus' ministry as disciples.

Women in the First Century of Christianity

After the death of Jesus, women continued to play prominent roles in the early movement. Some scholars have even suggested that the majority of Christians in the first century may have been women.

The letters of Paul—dated to the middle of the first century CE—and his casual greetings to acquaintances offer fascinating and solid information about many Jewish and Gentile women who were prominent in the movement. His letters provide vivid clues about the kind of activities in which women engaged more generally. He greets Prisca, Junia, Julia, and Nereus' sister, who worked and traveled as missionaries in pairs with their husbands or brothers (Romans 16:3, 7, 15). He tells us that Prisca and her husband risked their lives to save his. He praises Junia as a prominent apostle, who had been imprisoned for her labor. Mary and Persis are commended for their hard work (Romans 16:6, 12). Euodia and Syntyche are called his fellow-workers in the gospel (Philippians 4:2–3). Here is clear evidence of women apostles active in the earliest work of spreading the Christian message.

Paul's letters also offer some important glimpses into the inner workings of ancient Christian churches. These groups did not own church buildings but met in homes, no doubt due in part to the fact that Christianity was not legal in the Roman world of its day and in part because of the enormous expense to such fledgling societies. Such homes were a domain in which women played key roles. It is not surprising then to see women taking leadership roles in house churches. Paul tells of women who were the leaders of such house churches (Apphia in Philemon 2; Prisca in I Corinthians 16:19). This practice is confirmed by other texts that also mention women who headed churches in their homes, such as Lydia of Thyatira (Acts 16:15) and Nympha of Laodicea (Colossians 4:15). Women held offices and played significant roles in group worship. Paul, for example, greets a deacon named Phoebe (Romans 16:1) and assumes that women are praying and prophesying during worship (I Corinthians 11). As prophets, women's roles would have included not only ecstatic public speech, but preaching, teaching, leading prayer, and perhaps even performing the eucharist meal. (A later first century work, called the Didache, assumes that this duty fell regularly to Christian prophets.)

Mary Magdalene: A Truer Portrait

Later texts support these early portraits of women, both in exemplifying their prominence and confirming their leadership roles (Acts 17:4, 12). Certainly the most prominent among these in the ancient church was Mary Magdalene. A series of spectacular 19th and 20th century discoveries of Christian texts in Egypt dating to the second and third century have yielded a treasury of new information. It was already known from the New Testament gospels that Mary was a Jewish woman who followed Jesus of Nazareth. Apparently of independent means, she accompanied Jesus during his ministry and supported him out of her own resources (Mark 15:40–41; Matthew 27:55–56; Luke 8:1–3; John 19:25).

Although other information about her is more fantastic, she is repeatedly portrayed as a visionary and leader of the early movement. (Mark 16:1–9; Matthew 28:1–10; Luke 24:1–10; John 20:1, 11–18; Gospel of Peter). In the Gospel of John, the risen Jesus gives her special teaching and commissions her as an apostle to the apostles to bring them the good news. She obeys and is thus the first to announce the resurrection and to play the role of an apostle, although the term is not specifically used of her. Later tradition, however, will herald her as "the apostle to the apostles." The strength of this literary tradition makes it possible to suggest that historically Mary was a prophetic visionary and leader within one sector of the early Christian movement after the death of Jesus.

The newly discovered Egyptian writings elaborate this portrait of Mary as a favored disciple. Her role as "apostle to the apostles" is frequently explored, especially in considering her faith in contrast to that of the male disciples who refuse to believe her testimony. She is most often portrayed in texts that claim to record dialogues of Jesus with his disciples, both before and after the resurrection. In the Dialogue of the Savior, for example, Mary is named along with Judas (Thomas) and Matthew in the course of an extended dialogue with Jesus. During the discussion, Mary addresses several questions to the Savior as a representative of the disciples as a group. She thus appears as a prominent member of the disciple group and is the only woman named. Moreover, in response to a particularly insightful question, the Lord says of her, "You make clear the abundance of the revealer!" (140.17–19). At another point, after Mary has spoken, the narrator states, "She uttered this as a woman who had understood completely" (139.11–13). These affirmations make it clear that Mary is to be counted among the disciples who fully comprehended the Lord's teaching (142.11–13).

In another text, the Sophia of Jesus Christ, Mary also plays a clear role among those whom Jesus teaches. She is one of the seven women and twelve men gathered to hear the Savior after the resurrection, but before his ascension. Of these only five are named and speak, including Mary. At the end of his discourse, he tells them, "I have given you authority over all things as children of light," and they go forth in joy to preach the gospel. Here again Mary is included among those special disciples to whom Jesus entrusted his most elevated teaching, and she takes a role in the preaching of the gospel.

In the Gospel of Philip, Mary Magdalene is mentioned as one of three Marys "who always walked with the Lord" and as his companion (59.6–11). The work also says that Lord loved her more than all the disciples, and used to kiss her often (63.34–36). The importance of this portrayal is that yet again the work affirms the special relationship of Mary Magdalene to Jesus based on her spiritual perfection.

In the Pistis Sophia, Mary again is preeminent among the disciples, especially in the first three of the four books. She asks more questions than all the rest of the disciples together, and the Savior acknowledges that: "Your heart is directed to the Kingdom of Heaven more than all your brothers" (26:17–20). Indeed, Mary steps in when the other disciples are despairing in order to intercede for them to the Savior (218:10–219:2). Her complete spiritual comprehension is repeatedly stressed.

She is, however, most prominent in the early second century Gospel of Mary, which is ascribed pseudonymously to her. More than any other early Christian text, the Gospel of Mary presents an unflinchingly favorable portrait of Mary Magdalene as a woman leader among the disciples. The Lord himself says she is blessed for not wavering when he appears to her in a vision. When all the other disciples are weeping and frightened, she alone remains steadfast in her faith because she has grasped and appropriated the salvation offered in Jesus' teachings. Mary models the ideal disciple: she steps into the role of the Savior at his departure, comforts, and instructs the other disciples. Peter asks her to tell any words of the Savior which she might know but that the other disciples have not heard. His request acknowledges that Mary was preeminent among women in Jesus' esteem, and the question itself suggests that Jesus gave her private instruction. Mary agrees and gives an account of "secret" teaching she received from the Lord in a vision. The vision is given in the form of a dialogue between the Lord and Mary; it is an extensive account that takes up seven out of the eighteen pages of the work. At the conclusion of the work, Levi confirms that indeed the Saviour loved her more than the rest of the disciples (18.14–15). While her teachings do not go unchallenged, in the end the Gospel of Mary affirms both the truth of her teachings and her authority to teach the male disciples. She is portrayed as a prophetic visionary and as a leader among the disciples.

Other Christian Women

Other women appear in later literature as well. One of the most famous woman apostles was Thecla, a virgin-martyr converted by Paul. She cut her hair, donned men's clothing, and took up the duties of a missionary apostle. Threatened with rape, prostitution, and twice put in the ring as a martyr, she persevered in her faith and her chastity. Her lively and somewhat fabulous story is recorded in the second century Acts of Thecla. From very early, an order of women who were widows served formal roles of ministry in some churches (I Timothy 5:9–10). The most numerous clear cases of women's leadership, however, are offered by prophets: Mary Magdalene, the Corinthian women, Philip's daughters, Ammia of Philadelphia, Philumene, the visionary martyr Perpetua, Maximilla, Priscilla (Prisca), and Quintilla. There were many others whose names are lost to us. The African church father Tertullian, for example, describes an unnamed woman prophet in his congregation who not only had ecstatic visions during church services, but who also served as a counselor and healer (On the Soul 9.4). A remarkable collection of oracles from another unnamed woman prophet was discovered in Egypt in 1945. She speaks in the first person as the feminine voice of God: Thunder, Perfect Mind. The prophets Prisca and Quintilla inspired a Christian movement in second century Asia Minor (called the New Prophecy or Montanism) that spread around the Mediterranean and lasted for at least four centuries. Their oracles were collected and published, including the account of a vision in which Christ appeared to the prophet in the form of a woman and "put wisdom" in her (Epiphanius, Panarion 49.1). Montanist Christians ordained women as presbyters and bishops, and women held the title of prophet. The third century African bishop Cyprian also tells of an ecstatic woman prophet from Asia Minor who celebrated the eucharist and performed baptisms (Epistle 74.10). In the early second century, the Roman governor Pliny tells of two slave women he tortured who were deacons (Letter to Trajan 10.96). Other women were ordained as priests in fifth century Italy and Sicily (Gelasius, Epistle 14.26).

Women were also prominent as martyrs and suffered violently from torture and painful execution by wild animals and paid gladiators. In fact, the earliest writing definitely by a woman is the prison diary of Perpetua, a relatively wealthy matron and nursing mother who was put to death in Carthage at the beginning of the third century on the charge of being a Christian. In it, she records her testimony before the local Roman ruler and her defiance of her father's pleas that she recant. She tells of the support and fellowship among the confessors in prison, including other women. But above all, she records her prophetic visions. Through them, she was not merely reconciled passively to her fate, but claimed the power to define the meaning of her own death. In a situation where Romans sought to use their violence against her body as a witness to their power and justice, and where the Christian editor of her story sought to turn her death into a witness to the truth of Christianity, her own writing lets us see the human being caught up in these political struggles. She actively relinquishes her female roles as mother, daughter, and sister in favor of defining her identity solely in spiritual terms. However horrifying or heroic her behavior may seem, her brief diary offers an intimate look at one early Christian woman's spiritual journey.

Early Christian Women's Theology

Study of works by and about women is making it possible to begin to reconstruct some of the theological views of early Christian women. Although they are a diverse group, certain reoccurring elements appear to be common to women's theology-making. By placing the teaching of the Gospel of Mary side-by-side with the theology of the Corinthian women prophets, the Montanist women's oracles, Thunder Perfect Mind, and Perpetua's prison diary, it is possible to discern shared views about teaching and practice that may exemplify some of the contents of women's theology:

- Jesus was understood primarily as a teacher and mediator of wisdom rather than as ruler and judge.
- Theological reflection centered on the experience of the person of the risen Christ more than the crucified savior. Interestingly enough, this is true even in the case of the martyr Perpetua. One might expect her to identify with the suffering Christ, but it is the risen Christ she encounters in her vision.
- Direct access to God is possible for all through receiving the Spirit.
- In Christian community, the unity, power, and perfection of the Spirit are present now, not just in some future time.
- Those who are more spiritually advanced give what they have freely to all without claim to a fixed, hierarchical ordering of power.
- An ethics of freedom and spiritual development is emphasized over an ethics of order and control.
- A woman's identity and spirituality could be developed apart from her roles as wife and mother (or slave), whether she actually withdrew from those roles or not. Gender is itself contested as a "natural" category in the face of the power of God's Spirit at work in the community and the world. This meant that potentially women (and men) could exercise leadership on the basis of spiritual achievement apart from gender status and without conformity to established social gender roles.
- Overcoming social injustice and human suffering are seen to be integral to spiritual life.

Women were also actively engaged in reinterpreting the texts of their tradition. For example, another new text, the Hypostasis of the Archons, contains a retelling of the Genesis story ascribed to Eve's daughter Norea, in which her mother Eve appears as the instructor of Adam and his healer.

The new texts also contain an unexpected wealth of Christian imagination of the divine as feminine. The long version of the Apocryphon of John, for example, concludes with a hymn about the descent of divine Wisdom, a feminine figure here called the Pronoia of God. She enters into the lower world and the body in order to awaken the innermost spiritual being of the soul to the truth of its power and freedom, to awaken the spiritual power it needs to escape the counterfeit powers that enslave the soul in ignorance, poverty, and the drunken sleep of spiritual deadness, and to overcome illegitimate political and sexual domination. The oracle collection Thunder Perfect Mind also adds crucial evidence to women's prophetic theology-making. This prophet speaks powerfully to women, emphasizing the presence of women in her audience and insisting upon their identity with the feminine voice of the Divine. Her speech lets the hearers transverse the distance between political exploitation and empowerment, between the experience of degradation and the knowledge of infinite self-worth, between despair and peace. It overcomes the fragmentation of the self by naming it, cherishing it, insisting upon the multiplicity of self-hood and experience.

These elements may not be unique to women's religious thought or always result in women's leadership, but as a constellation they point toward one type of theologizing that was meaningful to some early Christian women, that had a place for women's legitimate exercise of leadership, and to whose construction women contributed. If we look to these elements, we are able to discern important contributions of women to early Christian theology and praxis. These elements also provide an important location for discussing some aspects of early Christian women's spiritual lives: their exercise of leadership, their ideals, their attraction to Christianity, and what gave meaning to their self-identity as Christians.

Undermining Women's Prominence

Women's prominence did not, however, go unchallenged. Every variety of ancient Christianity that advocated the legitimacy of women's leadership was eventually declared heretical, and evidence of women's early leadership roles was erased or suppressed.

This erasure has taken many forms. Collections of prophetic oracles were destroyed. Texts were changed. For example, at least one woman's place in history was obscured by turning her into a man! In Romans 16:7, the apostle Paul sends greetings to a woman named Junia. He says of her and her male partner Andronicus that they are "my kin and my fellow prisoners, prominent among the apostles and they were in Christ before me." Concluding that women could not be apostles, textual editors and translators transformed Junia into Junias, a man.

Or women's stories could be rewritten and alternative traditions could be invented. In the case of Mary Magdalene, starting in the fourth century, Christian theologians in the Latin West associated Mary Magdalene with the unnamed sinner who anointed Jesus' feet in Luke 7:36–50. The confusion began by conflating the account in John 12:1–8, in which Mary (of Bethany) anoints Jesus, with the anointing by the unnamed woman sinner in the accounts of Luke. Once this initial, erroneous identification was secured, Mary Magdalene could be associated with every unnamed sinful woman in the gospels, including the adulteress in John 8:1–11 and the Syro-phoenician woman with her five and more "husbands" in John 4:7–30. Mary the apostle, prophet, and teacher had become Mary the repentant whore. This fiction was invented at least in part to undermine her influence and with it the appeal to her apostolic authority to support women in roles of leadership.

Until recently the texts that survived have shown only the side that won. The new texts are therefore crucial in constructing a fuller and more accurate portrait. The Gospel of Mary, for example, argued that leadership should be based on spiritual maturity, regardless of whether one is male or female. This Gospel lets us hear an alternative voice to the one dominant in canonized works like I Timothy, which tried to silence women and insist that their salvation lies in bearing children. We can now hear the other side of the controversy over women's leadership and see what arguments were given in favor of it.

It needs to be emphasized that the formal elimination of women from official roles of institutional leadership did not eliminate women's actual presence and importance to the Christian tradition, although it certainly seriously damaged their capacity to contribute fully. What is remarkable is how much evidence has survived systematic attempts to erase women from history, and with them the warrants and models for women's leadership. The evidence presented here is but the tip of an iceberg.

KAREN L. KING is Professor of New Testament Studies and the History of Ancient Christianity at Harvard University in the Divinity School. She has published widely in the areas of Gnosticism, ancient Christianity, and Women's Studies.

UNIT 6

The World of the Middle Ages, 500–1500

Unit Selections

Key Points to Consider

- Why did the Eastern Roman Empire survive more than a thousand years longer than its Western counterpart? What effect did this have on the history of both empires?

- What was the traditional interpretation regarding the Maya and their civilization? How have recent archaeological discoveries changed that interpretation?

- Why were the medieval Holy Roman Emperors unable to unify Europe? Why does the ideal of unity still ring clear for many Europeans today?

- To what extent were Arab sources responsible for the development of European medicine? What does this reveal about both civilizations during the Middle Ages?

- What was the traditional interpretation of the Vikings' role in European history? How has this interpretation been modified in recent years?

- What factors contributed to the fall of Constantinople to the Turks in 1453? What effect did this have on both eastern and western worlds?

Student Web Site
www.mhcls.com

Internet References

Labyrinth Home Page to Medieval Studies
   http://www.georgetown.edu/labyrinth/
Lords of the Earth: Maya/Aztec/Inca Exchange
   http://www.mayalords.org/
The Maya Astronomy Page
   http://www.michielb.nl/maya/astro_content.html?t2 _ 1021391248914
WWW Medieval Resources
   http://ebbs.english.vt.edu/medieval/medieval.ebbs.html

World historians have some difficulty with this period of time. In the history of Europe, the Middle Ages, or the medieval period, is a time of retreat after the fall of Rome. This thousand-year span covers feudalism, the growth of national states, the bubonic plague (called the Black Death), reestablishment of long-distance trade, the domination of the Roman Catholic church, and the emergence of Western civilization. For world historians, Western developments during this period of time are important for the future, but they pale in comparison with the achievements of Islamic civilization and with the changes that people elsewhere in the world were experiencing.

Lifespan and comfort for most European and West Asian people in the year 1000 were little improved from conditions in the previous years, during the reign of the Roman Empire. In the Americas, however, the Maya had created a sophisticated culture that, at its zenith, rivaled that of ancient Egypt. The North American Indian town of Cahokia flourished and then declined. It provided a less sophisticated example of town and temple building in the north of Mesoamerican civilization.

In the New World, civilization evolved later than it did in the Old World. Perhaps this was due to the pattern of migration to the Western Hemisphere and the later development of agriculture in that part of the world. The Maya, nonetheless, constructed magnificent stone cities and developed complex social and economic institutions. Classics from the Maya culture, such as the *Popol Vuh*, have given scholars access to myths and rituals that gave life meaning. Unfortunately, much of this sophisticated New World civilization was destroyed in the Spanish conquest. And, the diseases brought by Europeans wreaked havoc among populations that had no exposure, and therefore no immunity, to measles, chickenpox, or scarlet fever.

Meanwhile, this period of time represents a golden age for Islamic power and culture. The Arabs preserved Greek writings, studying and commenting on the dialogues and treatises of Plato and Aristotle that were lost to the Western world. They also became interested in astronomy, and impressed the world with their architecture and advanced medicine. People in the Middle East established the first hospitals and pharmacies, as well as the first universities.

By the 5th century C.E, the Roman Empire had established a durable Eastern capital in Constantinople—at the intersection of Europe and Asia—that would survive barbarian attacks and last another thousand years. The Holy Roman Empire, created when Charlemagne was crowned by Pope Leo III on Christmas Day, 800, symbolized an enduring European ideal of unity. This might explain the valiant defense of Constantinople in the face of overwhelming force, before it fell to the Ottoman Turks in 1453.

© Pixtgal/age Fotostock

Explanations for the fall of the Roman Empire have occupied historians for centuries, with internal decay and barbarian invasions being most often-cited as causes. What is certain, however, is that Rome did weaken and eventually disappear. At least, this is true for the Western Roman Empire. Although the Eastern Empire today is no longer a world power, its former capital city (Constantinople, now Istanbul), in the heart of Muslim Turkey, remains the seat of Orthodox Christianity.

Toward the end of this period, farming improved in the West and nations formed. In England, the first halting step toward civil liberties was taken with the signing of the Magna Carta. And in the same century, an Italian named Marco Polo changed the course of history by exploring the East and living to tell about his discoveries. His writings inspired others to go where he had gone and, for better or worse, neither East nor West would ever be the same.

The Survival of the Eastern Roman Empire

Stephen Williams and Gerard Friell analyse why Constantinople survived the barbarian onslaughts in the fifth century, whereas Rome fell.

STEPHEN WILLIAMS AND GERARD FRIELL

The old attitude still prevails in some quarters that what we know of as the Roman Empire was dismembered in the fifth century, and that what survived in the East was something different—Byzantium, Greek and Christian; fascinating, no doubt, but no longer the real Rome. This quite misleading picture is often accompanied by another: that the survival of the Eastern half in the terrible fifth century, when the West went under, was a more or less natural development—even unconsciously anticipated by Constantine's wise foundation of his new capital in the wealthier, more urbanised East.

The reality of course was very different. Despite the administrative division into East and West, which predated Constantine, the empire was everywhere seen as one and indivisible. At the beginnings of the fifth century both halves faced similar chronic problems: immature or inept emperors, rebellious armies, external barbarian invaders and the large and dangerous settlements of barbarian 'allies' within imperial territories. By difficult expedients and innovations the East was eventually able to overcome these problems, while the West was not. After several attempts, Constantinople accepted that it had not the strength to save the West, but it still treated it as a group of temporarily lost provinces to be recovered when the situation permitted—a view that the emperor Justinian in the sixth century took entirely literally.

After the disastrous defeat by the immigrant Visigoths at Adrianople (Edirne) in 378, the new Eastern emperor, Theodosius, was eventually able to fight and manoeuvre them into signing a treaty in 382, settling them in the Balkans as 'allies' (*foederati*), since they could not possibly be expelled. They were obliged to support the emperor, militarily, on request, but this was nonetheless a radically new departure in foreign policy, the result of Roman weakness. Instead of mere farmer-settlers under Roman administration, this was an entire armed Germanic nation established deep within Roman territory under its own tribal leaders. It could not help but be a precedent for other land-hungry barbarians. Theodosius, however, had no option but to hope that in time the Goths could be assimilated as others had been.

After Theodosius's death in 395, his two young sons, Arcadius (377–408) and Honorius (384–423), inherited the thrones of East and West respectively. Both boy-emperors were immature and

incapable (Honorius was practically retarded), and although strong loyalty to the dynasty kept them on their thrones, they were entirely managed by individuals or factions within the two courts. Instead of the cooperation that was badly needed, the two governments of East and West intrigued and manoeuvred against each other like hostile states for over ten years, with damaging consequences.

On Theodosius's death the Visigoths immediately broke out of their assigned territories and ravaged the Eastern provinces, under their leader Alaric, who now declared himself king. Temporarily without their main army, the Eastern government, dominated by the eunuch chamberlain Eutropius, was able to deflect Alaric westwards by granting him a top military command in Illyricum (Yugoslavia). The combined status of Roman general and tribal warlord created yet another dangerous precedent. Alaric was able to exploit the deep hostility between the two governments, becoming a destabilising force over the next fifteen years.

In the West, real power was legitimately in the hands of the commander-in-chief Stilicho, of Vandal origin, who had been appointed guardian of the boy-emperor Honorius. He was resented and feared by the ruling circles at Constantinople, who had him declared a public enemy. Stilicho, hoping in vain to force Alaric back into his former alliance, was able to defeat him several times but not destroy him. He had to crush a revolt in Africa (encouraged by Constantinople) and then defeat an Ostrogothic invasion of Italy itself. He was by now forced to buy barbarian fighting men from any source and on any terms, often with personal promises, and even grants of land.

To defend Italy, Stilicho had to strip Britain and the Rhine frontier of troops, and at New Year 407 multiple barbarian invaders crossed the frozen Rhine into Gaul virtually unopposed, never to be expelled again. For this, Stilicho's political enemies in the Senate contrived to have him condemned and executed on the weak emperor's orders, whereupon thousands of his loyal barbarian troops, fearing for themselves and their families, fled over to join Alaric. With Stilicho removed, nothing could prevent Alaric from besieging and finally sacking Rome in 410.

The East had rid itself of the menace of Alaric by propelling him westwards, but this did not free it from other barbarian dangers. What Alaric's Visigoths could do, others could imitate. A new revolt broke out in 399 among the recently-settled Ostrogothic federates. Gainas, the general sent to suppress it, mistrusted the government and was himself of Gothic origin and the commander of other Gothic federate troops. The two Gothic groups joined forces, marched on Constantinople and occupied it, with Gainas dictating his terms to the emperor. However, he was met by a violent anti-Gothic, popular backlash and total hostility from the civil government. Having achieved nothing, he attempted a clumsy withdrawal from the capital in which many Goths and their families were massacred by the mob. Those that escaped were later defeated by loyal units (also commanded by a Goth).

These events had a profound effect on the civilian ruling circles in Constantinople. Henceforth they were determined to keep a firm grip on imperial power and curb ambitious generals, especially those of Gothic origin, even though many were entirely loyal. For several years Goths were excluded from top commands, armies were thinned in numbers, and care was taken to avoid any new settlements of barbarian federates. The Praetorian Prefect, Anthemius, the acknowledged leader of the state, invested instead in strengthening the defences on the Danube frontier, building a new and massive belt of land walls to protect Constantinople, its emperor and government, from both barbarian invasions and its own potentially dangerous armies.

The exclusion of Gothic generals did not last long. With the federate crises past, and a growing external threat from the Huns, able professional commanders such as Plinta, Aspar and Areobindus once again rose to the top *Magister* posts. The fact that they were divorced from any federate or tribal power base (unlike Alaric and Gainas) made them acceptable. They remained what they had been in the previous century—loyal members of the Roman ruling class.

The really farsighted achievement of the Eastern empire during this period was not so much the weakening of the power of the army, as the institutionalising of it within a central ruling establishment at Constantinople, which included the palace and civil bureaucracy. The Eastern field army, about 100,000 strong, was already divided into five regional mobile groups, and the commands carefully balanced between men of Gothic and Roman origin. Two of these groups—the Praesental armies—were stationed in the vicinity of Constantinople and their commanders, of whatever background, were senior members of the senate and members of the emperor's inner council of state, the Consistory.

Any successful, ambitious general was faced with a choice and a temptation. He could use external military violence to try to dominate the emperor at Constantinople, perhaps even making himself emperor, or at least military dictator. Or he could use the army's indispensability and natural leverage within the legitimate, established power structure where there was a place for him at the top table.

Gainas had attempted the first option and had been ruined. Other military leaders overwhelmingly chose the second. Though politically powerful, the army was only one of several competing, but also interlocking, forces around the throne. To break out of this careful web of power risked losing everything. Certainly, there were bitter conflicts within the Constantinople establishment. For many years the deficiencies of the pious and bookish emperor Theodosius II (408–450) were heavily compensated by his dominating sister Pulcheria, who did everything possible to keep power within the palace and the imperial family rather than the civil ministers and generals. But even she had to negotiate with these other power centres.

The solidarity of the inner establishment was strikingly demonstrated when confronted by the end of an imperial dynasty, when all the old threats of factional coup, military violence and even civil war reared their heads in the struggle to place a new emperor on the throne. Aware of what each stood to lose, palace, bureaucracy, army and, later, church found ways to fight their conflicts behind closed doors and then present an agreed imperial choice to be acclaimed by the senate, the troops, the people and the wider world.

This orderly transmission of imperial power was achieved in the elevation of Marcian in 450, Leo in 457 and Anastasius in 491, all of them dynastic breaks. Through these precedents, buttressed by an increasingly elaborate ceremony of emperor-making, violent coups and civil wars became the exception. Even if a declared rebel succeeded in gaining wide support outside, he still had to cash in his imperial claims in the capital itself, in the face of the central establishment and the city's virtually impregnable defences: if he did not already enjoy powerful allies within the city this was a daunting task.

Thus, an important factor in the durability of the establishment was simply the acknowledged geographical concentration of power and authority in a single capital, Constantinople, which was in every sense what Rome had once been. The emergence of a viable, rival power base was made very difficult, and this, as much as the city's strategic position and fortifications, contributed heavily to the stability and survival of the Eastern state.

Of all the elements in the establishment, stability was most steadfastly provided by the civil bureaucracy, which provided experience, statecraft and continuity. They kept the impersonal, administrative machine functioning even during violent conflicts within the palace, or purges of this or that faction. These senatorial mandarins, in fact, represented a new service aristocracy created by Constantine. Frequently of modest origins, they owed their power and status not to birth or landed wealth, but entirely to government service. Consequently, regardless of whether a particular emperor was strong or weak, they took great care to uphold and strengthen the imperial authority itself, since their careers, and hence their prosperity, completely depended on it.

In contrast, the great Western senatorial clans such as the Anicii and Scipiones were only concerned to husband their already huge accumulated family wealth, and treated high state positions as no more than honorific perquisites. Part of the East's undoubtedly greater financial muscle, therefore, was due not just to its inherently greater wealth but also to these mandarins' more honest management of the tax machine, even when it bore on their own aspiring social order.

In the West, the response to the problem of a weak unmilitary emperor was quite different. Real power was concentrated in a military strongman such as Stilicho who ruled on his behalf and enjoyed extraordinary authority, making appointments and issuing laws in the emperor's name. The long reign of the feeble Honorius, the multiple military emergencies and the need to raise and move armies rapidly made this new ruling figure indispensable. After a few years of turmoil the general Constantius stepped into this new position, now vaguely designated 'Patrician' and perhaps better described as military dictator or *generalissimo*. After him came Aetius. Both were patriotic and energetic rulers but had no legally acknowledged position beyond their monopoly of military force, and no regular way of transferring their power to a successor. Each had to intrigue or fight his way to dominant power, which was destructive and destabilising.

Inevitably they came to depend more on their personal popularity and prestige among the troops, whom they recruited and paid. A gulf steadily grew up between the real power of the warlord with his army, and the symbolic, legal authority with the emperor in his palace. During the invasion of Italy, Stilicho had persuaded Honorius to shift the imperial capital from Milan to the safe refuge of Ravenna, creating a geographical split in addition to the political one.

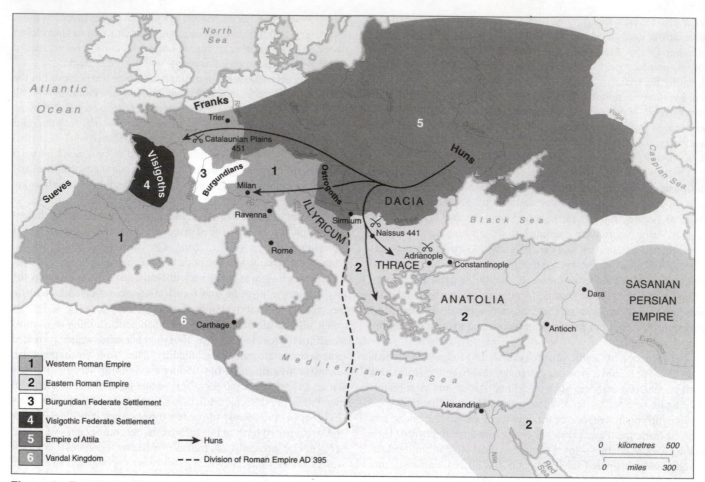

Figure 1 By 450, the Western empire was already a patchwork of barbarian settlements whereas the East retained its integrity.

Constantius achieved a degree of stability in the West, but at enormous cost. Visigoths, Burgundians, Franks, Suevi and Vandals were all settled as federates on large tracts of Gaul and Spain, and were evolving into Germanic kingdoms under only the most nominal Roman overlordship. Constantius and Aetius skillfully exploited their rivalries to maintain some ascendancy. But having relinquished control of so much taxable land and its populations, the regular Roman armies were only one force among many, and no responsible leader could do more than hold the balance, and avoid risking this force if possible.

The Hun menace took on an entirely new dimension with Attila, who had unified them under a single king and subjected all the remaining tribes to Hun rule. His object was not land to settle, but plunder, tribute and glory, and once again the blow fell initially on the East. His hordes ravaged the Balkans three times in the 440s, sacking and ruining many major cities and enslaving their populations. The Roman armies that met him in the field were repeatedly beaten by his cavalry, but he was always deterred by Constantinople whose defences he could not storm. After each invasion he had to be bought off by an increasingly ignominious 'treaty' and larger annual payments, involving heavier taxation of the senatorial classes. In all, the East paid him about nine tons of gold, until the new emperor Marcian finally tore up the treaties and defied him.

Yet here, the two great resources of the East came to the rescue: the impassable fortifications of Constantinople and the enormous taxable wealth of the Asiatic provinces—Anatolia, Syria, Palestine, Egypt. So long as this great land gate was kept shut and so long as these provinces remained secure—meaning peaceful relations with Persia—Attila could always be bought off and much of the Balkan territories temporarily lost without mortal damage to the empire.

Relations with Persia were always a crucial consideration if the empire was to avoid the perils of fighting on two frontiers simultaneously. Unlike other potential enemies, Persia was a centralised, sophisticated state, and both empires were continually involved in a chess game of military and diplomatic manoeuvres which at intervals broke down into open war. In set battle the Romans could usually win, but at quite huge logistical costs. The 1,400-mile frontier zone along the Euphrates was already the most expensive in terms of providing troops and resources. The danger was not so much that Persia would conquer the Roman provinces, as that they would disrupt the whole delicate defensive system of Arab alliances and force the empire to a great commitment of forces, imperilling other frontiers.

But, although Persia tried to take advantage of the empire's difficulties elsewhere, its war aims were limited and it was usually amenable to negotiation. After nearly twenty years of peace, a brief Persian attack in 441 was halted and led to a new treaty involving Roman payments. At the same time, Persia's ambitions were severely checked by pressure from their own northern enemies, the Ephthalite horse peoples, akin to the Huns, who were tacitly encouraged by Constantinople. Whatever martial propaganda they

134

still broadcast to their peoples, the two empires gradually came to accept the advantages of avoiding costly and unrewarding wars, and sought if possible to resolve conflicts by other means. As a result, a mature and structured diplomacy became as important as the military strategy.

Finally, after suffering heavier casualties in battle for diminishing returns of plunder, Attila decided to cut his losses and invade westward. Here Aetius, with all his carefully cultivated barbarian friendships, performed a diplomatic miracle in uniting and commanding the mutually hostile Germanic kingdoms in a great coalition to stop Attila in 451. After a huge and bloody battle on the Catalaunian plains of northern Gaul, Attila was forced for the first time to retreat. The next year he mounted an abortive invasion of Italy. Soon afterwards, he died suddenly in a drunken stupor. Within a short time his always personal and charismatic 'empire' collapsed.

In the West, Aetius was immediately concerned to disperse the more numerous and powerful Germanic armies as quickly as possible. But now that the main barbarian threat seemed removed, he was treacherously murdered by the emperor Valentinian III (425–455) who had long hated him. In revenge, Aetius's partisans assassinated Valentinian shortly afterwards, ending the Theodosian dynasty.

The next *generalissimo* figure, Ricimer, was himself a barbarian and naturally well-qualified to deal with the overwhelmingly barbarian army and allies. He was related both to the Visigoth and Sueve royal houses, and very willing to allow more federate settlements. Ricimer was a leader spanning two worlds. He saw the Roman empire more as a prestigious, unifying symbol than a political reality, and he set up and deposed puppet emperors at will. In the end it was only logical that a barbarian king should step into the ruling role of patrician and *generalissimo*. When that happened there was no need to retain even a figurehead emperor in the West. In 476 the barbarian king Odovacer forced the emperor Romulus Augustulus to abdicate, and sent an embassy to Constantinople declaring that he would henceforth rule as the viceroy of the Eastern emperor. The fiction of a single united Roman empire was still retained.

The East had tried, and partially succeeded, in arranging the fragments of Attila's old empire to its advantage, but it had been forced to accept two large blocs of Ostrogoths, formerly subjects of Attila, as federates in Illyricum (Yugoslavia) and Thrace (Bulgaria-Romania). These were a destabilising element, each too strong to be defeated by a single Roman field army. In the confused reign of Zeno (474–491) all the dangerous elements erupted again: open conflict in the imperial family, civil wars for the throne, rebellion by the Gothic federates. At one point there was fighting within the capital itself. There seemed a real danger that the Ostrogoths would carve out permanent kingdoms for themselves in the way this had happened in the West.

For a time, the central establishment lost control, but they had several strong advantages. There was always a strong core of regular Roman troops to balance the federates, and they continued to be steadily recruited. All the soldiers, Roman or federate, could only be paid from the central treasuries, which were a potent lever

in negotiations, as were timely bribes of gold. The Goths also suffered periodic food shortages which the imperial government, with its network of cities and supply depots, naturally exploited. The two Gothic blocs were often in competition and could easily be played off against each other. Their aims were opportunistic and their long-term goals uncertain. One king, Theoderic (471–526), wanted larger, more secure territories for his people, while the other, Strabo, aimed at a top Roman command and a seat at the centre of government.

By the time Zeno had managed to crush or conciliate his other domestic enemies, by adroit and unscrupulous manoeuvring, Strabo was dead and all the Goths followed Theoderic. In 488, with only one king to deal with, Zeno played the masterstroke. Instead of poor and precarious lands in the Balkans, he invited Theoderic to take Italy from Odovacer. Theoderic did so, finally freeing the East of the federate problem.

It was left to the next emperor Anastasius (491–518) to consolidate these gains. Himself a civil bureaucrat who knew the government machinery intimately, he overhauled and improved the entire fiscal system to produce considerably greater sums for the treasury without injuring the mass of taxpayers. With these funds he expanded the armies by raising pay, built new defences, revived and repopulated much of the Balkans, and fought a successful war against Persia, still leaving a healthy surplus. It was with these great resources that Justinian was soon to embark on his ambitious schemes of reconquest.

The East had certain long-term advantages: a strategically placed capital, shorter vulnerable frontiers, a wealthier agricultural base. But it demanded a high order of statecraft to overcome all the external and internal threats of the fifth century. Individually, its leaders were no more skilful than their Western counterparts, but they managed to evolve institutions and practices which applied these skills and perpetuated them. The Constantinople establishment; the constitutional rituals of imperial succession; the integration of the top army commands; the opposition to federate settlements; the centralised pool of administrative, fiscal and diplomatic experience—all these enabled the East to avoid the unravelling process of diminishing control which occurred in the West.

For Further Reading

A.H.M. Jones, *The Later Roman Empire* (2 vols, Oxford University Press, 1990); J.B. Bury, *History of The Later Roman Empire,* (Dover paperbacks, 1958); R.C. Blockley, *East Roman Foreign Policy* (ARCA, 1992); J.H.W.G. Liebeschuetz, *From Diocletian to the Arab Conquest,* (Oxford University Press, 1990); J.H. W.G. Liebeschuetz, *Barbarians and Bishops: Army, Church and State in the Age of Arcadius and Chrysostom* (Oxford University Press, 1991); C. Mango, *Byzantium. The Empire of New Rome* (London, 1980).

STEPHEN WILLIAMS and GERARD FRIELL are also the authors of *Theodosius: the Empire at Bay* (Batsford, 1994).

The New Maya

Having dispelled the myth of a model society led by gentle priest-kings, scholars are piecing together a fresh picture of the rise and fall of a complex civilization.

T. Patrick Culbert

The Maya inscriptions treat primarily of chronology, astronomy . . . and religious matters. . . . They tell no story of kingly conquests, recount no deeds of imperial achievement . . . indeed they are so utterly impersonal, so completely nonindividualistic, that it is even probable that the name glyphs of specific men and women were never recorded upon the Maya monuments.

Sylvanus Morley
The Ancient Maya (1946)

When Archaeology debuted in 1948, the views of Sylvanus Morley and J. Eric S. Thompson, the leading Mayanists at the time, prevailed. The majority of the Maya, they believed, were devout peasants who practiced slash-and-burn agriculture and lived in small, sparsely populated settlements on the outskirts of temple precincts. They were guided by priest-kings, gentle men without egos, devoted to prayer and temple building. This utopian view of Maya civilization persisted until a new generation of scholars took to the field on the heels of the Second World War.

Unlike their predecessors, concerned only with temples and tombs, postwar archaeologists wanted to study the lives of common people, whose labor had built the great sites. In the early 1950s Tulane, Harvard, and the University of Pennsylvania, among other institutions, undertook the first systematic mapping of large portions of sites like Tikal in the Petén region of Guatemala. These projects revealed thousands of small structures surrounding pyramid complexes, proving that Maya cities were bustling metropolises, not vacant ceremonial centers reserved for a priestly class.

Following the gradual decipherment of the hieroglyphs, which began in the 1960s with the pioneering work of Tatiana Proskouriakoff of the Carnegie Institution and Russian epigrapher Yuri Knorosov, the mystical, spiritual society the ancient Maya were thought to have enjoyed began to crumble. Though decipherment of Maya inscriptions is far from complete—epigrapher Peter Mathews of the University of Calgary estimates that 60 percent of the hieroglyphs can now be read with some certainty—we know the names of those responsible for the great buildings and of those buried in royal tombs. What is clear from the inscriptions is that Maya rulers were not devoted to esoteric matters and calendar keeping, but rather to self-aggrandizement. Egomaniacs all, they warred incessantly and sacrificed prisoners to build prestige.

Based on settlement pattern analysis, archaeologists estimate that by the Late Classic, ca. A.D. 600, Maya population had reached a density of 600 people per square mile across a 36,000-square-mile area in the forested lowlands of northern Guatemala and adjacent parts of Mexico and Belize. This is a staggering figure, comparable to the most heavily populated parts of rural China today. Slash-and-burn agriculture alone could not have supported populations this dense. To feed the multitudes, the Maya had to turn to new agricultural techniques that included shortening the fallow cycle to put more land under cultivation, terracing, and cultivating the wetlands that make up 40 percent of the southern Lowlands. The exact mix of techniques used is still a matter of debate.

Population estimates also figure in our interpretation of the mid-ninth-century Maya collapse. We now know that populations grew at an exponential rate for centuries, peaking around A.D. 750. Within a few decades, however, both urban and rural populations plummeted. By 850, two-thirds of the people living in the Southern Lowlands were gone, and most of the remainder disappeared by 1100. Archaeologists agree that to point to any single factor as the cause of the collapse would be naive. Most concur that centuries of uninterrupted growth put the Maya in a perilous position from which almost any disaster—drought, erosion, or social disorder—could have triggered a decline.

There has been a recent surge of interest in household archaeology aimed at informing us about the lives of non-elite people. The vast majority, perhaps 90 percent, of the Maya populace was devoted to some level of agricultural production, but there is increasing evidence of specialization in the manufacture of everyday items such as pottery. There are also indications of a middle class of specialists whose status was above those of full-time farmers.

Some of the most exciting work is in the area of Maya political organization, made possible by continued progress in hieroglyphic decipherment. In the 1970s, it was generally thought that a few great Maya cities served as the centers of regional states. By the late 1980s many scholars began to view the very large centers as city-states with limited areas of political control. A minority argued for larger political units. Epigraphers Simon Martin and Nikolai Grube have discovered phrases within inscriptions that indicate hierarchical relationships among Maya rulers of different cities (see ARCHAEOLOGY, November/December 1995, pp. 41–46). They see Late Classic history as a competition between two superpowers, Tikal and Calakmul, a massive site in Mexico just to the north of the Guatemalan border. In a masterful political strategy, Calakmul amassed allies in the sixth and seventh centuries who attacked Tikal and greatly diminished its power. Not until a new ruler (known as Ruler A) took the Tikal throne in 682, after his father had been captured and sacrificed by one of Calakmul's allies, did Tikal begin to recover. Ruler A's major accomplishment was to capture and sacrifice the ruler of Calakmul. He went on to build the two giant temples at the ends of Tikal's great plaza and a number of the other buildings at the site today.

The late Linda Schele probably did more than anyone to bring the results of Maya hieroglyphic decipherment to public and professional attention. In a series of books with various coauthors, Schele vividly presented the lives and world view of the ancient Maya. Like a growing number of Mayanists in recent years, she focused on ideology as a mainspring for society. The Maya view of the universe underscored the actions of powers and principalities, and the ruler, as mediator between subjects, gods, and ancestors, maintained the universe. Her most recent book, *Code of Kings,* "recounts" the funeral of Palenque's Pacal (A.D. 603–683), whose tomb in the Temple of the Inscriptions is perhaps the most famous of all Maya royal burials.

Some scholars have taken a more materialistic view of Maya rulers. Ideology, they say, could be manipulated to suit the purposes of those in power and was backed with spears for those who chose not to believe. We now know that war was commonplace in the Classic period and that it was accompanied by the capture and sacrifice of prisoners amid much fanfare. But were sacrifices the chief reason that the Maya went to war or were they simply the ceremonial trappings of campaigns motivated by the desire for tribute and territory? Perhaps the two were inextricably linked.

Despite differences in opinion and approaches inherent in the wide variety of disciplines involved in the study of the Maya, it is possible for scholars to integrate their data in an effort to understand these ancient people. Copán in western Honduras, the first major Maya site to be extensively excavated since the decipherment of hieroglyphic writing, provides an example of a happy marriage of archaeology, epigraphy, and art history.

Research by a variety of institutions and investigators has been under way there for more than 30 years. Archaeology has provided information about not only the site itself, but the whole Copán Valley, along with indications of ecological stress that resulted in the erosion of the surrounding hillsides, which may have contributed to the site's eventual abandonment.

At the main site, archaeological investigations and the study of inscriptions and iconography have provided a vivid image of elite life and a history of victories and defeats. Most stunning, perhaps, of all the discoveries are those that have been made in the tunnels dug into centuries of early construction underlying the Temple of the Hieroglyphic Stairway and the Acropolis. Just a few years ago, it was thought that the early fifth-century ruler Yax K'uk Mo' (Blue Green Quetzal Macaw), repeatedly acknowledged by later kings to have been the founder of the Copán dynasty, was either mythical or a vaguely remembered leader of a small village that once stood at the site. How wrong these guesses were. Deep beneath the Acropolis, archaeologists have uncovered buildings dating to the time of this reign, including a stela erected by his son and a small temple containing what are probably the remains of Yax K'uk Mo' himself.

Even with the enormous advances that have been made in the last few years, there are a multitude of questions still to be answered. We need to know far more about how commoners, who supplied food for the upper classes and labor for building the great structures, were integrated into the larger social picture. Was most land held privately by individuals or families, or communally by neighborhoods or villages, a proportion of whose production was collected as taxes? Or were there great estates held by Maya nobles, farmed by serfs or corvée labor? And what of the religious life of the commoners? Even in small groups of structures there are flat-topped pyramids that were once topped by perishable religious structures. Were the ceremonies that took place there simply a small-scale reflection of those performed in the great temples, or were there whole cults largely confined to poorer people? Were the ceremonies conducted by local lineage heads, or by "parish priests" who came to conduct rites that demanded special training or an equivalent of ordination? The crux of these questions is the extent to which the lives of the majority of the Maya population were separate from those of the upper classes in kind as well as in degree.

It no longer seems profitable to look at each site in isolation. Beyond the great cities, there are hundreds of Maya sites, and neighborhoods within large sites, of intermediate size that have stone temples and palaces whose construction involved considerable investments of labor, but which lack the inscriptions that would tell us about their ties to the great rulers. Those who governed these sites were certainly elite, but who were they? Were they members of the great royal families, sons and cousins who had been granted small domains in the interlands? Or were they local lords, ruling areas that had belonged to their families long before the mighty became mighty? We know from the inscriptions that ruling families visited each other, intermarried, and fought. But if there were long-distance alliances and enmities, how did they work? How strong were superpowers

ANNUAL EDITIONS

such as Calakmul and Tikal? Texts suggest that rulers in allied cities acknowledged the authority of the great centers, but how dependent they were is still unclear. Did they participate willingly in political campaigns or did superpower lords have to beg, wheedle, or threaten them into joining their causes? Answers to these questions can only come from research by investigators with different interests.

Today, Maya sites attract crowds of tourists. Roads are being opened to previously inaccessible sites such as Calakmul and Uaxactún. While the environmental impact of the new roads is a matter of concern, tourism may be far easier on the landscape than cutting and burning the forest for agriculture, as is currently being done. The Classic Maya collapse may be an example of the price paid for mismanaging the environment. Those concerned with managing the remaining tracts of tropical forest would do well to learn from the experience of this ancient people.

T. PATRICK CULBERT is a professor of anthropology at the University of Arizona.

From *Archaeology,* September/October 1998, pp. 47–51. Copyright © 1998 by T. Patrick Culbert. Reprinted by permission of the author.

The Ideal of Unity

Russell Chamberlin examines the origins and development of Europe's persistent vision of unity from the birth of the Holy Roman Empire to its fall.

RUSSELL CHAMBERLIN

'Neither holy, nor Roman, nor an empire'. Voltaire's gibe about the Holy Roman Empire was literally true but, like all such glib gibes missed the essential point. For a thousand years people believed it existed or thought it ought to exist. For a thousand years, as they tore at each other in fratricidal wars, Europeans nevertheless nursed the idea of a unity that would bind, not destroy, their racial identities. The Treaty of Rome of 1957, which established the European Economic Community, might lack the drama of the events of Christmas Day, 800, but it shared the same dynamic, and the Treaty may yet prove more durable than the crown.

On that day, Karl der Grosse, King of the Franks, King of the Lombards, Patrician of Rome, better known to English and French posterity as Charlemagne, had bent in prayer in the basilica of St Peter's in Rome. He was startled (some said later) when, without warning, Pope Leo III advanced and placed a circlet of gold on his head. The congregation, in a well-rehearsed chorus, acclaimed him as Roman law prescribed, 'To Carolus Augustus, crowned by God, mighty and pacific emperor, be life and victory'.

The giant silver-haired Frank rose to his feet, towering above the slighter-built Latins and, according to his biographer, Einhard, protested—just a little too much, in the view of posterity. His counsellor, the Englishman Alcuin, who had wide contacts in Rome, must have been well aware of the tide moving in Rome and had surely informed his master of the plans to revive the Roman empire with him at its head. Indeed, after the acclamation the rituals of coronation went smoothly, suggesting that all had been prepared long beforehand. And whatever his private thoughts, the new Emperor voluntarily took part in the ceremonies that followed.

Whoever stage-managed the event in St Peter's had done his work well by arranging that 'acclamation' by the Roman people and clergy. Even in the most dictatorial and tyrannical days of the classical empire the emperor was in theory chosen—acclaimed—by the army and the people, and the idea that the Roman empire was a *res publica* had never been abandoned, even when it had become a formality.

Charlemagne's protests were diplomatic and political: he was objecting to the time and manner of Leo's act and its heavy symbolism. Moreover, he realised that the man who bestowed a crown could take it back. Charlemagne was having none of that. When, eleven years later, he made his last surviving son Louis co-emperor it was he who, personally, placed the crown on the young man's head. Centuries later, Napoleon took the hint and, in making himself 'emperor' of the French, took care to crown himself.

There was another reason for Charlemagne to protest: Leo's action was illegal. There could be only one *imperator* on earth and he (or, to be exact, she, Irene) was already reigning in Constantinople. Strictly speaking, the Roman Empire—the empire of Augustus, Nero, Virgil and Tacitus—endured until 1453 when the last true Roman emperor fell beneath Turkish swords. Leo's act began the long degradation of the once awesome title, so that, in due course, there would emerge an 'emperor' of Austria, an 'emperor' of Mexico, of Haiti, and, ultimate absurdity, the British style, 'king-emperor', adopted after the acquisition of the Indian Empire even as, ironically, the mighty empire itself would dwindle down to a 'loose federation of German princes under the presidency of the House of Habsburg'.

The Byzantines derided the coronation of Charlemagne. To them he was simply another barbarian general with ideas above his station. Indeed, he took care never to style himself *Imperator Romanorum*. His jurists, dredging through the detritus of empire, came up with a title which met with his approval: *Romanum gubernas imperium* 'Governing the Roman Empire'. The resounding title of this first of the post-classical Western Emperors was 'Charles, Most Serene Augustus, crowned by God, great and merciful Emperor, governing the Roman empire and by the mercy of God, King of the Lombards and the Franks'.

Although illegal, the coronation and acclamation were perhaps inevitable. In the Western world, the rule of law had broken down. Alcuin, a stickler for law and conventions, gave his opinion:

> Upon you alone reposes the whole salvation of the Churches of Christ. You are the avenger of crime, the guide of the wanderers, the comforter of the mourners, the exaltation of the righteous.

A thousand years later, James Bryce, the great historian of the Holy Roman Empire, agreed that a vacuum had been created in Europe by the rise of Byzantium. The coronation of Charlemagne 'was the revolt of the ancient Western capital against a daughter who had become a mistress, an exercise of the sacred right of insurrection justified by the weakness and wickedness of the Byzantine'. That wickedness had plumbed new depths a few years earlier when the reigning emperor Constantine had been blinded and, deposed by his mother who claimed to reign as 'emperor': to Western apologists, the Byzantine throne was vacant and the Frankish monarch was merely taking up the sceptre laid down by the Latin Caesars. One of the great myths of history is the portrayal of the 'Fall of the Roman Empire' as a Hollywood-type scenario in which shaggy, skin-clad Germanic 'barbarians' hurl themselves upon elegant, toga-clad 'Romans', raping, murdering, destroying what they could not eat, wear or carry off. In reality the 'barbarians' were inferior only in culture, not intelligence. They could, and did, respond to the majesty of the Empire. For a people without written records, that Empire must have seemed, quite literally, eternal: an almost supernatural structure around which the world always had and always would revolve. But they realised that behind this outward show was a hugely complex human system that had brought stability out of chaos. In the early 5th century, the Visigothic chieftain, Arhalhauf, spoke for most of his fellow barbarians:

> It was at first my wish to destroy the Roman name and erect in its place a Gothic empire. But when experience taught me that the untameable barbarism of the Goths would not suffer them to live under the sway of law I chose the glory of renewing and maintaining by Gothic strength the fame of Rome.

The Franks themselves had entered history fighting alongside the Roman army at one of its last great battles, that of Chalons in 451 A.D. when it turned back the invasion of Attila the Hun. The captain of the Frankish host was Merovech, who founded the first Frankish dynasty, the Merovings, but they were gradually shouldered aside by their own Mayors of the Palace. The dynasty ended bloodlessly in 751, when Charlemagne's father Pippin appealed to Rome, asking, in effect, who should wear the crown: he who was the puppet or he who truly ruled? Pope Zarachias came down in Pippin's favour. He thus began that link between pope and Germanic king that was to dominate the notion of the Western Christian empire for centuries.

Meanwhile, a debt had been contracted and four years later the papacy sent Pippin the bill. In January 754 Pope Stephen and a small entourage braved the Alps in mid-winter to throw himself at the feet of Pippin and plead for help against Aistulf, King of the Lombards, who had dared to seize the property of the Church. Pippin avoided the tricky business of precedence between pope and monarch by sending his fourteen-year-old son to escort Stephen to the palace, thus providing posterity with its first glimpse of the future Charlemagne.

The historiography of Charlemagne is tantalising. Later, he had his own biographer, in his devoted secretary and architect Einhard. But though Einhard declared he would record nothing through hearsay, he also glossed over facts unfavourable to his hero. The surviving evidence of the development of the relationship between the papal and Frankish courts is one-sided, for while all the popes' letters survived in the Frankish archives, the letters from Pippin and his sons have disappeared from the Vatican, probably looted on the orders of Napoleon.

After Charlemagne's debut, little is heard of him directly until the death of his father in 768. He emerged on the European stage with his capture of the Lombard capital of Pavia in 774, thereby acquiring the Iron Crown of the Lombards and establishing the Frankish control beyond the Alps. The young king began to lay the foundations of what was to become an imperial regime and which, eventually, would provide a blueprint for Europe for centuries.

Distance and communication were the greatest problems he faced, as for all medieval monarchs. He tackled these by establishing *missi domini,* trusted counsellors with delegated powers who penetrated every part of his enormous realm, which ran from the Elbe to the Tiber, conveying his will in documents known as 'capitularies'. These provide a means for historians to follow the thought processes by which he governed his expanding realm. Named after the articles or capitula into which they were divided, each was nominally concerned with a specific subject but tended to be wide-ranging, as though the King were saying, 'Oh, yes that reminds me . . .'. Nothing was too small: the provision of a dowry for a young girl; the number and type of tools to be kept in a manor. Nothing was too large: the composition of the Host in the mass; the conduct of priests.

The deeply religious Charlemagne, through his relationship with a succession of six popes, strove to advance the ideal of a theocratic state governed by a priest and a king in harmony. But there was no doubt as to which he considered the dominant partner. When Pope Leo III announced that a vial of the Precious Blood had been found in Mantua the sceptical King ordered an enquiry. Nothing more was heard of the miraculous substance. His restless, questing, creative mind stimulated the so-called Carolingian renaissance, that sudden flowering of learning which was doomed to disappear after his death. But it left its permanent mark, in the form of the Carolingian miniscule script, which replaced the ugly, spiky Merovingian script, and was adopted by the humanist Poggio Bracciolini in the fifteenth century and through him became the model for all fonts of print.

The King's transmutation into Emperor made little personal difference to him. He did not fall into the trap of trying to pass himself off as a Roman and in so doing losing contact with his roots. Only twice did he wear the robes of the Patrician, both times by direct request of the pope. He dressed and acted in a manner indistinguishable from his subjects. He took literally the precept 'where the emperor is, there is Rome' and his beloved city of Aachen became the Rome of the North.

Charlemagne's imprint on Aachen remains evident over a thousand years later. The city's *rathaus* is built on the foundations of his palace, making it the world's longest occupied seat of administration. Even more astonishing is his chapel, designed by Einhard on the basis of the mystic octagon. Nothing has changed in its interior. The Emperor Frederick Barbarossa (r. 1152–90) provided an immense candelabra to celebrate Charlemagne's canonisation in 1165: the Emperor Henry II (r. 1002–24) provided the golden front of the altar, but nothing else has been added. The mezzanine gallery, on which the throne is placed, is approached by a flight of stairs which could be in a modest town church. The throne itself, composed of plain slabs of stone, is unchanged; Thirty emperors have been crowned in it: each resisted the temptation to add his symbols to its simple expression of majesty.

With the death of Charlemagne in 814, cracks in the state opened up in the Empire, as warlords struggled for dominance. Yet the memory continued of that compact made on Christmas Day 800, and those boasting Carolingian blood, no matter how remote or illegitimate, advanced their claims over the rest. But without effect. It seemed that the Empire was at an end before it had started.

It was revived only by bizarre events in Rome in the mid-tenth century. By this time, Rome was on the edge of collapse. The aqueducts had long since failed, forcing the population, now shrunk to less than 20,000, to huddle in the unhealthy lower areas. Bandit families holed up in the once-great buildings, fighting each other and preying on the populace. The Donation of Constantine, an eighth-century forgery according to which the first Christian Emperor had supposedly granted the Church vast territories in central Italy, had turned the papacy into a territorial monarchy, to be fought for as any other secular prize. The papacy itself was in a state of grotesque degradation, with popes murdering or being murdered, placed on the throne by their paramours, hurled off it by their rivals. Two extraordinary women ruled both the city and the papacy, Theodora and her daughter Marozia, the probable model for the later legend of Pope Joan. The sober papal historian, Cardinal Baronius, writing in the sixteenth century, labelled this period the 'Pornocracy'. In 961 the Apostolic throne was occupied by Marozia's grandson, a dissolute twenty-year-old called John XII. Threatened by a Lombard warlord, Berengar, he summoned a Germanic monarch, the Saxon Otto I, to his aid, promising that crown of empire which—it was now believed—only a pope could bestow.

Like Charlemagne before his own imperial coronation, Otto was already a figure of European stature. At Lechfeld (955) near Augsburg, his army had destroyed an immense army of Magyars, true barbarians as murderous as the Huns. It was claimed that his warriors hailed him as *imperator* after the battle: inherently unlikely but testament to how he was seen.

Otto came at John's summons but he had no illusions about the fickle, violent Romans. He instructed his sword-bearer, Ansfried:

When I kneel today at the grave of the Apostle, stand behind me with the sword. I know only too well what my ancestors have experienced from these faithless Romans.

But all passed smoothly. John listened contritely to the lecture on morals by the pious Saxon, and made specious promises. Yet the moment Otto withdrew from Rome to commence the campaign against Berengar, John offered the crown of empire—to Berengar. That failing, he peddled it round, with no takers. It is difficult to interpret John's lunatic actions. It is possible that he wanted to show that he could make and unmake an emperor at will. It is possible that he was mentally unbalanced. Even his *curia* revolted. Otto convened a synod

to which the pope was summoned to account for himself. John dashed off a contemptuous response ignoring the emperor: 'To all the bishops. We hear that you wish to make another pope. If you do, I excommunicate you by almighty God and you have no power to ordain no one or celebrate mass. Ponderously humorous, Otto urged him to improve his morals and his grammar: 'We thought that two negatives made a positive' but followed this with a threat: unless the pope presented himself, he would be deposed. This too was ignored. At the synod a catalogue of John's crimes was presented, ranging from rape to sacrilege.

On December 1st, Pope John XII was formally deposed and a nominee of Otto's took his place. John ignored this too. In Otto's absence he returned to Rome and took bloody revenge on those who had testified against him and who had remained in the city. How the matter might have ended, with a Roman-born pope calling on the support of a Roman mob, is difficult to speculate—but a cuckold caught the Holy Father *in flagrante* and, enraged, cudgelled him to death.

The blows of the cudgel might have ended the theological debate but it did nothing to resolve the secular one. The Romans had seen their bishop, their prince, deposed by a German; and they rose in revolt. The papal crown was the symbol of Roman sovereignty and, to gain control of that symbol, emperor and city were now prepared to destroy each other and themselves. Otto subjected Rome to a terrible vengeance; but it rose again. Again he smashed it down. Again it rose. And again. The Emperor died and his son Otto II continued to pour out German blood and wealth seeking the double goal of a purified papacy and a Roman crown.

With the approach of the millennium, there was a pause in the cycle of violence. The pope was the pious and learned Sylvester, reputed to be a magician, so versed was he in the sciences. The emperor was his pupil, the youthful Otto III (r. 983–1002) who, with his pope, swore to restore the splendours of the Roman empire infused with Christian belief. He built himself a palace on the Aventine, dressed in the toga, cast a medal with the legend 'Otto Imperator Augustus' and on the reverse the proud claim *Renovatio Imperii Romanorum*. But the Romans rose against him, drove him and his pope out of the city, and reverted to murderous anarchy. He died outside the city in January 1002, not quite twenty-two years of age. Sylvester survived his brilliant but erratic protégé by barely sixteen months. His epitaph summed up the sorrow that afflicted all thoughtful men at the ending of a splendid vision:

The world, on the brink of triumph, its peace now departed, grew contorted in grief and the reeling Church forgot her rest.

The failure of Otto III and Sylvester marked the effective end of the medieval dream of a single state in which an emperor ruled over the bodies of all Christian men, and a pope over their souls. At Canossa in 1077 Pope Gregory VII avenged the deposition of John XII when the Emperor Henry IV was forced to beg for forgiveness in the snow. In 1300 Pope Boniface VIII displayed himself to pilgrims robed in imperial trappings, calling out 'I, I am the emperor'. But he, too, was eventually destroyed.

Looking down through the long perspective of the Holy Roman Empire is a melancholy experience of watching the dream fall apart. The Italians fought endless civic wars under the banner of Guelph or Ghibelline, Pope or Empire, but they were little more than pretexts for strife. Yet as the actual power of the emperor waned, the ideal of the universal monarch increased so that the imperial nadir coincided with its most able apologia, Dante's *De Monarchia*. Henry VII (r. 1312–13) came in 1310 in answer to Dante's summons to resolve the conflict, but became trapped in the complexities of Italian politics and died shamefully.

Dante's call for the risen majesty of empire became its requiem. Nevertheless, in 1354 a Germanic emperor was again summoned to Italy to take the crown and bring peace to a tortured land—but where Henry had come in majesty, the progress of his son Charles IV 'was more as a merchant going to Mass than an emperor going to his throne', as the Florentine merchant Villani observed sardonically. Petrarch, who had implored him to come, joined Villani in condemning him. 'Emperor of the Romans but in name, thou art in truth no more than the king of Bohemia'. But Petrarch was looking back to a mythical Golden Age, while Charles accepted he was living in an Age of Iron. Shrugging off the criticism he returned home and promulgated his Golden Bull, which effectively turned the crown of empire into a German crown.

The last word is perhaps best left to the sardonic Edward Gibbon:

> It is the duty of a patriot to prefer and promote the exclusive interest and glory of his native country; but a philosopher may be permitted to enlarge his views and to consider Europe as one great Republic.

For Further Reading

In 1965, Aachen put on an exhibition, embodied in four volumes edited by Wolfgang Braunfels, *Karl der Grosse: Lebenswerk und Nachleben*, D.A. Bullough, *Age of Charlemagne* (1965); James Bryce, *The Holy Roman Empire*, (8th ed. 1887); Russell Chamberlin, *Charlemagne, Emperor of the Western World*. (2nd ed. 2003); F.L. Ganshof, *Frankish Insitutions under Charlemagne:* trans S. Bruce and Mary Lyon. (1968); Gregorovius, Ferdinand *History of the City of Rome in the Middle Ages*, trans. Annie Hamilton. (1912); Thomas Hodgkin, *Italy and Her Invaders* (1899); Friedrich Heer, *The Holy Roman Empire* (Phoenix, 2003); Horace K. Mann, *The Lives of the Popes in the Early Middle Ages* (1902–32); W. Ullman, *Medieval Papalism* (1949).

RUSSELL CHAMBERLIN is the author of some thirty books on European travel and history. He has been awarded an honorary degree by the University of Surrey.

The Arab Roots of European Medicine

**Wel knew he the olde Esculapius and Deyscorides and eek Rufus
Olde Ypocras, Haly and Galeyn, Serapion, Razi and Avycen, Averrois,
Damascien and Constantyn, Bernard and Gatesden and Gilbertyn.**

DAVID W. TSCHANZ

In the "General Prologue" of *The Canterbury Tales,* Geoffrey Chaucer identifies the authorities used by his "Doctour of Physic" in the . . . lines quoted above. The list includes four Arab physicians: Jesu Haly (Ibn'Isa), Razi (Al-Razi, or Rhazes), Avycen (Ibn Sina, or Avicenna) and Averrois (Ibn Rushd, or Averroes). These four did not make Chaucer's list only to add an exotic flavor to his late-14th-century poetry. Chaucer cited them because they were regarded as among the great medical authorities of the ancient world and the European Middle Ages, physicians whose textbooks were used in European medical schools, and would be for centuries to come. First collecting, then translating, then augmenting and finally codifying the classical Greco-Roman heritage that Europe has lost, Arab physicians of the eighth to eleventh century laid the foundations of the institutions and the science of modern medicine.

After the collapse of the western Roman empire in the fifth century, Europe lost touch with much of its intellectual heritage. Of Greek science, all that remained were Pliny's *Encyclopedia* and Boethius's treatises on logic and mathematics; the Latin library was so limited that European theologians found it nearly impossible to expand their knowledge of their own scriptures.

The center of Europe's new world view became the church, which exerted profound new influences in medicine. Because Christianity emphasized compassion and care for the sick, monastic orders ran fine hospitals—but they did not function as hospitals do today. They were simply places to take seriously ill people, where they were expected to either recover or die as God willed. There were no learned physicians to attend them, only kindly monks who dispensed comfort and the sacraments, but not medicines.

Because the Christian church viewed care of the soul as far more important than care of the body, medical treatment and even physical cleanliness were little valued, and mortification of the flesh was seen as a sign of saintliness. In time, nearly all Europeans came to look upon illness as a condition caused by supernatural forces, which might take the form of diabolical possession. Hence, cures could only be effected by religious means. Every malady had a patron saint to whom prayers were directed by the patient, family, friends and the community. Upper respiratory infections were warded off by a blessing of the throat with crossed candles on the feast of Saint Blaise. Saint Roch became the patron of plague victims. Saint Nicaise was the source of protection against smallpox. Kings, regarded as divinely appointed, were believed to be able to cure scrofula and skin diseases, among other maladies, with the "royal touch."

With the study of disease and of patients neglected, licensed medicine as an independent craft virtually vanished. Those physicians who endured were mostly connected with monasteries and abbeys. But even for them, the generally accepted goal was less to discover causes, or even to heal, than to study the writings of other physicians and comment on their work. In the middle of the seventh century, the Catholic church banned surgery by monks, because it constituted a danger to their souls. Since nearly all of the surgeons of that era were clerics, the decree effectively ended the practice of surgery in Europe.

At roughly the same time, another civilization was rising in the east. The coming of Islam, also in the seventh century (See *Aramco World,* November/December 1991), led to a hundred years of continuous geographical expansion and an unprecedented era of ferment in all branches of learning. The Arabs rapidly melded the various cultures of the Islamic domain, and Arabic—the language of the Qur'an—became the universal language. By the 10th century a single language linked peoples from the Rann of Kutch to the south of France, and Arabic became to the East what Latin and Greek had been to the West—the language of literature, the arts and sciences, and the common tongue of the educated.

Medicine was the first of the Greek sciences to be studied in depth by Islamic scholars. After Plato's Academy was closed in 529, some of its scholars found refuge at the university at Jundishahpur, the old Sassanid capital of Persia, which had also sheltered excommunicated Nestorian Christian scholars—among them physicians—in 431. Persia became part of the Islamic world in 636, and Arab rulers supported the medical school at Jundishahpur; for the next 200 years it was the

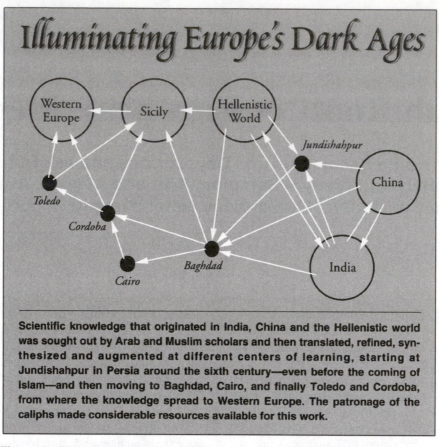

Illuminating Europe's Dark Ages

Scientific knowledge that originated in India, China and the Hellenistic world was sought out by Arab and Muslim scholars and then translated, refined, synthesized and augmented at different centers of learning, starting at Jundishahpur in Persia around the sixth century—even before the coming of Islam—and then moving to Baghdad, Cairo, and finally Toledo and Cordoba, from where the knowledge spread to Western Europe. The patronage of the caliphs made considerable resources available for this work.

Figure 1 Diagram and caption adapted from *The Crest of The Peacock: Non-European Roots of Mathematics* by George Gheverghese Joseph (Penguin Books/ I.B. Tauris) © 1991. Used by permission of Penguin Books Ltd.

greatest center of medical teaching in the Islamic world. There, Islamic physicians first familiarized themselves with the works of Hippocrates, Galen and other Greek physicians. At the same time, they were also exposed to the medical knowledge of Byzantium, Persia, India and China.

Recognizing the importance of translating Greek works into Arabic to make them more widely available, the Abbasid caliphs Harun al-Rashid (786–809) and his son, al-Ma'mun (813–833) established a translation bureau in Baghdad, the Bayt al-Hikmah, or House of Wisdom, and sent embassies to collect Greek scientific works in the Byzantine Empire. (See *Aramco World*, May/June 1982.) This ushered in the first era in Islamic medicine, whose effects we feel today: the period of translation and compilation.

The most important of the translators was Hunayn ibn Ishaq al-'Ibadi (809–73), who was reputed to have been paid for his manuscripts by an equal weight of gold. He and his team of translators rendered the entire body of Greek medical texts, including all the works of Galen, Oribasius, Paul of Aegin, Hippocrates and the *Materia Medica* of Dioscorides, into Arabic by the end of the ninth century. These translations established the foundations of a uniquely Arab medicine.

Muslim medical practice largely accepted Galen's premise of humors, which held that the human body was made up of the same four elements that comprise the world—earth, air, fire and water. These elements could be mixed in various proportions,

and the differing mixtures gave rise to the different temperaments and "humors." When the body's humors were correctly balanced, a person was healthy. Sickness was due not to supernatural forces but to humoral imbalance, and such imbalance could be corrected by the doctor's healing arts.

Muslim physicians therefore came to look upon medicine as the science by which the dispositions of the human body could be discerned, and to see its goal as the preservation of health and, if health should be lost, assistance in recovering it. They viewed themselves as practitioners of the dual art of healing and the maintenance of health.

Even before the period of translation closed, advances were made in other health-related fields. Harun al-Rashid established the first hospital, in the modern sense of the term, at Baghdad about 805. Within a decade or two, 34 more hospitals had sprung up throughout the Islamic world, and the number grew each year.

These hospitals, or *bimaristans,* bore little resemblance to their European counterparts. The sick saw the *bimaristan* as a place where they could be treated and perhaps cured by physicians, and the physicians saw the *bimaristan* as an institution devoted to the promotion of health, the cure of disease and the expansion and dissemination of medical knowledge. Medical schools and libraries were attached to the larger hospitals, and senior physicians taught students, who were in turn expected to apply in the men's and women's wards what they had learned

The Caliphs' Researches

Fourteenth-century historian and political scientist Ibn Khaldun wrote about the intellectual curiosity that helped to preserve Greek learning.

When the Byzantine emperors conquered Syria, the scientific works of the Greeks were still in existence. Then God brought Islam, and the Muslims won their remarkable victories, conquering the Byzantines as well as all other nations. At first, the Muslims were simple, and did not cultivate learning, but as time went on and the Muslim dynasty flourished, the Muslims developed an urban culture which surpassed that of any other nation.

They began to wish to study the various branches of philosophy, of whose existence they knew from their contact with bishops and priests among their Christian subjects. In any case, man has always had a penchant for intellectual speculation. The caliph al-Mansur therefore sent an embassy to the Byzantine emperor, asking him to send him translations of books on mathematics. The emperor sent him Euclid's *Elements* and some works on physics.

Muslim scholars studied these books, and their desire to obtain others was whetted. When al-Ma'mun, who had some scientific knowledge, assumed the caliphate, he wished to do something to further the progress of science. For that purpose, he sent ambassadors and translators to the Byzantine empire, in order to search out works on the Greek sciences and have them translated into Arabic. As a result of these efforts, a great deal of material was gathered and preserved.

—Bodleian Library

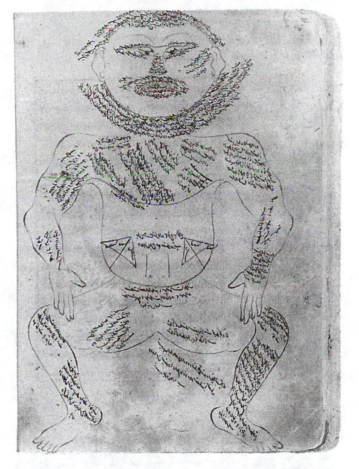

Figure 2 Seeds of *Silene gallica* (top left) called *hashishat al-thubban,* or flyweed, in Arabic, were effective in a snake-bite antidote, according to Dioscorides. Above, Persian notations detail the human muscle system in Mansur ibn Ilyas' late-14th-century *Tashrih-i Badan-i Insan (The Anatomy of the Human Body).*

Note: Bibliothèque Nationale de France.

in the lecture hall. Hospitals set examinations for their students, and issued diplomas. By the 11th century, there were even traveling clinics, staffed by the hospitals, that brought medical care to those too distant or too sick to come to the hospitals themselves. The *bimaristan* was, in short, the cradle of Arab medicine and the prototype upon which the modern hospital is based.

Like the hospital, the institution of the pharmacy, too, was an Islamic development. Islam teaches that "God has provided a remedy for every illness," and that Muslims should search for those remedies and use them with skill and compassion. One of the first pharmacological treatises was composed by Jabir ibn Hayyan (ca. 776), who is considered the father of Arab alchemy.

The Arab pharmacopoeia of the time was extensive, and gave descriptions of the geographical origin, physical properties and methods of application of everything found useful in the cure of disease. Arab pharmacists, or *saydalani,* introduced a large number of new drugs to clinical practice, including senna, camphor, sandalwood, musk, myrrh, cassia, tamarind, nutmeg, cloves, aconite, ambergris and mercury. The *saydalani* also developed syrups and juleps—the words came from Arabic and Persian, respectively—and pleasant solvents such as rose water and orange-blossom water as means of administering drugs. They were familiar with the anesthetic effects of Indian hemp and henbane, both when taken in liquids and inhaled.

By the time of al-Ma'mun's caliphate, pharmacy was a profession practiced by highly skilled specialists. Pharmacists were required to pass examinations and be licensed, and were then monitored by the state. At the start of the ninth century, the first private apothecary shops opened in Baghdad. Pharmaceutical preparations were manufactured and distributed commercially, then dispensed by physicians and pharmacists in a variety of forms—ointments, pills, elixirs, confections, tinctures, suppositories and inhalants.

Figure 3 Surgical instruments are shown in detail in a 13th-century Latin translation of *The Method* (above), a 30-part medical text written by Islam's greatest medieval surgeon, Abu al-Qasim, who practised in 10th-century Córdoba.

Note: Bibliothèque Nationale de France.

The blossoming of original thought in Arab medicine began as the ninth century drew to a close. The first major work appeared when Abu Bakr Muhammad ibn Zakariya Al-Razi (ca. 841–926) turned his attention to medicine.

Al-Razi, known to the West as Rhazes, was born in Persia in the town of Rayy, near Tehran. After a youth spent as a musician, mathematician and alchemist, Al-Razi went to Baghdad to take up the study of medicine at the age of 40. Completing his studies, he returned to Rayy and assumed the directorship of its hospital. His reputation grew rapidly and within a few years he was selected to be the director of a new hospital to be built in Baghdad. He approached the question of where to put the new facility by hanging pieces of meat in various sections of the city and checking the rate at which they spoiled. He then ordered the hospital built at the site where the meat showed the least putrefaction.

A Physician Observes

In Al-Judari wa al-Hasbah, *Al-Razi distinguished small-pox from measles for the first time in medical history. This passage shows his skill as a medical observer, a competence on which he placed great importance.*

The eruption of the smallpox is preceded by a continued fever, pain in the back, itching in the nose and terrors in the sleep. These are the more peculiar symptoms of its approach, especially a pain in the back with fever; then also a pricking which the patient feels all over his body; a fullness of the face, which at times comes and goes; an inflamed color, and vehement redness in both cheeks; a redness of both the eyes, heaviness of the whole body; great uneasiness, the symptoms of which are stretching and yawning; a pain in the throat and chest, with slight difficulty in breathing and cough; a dryness of the breath, thick spittle and hoarseness of the voice; pain and heaviness of the head; inquietude, nausea and anxiety; (with this difference that the inquietude, nausea and anxiety are more frequent in the measles than in the smallpox; while on the other hand, the pain in the back is more peculiar to the smallpox than to the measles;) heat of the whole body; an inflamed colon, and shining redness, and especially an intense redness of the gums.

—Bodleian Library

Above: Mandrake (Mandragora officinalis; al-luffah in Arabic) was described in the 10th-century by Al-Biruni as a useful soporific.

Al-Razi is regarded as Islamic medicine's greatest clinician and its most original thinker. A prolific writer, he turned out some 237 books, about half of which dealt with medicine. His treatise *The Diseases of Children* has led some historians to regard him as the father of pediatrics. He was the first to identify hay fever and its cause. His work on kidney stones is still considered a classic. In addition, he was instrumental in the introduction of mercurial ointments to treat scabies. Al-Razi advocated reliance on observation rather than on received authority; he was a strong proponent of experimental medicine and the beneficial use of previously tested medicinal plants and other drugs. A leader in

Testing New Medicines

In his voluminous writings, Ibn Sina laid out the following rules for testing the effectiveness of a new drug or medication. These principles still form the basis of modern clinical drug trials.

1. The drug must be free from any extraneous accidental quality.
2. It must be used on a simple not a composite, disease.
3. The drug must be tested with two contrary types of diseases, because sometimes a drug cures one disease by its essential qualities and another by its accidental ones.
4. The quality of the drug must correspond to the strength of the disease. For example, there are some drugs whose heat is less than the coldness of certain diseases, so that they would have no effect on them.
5. The time of action must be observed, so that essence and accident are not confused.
6. The effect of the drug must be seen to occur constantly or in many cases, for if this did not happen, it was an accidental effect.
7. The experimentation must be done with the human body, for testing a drug on a lion or a horse might not prove anything about its effect on man.

—Bodleian Library

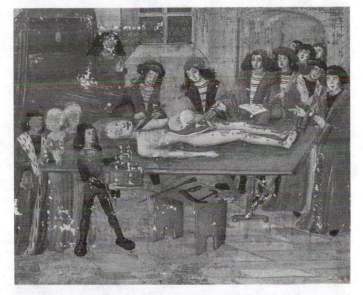

Figure 4 This depiction of mandrake before flowering (left) appeared in an Arabic version of *De Materia Medica* titled *Khawass al-Ashjar (The Properties of Plants),* translated in Baghdad in 1240. Above, an anatomy lesson at the medical school at Montpelier—one of Europe's earliest—from de Chauliac's *1363 Grande Chirurgie.*

Note: Art Resource/Museé Alger.

the fight against quacks and charlatans—and author of a book exposing their methods—he called for high professional standards for practitioners. He also insisted on continuing education for already licensed physicians. Al-Razi was the first to emphasize the value of mutual trust and consultation among skilled physicians in the treatment of patients, a rare practice at that time.

Following his term as hospital director in Baghdad, he returned to Rayy where he taught the healing arts in the local hospital, and he continued to write. His first major work was a 10 part treatise entitled *Al-Kitab al-Mansuri,* so called after the ruler of Rayy, Mansur ibn Ishaq. In it, he discussed such varied subjects as general medical theories and definitions; diet and drugs and their effect on the human body; mother and child care, skin disease, oral hygiene, climatology and the effect of the environment on health; epidemiology and toxicology.

Al-Razi also prepared *Al-Judari wa al Hasbah,* the first treatise ever written on smallpox and measles. In a masterful demonstration of clinical observation (*see box* "A Physician Observes"), Al-Razi became the first to distinguish the two diseases from each other. At the same time, he provided still-valid guidelines for the sound treatment of both.

His most esteemed work was a medical encyclopedia in 25 books, *Al-Kitab al-Hawi,* or *The Comprehensive Work,* the *Liber Continens* of Al-Razi's later Latin translators. Al-Razi spent a lifetime collecting data for the book, which he intended as a summary of all the medical knowledge of his time, augmented by his own experience and observations. In *Al-Hawi,* Al-Razi emphasized the need for physicians to pay careful attention to what the patients' histories told them, rather than merely consulting the authorities of the past. In a series of diagnosed case histories entitled "Illustrative Accounts of Patients," Al-Razi demonstrated this important tenet. One patient, who lived in a malarial district, suffered from intermittent chills and fever that had been diagnosed as malaria, but nonetheless seemed incurable. Al-Razi was asked to examine him. Upon noting pus in the urine, he diagnosed an infected kidney, and he treated the patient successfully with diuretics.

Al-Razi's clinical skill was matched by his understanding of human nature, particularly as demonstrated in the attitudes of patients. In a series of short monographs on the doctor-patient relationship, he described principles that are still taught a millennium later: Doctors and patients need to establish a mutual bond

Figure 5 At the Benedictine monastery at Monte Cassino in the 10th century, the Middle Eastern traveler Leo Africanus translated Arab medical texts and supervised a hospital run on Arab principles. Between that time and the Renaissance, European hospitals, like the one above, from an undated Italian manuscript, were increasingly modeled on the Arab bimaristan.
Note: Art Resource/Biblioteca Laurenziana.

of trust, he wrote; positive comments from doctors encourage patients, make them feel better and speed their recovery; and, he warned, changing from one doctor to another wastes patients' health, wealth and time.

Not long after Al-Razi's death, Abu'Al al-Husayn ibn 'Abd Allah ibn Sina (980–1037) was born in Bukhara, in what today is Uzbekistan. Later translators Latinized his name to Avicenna. It is hard to describe Ibn Sina in anything other than superlatives. He was to the Arab world what Aristotle was to Greece, Leonardo da Vinci to the Renaissance and Goethe to Germany. His preeminence embraced not only medicine, but also the fields of philosophy, science, music, poetry and statecraft. His contemporaries called him "the prince of physicians."

Ibn Sina's life was in fact the stuff of legend. The son of a tax collector, he was so precocious that he had completely memorized the Qur'an by age 10. Then he studied law, mathematics, physics, and philosophy. Confronted by a difficult problem in Aristotle's *Metaphysics,* Ibn Sina re-read the book 40 times in his successful search for a solution. At 16 he turned to the study of medicine, which he said he found "not difficult." By 18, his fame as a physician was so great that he was summoned to treat the Samanid prince Nuh ibn Mansur. His success with that patient won him access to the Samanid royal library, one of the greatest of Bukhara's many storehouses of learning.

At 20, Ibn Sina was appointed court physician, and twice served as vizier, to Shams al-Dawlah, the Buyid prince of Hamadan, in western Persia. His remaining years were crowded with adventure and hard work, yet he somehow found time to write 20 books on theology, metaphysics, astronomy,

philology and poetry and 20 more on medicine—including *Kitab al-Shifa',* or *The Book of Healing,* a medical and philosophical encyclopedia.

His supreme work, however, is the monumental *Al-Qanun fi al-Tibb, The Canon of Medicine.* Over one million words long, it was nothing less than a codification of all existing medical knowledge. Summarizing the Hippocratic and Galenic traditions, describing Syro-Arab and Indo-Persian practice and including notes on his own observations, Ibn Sina strove to fit each bit of anatomy, physiology, diagnosis and treatment into its proper niche.

The Canon stressed the importance of diet and the influence of climate and environment on health. It included discussions of rabies, hydrocele, breast cancer, tumors, labor and poisons and their treatment. Ibn Sina differentiated meningitis from the meningismus of other acute diseases; and described chronic nephritis, facial paralysis, ulcer of the stomach and the various types of hepatitis and their causes. He also expounded the dilation and contraction of the pupils and their diagnostic value, described the six motor muscles of the eye and discussed the functions of the tear ducts, and he noted the contagious nature of some diseases, which he attributed to "traces" left in the air by a sick person.

The Canon also included a description of some 760 medicinal plants and the drugs that could be derived from them. At the same time Ibn Sina laid out the basic rules of clinical drug trials, principles that are still followed today. (*See box,* "Testing New Medicines".)

Not surprisingly, *The Canon* rapidly became the standard medical reference work of the Islamic world. Nizami-i Arudi of Samarkand spoke for generations of physicians when he wrote, in the early 12th century, "From him who manages the first volume [*of The Canon*], nothing will be hidden concerning the general theory and principles of medicine." *The Canon* was used as a reference, a teaching guide and a medical textbook until well into the 19th century, longer than any other medical work.

During the 10th century, when Arab astronomical texts were first translated in Catalonia, Europe began to reap the intellectual riches of the Arabs and, in so doing, to seek out its own classical heritage. The medical works of Galen and Hippocrates returned to the West by way of the Middle East and North Africa, recovered through Latin translations of what had become the Arab medical classics. Through the intellectual ferment of the Islamic present, Europe recovered some of its past.

The two main translators of classical material from Arabic into Latin were Constantinus (also known as Leo) Africanus (1020–1087), who worked at Salerno and in the cloister of Monte Cassino, and Gerard of Cremona (1140–1187), who worked in Toledo. It was no accident that both translators lived in the Arab-Christian transition zone, where the two cultures fructified each other. And it was no coincidence that Salerno, Europe's first great medical faculty of the Middle Ages, was close to Arab Sicily, nor that the second, Montpellier, was founded in 1221 in southern France, near the Andalusian border.

Ibn Sina's *Canon* made its first appearance in Europe by the end of the 12th century, and its impact was dramatic. Copied and recopied, it quickly became the standard European medical reference work. In the last 30 years of the 15th century, just before the European invention of printing, it was issued in 16 editions; in the century that followed more than 20 further editions were printed. From the 12th to the 17th century, its *materia medica* was the pharmacopoeia of Europe, and as late as 1537 *The Canon* was still a required textbook at the University of Vienna.

Translations of Al-Razi's *Al-Kitab al-Hawi* and other works followed rapidly. Printed while printing was still in its infancy, all of Al-Razi's works gained widespread acceptance. The ninth book of *Al-Kitab al-Mansuri* ("Concerning Diseases from the Head to the Foot") remained part of the medical curriculum at the University of Tübingen until the end of the 15th century.

Contemporary Europeans regarded Ibn Sina and Al-Razi as the greatest authorities on medical matters, and portraits of both men still adorn the great hall of the School of Medicine at the University of Paris. In *The Inferno,* Dante placed Ibn Sina side by side with antiquity's two greatest physicians, Hippocrates and Galen. Roger Bacon consulted Ibn Sina to further his own inquiries into vision.

But it was not only Al-Razi and Ibn Sina who influenced Europe. Translations of more than 400 Arab authors, writing on such varied topics as ophthalmology, surgery, pharmaceuticals, child care and public health, deeply influenced the rebirth of European science.

Despite their belief in now superseded theories such as humors and miasmas, the medicine of Ibn Sina, Al-Razi and their contemporaries is the basis of much of what we take for granted today.

It was those Arab physicians who made accurate diagnoses of plague, diphtheria, leprosy, rabies, diabetes, gout, cancer and epilepsy. Ibn Sina's theory of infection by "traces" led to the introduction of quarantine as a means of limiting the spread of infectious diseases. Arab doctors laid down the principles of clinical investigation and drug trials, and they uncovered the secret of sight. They mastered operations for hernia and cataract, filled teeth with gold leaf and prescribed spectacles for defective eyesight. And they passed on rules of health, diet and hygiene that are still largely valid today.

Thus the Islamic world not only provided a slender but ultimately successful line of transmission for the medical knowledge of ancient Greece and the Hellenic world, it also corrected and enormously expanded that knowledge before passing it on to a Europe that had abandoned observation, experimentation and the very concept of earthly progress centuries before. Physicians of different languages and religions had cooperated in building a sturdy structure whose outlines are still visible in the medical practices of our own time.

DAVID W. TSCHANZ lives and works in Saudi Arabia as an epidemiologist with Saudi Aramco. He holds master's degrees in both history and epidemiology, and writes about the history of medicine.

The Age of the Vikings

Norse seafarers plundered, traded, and settled from Canada to Russia.

A.D. 793 was a particularly nasty year along the northeastern coast of England. First came the "fierce, foreboding omens," and the "wretchedly terrified" populace watched fiery dragons dance across the sky. A great famine struck. And then "the ravaging of heathen men destroyed God's church at Lindisfarne through brutal robbery and slaughter." And so began the Age of the Vikings.

ARNE EMIL CHRISTENSEN

This *Anglo-Saxon Chronicle* description of the first major Viking raid is typical of contemporary accounts of the Norsemen. In a remarkably violent time, the Vikings were feared above all others in Europe. Yet they were much more than brutal warriors. The Norse proved themselves to be colonizers, city-builders, law-givers, architects, explorers, and merchants.

For 250 years, from about A.D. 800 until 1050, people of Denmark, Sweden, and Norway played a potent role in European history far out of proportion to the size and population of their mother countries. They plundered, traded, and settled from deep into Russia all the way to Newfoundland on the edge of the New World. They terrorized powerful, established kingdoms like France and England.

The Norse sailed up the rivers of France and Spain, laid siege to Paris, and attacked coastal towns in Italy. In the east, they traded with Arab merchants at Bulgar on the Volga and raided as far east as the Caspian Sea. From Kiev, they traveled downriver to the Black Sea and attempted an attack on the Byzantine capital of Constantinople.

The Vikings' Reach

From Scandinavia, Norse seafarers carried raids, trade, and colonies throughout their expanding world. They swept the coasts of Europe, followed rivers deep into Russia, and crossed the seas to settle Iceland, Greenland, and (briefly) North America.

Norse Graves Reveal the Paradox of War and Peace
Burying Vikings

An Arab traveling through Russia nearly 1,200 years ago happened upon an extraordinary sight: the fiery burial of a Viking chieftain.

The leader's great ship was hauled ashore and his valuables loaded aboard it. The body was dressed in fine clothes and placed on the ship. A slave woman who had chosen to follow her master into the afterlife was killed and her body was placed aboard. Then the chieftain's horse and dog were sacrificed for the grave. Finally, the ship was set ablaze and a mound built over the ashes of the funeral pyre.

Ibn Fadlans described the ninth-century A.D. scene in his journal—the only eyewitness account of a Viking burial. Fortunately for archaeologists, not all Norse funerals involved burning the remains; sometimes whole ships were buried with their owners and property, offering a remarkable glimpse into the life and times of the Norsemen.

The graves give mute testimony to the violence of the Viking age. Nearly all males were buried with weapons. A warrior fully equipped for the next world was interred with his sword, ax, and spear, and often with a bow and arrows. A wooden shield with a central iron boss was the usual protection. The helmets and armor seen on modern representations are extremely rare, and the horned helmet of cartoon Vikings has never been seen in a real Norse grave.

The graves also reveal the paradox of the Vikings: Alongside the fearsome set of arms, the accouterments of peace are also found. Craftsmen were buried with their tools, blacksmiths with their hammer, tongs, and files. Farmers had their hoe, scythe, and sickle; and along the coasts, the dead were often buried with their boats and fishing equipment. Women took with them their personal jewelry, as well as textiles and kitchen tools.

Only metal objects survive the centuries in most graves, but conditions at a few, especially beneath the blue clay on the Oslo Fjord, preserved even wood, leather, and textiles. The clay and tightly stacked turf used in some of the burials produced graves as well sealed as hermetic jars. Everything sacrificed in such graves has been preserved in the moist, oxygen-free conditions.

The preserved contents of three extremely rich ship graves— from *Oseberg, Gokstad,* and *Tune*—are among Norway's national treasures. At the time of the burial, the ships were pulled ashore on rollers and placed in a pit dug into the ground. A burial chamber was built on board to hold the body and provisions needed for a life after death. Then a huge mound was built over the grave.

The remains of a man were found in the *Gokstad* grave, and the *Tune* ship probably also held a male. But the *Oseberg* grave was the resting place for two women, one 50 to 60 years old and the other in her 20s. The *Oseberg* and *Gokstad* graves had been robbed, so the fine weapons and jewelry that must have been among the original grave goods were not found. Articles of wood, leather, and textiles, however, did not interest the robbers and have survived.

UDO Archives/courtesy of Smithsonian Institution.
The most famous of Viking ships came from the Oseberg Burial Mound, shown here during excavations in 1904. The impermeable blue clay of the mound in the Oslo Fjord protected the ship and its contents for more than 1,000 years.

It is unclear which of the *Oseberg* women was the recipient of the grave, and which was the after-death companion. Women often held high status in Norse society, and the *Oseberg* grave belonged to a high-ranking women.

Her grave held the evidence of her role as the main administrator of a manor. Even after death, she was equipped to spin and weave and supervise milking, cheese-making, and work in the fields. For land travel, she had three sleds and a wagon complete with sacrificed horses and two tents. Cooking equipment, wooden troughs and buckets, a cauldron, a frying pan, and a carving knife were at hand, as were two oxen, grain, apples, and blueberries.

Objects such as the wagon and several finely carved wooden animal heads probably were religious icons, suggesting the woman may have been both a political and religious leader. The many decorated wooden objects seem to be the work of several different woodcarvers. Except for this grave, our knowledge of Viking art is based mainly on preserved metalwork that generally is smaller than the wooden objects. But whether metal or wood, the artistic goal was the same: to create a carpet of inter-twined, fantastic animals.

The number of different artisans represented suggests the "Oseberg" queen was a patron of the arts who assembled the best wood-carvers and weavers at her court. The woodcarvings prove that some Vikings were as handy with chisel and knife as with sword and spear.

Scandinavian Ships Drove the Vikings' Fierce Amphibious Warfare
The Perfect War Machine

Viking warships were fearsome works of art. The sight of that curved prow suddenly cresting the horizon could send whole cities into panic a millennium ago.

The Scandinavian shipbuilders who created these unique and pioneering craft were quite possibly the most important factor in establishing Norse military supremacy and creating a far-flung web of trade and colonization. A leading Swedish archaeologist, Bertil Almgren, called Viking ships the only ocean-going landing craft ever devised—which would explain how small bands of warriors could terrorize settled societies.

Early accounts of Norse attacks demonstrate the military value of these unique craft and the shattering amphibious tactics they permitted. The ships—light, flexible, and free to maneuver in shallow water—had no need of harbors. They could be easily beached by their crews, who then transformed themselves from oarsmen to fierce shock troops who swarmed over their terrified targets.

A surprise amphibious attack could hit almost anywhere along Europe's coasts and rivers. Then after a quick and bloody battle, the Norsemen were gone—far out to sea again before a counterattack could be mounted. The Vikings learned early how to tack their ships against the wind, allowing immediate escape even with the wind at their faces. At a time when civilized armies were supposed to march overland, the amphibious tactics of the Norsemen were devastating.

The Viking ship, that near-perfect war machine of its day, was the culmination of a long Scandinavian shipbuilding tradition that dates back to at least 350 B.C. Many of the techniques developed by Norse shipbuilders are still used for small boats today, so 1,000-year-old problems can be answered by living boatbuilders.

The sail came rather late to Viking ships, probably not until early in the eighth century. But the new sailing ships were perfected through four generations to serve raiders and traders alike.

Even with a full crew, the *Gokstad* could float in one meter (just over three feet) of water. She could be beached by the crew and was well suited for surprise attacks on foreign shores.

The Viking ships were clinker built: Long planks were overlapped and fastened together with iron rivets to form the hull. This planking shell was built first, then the ribs inserted afterwards for strength and stability. This method produces much lighter, more flexible ships than those that began with the stout interior frame to which outer planking was added.

Norse shipbuilders gained even more flexibility by lashing the ship's ribs and planking together. The backbone of keel and stems fore and aft increased strength. Most ships were built of oak; pine was also used.

As society changed during the Viking Age, different kinds of ships were developed. Warships were long and slender, built for speed with large crews who could man the oars. Cargo ships were much wider and slower and relied more on sails than did the warships. Busy trade routes from Western Norway to Iceland and Greenland required seaworthy ships.

Much of what we know about Viking shipbuilding comes from the Norse practice of burying important personages in their ships. Three especially notable excavated ship burials come from Oseberg, Gokstad and Tune in Norway. All three are exhibited in the Viking Ship Museum at Bygdoy in Oslo.

Norway's National Museum recently used tree-ring analysis to date these three pristine ships. The *Oseberg* was built between A.D. 815 and 820, the other two in the A.D. 890s. The *Oseberg* is 22 meters (72 feet) long and could be rowed by 30 men. The *Gokstad* stretches 24 meters (78 feet) with room for 32 oarsmen, while the *Tune* was probably about 20 meters (65 feet) long.

All three had a mast amidships, with the sail of *Gokstad* estimated at about 120 square meters (1,300 square feet). Sails were made of wool, and the task of collecting wool, and sorting, spinning, weaving, and sewing such a sail must have been a greater task than building the ship.

The *Oseberg* was less seaworthy than the later *Gokstad* and *Tune* ships, but still well-suited for trips across the North Sea in summer. It is probably typical of the warship used for the early raids. The seaworthiness of the *Gokstad* has been proved by the three replicas which have crossed the North Atlantic in modern times, yet the ship could float freely in as little as one meter (just over three feet) of water.

Most of the routes taken by Viking Age seafarers were in coastal waters or across fairly short stretches of open sea. Navigation was based on landmarks; and in coastal waters, it was usual to find a good harbor for the night and camp on the shore. Only on the long stretches of open water from Western Norway to Iceland and Greenland would sailors be out of sight of land for several days.

M en from the sea. Scandinavia was hardly unknown to the rest of Europe when the surprise raids began. Archaeological evidence shows cultural contacts dating back several millennia, but the distant Nordic area was of little import to the rest of Europe.

That changed suddenly in A.D. 793, when "men from the sea" plundered Lindisfarne monastery on Northumberland Island. Within a few years, every summer brought a wave of attacks on Ireland, England, France, and the North Sea's Frisian Islands.

Some of the Viking raiders stayed behind to build well-planned cities like Dublin and Kiev or take over existing ones like York. Others came with family and livestock to settle as farmers in England, Scotland, Normandy, and Russia. For 200 years, their ships sailed all the known waters of Europe and ventured where ships had never been.

Great ventures under famous chiefs often involved men from throughout Scandinavia, but the three countries divided their world into distinct spheres of interest.

The Swedes sailed mainly to the east, trading and settling along the Russian rivers and settling in towns as far south as Kiev. They must have played a role in creating the Russian state, although the importance of the role is debated. The Norsemen's eastern expansion was less warlike than the move against Western Europe. Trade was key in the east, and the enormous quantities of ancient Arab coins found in Sweden demonstrate how far the trade networks reached.

Sweeping across Europe the Danes sailed south to Friesland (in northern Europe), France, and southern England, occasionally reaching even Spain and Italy. Much of England became known as the "danelaw." In France, the embattled king invited Rollo, a Norse chieftain, to settle in Normandy as a French duke—in exchange for keeping other Vikings at bay.

Norway held sway in the west and northwest. Norwegian settlements on Orkney and Shetland may predate the Viking Age, when Norway drilled deep roots into northern England, Scotland, and Ireland. Scandinavian jewelry recovered from English graves tell of whole families emigrating, while Celtic names in Iceland suggest some settlers came from Ireland with Irish wives.

Farther west, the settlers came upon virgin land: the Faroe Islands, Iceland, and Greenland. The settlement of Iceland intensified around A.D. 900, when Norwegian kings strengthened their central government, according to a unique source, *Land-namabok*, which tells the story of the settlement and names many of the settlers.

Chiefs often preferred to emigrate rather than submit to higher authority; family and friends usually followed. Some settlers had no choice after being outlawed at home. The man who led the colonization of Greenland, Eirik the Red, was expelled from Iceland for killing and other mayhem.

New world colony. Sailing still farther westward, the Norse reached North America and launched a settlement around A.D. 1000. Conflicts with the original inhabitants of the New World doomed the colony, however, and the settlers returned to Greenland.

The location—and even the existence—of the Norsemen's North American settlement has been hotly debated for more than a century, with suggestions ranging from Labrador to Manhattan. Unassailable proof was discovered in the 1960s by Helge and Anne Stine Ingstad with their excavations at L'Anse aux Meadows on northern Newfoundland. Houses like those excavated on Iceland and Greenland, Viking artifacts, and radiocarbon dates of about A.D. 1000 proved this to be a site built and used by Norse people.

What accounts for this rapid, violent expansion? Well-organized states such as France and the Anglo-Saxon kingdoms of England were taken by complete surprise and were rarely able to resist the amphibious attacks.

Written accounts from the time, which were hardly objective, paint the Vikings as merciless pirates, robbers, and brigands. And, indeed, they no doubt were. But these were violent times. Accounts from Ireland state that the Irish themselves plundered about as many monasteries and churches as the Vikings. The Frankish Empire grew via long and bloody wars, and the Anglo-Saxon kingdoms fought one another repeatedly. The Vikings may well have been just the most efficient raiders of their day.

But they were more than warriors. Some of their leaders not only won great battles, but founded kingdoms in conquered lands, planned cities, and gave laws that are still in force. The remains of fortresses that could house an army have been found in Denmark. Dating to the end of the Viking Age, the circular forts are laid out with a precision that impresses modern surveyors. The forts testify to an advanced knowledge of geometry and surveying.

Farmers and blacksmiths in their homelands, the Norse mostly were farmers and stockbreeders who supplemented their larder by fishing and hunting. Barley, oats, and some wheat were cultivated; and cattle, horses, sheep, goats, and pigs were raised. Iron-making was an important resource in Sweden and in Norway, with bog ore to supply the iron and ample wood to fuel the furnace pits. Some areas quarried steatite for cooking vessels and slate for whetstones.

The farmers were generally self-reliant, although luxury goods and such necessities as salt formed the basis of thriving trade. Steatite items survive the centuries well and turn up in excavations outside Scandinavia; but such perishable goods as furs, ropes of seal and walrus skins, and dried fish must also have been important trade items. Many Arab coins have been found in Scandinavia, and although we do not know what was purchased with the coins, iron and slaves are possibilities.

Warfare was rarely allowed to interfere with trade. As Alfred of Wessex fought desperately to block a Viking invasion, he was visited by Ottar, a Norwegian merchant. Ottar's story was written down and survives as the only contemporary report on Viking society by a Viking. Ottar lived in the far north of Norway and collected his trade goods as taxes paid by nearby indigenous people, the Saami. He mentions furs, eiderdown, and skin ropes, as well as walrus teeth—the "ivory of the Arctic."

A source of warriors. One force driving Norse expansion may have been the *odel*, which seems to extend back to Viking times. The *odel* dictated that a farm should not be divided but inherited intact by the oldest son. Younger sons and daughters received far less and likely had to clear new land or go abroad to acquire a farm. Landless younger sons may have given chieftains the manpower they needed to raid Europe.

Although West European sources tell a grim story of the Vikings, archaeological excavations paint a much more varied picture. Excavated farms and graves reveal artifacts from a peaceful life centered on the rhythm of a year that revolved around agriculture. Piles of stones tell of careful clearing of the land, and we have found the furrows left by a plowing 1,100 years ago.

153

Roland Hejdström.

This oval brooch from Sweden's Gotland Island was made in Karelia, Russia.

As the years progressed, Norse society changed. Fewer chieftains controlled more and more resources, forming the basis of kingdoms until each of the three countries united into a central kingdom along roughly the same borders as today. Marketplaces grew into towns with well-planned streets and plots for homes.

From Staraya Ladoga and Kiev in Russia to Dublin in Ireland, we find evidence of townspeople basing their life on trade and handicraft. Garbage disposal was not a high priority, and the thick layers of ancient refuse are now gold mines for archaeologists. Excavations illuminate everything from changing fashions to the kinds of lice that bedeviled the townspeople.

Christian Vikings. The Viking age ended in the eleventh century, as Scandinavian kingdoms adopted Christianity. The raids gradually ended, and the pantheon of warrior gods faded. Viking gods lived on as our days of the week: Tuesday, Wednesday, Thursday and Friday. Ty and Thor were war gods; Wotan (or Odin) was the chief god with power over life, death, and poetry; Frey and his sister Freya were the gods of fertility. We know little of Viking religion, as written sources are late and colored by Christian belief. The gods demanded sacrifice, and temples and holy forests were probably dedicated to these deities. Like their Greek and Roman counterparts, the Viking gods had human traits.

The northern countries, once the scourge of a continent, became a regular part of Christian Europe and great changes ensued. But for the people of the Norselands, life went on. They continued to sow and reap, and herd and hunt as they had for generations beyond counting.

ARNE EMIL CHRISTENSEN, of the University Museum of National Antiquities in Oslo, specializes in shipbuilding history and craftsmanship in the Iron Age and Viking period.

From *Scientific American Discovering Archaeology,* September/October 2000, pp. 40–47. Copyright © 2000 by Arne Emil Christensen. Reprinted by permission of the author.

The Fall of Constantinople

Judith Herrin tells the dramatic story of the final moments of Byzantine control of the imperial capital.

JUDITH HERRIN

"At this moment of confusion, which happened at sunrise, our omnipotent God came to His most bitter decision and decided to fulfil all the prophecies, as I have said, and at sunrise the Turks entered the city near San Romano, where the walls had been razed to the ground by their cannon . . . anyone they found was put to the scimitar, women and men, old and young, of any conditions. This butchery lasted from sunrise, when the Turks entered the city, until midday . . . The Turks made eagerly for the piazza five miles from the point where they made their entrance at San Romano, and when they reached it at once some of them climbed up a tower where the flags of Saint Mark and the Most Serene Emperor were flying, and they cut down the flag of Saint Mark and took away the flag of the Most Serene Emperor and then on the same tower they raised the flag of the Sultan . . . When their flag was raised and ours cut down, we saw that the whole city was taken, and that there was no further hope of recovering from this."

With these words, and much longer descriptions of the slaughter that followed, the Venetian Nicolo Barbaro recorded the fall of Constantinople to the Ottoman Turks. His eyewitness account describes the progressive stranglehold devised by the Turks and the sense of fatalism that developed within the city. As the major trading partner of the empire, Venice had strong links with Constantinople and its citizens fought bravely in its defence. Barbaro's account of their loyalty is impressive. Although he is less favourably inclined to the Genoese, who also played a leading role in the defence of the city, his account has the immediacy of one who lived through the siege.

There is no shortage of records of the fall, although some were concocted long after the event and claim a presence that turns out to be quite inauthentic. Greeks, Italians, Slavs, Turks and Russians all composed their own versions; they cannot possibly be reconciled. But those written closer to the date, May 29th, 1453, and by people involved in some capacity all share a sense of the disaster they documented. Taking account of many of their variations and contradictions, they permit a basic outline of events to be constructed.

The leaders of what became such a mythic battle were both younger sons who had never expected to become rulers. The Ottoman sultan Mehmet II, born in 1432, was made sole heir at the age of eleven by the death of his two elder brothers; Constantine XI, born in 1404, was the fourth of six sons of Manuel II, whose imperial authority was inherited by the eldest John VIII. When John died in 1448, the Empress-Mother Helena insisted that Constantine should be crowned in a disputed succession. His two younger brothers, Demetrios and Thomas, were appointed Despots in the Morea (southern Greece), and took no interest in the fate of Constantinople. In 1453 the Sultan was twenty-one years old, the Emperor forty-nine, and the Ottomans far out-numbered the Christian forces who undertook the defence of the city.

The imperial capital dedicated by Constantine I in TD 330 had resisted siege on numerous occasions. The triple line of fortifications constructed on the land side in the fifth century had held off attacks by Goths, Persians, Avars, Bulgars, Russians, and especially Arabs. Even today they make an impressive sight. Over the centuries new aqueducts and cisterns were built to ensure an ample water supply, and the imperial granaries stored plentiful amounts of grain.

From the first attempt by the Arabs to capture the city in 674–78, Muslim forces aimed to make Constantinople their own capital. Using this ancient foundation as their base, they hoped to extend their power across Thrace and the Balkans into Europe, in the same irresistible way that they advanced across North Africa into Spain. Frustrated in these efforts, the centre of their operations was moved to Baghdad, and they occupied the Fertile Crescent and vast areas further east. In the eleventh century these same ambitions were taken up by Turkish tribes from central Asia, who constantly harried the empire. First Seljuks and later Ottomans maintained pressure on Constantinople, hoping to take a symbol of unconquered strength and great strategic importance.

Their aim was not merely political and military. For centuries Constantinople was the largest metropolis in the known world, the impregnable core of a great empire, served by a deep-water port that gave access to the sea. Known as New Rome and the Queen City, it had been built to impress, its magnificent public monuments, decorated with statuary set in an elegant classical urban landscape. Its apparent invincibility and famous reputation made it a great prize. The city was also reputed to be hugely wealthy. While the Turks had no interest in its famous collection of Christian relics, the fact that many were made of solid gold and silver, decorated with huge gems and ancient cameos, was of importance. Their existence added weight to the rumour that Constantinople contained vast stores of gold, a claim which cannot have been true by 1453. By the early fifteenth century the city had lost all its provinces to Turkish occupation and was totally isolated. The surviving Greek territories of Trebizond and the Morea were similarly surrounded and made no effort to assist the ancient capital.

It is notoriously difficult to reconstruct the early history of the Ottoman Turks from the sparse sources that survive. They seem to have been a tribe of *ghazi* warriors (men devoted to holy war) who gradually adopted a more organised monarchy. Their leader Osman (1288–1326) gave his name to the group, which is now associated with one of the most successful empires of all time. During the fourteenth century these Ottoman Turks took full advantage of the civil war in Byzantium. From his capital at Nikomedia Sultan Orhan offered assistance to John VI, claimant to the throne, and married his daughter Theodora, thus setting up an excellent excuse for invading the empire.

At the same time, he was able to exploit unexpected developments at Gallipoli when an earthquake shook the castle fortifications so violently that they collapsed in 1354. Orhan ferried an entire army across the Dardanelles and opened a bridgehead on the European shore. The conquest of Thrace, the last province loyal to the empire, and the capture of Adrianople, which became the Ottoman capital as Edirne, meant that the Turks were now in a position to threaten the capital from the west. Once they could mount an attack by land as well as by sea, Constantinople was totally surrounded. This stranglehold on the empire was symbolised by the treaty of 1373, which reduced the emperor to the status of a Turkish vassal. John V agreed to pay Sultan Murad an annual tribute, to provide military aid whenever

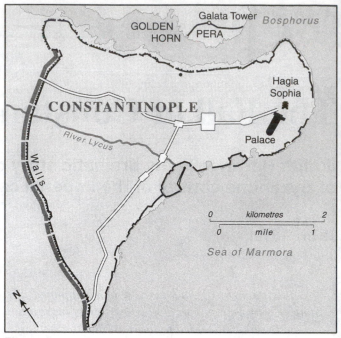

Figure 1

it was required, and to allow his son Manuel to accompany the Turks back to their court as a hostage.

Despite a surprising defeat by the Mongols in 1402, Ottoman attempts to capture Constantinople continued. In preparation for the campaign of 1452–53, Sultan Mehmet II ordered the blockade of the city. Since the southern entrance to the Bosphorus from the Aegean at the Dardanelles was already in Ottoman hands, he concentrated on the northern entrance from the Black Sea. Two castles were constructed close to the mouth of the Bosphorus on the Asian and European shores, to prevent any aid arriving from the Black Sea. Barbaro gives a vivid description of how the garrison at Rumeli Hisar on the European shore tried to control shipping by firing on any galleys entering the Bosphorus until they lowered their sails:

> From the walls of the castle, the Turks began to shout 'Lower your sails, Captain' . . . and when they saw that he was unwilling to lower them, they began to fire their cannon and many guns and a great number of arrows, so that they killed many men . . . After he had lowered his sails, the Turks stopped firing, and then the current carried the galleys towards Constantinople. And when they had passed the castle and the Turks could not reach them any longer with their cannon, the captain quickly raised his sails and got through safely.

Ships also carried oars so that sailors could row with the current in order to avoid the blockade.

Byzantine rulers had made too many appeals to Western powers to come to the aid of their Christian city. The crusading movement had been exhausted by numerous military disasters. After the failure of the crusade of 1396 at

Nicopolis on the Danube, the young emperor Manuel II made a long tour of western capital cities between 1399 and 1403 in the hope of gaining financial and above all military support for the defence of the city. In Paris he noticed a fine tapestry hanging in the palace of the Louvre and wrote a letter to his old tutor describing its beauty. In London he was invited to the Christmas dinner hosted by Henry IV at the palace of Eltham. Manuel's attempts to obtain aid were enhanced, as so many times before, by a promise to unite the Latin and Greek churches.

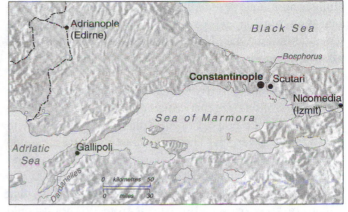

Figure 2

In this respect Manuel and his son John VIII proved that they could achieve the desired ecclesiastical union. At the Council of Ferrara-Florence in 1438–39 the union of the churches was finally realised. But even after this major compromise, help from the papacy, the Italian city republics and the monarchs who had received Manuel during his trip was slow to materialise. In the autumn of 1452, the papal legate Cardinal Isidore and Bishop Leonard of Chios arrived in the city with a body of archers recruited and paid for by the papacy. The Cardinal then celebrated the official union of the Latin and Greek churches in the cathedral of Hagia Sophia on December 12th.

As Bishop Leonard of Chios reports the event:

Through the diligence and honesty of the said Cardinal, Isidore of Kiev, and with the assent (if it was not insincere) of the emperor and the senate, the holy union was sanctioned and solemnly celebrated on December 12th, the feast of Saint Spiridon, the bishop.

But even with the union in place, Western promises to assist the last great Christian centre in the East Mediterranean proved empty, while a large portion of the Greek population of Constantinople remained obstinately opposed to it.

Among those who joined the Greek inhabitants in the city to defend it against the expected siege, were numerous representatives of the Italian republics of Venice and Genoa. Both enjoyed commercial privileges from trading in Constantinople but were staunch rivals. Some of those who fought had been residents for many years, had adopted Byzantine citizenship and married Greek wives. A significant number of Armenians were present and the resident Catalan traders took part under their consul. Prince Orhan, pretender to the Ottoman throne, who had lived for years as a guest of the Byzantine court, offered his services with his Turkish companions. Ships from Ancona, Provence and Castile added to the naval forces, and a group of Greeks from Crete elected to remain in the city. When they saw what would happen, though, on February 26th, 1453, six of their ships slipped away with one Venetian.

The inhabitants were greatly cheered by the arrival in January 1453 of the Genoese *condottieri,* who braved the Turkish blockade and got through with his two ships and about 700 men. This was Giovanni Giustiniani Longo, identified in many sources as Justinian, a friend of the emperor, whose determination to assist the city was greatly appreciated. Constantine XI put him in charge of the weakest part of the land walls, the section by the Gate of Romanos, and, as Nestor-Iskander says:

... he invigorated and even instructed the people so that they would not lose hope and maintain unswerving trust in God ... All people admired and obeyed him in all things.

After masterminding the defence Justinian was hit on the chest during the last days of the assault. The Genoese managed to get him out of the city on one of the first ships to leave after the capture but he died at Chios. His disappearance lowered the spirits of the Christian forces.

Also among the defenders was a young man called Nestor, who had been taken captive by a Turkish regiment in Moldavia, southern Russia, forcibly converted to Islam and enrolled in the unit. Since he had some education, Nestor, renamed Iskander, was employed in military administration and learned about Turkish artillery practices. He accompanied the unit on its march to Constantinople and then ran away, 'that I might not die in this wretched faith'. His account of the siege may have been written many years later when he was a monk in a Greek monastery, but it has the quality of a lived experience, a first-hand account of what he witnessed as a noncombatant. It has been suggested that he was attached to Giustiniani's forces at the Romanos Gate and helped them to identify the Ottoman commanders and their weaponry.

Siege warfare was revolutionised in the fifteenth century by the invention of cannon. In the 1420s when the Byzantines had their first experience of bombardment by cannon, they reduced the effectiveness of the new weapon by suspending bales of material, wood and anything that might absorb and diffuse its impact. But the fifth-century fortifications of Constantinople presented an easy target. Now Byzantium needed new technology as well as new warriors to match the enemy. Appreciating this vital combination, in 1451 Constantine XI employed a Christian engineer, a

Hungarian named Urban, to assist with the first, while he sent numerous appeals to the West for extra soldiers. But when he failed to pay Urban adequately, the cannon expert offered his skills to the Turkish side. The former allies of the Empire, meanwhile, sent little or no assistance.

It was undoubtedly Byzantine inability to invest in this technology of warfare that sealed the fate of the city. Once Urban was in the employ of the Sultan, who was happy to pay what he asked, the Hungarian cast the largest cannon ever produced, a 29 foot-long bore which fired enormous stones variously identified as weighing 1,200–1,300 lbs. This was called Imperial (*Basilica*) and was so heavy that a team of sixty oxen had to haul it from Edirne. It could only be fired seven times a day because it overheated so greatly. But once correctly positioned opposite the Gate of Romanos and fired, it brought down the ancient walls and created the historic breach through which the Ottoman forces entered the city on the morning of May 29th.

Against this monster weapon, the defenders set up their own much smaller cannon. But when fired they caused more damage to the ancient structures of the city than to the enemy. All the regular techniques of siege warfare were employed: the attackers dug tunnels under the walls, and built tall siege towers which they rolled up to the walls, in order to fix their scaling ladders. The defenders dug counter tunnels and threw burning material into those of the invaders; they poured hot pitch from the walls and set fire to anything wooden set against them. The smoke of fires, as well as cannon, meant that the combatants fought without seeing clearly what was around them.

In 1453 Easter was celebrated on Sunday April 1st, and the next day the Emperor ordered the boom which protected the city's harbour on the Golden Horn to be set in place. Once it was stretched between Constantinople and the Genoese colony of Pera it prevented ships from entering the harbour. As they watched the Turks bringing up their forces, the inhabitants must have realised that battle was about to commence. From April 11th, the cannon bombardment began and the following day the full Turkish fleet of 145 ships anchored two miles off from Constantinople. Fighting occurred on land and sea, with a major onslaught on the walls on April 18th, and a notable naval engagement on April 20th. After the land battle Constantine XI ordered the clergy and monks to gather up the dead and bury them: a total of 1,740 Greeks and 700 Franks (i.e. Westerners) and Armenians, against 18,000 Turks. This duty was repeated on April 25th, when 5,700 defenders were slain, and 35,000 enemy. While the figures (which vary from source to source) are not reliable, the sense of loss and disaster permeates all accounts. Constantinople had been under siege in effect for many years. In 1453 the actual conquest took forty-six days.

Towards the middle of May after stalwart resistance, the Sultan sent an envoy into the city to discuss a possible solution. Mehmet still wished to take the city, but he announced that he would lift the siege if the Emperor paid an annual tribute of 100,000 gold bezants. Alternatively, all the citizens could leave with their possessions and no one would be harmed. The Emperor summoned his council to discuss the proposal. No one seriously believed that such a huge sum could be raised as tribute, nor were they prepared to abandon the city. As in many earlier meetings he had with Cardinal Isidore and the clergy of Hagia Sophia, the Emperor refused to consider flight. Further discussion on the issue was useless. He had embraced his heroic role.

One aspect of the siege emphasised by many authors is the immense din of battle. The Turks made their dawn prayers and then advanced with castanets, tambourines, cymbals and terrifying war cries. Fifes, trumpets, pipes and lutes also accompanied the troops. Three centuries later this manifestation of Turkish military music inspired Mozart to some of his most exciting compositions. In response to the Turks' percussive noise, the Emperor ordered the bells of the city to be rung, and from the numerous churches the tolling of bells inspired the Christians to greater zeal. Trumpets blared at the arrival of troops in support of the city. Nestor-Iskander records how the sound of church bells summoned the noncombatants, priests, monks, women and children to collect the crosses and holy icons and bring them out to bless the city. He also says that women fought among the men and even children threw bricks and paving stones at the Turks once they were inside the city. His account reminds us of the long clash of Muslim and Christian forces which can still be heard today.

George Sprantzes, Constantine XI's loyal secretary, recorded the outcome of the final battle and the way the last emperor of Byzantium conducted himself:

> On Tuesday May 29th, early in the day, the sultan took possession of our City; in this time of capture my late master and emperor, Lord Constantine, was killed. I was not at his side at that hour but had been inspecting another part of the City according to his orders . . . What did my late lord the emperor not do publicly and privately in his efforts to gain some aid for his house, for the Christians and for his own life? Did he ever think that it was possible and easy for him to abandon the City, if something happened? . . . Who knew of our emperor's fastings and prayers, both his own and those of priests whom he paid to do so; of his services to the poor and of his increased pledges to God, in the hope of saving his subjects from the Turkish yoke? Nevertheless, God ignored his offerings, I know not why or for what sins, and men disregarded his efforts, as each individual spoke against him as he pleased.

In many respects the city of Constantinople which had for so long eluded the Arabs and Turks was no longer the great Queen of Cities it had once been. That city had already been destroyed in 1204 by Western forces of the Fourth Crusade who had plundered its wealth and then occupied it for fifty-seven years. When the Byzantines reconquered their capital in 1261, they attempted to restore its past glory but could never recreate its former strength. As the Ottomans closed in on their prize, Constantinople became the last outpost of Christian faith in the Middle East, and its inhabitants had to face their historic destiny. The battle between Christianity and Islam was joined around the city.

Constantine XI was the first to realise this and his disappearance during the last day of fighting heightened the myth of 1453. Although a head was solemnly presented to Sultan Mehmet and a corpse given to the Greeks for formal burial, Constantine's body was never found. As a result many stories of his escape and survival circulated. The idea that he had found shelter within the walls of the city and would emerge to triumph over the Muslims is typical. The prolonged resistance and bravery of the defenders made heroes of them all. And within a few years, to have been present in the city on May 29th, 1453, became a badge of honour, claimed by many who had been elsewhere. By the same token Sultan Mehmet would have delighted in the nickname which recognised his role in the fall: from the late fifteenth century onwards, and even today, 550 years later, he is still known as Mehmet the Conqueror.

For Further Reading

J. R. Melville Jones, *The Fall of Constantinople 1453: Seven Contemporary Accounts* (Amsterdam 1972); J. R. Jones, *Nicolo Barbaro: A Diary of the Siege of Constantinople 1453* (New York 1969); Nestor-Iskander, *The Tale of Constantinople (of Its Origin and Capture by the Turks in the Year 1453)*, translated and annotated by Walter K. Hanak and Marios Philippides (New Rochelle NY and Athens 1998); M. Philippides, *The Fall of the Byzantine Empire: A Chronicle by George Sphrantzes 1401–1477* (Amherst, 1980); Steven Runciman, *The Fall of Constantinople 1453* (Cambridge 1965); Mark Bartusis, *The Late Byzantine Army: Arms and Society, 1204–1453* (Philadelphia, 1992)

JUDITH HERRIN is Professor of Late Antique and Byzantine Studies at King's College London. Her most recent book is *Women in Purple. Rulers of Medieval Byzantium* (Weidenfeld and Nicolson, 2002).

UNIT 7

1500: The Era of Global Expansion

Unit Selections

Key Points to Consider

- To what extent could the 15th-century Chinese fleet have been a deterrent to western expansion in Asia? Why did the Chinese scuttle their fleet later in the century?

- Why were Jews and Muslims being expelled from Spain in 1492? Why is it ironic that this occurred at the same time Columbus's ships were leaving?

- What factors allowed the West to dominate the world during the age of exploration? What were the results of this domination?

- Why were spices a desired commodity? Why were the Portuguese able to dominate the trade in spices?

- What is the significance of Magellan's round-the-world voyage? What did it signify for both Western civilization and the world?

- What were the immediate results of the Battle of Lepanto? What were its long-term implications?

Student Web Site

www.mhcls.com

Internet References

Gander Academy's European Explorers Resources on the World Wide Web
   http://www.stemnet.nf.ca/CITE/explorer.htm
The Great Chinese Mariner Zheng He
   www.chinapage.com/zhenghe.html
Internet Medieval Sourcebook
   http://wwwfordham.edu/halsall/Sbook12.html
Magellan's Voyage Around the World
   www.fordham.edu/halsall/mod/1519magellan.html
NOVA Online: The Vikings
   http://www.pbs.org/wgbh/nova/vikings/

It might be argued that the most important event in the formation of the modern world is the industrial revolution. In that case, textbooks should divide at that point. A date of 1800 could roughly mark the start not only of the industrial revolution, but also the liberal, political revolts in France, the United States, and Latin America. Yet, 1500 is the time of the Reformation, the Renaissance, and the great global explorations. This is the start of the Western domination of the world that continues into the present. Therefore, most world historians accept 1500 as a suitable breaking point for teaching purposes. So it is with the two volumes of *Annual Editions: World History*.

In global exploration, the Scandinavians might have led the way with their colonies in Iceland, Greenland, and Nova Scotia. But, their attempt failed for ecological reasons. The Chinese also might have led the way if it had not been for indifference, internal economic problems, politics, and perhaps, arrogance. Zheng He, a court eunuch and Muslim, directed a powerful fleet westward on successful explorations that carried him to India and the eastern coast of Africa. But, the Chinese government stopped the voyages and destroyed the ships. Like those of the Vikings, the Chinese discoveries were left unexploited.

Subsequent explorations were left to the Europeans, who had the ambition as well as the technology to undertake them. The Portuguese sailed southward around Africa, while Christopher Columbus headed westward. His encounter with a new world changed the course of history and paved the way for other Europeans to follow and share in the exploitation of lands and peoples. The quincentenary of his 1492 voyage brought unprecedented criticism from native activist groups, who see Columbus as the symbol of their subsequent oppression.

Another group of people left Spain the day before Columbus sailed toward the Americas. Jews and Muslims who refused to convert to Christianity were expelled from Spain by the Catholic monarchs Ferdinand and Isabella. Cordoba, Spain had been a seat of Islamic culture during the classical period of Islamic civilization, while the rest of Europe was immersed in the so-called Dark Ages. During this *reconquista* or re-conquest of Spain, the king and queen engaged in an early form of ethnic cleansing.

Global expansion led rapidly to western world dominance. Non-Western cultures after 1500 were progressively less able to preserve their own cultural and political autonomy, and thousands if not millions perished through the spread of European diseases. Driven by a combination of greed and religious fervor, Europeans explored the world. The search for spices drove the Portuguese to India, and a competitive spirit led Magellan to circumnavigate the globe, a feat accomplished by no other civilization.

Through these voyages, Europeans were able to bypass the Middle East and open up new trade lanes. That marked the beginning of a global shift in commerce. Time and technology were on the side of the West.

1492: The Prequel

Decades before Columbus, Zheng He sailed from China with 300 ships and 28,000 men. His fleet got as far as Africa and could have easily reached America, but the Chinese turned back. What happened?

NICHOLAS D. KRISTOF

From the sea, the tiny East African island of Pate, just off the Kenyan coast, looks much as it must have in the 15th century: an impenetrable shore of endless mangrove trees. As my little boat bounced along the waves in the gray dawn, I could see no antennae or buildings or even gaps where trees had been cut down, no sign of human habitation, nothing but a dense and mysterious jungle.

The village's inhabitants, much lighter-skinned than people on the Kenyan mainland, emerged barefoot to stare at me with the same curiosity with which I was studying them. These were people I had come halfway around the world to see, in the hope of solving an ancient historical puzzle.

The boatman drew as close as he could to a narrow black-sand beach, and I splashed ashore. My local Swahili interpreter led the way through the forest, along a winding trail scattered with mangoes, coconuts and occasional seashells deposited by high tides. The tropical sun was firmly overhead when we finally came upon a village of stone houses with thatched roofs, its dirt paths sheltered by palm trees. The village's inhabitants, much lighter-skinned than people on the Kenyan mainland, emerged barefoot to stare at me with the same curiosity with which I was studying them. These were people I had come halfway around the world to see, in the hope of solving an ancient historical puzzle.

"Tell me," I asked the first group I encountered, "where did the people here come from? Long ago, did foreign sailors ever settle here?"

The answer was a series of shrugs. "I've never heard about that," one said. "You'll have to ask the elders."

I tried several old men and women without success. Finally the villagers led me to the patriarch of the village, Bwana Mkuu Al-Bauri, the keeper of oral traditions. He was a frail old man

with gray stubble on his cheeks, head and chest. He wore a yellow sarong around his waist; his ribs pressed through the taut skin on his bare torso. Al-Bauri hobbled out of his bed, resting on a cane and the arm of a grandson. He claimed to be 121 years old; a pineapple-size tumor jutted from the left side of his chest.

"I know this from my grandfather, who himself was the keeper of history here," the patriarch told me in an unexpectedly clear voice. "Many, many years ago, there was a ship from China that wrecked on the rocks off the coast near here. The sailors swam ashore near the village of Shanga—my ancestors were there and saw it themselves. The Chinese were visitors, so we helped those Chinese men and gave them food and shelter, and then they married our women. Although they do not live in this village, I believe their descendants still can be found somewhere else on this island."

I almost felt like hugging Bwana Al-Bauri. For months I had been poking around obscure documents and research reports, trying to track down a legend of an ancient Chinese shipwreck that had led to a settlement on the African coast. My interest arose from a fascination with what to me is a central enigma of the millennium: why did the West triumph over the East?

For most of the last several thousand years, it would have seemed far likelier that Chinese or Indians, not Europeans, would dominate the world by the year 2000, and that America and Australia would be settled by Chinese rather than by the inhabitants of a backward island called Britain. The reversal of fortunes of East and West strikes me as the biggest news story of the millennium, and one of its most unexpected as well.

As a resident of Asia for most of the past 13 years, I've been searching for an explanation. It has always seemed to me that the turning point came in the early 1400's, when Admiral Zheng He sailed from China to conquer the world. Zheng He (pronounced JUNG HUH) was an improbable commander of a great Chinese fleet, in that he was a Muslim from a rebel family and had been seized by the Chinese Army when he was still a boy. Like many other prisoners of the time, he was castrated—his sexual organs completely hacked off, a process that killed many of those who suffered it. But he was a brilliant and tenacious boy who grew up to be physically imposing. A natural leader, he had the good fortune to be assigned, as a houseboy, to the household of a great prince, Zhu Di.

In time, the prince and Zheng He grew close, and they conspired to overthrow the prince's nephew, the Emperor of China. With Zheng He as one of the prince's military commanders, the revolt succeeded and the prince became China's Yongle Emperor. One of the emperor's first acts (after torturing to death those who had opposed him) was to reward Zheng He with the command of a great fleet that was to sail off and assert China's pre-eminence in the world.

Between 1405 and 1433, Zheng He led seven major expeditions, commanding the largest armada the world would see for the next five centuries. Not until World War I did the West mount anything comparable. Zheng He's fleet included 28,000 sailors on 300 ships, the longest of which were 400 feet. By comparison, Columbus in 1492 had 90 sailors on three ships, the biggest of which was 85 feet long. Zheng He's ships also had advanced design elements that would not be introduced in Europe for another 350 years, including balanced rudders and watertight bulwark compartments.

The sophistication of Zheng He's fleet underscores just how far ahead of the West the East once was. Indeed, except for the period of the Roman Empire, China had been wealthier, more advanced and more cosmopolitan than any place in Europe for several thousand years. Hangzhou, for example, had a population in excess of a million during the time it was China's capital (in the 12th century), and records suggest that as early as the 7th century, the city of Guangzhou had 200,000 foreign residents: Arabs, Persians, Malays, Indians, Africans and Turks. By contrast, the largest city in Europe in 1400 was probably Paris, with a total population of slightly more than 100,000.

A half-century before Columbus, Zheng He had reached East Africa and learned about Europe from Arab traders. The Chinese could easily have continued around the Cape of Good Hope and established direct trade with Europe. But as they saw it, Europe was a backward region, and China had little interest in the wool, beads and wine Europe had to trade. Africa had what China wanted—ivory, medicines, spices, exotic woods, even specimens of native wildlife.

In Zheng He's time, China and India together accounted for more than half of the world's gross national product, as they have for most of human history. Even as recently as 1820, China accounted for 29 percent of the global economy and India another 16 percent, according to the calculations of Angus Maddison, a leading British economic historian.

Asia's retreat into relative isolation after the expeditions of Zheng He amounted to a catastrophic missed opportunity, one that laid the groundwork for the rise of Europe and, eventually, America. Westerners often attribute their economic advantage today to the intelligence, democratic habits or hard work of their forebears, but a more important reason may well have been the folly of 15th-century Chinese rulers. That is why I came to be fascinated with Zheng He and set out earlier this year to retrace his journeys. I wanted to see what legacy, if any, remained of his achievement, and to figure out why his travels did not remake the world in the way that Columbus's did.

Westerners often attribute their economic advantage today to the intelligence or hard work of their forebears, but a more important reason may well have been the folly of the 15th-century Chinese rulers who dismantled Zheng He's fleet.

Zheng He lived in Nanjing, the old capital, where I arrived one day in February. Nanjing is a grimy metropolis on the Yangtze River in the heart of China. It has been five centuries since Zheng He's death, and his marks on the city have grown faint. The shipyards that built his fleet are still busy, and the courtyard of what had been his splendid 72-room mansion is now the Zheng He Memorial Park, where children roller-skate and old couples totter around for exercise. But though the park has a small Zheng He museum, it was closed—for renovation, a caretaker told me, though he knew of no plans to reopen it.

I'd heard that Zheng He's tomb is on a hillside outside the city, and I set out to find it. It wasn't long before the road petered out, from asphalt to gravel to dirt to nothing. No tomb was in sight, so I approached an old man weeding a vegetable garden behind his house. Tang Yiming, 72, was still lithe and strong. His hair was gray and ragged where he had cut it himself, disastrously, in front of a mirror. Evidently lonely, he was delighted to talk, and offered to show me the path to the tomb. As we walked, I mentioned that I had read that there used to be an old Ming Dynasty tablet on Zheng He's grave.

"Oh, yeah, the old tablet," he said nonchalantly. "When I was a boy, there was a Ming Dynasty tablet here. When it disappeared, the Government offered a huge reward to anyone who would return it—a reward big enough to build a new house. Seemed like a lot of money. But the problem was that we couldn't give it back. People around here are poor. We'd smashed it up to use as building materials."

A second mystery concerned what, if anything, is actually buried in Zheng He's tomb, since he is believed to have died on his last voyage and been buried at sea. So I said in passing that I'd heard tell the tomb is empty, and let my voice trail off.

"Oh, there's nothing in there," Tang said, a bit sadly. "No bones, nothing. That's for sure."

"How do you know?"

"In 1962, people dug up the grave, looking for anything to sell. We dug up the ground to one and a half times the height of a man. But there was absolutely nothing in there. It's empty."

The absence of impressive monuments to Zheng He in China today should probably come as no surprise, since his achievement was ultimately renounced. Curiously, it is not in China but in Indonesia where his memory has been most actively kept alive. Zheng He's expeditions led directly to the wave of Chinese immigration to Southeast Asia, and in some countries he is regarded today as a deity. In the Indonesia city of Semarang, for example, there is a large temple honoring Zheng He, located near a cave where he once nursed a sick friend. Indonesians still pray to Zheng He for a cure or good luck.

Not so in his native land. Zheng He was viewed with deep suspicion by China's traditional elite, the Confucian scholars, who made sure to destroy the archives of his journey. Even so, it is possible to learn something about his story from Chinese sources—from imperial archives and even the memoirs of crewmen. The historical record makes clear, for example, that it was not some sudden impulse of extroversion that led to Zheng He's achievement. It grew, rather, out of a long sailing tradition. Chinese accounts suggest that in the fifth century, a Chinese monk sailed to a mysterious "far east country" that sounds very much like Mayan Mexico, and Mayan art at that time suddenly began to include Buddhist symbols. By the 13th century, Chinese ships regularly traveled to India and occasionally to East Africa.

Zheng He's armada was far grander, of course, than anything that came before. His grandest vessels were the "treasure ships," 400 feet long and 160 feet wide, with nine masts raising red silk sails to the wind, as well as multiple decks and luxury cabins with balconies. His armada included supply ships to carry horses, troop transports, warships, patrol boats and as many as 20 tankers to carry fresh water. The full contingent of 28,000 crew members included interpreters for Arabic and other languages, astrologers to forecast the weather, astronomers to study the stars, pharmacologists to collect medicinal plants, ship-repair specialists, doctors and even two protocol officers to help organize official receptions.

In the aftermath of such an incredible undertaking, you somehow expect to find a deeper mark on Chinese history, a greater legacy. But perhaps the faintness of Zheng He's trace in contemporary China is itself a lesson. In the end, an explorer makes history but does not necessarily change it, for his impact depends less on the trail he blazes than on the willingness of others to follow. The daring of a great expedition ultimately is hostage to the national will of those who remain behind.

I n February I traveled to Calicut, a port town in southwestern India that was (and still is) the pepper capital of the world. The evening I arrived, I went down to the beach in the center of town to look at the coastline where Zheng He once had berthed his ships. In the 14th and 15th centuries, Calicut was one of the world's great ports, known to the Chinese as "the great country of the Western ocean." In the early 15th century, the sight of Zheng He's fleet riding anchor in Calicut harbor symbolized the strength of the world's two greatest powers, China and India.

On this sultry evening, the beach, framed by long piers jutting out to sea, was crowded with young lovers and ice-cream vendors. Those piers are all that remain of the port of Calicut, and you can see at a glance that they are no longer usable. The following day I visited the port offices, musty with handwritten ledgers of ship visits dating back nearly a century. The administrator of the port, Captain E. G. Mohanan, explained matter-of-factly what had happened. "The piers got old and no proper maintenance was ever carried out," he said, as a ceiling fan whirred tiredly overhead. "By the time we thought of it, it was not economical to fix it up." So in 1989, trade was halted, and one of the great ports of the world became no port at all.

The disappearance of a great Chinese fleet from a great Indian port symbolized one of history's biggest lost opportunities—Asia's failure to dominate the second half of this millennium. So how did this happen?

While Zheng He was crossing the Indian Ocean, the Confucian scholar-officials who dominated the upper echelons of the Chinese Government were at political war with the eunuchs, a group they regarded as corrupt and immoral. The eunuchs' role at court involved looking after the concubines, but they also served as palace administrators, often doling out contracts in exchange for kickbacks. Partly as a result of their legendary greed, they promoted commerce. Unlike the scholars—who owed their position to their mastery of 2,000-year-old texts—the eunuchs, lacking any such roots in a classical past, were sometimes outward-looking and progressive. Indeed, one can argue that it was the virtuous, incorruptible scholars who in the mid-15th century set China on its disastrous course.

After the Yongle Emperor died in 1424, China endured a series of brutal power struggles; a successor emperor died under suspicious circumstances and ultimately the scholars emerged triumphant. They ended the voyages of Zheng He's successors, halted construction of new ships and imposed curbs on private shipping. To prevent any backsliding, they destroyed Zheng He's sailing records and, with the backing of the new emperor, set about dismantling China's navy.

By 1500 the Government had made it a capital offense to build a boat with more than two masts, and in 1525 the Government ordered the destruction of all oceangoing ships. The greatest navy in history, which a century earlier had 3,500 ships (by comparison, the United States Navy today has 324), had been extinguished, and China set a course for itself that would lead to poverty, defeat and decline.

Still, it was not the outcome of a single power struggle in the 1440's that cost China its worldly influence. Historians offer a host of reasons for why Asia eventually lost its way economically and was late to industrialize; two and a half reasons seem most convincing.

The first is that Asia was simply not greedy enough. The dominant social ethos in ancient China was Confucianism and in India it was caste, with the result that the elites in both nations looked down their noses at business. Ancient China cared about many things—prestige, honor, culture, arts, education, ancestors, religion, filial piety—but making money came far down the list. Confucius had specifically declared that it was wrong for a man to make a distant voyage while his parents were alive, and he had condemned profit as the concern of "a little man." As it was, Zheng He's ships were built on such a grand scale and carried such lavish gifts to foreign leaders that the voyages were not the huge money spinners they could have been.

In contrast to Asia, Europe was consumed with greed. Portugal led the age of discovery in the 15th century largely because it wanted spices, a precious commodity; it was the hope of profits that drove its ships steadily farther down the African coast and eventually around the Horn to Asia. The profits of this trade could be vast: Magellan's crew once sold a cargo of 26 tons of cloves for 10,000 times the cost.

A second reason for Asia's economic stagnation is more difficult to articulate but has to do with what might be called a culture of complacency. China and India shared a tendency to look inward, a devotion to past ideals and methods, a respect for authority and a suspicion of new ideas. David S. Landes, a Harvard economist, has written of ancient China's "intellectual xenophobia"; the former Indian Prime Minister Jawaharlal Nehru referred to the "petrification of classes" and the "static nature" of Indian society. These are all different ways of describing the same economic and intellectual complacency.

Chinese elites regarded their country as the "Middle Kingdom" and believed they had nothing to learn from barbarians abroad. India exhibited much of the same self-satisfaction. "Indians didn't go to Portugal not because they couldn't but because they didn't want to," mused M. P. Sridharan, a historian, as we sat talking on the porch of his home in Calicut.

The 15th-century Portuguese were the opposite. Because of its coastline and fishing industry, Portugal always looked to the sea, yet rivalries with Spain and other countries shut it out of the Mediterranean trade. So the only way for Portugal to get at the wealth of the East was by conquering the oceans.

The half reason is simply that China was a single nation while Europe was many. When the Confucian scholars reasserted control in Beijing and banned shipping, their policy mistake condemned all of China. In contrast, European countries committed economic suicide selectively. So when Portugal slipped into a quasi-Chinese mind-set in the 16th century, slaughtering Jews and burning heretics and driving astronomers and scientists abroad, Holland and England were free to take up the slack.

When I first began researching Zheng He, I never thought I'd be traveling all the way to Africa to look for traces of his voyages. Then I came across a few intriguing references to the possibility of an ancient Chinese shipwreck that might have left some Chinese stranded on the island of Pate (pronounced PAH-tay). One was a skeptical reference in a scholarly journal, another was a casual conversation with a Kenyan I met a few years ago and the third was the epilogue of Louise Levathes's wonderful 1994 book about China's maritime adventures, "When China Ruled the Seas." Levathes had traveled to Kenya and found people who believed they were descended from survivors of a Chinese shipwreck. So, on a whim and an expense account, I flew to Lamu, an island off northern Kenya, and hired a boat and an interpreter to go to Pate and see for myself.

Pate is off in its own world, without electricity or roads or vehicles. Mostly jungle, it has been shielded from the 20th century largely because it is accessible from the Kenyan mainland only by taking a boat through a narrow tidal channel that is passable only at high tide. Initially I was disappointed by what I found there. In the first villages I visited, I saw people who were light-skinned and had hair that was not tightly curled, but they could have been part Arab or European rather than part Chinese. The remote villages of Chundwa and Faza were more promising, for there I found people whose eyes, hair and complexion hinted at Asian ancestry, though their background was ambiguous.

And then on a still and sweltering afternoon I strolled through the coconut palms into the village of Siyu, where I met a fisherman in his 40's named Abdullah Mohammed Badui. I stopped and stared at the man in astonishment, for he had light skin and narrow eyes. Fortunately, he was as rude as I was, and we stared at each other in mutual surprise before venturing a word. Eventually I asked him about his background and appearance.

"I am in the Famao clan," he said. "There are 50 or 100 of us Famao left here. Legend has it that we are descended from Chinese and others.

"A Chinese ship was coming along and it hit rocks and wrecked," Badui continued. "The sailors swam ashore to the village that we now call Shanga, and they married the local women, and that is why we Famao look so different."

Another Famao, with the same light complexion and vaguely Asian features, approached to listen. His name was Athman Mohammed Mzee, and he, too, told of hearing of the Chinese shipwreck from the elders. He volunteered an intriguing detail: the Africans had given giraffes to the Chinese.

Salim Bonaheri, a 55-year-old Famao man I met the next day, proudly declared, "My ancestors were Chinese or Vietnamese or something like that." I asked how they had got to Pate.

"I don't know," Bonaheri said with a shrug. Most of my conversations were like that, intriguing but frustrating dead ends. I was surrounded by people whose appearance seemed tantalizingly Asian, but who had only the vaguest notions of why that might be. I kept at it, though, and eventually found people like Khalifa Mohammed Omar, a 55-year-old Famao fisherman who looked somewhat Chinese and who also clearly remembered the stories passed down by his grandfather. From him and others, a tale emerged.

Countless generations ago, they said, Chinese sailors traded with local African kings. The local kings gave them giraffes to take back to China. One of the Chinese ships struck rocks off the eastern coast of Pate, and the sailors swam ashore, carrying with them porcelain and other goods from the ship. In time they married local women, converted to Islam and named the village Shanga, after Shanghai. Later, fighting erupted among Pate's clans, Shanga was destroyed and the Famao fled, some to the mainland, others to the village of Siyu.

Every time I heard the story about the giraffes my pulse began to race. Chinese records indicate that Zheng He had brought the first giraffes to China, a fact that is not widely known. The giraffe caused an enormous stir in China because it was believed to be the mythical *qilin,* or Chinese unicorn. It is difficult to imagine how African villagers on an island as remote as Pate would know about the giraffes unless the tale had been handed down to them by the Chinese sailors.

Chinese ceramics are found in many places along the east African coast, and their presence on Pate could be the result of purchases from Arab traders. But the porcelain on Pate was overwhelmingly concentrated among the Famao clan, which could mean that it had been inherited rather than purchased. I also visited some ancient Famao graves that looked less like traditional Kenyan graves than what the Chinese call "turtle-shell graves," with rounded tops.

165

Researchers have turned up other equally tantalizing clues. Craftsmen on Pate and the other islands of Lamu practice a kind of basket-weaving that is common in southern China but unknown on the Kenyan mainland. On Pate, drums are more often played in the Chinese than the African style, and the local dialect has a few words that may be Chinese in origin. More startling, in 1569 a Portuguese priest named Monclaro wrote that Pate had a flourishing silk-making industry—Pate, and no other place in the region. Elders in several villages on Pate confirmed to me that their island had produced silk until about half a century ago.

When I asked my boatman, Bakari Muhaji Ali, if he thought it was possible that a ship could have wrecked off the coast near Shanga, he laughed. "There are undersea rocks all over there," he said. "If you don't know exactly where you're going, you'll wreck your ship for sure."

If indeed there was a Chinese shipwreck off Pate, there is reason to think it happened in Zheng He's time. For if the shipwreck had predated him, surviving sailors would not have passed down stories of the giraffes. And if the wreck didn't occur until after Zheng He, its survivors could not have settled in Shanga, since British archeological digs indicate that the village was sacked, burned and abandoned in about 1440—very soon after Zheng He's last voyage.

Still, there is no hard proof for the shipwreck theory, and there are plenty of holes in it. No ancient Chinese characters have been found on tombs in Pate, no nautical instruments have ever turned up on the island and there are no Chinese accounts of an African shipwreck. This last lacuna might be explained by the destruction of the fleet's records. Yet if one of Zheng He's ships did founder on the rocks off Pate, then why didn't some other ships in the fleet come to the sailors' rescue?

As I made my way back through the jungle for the return trip, I pondered the significance of what I'd seen on Pate. In the faces of the Famao, in those bits of pottery and tantalizing hints of Chinese culture, I felt as though I'd glimpsed the shadowy outlines of one of the greatest might-have-beens of the millennium now ending. I thought about the Columbian Exchange, the swap of animals, plants, genes, germs, weapons and peoples that utterly remade both the New World and the Old, and I couldn't help wondering about another exchange—Zheng He's—that never took place, yet could have.

If ancient China had been greedier and more outward-looking, if other traders had followed in Zheng He's wake and then continued on, Asia might well have dominated Africa and even Europe. Chinese might have settled in not only Malaysia and Singapore, but also in East Africa, the Pacific Islands, even in America. Perhaps the Famao show us what the mestizos of such a world might have looked liked, the children of a hybrid culture that was never born. What I'd glimpsed in Pate was the high-water mark of an Asian push that simply stopped—not for want of ships or know-how, but strictly for want of national will.

All this might seem fanciful, and yet in Zheng He's time the prospect of a New World settled by the Spanish or English would have seemed infinitely more remote than a New World made by the Chinese. How different would history have been had Zheng He continued on to America? The mind rebels; the ramifications are almost too overwhelming to contemplate. So consider just one: this magazine would have been published in Chinese.

NICHOLAS D. KRISTOF is the Tokyo bureau chief of *The New York Times.* He is the author, with Sheryl WuDunn, of "China Wakes."

The Other 1492: Jews and Muslims in Columbus's Spain

Fouad Ajami

The Edict of Expulsion issued by Ferdinand and Isabella on March 31, 1492, had the Jews quitting Spain on the last day of July of the same year. All Don Isaac Abravanel could do for his people was secure them a two-day stay of execution. Abravanel, one of the great figures of Iberian Jewry, had given Ferdinand and Isabella eight years of service: he had organized the chaotic finances of Castile and Aragon and helped the sovereigns in their final push against the Muslim stronghold of Granada. The work of the Reconquista against Muslim Spain completed, Don Isaac was suddenly thrown into the supreme challenge of his life.

Fragments survive of Abravanel's futile pleas to the Spanish sovereigns. There is the narrative by Don Isaac himself recorded in exile: "Thrice on my knees I besought the King. 'Regard us, O king, use not thy subjects so cruelly.' But as the adder closes its ear with dust against the voice of the charmer, so the King hardened his heart against entreaties of his supplicants."

Ferdinand and Isabella offered Don Isaac the chance to stay in Spain with his wealth and position intact—the edict had prohibited the Jews from taking any gold, coins, or silver with them. In return, he would of course have to undergo baptism and conversion. Abravanel chose dispossession and exile. There were lands where the life of the faith could be lived—the Italian city-states, Portugal, the Netherlands, the Muslim domains of the Ottoman Sultan, the Barbary states of Tunis, Algiers, and Tripoli, and there was a haven in Egypt.

Thanks to the two-day extension secured by Abravanel the last ships that took the Jews to these lands left Spain on the second of August. "This fleet of woe and misery," says one chronicler, was to sail parallel to a fleet of high promise. Christopher Columbus's fleet was ready for sea on the second of August: the men received their communion at the Church of St. George in Palos on that day. The Captain General set sail in the early hours of the third day of August.

Months earlier there had been another departure: Boabdil, the last Muslim king of Granada, took to the road. History and grief and yearning have touched and ennobled that story. On the last ridge, overlooking Granada, the storytellers say, Boabdil paused to catch a final glimpse of his realm. The ridge came to be known as El Ultimo Sospiro del Moro, the Moor's last sigh. Boabdil's unsentimental mother is said to have taunted him during his moment of grief. "You should weep like a woman for the land you could not defend like a man." In truth, there was not much that Boabdil could have done. Granada was living on borrowed time. Boabdil cut the best possible deal with the Spanish: an estate for himself, a pledge of safety for the people of his city, safe passage for those who could not bear to live under Christian rule. The victors made another promise: Muslims who stayed behind were not to be molested; their religious rights were to be honored. That pledge would be violated. The remaining Muslims would face, a decade hence, the same choice offered the Jews: conversion or exile. A century later the Moriscos—the Moorish converts to Christianity—were also expelled.

Men invent and reinvent the past. In the legend of Moorish Spain, the Jews of Toledo opened the gates of the city to the Muslim conquerors when they came in 711. They were eager to welcome the Muslim armies that had overrun the Visigothic kingdom. The legend is groundless. In the war between the Goths and the Muslim armies, the Jews were, for the most part, quiet spectators. To be sure, they were glad to see the defeat of the Goths. The same must have been true of the Ibero-Roman natives of the peninsula. The Goths had been severe rulers. They had not allowed the Jews to sing their Psalms, to celebrate Passover, to testify in court against Christians, or to observe their dietary laws. Forced baptisms of Jews was a recurring phenomenon under Visigothic rule. Centuries later Montesquieu was to observe that "all the laws of the Inquisition had been part of the Visigothic code" that regulated the conduct of the Jews in seventh-century Spain.

It was a polyglot world that the Muslims came to rule in the Iberian peninsula. There were Arabs, Berbers, Jews, and blacks, Muslims of native Spanish stock, native Christians. Islam was overextended in Spain; it thus made its accommodation with its habitat, ruled with a light touch. At its zenith in the tenth and eleventh centuries, it was to fashion a society of tranquillity and brilliance. Its cities thrived. Cordoba's population approximated a quarter million people; it was unmatched by any European city of the time. Its only rivals were the cities of Baghdad and Constantinople. The economy of Muslim Spain boomed, tied as it was to the larger Muslim economy. The Jews came into their own during these two centuries of prosperity. Literacy spread; Jewish academies opened in Cordoba, Granada, Toledo, Barcelona. Hispano-Arabic culture thrived in the cities of the south. A rich body of Judeo-Arabic philosophy was to become the distinctive gift of this age. Spanish Jewry declared its intellectual independence from the religious authority of the Iraqi academies that had been pre-eminent down through the ages. The Arabs had prided themselves on their poetry and literature; the Jews were to run a close race.

This was a world in flux, an ideal setting for a community of outsiders. There was room for talent; it was easy for Jews to find their way into all walks of public life. "No office, except that of the ruler, seemed to be out of the reach of a talented and ambitious Jew," Norman Stillman writes in his historical survey, *The Jews in Arab Lands*. Success at court was not without its hazards though. It called forth its steady companion—the wrath of the crowd. A Jew by the name of Samuel ben Naghrela was the ruler's minister in the Berber kingdom of Granada until his death in 1056. Ten years later his son, Joseph, was crucified by a mob on the city's main gate in an anti-Jewish riot. The father had risen on his own: he knew the hazards of success. The son had taken success for granted. He was, says one chronicle, "proud to his own hurt and the Berber princes were jealous of him." This riot was the first massacre of Jews in Muslim Spain. The date was December 30, 1066. About 1,500 families perished in that riot.

No measure of cultural brilliance would compensate for the political fragility of the edifice. A Muslim poet of Granada may have intuited the weakness underneath the cultural glitter when he wrote that he had "the fault of rising in the West." The Muslims had conquered the plains and the Mediterranean coast. The mountains in the north, the poorer regions of old Castile, were in Christian hands. This set the stage for a bloody and long struggle.

Trouble came to paradise as the eleventh century drew to a close. The Jews were caught between the pressures of the Reconquista and a Muslim society awakening to a new sense of vulnerability—and intolerance. Moses Ben Maimon, better known as Maimonides (1131–1204), the great figure of medieval Jewish life, quit his native birthplace in Cordoba and sought shelter in Cairo. (Maimonides became a luminary in the life of Cairo; he rose to become the physician of Saladin.) A yearning for Zion, for life in the land of Israel, was to find its way into the poetry of the time. The "Golden Age" of the Jews of Muslim Spain had drawn to a close. Small messianic Jewish movements made their appearance—an expression of the malaise of the Jews as the Andalusian cocoon was to be torn asunder.

Little was to remain of the Moorish realms in the peninsula. Toledo had been lost in 1085; Cordoba itself in 1236, Valencia in 1238, Seville two years later. By 1264 all that remained were Granada and its surroundings. That Muslim foothold was spared because the warring kingdoms to its north—Castile, Aragon, Navarre, Portugal—had been busy with their own feuds. Reconquista remained in abeyance, while Granada became a veritable protectorate of Castile. The loss of Constantinople to the Ottoman Turks in 1453 would help focus the attention of Christendom on Granada. Granada would now become a matter of faith rather than realpolitik. The unification of Castile and Aragon under Ferdinand and Isabella sealed Granada's fate.

Hope had deluded the Jews in the domains of Ferdinand and Isabella. The Crown, traditionally the protector of the Jews against the Church and townsmen, would be more audacious now. The Jews would be dispossessed and fed to the mob in the service of royal absolutism.

Pick up the trail a good century before the Inquisition and Edict of Expulsion: over the course of that pivotal century the place of the Jews in Spain had become untenable. The Jews farmed the taxes of the state; they were the ideal scapegoat for all the disgruntled. The mob and the priests who led the mob in intermittent outbursts against the Jews saw a Jewish conspiracy behind every cruel turn of fate. Jewish physicians were carrying poison under their fingernails, Jewish sorcerers were everywhere, a Jewish cabal was out to undo Christianity.

The Jewish world was hit with great ferocity in a wave of massacres that took place in 1391. The troubles began in Seville and spread to Cordoba, Valencia, and Barcelona. Before the great terror subsided, some 25,000 may have been killed. A new law was passed in 1412: the so-called "Ordinance on the Enclosure of the Jews and Moors" at Valladolid. The Jews were now to wear a distinctive yellow garment; Jews and Moors were banned from serving as spice dealers, tax farmers, moneylenders, physicians, or surgeons; they were to live in separate enclosures locked and guarded at night. A massive wave of conversion was to take place in 1412–15.

Baptism bought time for those who chose it. But now a new crisis threatened. Where they had been a people apart, the sin of the Jews was separation. Now it was their assimilation that agitated their enemies. The Grand Inquisitor doing his work in the 1480s would claim that he was hunting crypto-Jews among the conversos. We know better now, thanks to the able work of the Israeli historian Benzion Netanyahu. In a book titled *The Marranos of Spain* Netanyahu turns the story inside out. Conversion had worked, it had depleted the Jewish world and increased the self-confidence of the conversos. They were no longer a minority who had gone astray; they now outnumbered the Jews of the realm.

Mobility denied the Jews was now theirs. They flocked into professions from which they had been excluded: the law, the army, the universities, the church. One rabbi, Solomon Levi, christened as Paul de Santa Maria, rose to become bishop of Burgos. The Talmudist Joshua Halorqi left Judaism for the Church, took the name Jeronimo de Santa Fe, and became a zealous advocate of his new faith. By 1480 half the important offices in the court of Aragon were occupied by conversos or their children. The great energy of the conversos rankled the Jews, increasing numbers of whom dispensed with the cherished notion that the conversos were *anusim* (forced ones) who were destined to return to the faith. More important, though, it galvanized the forces that sought the eradication of the Jewish presence in Spain. If the Jews had slipped through the gate as converts, they had to be banished and destroyed. The line had to be redrawn. Tomas de Torquemada, the priest who was the evil genius of the Inquisition, knew where he was heading.

The conversos and those who remained true to the Jewish faith may have taken two separate paths. In one swift, terrible decade, Torquemada would bring them together. The Inquisition in 1481 against the conversos, the Edict of Expulsion in 1492.

A tale of dubious authenticity has the Ottoman Sultan Bayezid II (1481–1512) wondering about Ferdinand and about the folly of his expulsion of the Jews: "Do they call this Ferdinand a wise prince who impoverishes his kingdom and thereby enriches mine?" The tale aside, the lands of Islam provided safe havens for the Jews. The gates of many Muslim realms were opened before the Sephardim. The new lands were eager to accommodate them, as they brought with them new skills in the making of weaponry and gunpowder, in printing and medicine. They knew the languages of Europe. In the great struggle of the age between Islam and Christendom the Jews found a reprieve. For the rulers of the Ottoman Empire the Jews were ideal subjects.

By the standards of Europe in the High Middle Ages, the world of Islam was, on the whole, a tolerant world. It was not an "interfaith utopia" (to borrow the words of the distinguished historian of Islam Bernard Lewis). The life the Jews led was circumscribed. It was a life without illusions. There was a clear division of labor; political power, careers in the bureaucracy and the military were off limits. There was a body of discriminatory law: houses of worship could not be built higher than mosques; Jews and Christians were often required to wear distinctive garb. They could not bear arms or ride horses. They had to pay higher taxes than those paid by Muslims.

And some Muslim realms were harder than others. Morocco stood out in the degradation it heaped upon the Jews. Here Islam was frontier Islam, embittered by wars against Portugal and Spain. The Jews were the only non-Muslim community in Morocco. The limits imposed upon them—enclosed ghettos that functioned like the Juderias of Aragon and Castile—recalled the degradations of Europe. The Jews of Morocco lived at the mercy of the elements. It was feast or famine. Merciful sultans alternated with cruel ones. What the sultans gave, the preachers and the crowd frequently took away. The protection the rulers offered in this wild and anarchic realm could never withstand what one historian described as the three miseries of Morocco: plague, famine, and civil war.

It was easier in other Muslim lands. The private domain Islamic rule conceded, the freedom from forced conversions must have seemed particularly generous when compared with what prevailed in medieval Europe. A Jew writing to his co-religionists in Europe described Turkey as a land where "every man may dwell at peace under his own vine and fig tree." The Jews were a people on the run. The tolerance in the new surroundings seemed wondrous. A converso who made a new life in Turkey and returned to the faith spoke of Turkey in nearly messianic terms, described it as "a broad expansive sea which our Lord has opened with the rod of his mercy. Here the gates of liberty are wide open for you that you may fully practice your Judaism."

Jewish centers of learning and commerce sprouted throughout the Muslim world. Salonika, conquered by the Turks early in the 1400s, was to become, for all practical purposes, a Jewish city. Jews became the city's overwhelming majority. They dominated the life of the city until its loss to the Greeks in 1912. A substantial Jewish colony laid roots in Istanbul. The town of Safed, in Palestine, attracted Jewish textile makers and scholars, and became a famous center of learning. Close by there was a protected niche for the Jews in the life of Egypt. Baghdad's Jewry was perhaps in a league by itself. It had its academies, a vigorous mercantile elite with far-flung commercial operations.

Then the world of the Jews of Islam closed up. It happened over a long period of time. The civilization of Islam itself went into eclipse, its Ottoman standard-bearers were overtaken by Europe in the seventeenth century. The Jews who had done well by civilization in the midst of a surge were to suffer its demise. Increasingly the Christian European powers set the terms of the traffic with Islamic lands. For intermediaries these European powers preferred the local Christian communities—Greeks, Armenians, Christian Arabs. And these local Christians were sworn enemies of the Jews, bent on cutting them out of international commerce and diplomacy. The knowledge—of foreign languages, of science and medicine—that Jews had brought with them from Europe had receded and been rendered obsolete. European missions were busy at work shoring up the skills and the privileges of the Christians of the "east." On the defensive, the Islamic order itself was growing increasingly xenophobic and intolerant. The submission to Europe had to be hidden under displays of chauvinism. The Jews of Islam headed into a long night. The center of the Jewish world had long shifted westward. Lewis sums up the closing of that Jewish world in the east in his book *The Jews of Islam:*

"The growing segregation, the dwindling tolerance, the diminished participation, the worsening poverty, both material and intellectual, of the Jewish communities under Muslim rule."

From this long slumber the Jews of the east were awakened by a movement fashioned by their kinsmen in the west: modern Zionism. It came calling on them, summoned them to a new undertaking. The Jews of Islam had been spared both the gift of modern European history (the Enlightenment, the bourgeois age, the emancipation) and then the horrors visited on European Jewry. Zionism had been spun with European thread. But the Jews of the east took to it. To be sure, there were many who had wanted to sit out the fight between Arab and Jew in Palestine and to avert their gaze. Some of the leading figures of Egyptian Jewry the chief Rabbi Haim Nahum, the head of the community, a banker by the name of Joseph Aslan de Cattaoui Pasha whose family had presided over the community since the mid-nineteenth century—were men "devoted to king and country" who had wanted nothing to do with Zionism. But the ground burned in Egypt. Fascist doctrines of nationalism and a new Islamic militancy were sweeping through the place. Palestine and the struggle between Arab and Jew were too close: the world of Egyptian Jewry couldn't withstand all of this.

It was now past living those circumscribed lives. Modern nationalism—in its Arab and Jewish variants—blew away the world of the Arab Jews. The braver and younger souls among the Jews of Arab lands didn't care to live the quiet and worried lives of their elders. When the first Arab-Israeli war of 1948–49 opened, there were some 800,000 Jews in the Arab world; some 6 percent of world Jewry. A decade or so later, Harat al Yahud (the Jewish quarter) in Muslim cities belonged to memory. The large Jewish communities in Morocco, Algeria, Egypt, Iraq, packed up and left. There was a new and altered geography of Jewish life; the center of gravity had shifted again, toward two poles: the New World and Israel.

Setting sail to the New World, Columbus had had little to say about that "parallel fleet of woe and misery" that carried the Jews out of Spain. He was careful to note, though, that he wanted the Jews excluded from the lands he would discover and claim for Spain. Fate mocked him.

I t came to pass that in the midst of the retrospects and the celebration and the rampant revisionism of the quincentennial of Columbus's voyage of discovery, Arabs and Jews at an impasse came together in Madrid in October 1991. (Benjamin Netanyahu, Israel's deputy foreign minister, went to Madrid; his father, the distinguished historian Benzion Netanyahu, had chronicled the heartbreak of the Jews of Spain and the shattering of their world.) It was a "good venue," the innocent said of Madrid, the right place for Muslims and Jews to come together. Perhaps it was. The Spanish certainly thought so; the great irony would have been too much for them to ponder. Beyond the tumult of the conference and its utterances, those in the know, though, could have sworn that they could hear both the Moor's last sigh and the parting words of hurt and pride of Don Isaac Abravanel, and that plea that fell on deaf ears.

FOUAD AJAMI is professor of Middle East Studies at the School of Advanced Studies, Johns Hopkins University.

The Far West's Challenge to the World, 1500–1700 A.D.

WILLIAM H. MCNEILL

The year 1500 A.D. aptly symbolizes the advent of the modern era, in world as well as in European history. Shortly before that date, technical improvements in navigation pioneered by the Portuguese under Prince Henry the Navigator (d. 1460) reduced to tolerable proportions the perils of the stormy and tide-beset North Atlantic. Once they had mastered these dangerous waters, European sailors found no seas impenetrable, nor any ice-free coast too formidable for their daring. In rapid succession, bold captains sailed into distant and hitherto unknown seas: Columbus (1492), Vasco da Gama (1498), and Magellan (1519–22) were only the most famous.

The result was to link the Atlantic face of Europe with the shores of most of the earth. What had always before been the extreme fringe of Eurasia became, within little more than a generation, a focus of the world's sea lanes, influencing and being influenced by every human society within easy reach of the sea. Thereby the millennial land-centered balance among the Eurasian civilizations was abruptly challenged and, within three centuries, reversed. The sheltering ocean barrier between the Americas and the rest of the world was suddenly shattered, and the slave trade brought most of Africa into the penumbra of civilization. Only Australia and the smaller islands of the Pacific remained for a while immune; yet by the close of the eighteenth century, they too began to feel the force of European seamanship and civilization.

Western Europe, of course, was the principal gainer from this extraordinary revolution in world relationships, both materially and in a larger sense, for it now became the pre-eminent meeting place for novelties of every kind. This allowed Europeans to adopt whatever pleased them in the tool kits of other peoples and stimulated them to reconsider, recombine, and invent anew within their own enlarged cultural heritage. The Amerindian civilizations of Mexico and Peru were the most conspicuous victims of the New World balance, being suddenly reduced to a comparatively simple village level after the directing classes had been destroyed or demoralized by the Spaniards. Within the Old World, the Moslem peoples lost their central position in the ecumene as ocean routes supplanted overland portage. Only in the Far East were the effects of the new constellation of world relationships at first unimportant. From a Chinese viewpoint it made little difference whether foreign trade, regulated within traditional forms, passed to Moslem or European merchants' hands. As soon as European expansive energy seemed to threaten their political integrity, first Japan and then China evicted the disturbers and closed their borders against further encroachment. Yet by the middle of the nineteenth century, even this deliberate isolation could no longer be maintained; and the civilizations of the Far East—simultaneously with the primitive cultures of central Africa—began to stagger under the impact of the newly industrialized European (and extra-European) West.

The key to world history from 1500 is the growing political dominance first of western Europe, then of an enlarged European-type society planted astride the north Atlantic and extending eastward into Siberia. Yet until about 1700, the ancient landward frontiers of the Asian civilizations retained much of their old significance. Both India (from 1526) and China (by 1644) suffered yet another conquest from across these frontiers; and the Ottoman empire did not exhaust its expansive power until near the close of the seventeenth century. Only in Central America and western South America did Europeans succeed in establishing extensive land empires overseas during this period. Hence the years 1500–1700 may be regarded as transitional between the old land-centered and the new ocean-centered pattern of ecumenical relationships—a time when European enterprise had modified, but not yet upset the fourfold balance of the Old World.

The next major period, 1700–1850, saw a decisive alteration of the balance in favor of Europe, except in the Far East. Two great outliers were added to the Western world by the Petrine conversion of Russia and by the colonization of North America. Less massive offshoots of European society were simultaneously established in southernmost Africa, in the South American pampas, and in Australia. India was subjected to European rule; the Moslem Middle East escaped a similar fate only because of intra-European rivalries; and the barbarian reservoir of the Eurasian steppes lost its last shreds of military and cultural significance with the progress of Russian and Chinese conquest and colonization.

After 1850, the rapid development of mechanically powered industry enormously enhanced the political and cultural primacy of the West. At the beginning of this period, the Far Eastern citadel fell before Western gunboats; and a few of the European nations extended and consolidated colonial empires in Asia and Africa. Although European empires have decayed since 1945, and the separate nation-states of Europe have been eclipsed as centers of political power by the melding of peoples and nations occurring under the aegis of both the American and Russian governments, it remains true that, since the end of World War II, the scramble to imitate and appropriate science, technology, and other aspects of Western culture has accelerated enormously all round the world. Thus the dethronement of western Europe from its brief mastery of the globe coincided with (and was caused by) an unprecedented, rapid Westernization of all the peoples of the earth. The rise of the West seems today still far from its apogee; nor is it obvious, even in the narrower political sense, that the era of Western dominance is past. The American and Russian outliers of European civilization remain militarily far stronger than the other states of the world, while the power of a federally reorganized western Europe is potentially superior to both and remains inferior only because of difficulties in articulating common policies among nations still clinging to the trappings of their decaying sovereignties.

From the perspective of the mid-twentieth century, the career of Western civilization since 1500 appears as a vast explosion, far greater than any comparable phenomenon of the past both in geographic range and in social depth. Incessant and accelerating self-transformation, compounded from a welter of conflicting ideas, institutions, aspirations, and inventions, has characterized modern European history; and with the recent institutionalization of deliberate innovation in the form of industrial research laboratories, universities, military general staffs, and planning commissions of every sort, an accelerating pace of technical and social change bids fair to remain a persistent feature of Western civilization.

This changeability gives the European and Western history of recent centuries both a fascinating and a confusing character. The fact that we are heirs but also prisoners of the Western past, caught in the very midst of an unpredictable and incredibly fast-moving flux, does not make it easier to discern critical landmarks, as we can, with equanimity if not without error, for ages long past and civilizations alien to our own.

. . . Fortunately, a noble array of historians has traversed the ground already, so that it is not difficult to divide Western history into periods, nor to characterize such periods with some degree of plausibility. A greater embarrassment arises from the fact that suitable periods of Western history do not coincide with the benchmarks of modern world history. This is not surprising, for Europe had first to reorganize itself at a new level before the effects of its increased power could show themselves significantly abroad. One should therefore expect to find a lag between the successive self-transformations of European society and their manifestations in the larger theater of world history. . . .

The Great European Explorations and Their World-Wide Consequences

Europeans of the Atlantic seaboard possessed three talismans of power by 1500 which conferred upon them the command of all the oceans of the world within half a century and permitted the subjugation of the most highly developed regions of the Americas within a single generation. These were: (1) a deep-rooted pugnacity and recklessness operating by means of (2) a complex military technology, most notably in naval matters; and (3) a population inured to a variety of diseases which had long been endemic throughout the Old World ecumene.

The Bronze Age barbarian roots of European pugnacity and the medieval survival of military habits among the merchant classes of western Europe, as well as among aristocrats and territorial lords of less exalted degree, [are worth emphasizing]. Yet only when one remembers the all but incredible courage, daring, and brutality of Cortez and Pizarro in the Americas, reflects upon the ruthless aggression of Almeida and Albuquerque in the Indian Ocean, and discovers the disdain of even so cultivated a European as Father Matteo Ricci for the civility of the Chinese, does the full force of European warlikeness, when compared with the attitudes and aptitudes of other major civilizations of the earth, become apparent. The Moslems and the Japanese could alone compare in the honor they paid to the military virtues. But Moslem merchants usually cringed before the violence held in high repute by their rulers and seldom dared or perhaps cared to emulate it. Hence Moslem commercial enterprise lacked the cutting edge of naked, well-organized, large-scale force which constituted the chief stock-in-trade of European overseas merchants in the sixteenth century. The Japanese could, indeed, match broadswords with any European; but the chivalric stylization of their warfare, together with their narrowly restricted supply of iron, meant that neither *samurai* nor a sea pirate could reply in kind to a European broadside.

Supremacy at sea gave a vastly enlarged scope to European warlikeness after 1500. But Europe's maritime superiority was itself the product of a deliberate combination of science and practice, beginning in the commercial cities of Italy and coming to fruition in Portugal through the efforts of Prince Henry the Navigator and his successors. With the introduction of the compass (thirteenth century), navigation beyond sight of land had become a regular practice in the Mediterranean; and the navigators' charts, or *portolans,* needed for such voyaging showed coasts, harbors, landmarks, and compass bearings between major ports. Although they were drawn freehand, without any definite mathematical projection, *portolans* nevertheless maintained fairly accurate scales of distances. But similar mapping could be applied to the larger distances of Atlantic navigation only if means could be found to locate key points along the coast accurately. To solve this problem, Prince Henry brought to Portugal some of the best mathematicians and astronomers of Europe, who constructed simple astronomical instruments and trigonometrical tables by which ship captains could measure the latitude of newly discovered places along the African coast. The calculation of longitude was more difficult; and, until a satisfactory marine chronometer was invented in the eighteenth century, longitude could be approximated only by dead reckoning. Nevertheless, the new methods worked out at Prince Henry's court allowed the Portuguese to make usable charts of the Atlantic coasts. Such charts gave Portuguese sea captains courage to sail beyond sight of land for weeks and presently for months, confident of being able to steer their ships to within a few miles of the desired landfall.

The Portuguese court also accumulated systematic information about oceanic winds and currents; but this data was kept secret as a matter of high policy, so that modern scholars are uncertain how much the early Portuguese navigators knew. At the same time, Portuguese naval experts attacked the problem of improving ship construction. They proceeded by rule of thumb; but deliberate experiment, systematically pursued, rapidly increased the seaworthiness, maneuverability, and speed of Portuguese and presently (since improvements in naval architecture could not be kept secret) of other European ships. The most important changes were: a reduction of hull width in proportion to length; the introduction of multiple masts (usually three or four); and the substitution of several smaller, more manageable sails for the single sail per mast from which the evolution started. These innovations allowed a crew to trim the sails to suit varying conditions of wind and sea, thus greatly facilitating steering and protecting the vessel from disaster in sudden gales.

With these improvements, larger ships could be built; and increasing size and sturdiness of construction made it possible to transform seagoing vessels into gun platforms for heavy cannon. Thus by 1509, when the Portuguese fought the decisive battle for control of the Arabian Sea off the Indian port of Diu, their ships could deliver a heavy broadside at a range their Moslem enemies could not begin to match. Under such circumstances, the superior numbers of the opposing fleet simply provided the Portuguese with additional targets for their gunnery. The old tactics of sea fighting—ramming, grappling, and boarding—were almost useless against cannon fire effective at as much as 200 yards distance.

The third weapon in the European armory—disease—was quite as important as stark pugnacity and weight of metal. Endemic European diseases like smallpox and measles became lethal epidemics among Amerindian populations, who had no inherited or acquired immunities to such infections. Literally millions died of these and other European diseases; and the smallpox epidemic raging in Tenochtitlan when Cortez and his men were expelled from the citadel in 1520 had far more to do with the collapse of Aztec power than merely military operations. The Inca empire, too, may have been ravaged and weakened by a similar epidemic before Pizarro ever reached Peru.

On the other hand, diseases like yellow fever and malaria took a heavy toll of Europeans in Africa and India. But climatic conditions generally prevented new tropical diseases from penetrating Europe itself in any very serious fashion. Those which could flourish in temperate climates, like typhus, cholera, and bubonic plague, had long been known throughout the ecumene; and European populations had presumably acquired some degree of resistance to them. Certainly the new frequency of sea contact with distant regions had important medical consequences for Europeans, as the plagues for which Lisbon and London became famous prove. But gradually the infections which in earlier centuries had appeared sporadically as epidemics became merely endemic, as the exposed populations developed a satisfactory level of resistance. Before 1700, European populations had therefore successfully absorbed the shocks that came with the intensified circulation of diseases initiated by their own sea voyaging. Epidemics consequently ceased to be demographically significant. The result was that from about 1650 (or before), population growth in Europe assumed a new velocity. Moreover, so far as imperfect data allow one to judge, between 1550 and 1650 population also began to spurt upward in China, India, and the Middle East. Such an acceleration of population growth within each of the great civilizations of the Old World can scarcely be a mere coincidence. Presumably the same ecological processes worked themselves out in all parts of the ecumene, as age-old epidemic checks upon population faded into merely endemic attrition.

The formidable combination of European warlikeness, naval technique, and comparatively high levels of resistance to disease transformed the cultural balance of the world within an amazingly brief period of time. Columbus linked the Americas with Europe in 1492; and the Spaniards proceeded to explore, conquer, and colonize the New World with extraordinary energy, utter ruthlessness, and an intense missionary idealism. Cortez destroyed the Aztec state in 1519–21; Pizarro became master of the Inca empire between 1531 and 1535. Within the following generation, less famous but no less hardy conquistadores founded Spanish settlements along the coasts of Chile and Argentina, penetrated the highlands of Ecuador, Colombia, Venezuela, and Central America, and explored the Amazon basin and the southern United States. As early as 1571, Spanish power leaped across the Pacific to the Philippines, where it collided with the sea empire which their Iberian neighbors, the Portuguese, had meanwhile flung around Africa and across the southern seas of the Eastern Hemisphere.

Portuguese expansion into the Indian Ocean proceeded with even greater rapidity. Exactly a decade elapsed between the completion of Vasco da Gama's first voyage to India (1497–99) and the decisive Portuguese naval victory off Diu (1509). The Portuguese quickly exploited this success by capturing Goa (1510) and Malacca (1511), which together with Ormuz on the Persian Gulf (occupied permanently from 1515) gave them the necessary bases from which to dominate the trade of the entire Indian Ocean. Nor did they rest content with these successes. Portuguese ships followed the precious spices to their farthest source in the Moluccas without delay (1511–12); and a Portuguese merchant explorer traveling on a Malay vessel visited Canton as early as 1513–14. By 1557, a permanent Portuguese settlement was founded at Macao on the south China coast; and trade and missionary activity in Japan started in the 1540's. On the other side of the world, the Portuguese discovered Brazil in 1500 and began to settle the country after 1530. Coastal stations in both west and east Africa, established between 1471 and 1507, completed the chain of ports of call which held the Portuguese empire together.

No other European nations approached the early success of Spain and Portugal overseas. Nevertheless, the two Iberian nations did not long enjoy undisturbed the new wealth their enterprise had won. From the beginning, the Spaniards found it difficult to protect their shipping against French and Portuguese sea raiders. English pirates offered an additional and formidable threat after 1568, when the first open clash between English interlopers and the Spanish authorities in the Caribbean took place. Between 1516 and 1568 the other great maritime people of the age, the Dutch, were subjects of the same Hapsburg monarchs who ruled in Spain and, consequently, enjoyed a favored status as middlemen between Spanish and north European ports. Initially, therefore, Dutch shipping had no incentive to harass Iberian sea power.

This naval balance shifted sharply in the second half of the sixteenth century, when the Dutch revolt against Spain (1568), followed by the English victory over the Spanish armada (1588), signalized the waning of Iberian sea power before that of the northern European nations. Harassment of Dutch ships in Spanish ports simply accelerated the shift; for the Dutch responded by despatching their vessels directly to the Orient (1594), and the English soon followed suit. Thereafter, Dutch naval and commercial power rapidly supplanted that of Portugal in the southern seas. The establishment of a base in Java (1618), the capture of Malacca from the Portuguese (1641), and the seizure of the most important trading posts of Ceylon (by 1644) secured Dutch hegemony in the Indian Ocean; and during the same decades, English traders gained a foothold in western India. Simultaneously, English (1607), French (1608), and Dutch (1613) colonization of mainland North America, and the seizure of most of the smaller Caribbean islands by the same three nations, infringed upon Spanish claims to monopoly in the New World, but failed to dislodge Spanish power from any important area where it was already established.

T he truly extraordinary *élan* of the first Iberian conquests and the no less remarkable missionary enterprise that followed closely in its wake surely mark a new era in the history of the human community. Yet older landmarks of that history did not crumble all at once. Movement from the Eurasian steppes continued to make political history—for example, the Uzbek conquest of Transoxiana (1507–12) with its sequel, the Mogul conquest of India (1526–1688); and the Manchu conquest of China (1621–83).

Chinese civilization was indeed only slightly affected by the new regime of the seas; and Moslem expansion, which had been a dominating feature of world history during the centuries before 1500, did not cease or even slacken very noticeably until the late seventeenth century. Through their conquest of the high seas, western Europeans did indeed outflank the Moslem world in India and southeast Asia, while Russian penetration of Siberian forests soon outflanked the Moslem lands on the north also. Yet these probing extensions of European (or para-European) power remained tenuous and comparatively weak in the seventeenth century. Far from being crushed in the jaws of a vast European pincer, the Moslems continued to win important victories and to

penetrate new territories in southeast Europe, India, Africa, and southeast Asia. Only in the western and central steppe did Islam suffer significant territorial setbacks before 1700.

Thus only two large areas of the world were fundamentally transformed during the first two centuries of European overseas expansion: the regions of Amerindian high culture and western Europe itself. European naval enterprise certainly widened the range and increased the intimacy of contacts among the various peoples of the ecumene and brought new peoples into touch with the disruptive social influences of high civilization. Yet the Chinese, Moslem, and Hindu worlds were not yet really deflected from their earlier paths of development; and substantial portions of the land surface of the globe—Australia and Oceania, the rain forests of South America, and most of North America and northeastern Asia—remained almost unaffected by Europe's achievement.

Nevertheless, a new dimension had been added to world history. An ocean frontier, where European seamen and soldiers, merchants, missionaries, and settlers came into contact with the various peoples of the world, civilized and uncivilized, began to challenge the ancient pre-eminence of the Eurasian land frontier, where steppe nomads had for centuries probed, tested, and disturbed civilized agricultural populations. Very ancient social gradients began to shift when the coasts of Europe, Asia, and America became the scene of more and more important social interactions and innovation. Diseases, gold and silver, and certain valuable crops were the first items to flow freely through the new transoceanic channels of communication. Each of these had important and far-reaching consequences for Asians as well as for Europeans and Amerindians. But prior to 1700, only a few isolated borrowings of more recondite techniques or ideas passed through the sea lanes that now connected the four great civilization of the Old World. In such exchanges, Europe was more often the receiver than the giver, for its people were inspired by a lively curiosity, insatiable greed, and a reckless spirit of adventure that contrasted sharply with the smug conservatism of Chinese, Moslem, and Hindu cultural leaders.

Partly by reason of the stimuli that flowed into Europe from overseas, but primarily because of internal tensions arising from its own heterogeneous cultural inheritance, Europe entered upon a veritable social explosion in the period 1500–1650—an experience painful in itself but which nonetheless raised European power to a new level of effectiveness and for the first time gave Europeans a clear margin of superiority over the other great civilizations of the world. . . .

Conclusion

Between 1500 and 1700, the Eurasian ecumene expanded to include parts of the Americas, much of sub-Saharan Africa, and all of northern Asia. Moreover, within the Old World itself, western Europe began to forge ahead of all rivals as the most active center of geographical expansion and of cultural innovation. Indeed, Europe's self-revolution transformed the medieval frame of Western civilization into a new and vastly more powerful organization of society. Yet the Moslem, Hindu, and Chinese lands were not yet seriously affected by the new energies emanating from Europe. Until after 1700, the history of these regions continued to turn around old traditions and familiar problems.

Most of the rest of the world, lacking the massive self-sufficiency of Moslem, Hindu, and Chinese civilization, was more acutely affected by contact with Europeans. In the New World, these contacts first decapitated and then decimated the Amerindian societies; but in other regions, where local powers of resistance were greater, a strikingly consistent pattern of reaction manifested itself. In such diverse areas as Japan, Burma, Siam, Russia, and parts of Africa, an initial interest in and occasional eagerness to accept European techniques, ideas, religion, or fashions of dress was supplanted in the course of the seventeenth century by a policy of withdrawal and deliberate insulation from European pressures. The Hindu revival in India and the reform of Lamaism in Tibet and Mongolia manifested a similar spirit; for both served to protect local cultural values against alien pressures, though in these cases the pressures were primarily Moslem and Chinese rather than European.

A few fringe areas of the earth still remained unaffected by the disturbing forces of civilization. But by 1700 the only large habitable regions remaining outside the ecumene were Australia, the Amazon rain forest, and northwestern North America; and even these latter two had largely felt tremors of social disturbance generated by the approaching onset of civilization.

At no previous time in world history had the pace of social transformation been so rapid. The new density and intimacy of contacts across the oceans of the earth assured a continuance of cross-stimulation among the major cultures of mankind. The efforts to restrict foreign contacts and to withdraw from disturbing relationships with outsiders—especially with the restless and ruthless Westerners—were doomed to ultimate failure by the fact that successive self-transformations of western European civilization, and especially of Western technology, rapidly increased the pressures Westerners were able to bring against the other peoples of the earth. Indeed, world history since 1500 may be thought of as a race between the West's growing power to molest the rest of the world and the increasingly desperate efforts of other peoples to stave Westerners off, either by clinging more strenuously than before to their peculiar cultural inheritance or, when that failed, by appropriating aspects of Western civilization—especially technology—in the hope of thereby finding means to preserve their local autonomy.

A Taste of Adventure

Kerala, India, and the Molucca Islands, Indonesia

The history of spices is the history of trade.

Soon after dawn on May 21st, 1498, Vasco da Gama and his crew arrived at Calicut after the first direct sea voyage from Europe to Asia. If history's modern age has a beginning, this is it. Europe's ignorance of, and isolation from, the cosmopolitan intellectual and commercial life of Asia were ended forever. With ships, weaponry and a willingness to use them both, the countries of Europe were about to colonise the rest of the world. To support this expansion, its merchant classes would invent new forms of commercial credit and the first great corporations, vital parts of capitalism's operating system, and spread their trading networks across the seven seas. And what did the men shout as they came ashore? "For Christ and spices!"

And what did the men shout as they came ashore? "For Christ and spices!"

The proselytising part turned out to be disappointingly unnecessary: there were already plenty of Christians living on the Malabar coast, following the arrival of a Syrian contingent many centuries earlier. But as far as spice went, Da Gama and his crew were right on the money. Then, as now, Calicut was a gateway to the world's greatest pepper-growing region—indeed this was why the Syrians had moved there in the first place. As such it was at the heart of the spice trade, a network of sea routes and entrepots in the making for millennia: the world economy's oldest, deepest, most aromatic roots.

For thousands of years before Da Gama and hundreds of years afterwards, the secret of the spice trade was simple: great demand and highly controlled supply. Some of that control was enforced through political power or contrived through mercantile guile. Some was simply a gift from the gods of climate and botany. Legend has it that, before leaving, Da Gama dared to ask the zamorin of Calicut whether he could take a pepper stalk with him for re-planting. His courtiers were outraged, but the potentate stayed calm. "You can take our pepper, but you will never be able to take our rains." He knew how important the region's unusual twin monsoon, both phases of which bring heavy rain, was to its fickle crop. To this day, though regions elsewhere grow pepper, Kerala reigns supreme in its quality, dominating the high end of the market.

If those vital downpours have not washed away what passes for the road, a few days travel into Kerala's rolling Western Ghats, where waterfalls roar and herds of wild elephants loom from soft mist, brings you to the ancestral home of *Piper nigrum*. High up in the middle of nowhere, Iddicki produces the finest pepper in the world, its peppercorns always dark and heavy, bursting with flavour. Its vines wind their way around almost every tree in sight, climbing ten metres or more into the sky.

After such a journey you might expect Iddicki to be a sleepy backwater. In its own idyllic way, though, it is a boomtown worthy of the Wild West. Fancy jeeps clog the narrow streets; shops overflow with the latest necessities of rural life, like washing machines and stereos. Giant satellite dishes shove their expensive snouts at the heavens from every other house. One of the world's largest stashes of gold is in rural India, and to judge by its glittering jewellery shops this town has considerably more than its fair share. "Black gold," explains one pepper farmer with a broad grin, is fetching top prices on the world market.

Until you talk to them about that world market, Iddicki's residents seem much like farmers anywhere else in the developing world—scraping a living at the margins of the market economy. Thomas Thomas, one of the several hundred thousand smallholders who grow Kerala's pepper, is a good example. A humble man of the earth, he speaks softly and still wears his *dhothi,* a traditional loincloth, when he tills his soil. But with a little prompting he will give you an analysis of the pepper market sophisticated enough to make a Chicago commodities trader blush: current prices, the direction of the futures market, the costs versus benefits of holding stocks. A local spice dealer explains over a feast of fiery snapper and spiced tapioca at his spacious bungalow that "there is full price-discovery in this market." The farmers who sell their crops to him (for resale at the big market in Jewtown, which has replaced Calicut as the hub of Kerala's pepper trade) do so with the latest New York and Rotterdam prices in hand. One particularly sharp farmer, he moans, is cutting out the middlemen altogether and shipping his stocks directly to Europe.

The global aspect of the dealer's trade is nothing new. As far back as 2600 BC, there are records of the Egyptians feeding spices obtained from Asia to labourers building the great pyramid of Cheops, to give them strength. Archeological evidence suggests that cloves were quite popular in Syria not long after, despite the fact that, like nutmeg and mace, they came only from the spice islands of what is now Indonesia. Long before the 6th century BC, when Confucius advocated the use of ginger, the Chinese were obtaining spices from the tropics. Europe imported them before Rome was founded.

Today spices are chiefly flavourings for food, but a hundred other uses have contributed to the demand through history. In ancient Egypt cassia and cinnamon fetched a high price because they were essential for embalming; so too were anise, marjoram and cumin, used to rinse out the innards of the worthy dead. Hammurabi's legal code, which called for severe punishment of sloppy or unsuccessful surgeons, did much to encourage the use of medicinal spices in Sumeria.

Particularly in Europe, though, food came to matter most. Spices preserve, and they also make the poorly preserved palatable, masking the appetite-killing stench of decay. After bad harvests and in cold winters the only thing that kept starvation at bay was heavily salted meat—with pepper. And there was never enough of it. Thus pepper began the association with gold it still has in the streets of Iddicki, often at a one-to-one exchange rate. In order to call off their siege of Rome in 408 AD, the Visigoths demanded a bounty in gold, silver and pepper. In the Middle Ages plague added to the demand for medicinal spices; a German price table from the 14th century sets the value of a pound of nutmeg at seven fat oxen. At the same time "peppercorn rents" were a serious way of doing business. When the *Mary Rose*, an English ship that sank in 1545, was raised from the ocean floor in the 1980s, nearly every sailor was found with a bunch of pepper-corns on his person—the most portable store of value available.

The great beneficiaries of Europe's need were the Arabs. Spices could change hands a dozen times between their source and Europe, soaring in value with each transaction, and the Arabs were the greatest of the middlemen. Keen to keep it that way, they did everything possible to confuse consumers about the spices' origins. As early as the 5th century BC an Arab cover story fooled Herodotus into believing that cinnamon was found only on a mountain range somewhere in Arabia. The spices were jealously guarded by vicious birds of prey, he wrote, which made their nests of the stuff on steep mountain slopes. Arabs would leave out large chunks of fresh donkey meat for the birds to take back to their nests, which would crash to the ground under the weight. The brave Arabs then grabbed the nests, from under the talons of their previous owners.

Not everyone was fooled. In the 1st century AD the Roman historian Pliny grew concerned at the way the empire's gold flowed ever to the east, and set out to expose the truth and undercut the Arab monopolists who he reckoned to be selling pepper at prices a hundred times what they paid for it in India. It did not help that the gluttonous Romans were, in the words of Frederic Rosengarten, a spice historian, "the most extravagant users of aromatics in history". They used spices in every imaginable combination for their foods, wines and fragrances. Legionaries headed off to battle wearing perfume. The rich slept on pillows of saffron in the belief that it would cure hangovers.

Resentment against the Arab stranglehold had led Rome to launch an invasion of Arabia in 24 BC, an ill-fated expedition that ended in humiliation. But where military means failed, market intelligence prevailed. In 40 AD, Hippalus, a Greek merchant, discovered something the Arabs had long tried to obscure: that the monsoons which nourish India's pepper vines reverse direction mid-year, and that trips from Egypt's Red Sea coast to India and back could thus be shorter and safer than the empire had imagined. Roman trade with India boomed: the Arab monopoly broke.

Early in the 7th century, an obscure spice merchant named Muhammad re-established Arab dominance of the spice trade by introducing an aggressive, expansionary Islam to the world. When the muslims took Alexandria in 641 AD, they killed the trade which had long flourished between Rome and India. As they tightened their grip on the business over the next few centuries, prices in Europe rose dramatically. During the Middle Ages, spices became a luxury that only a few in Europe could afford. This was bad news for the poor and good news for Venice. Its shrewd merchants struck a deal with the Arabs that made them the trade's preferred—indeed almost exclusive—European distributors. Even during the crusades, the relationship bought wealth to all concerned.

The rest of Europe did not care at all for the Muslim Curtain, as the Islamic empire separating west from east came to be called, or for the Venetians. The final blow came in 1453 when the Ottoman Turks took Constantinople, shutting down the small overland trade that had previously evaded the Arab-Venetian monopoly. The Egyptians, gate-keepers of the trade with Venice, felt confident enough to impose a tariff amounting to a third of the value of spices passing through their fingers.

Salvation for the palates and exchequers of Europe's kings lay in finding a sea route to the Indies. In particular, the hunt was on for Malacca, the most important entrepôt in the spice trade and the fabled gateway to the Spice Islands. Spain and Portugal financed dozens of exploration parties in its general direction; half would never make it back home. The rationale for this expense and danger was simple: "He who is lord of Malacca has his hand on the throat of Venice."

He who is lord of Malacca has his hand on the throat of Venice.

It was as part of Portugal's *Drang nach Osten* that Vasco da Gama rounded Africa's Cape of Good Hope to reach India in 1498. As waves of Portuguese explorers returned to Lisbon with their loads of spices, the Venetians and the Egyptians were stunned: the price of pepper in Lisbon fell to one-fifth that in Venice.

The Spaniards, too, were less than happy. They had sent Christopher Columbus to find a route to the Indies via the west, but he had failed, hitting upon the previously unknown Americas instead. In his zeal to convince his paymasters and himself that he had succeeded, he named the new world's natives as Indians and their sacred *chiles* "red" pepper—two unpardonable obfuscations that have confused people to this day.

Pope Alexander IV was drafted in to keep the two expansionist powers apart; the result was the treaty of Tordesillas, which granted all discoveries west of a mid-Atlantic meridian to Spain, and those east of it to Portugal. But the Spanish clung to the possibility of a western end-run to the Spice Islands, and financed Ferdinand Magellan on what would become the first circumnavigation of the earth. Magellan himself was killed in the Philippines, but his sidekick, Sebastian del Cano, completed the momentous journey—with a landfall at the Spice Islands en route. In 1522 his *Victoria* returned to Europe with a tonne of spices on board. The king awarded him a coat of arms embellished with two cinnamon sticks, three nutmegs and twelve cloves.

But the Portuguese had pipped Spain to the post. They had captured the vibrant free-trading port of Malacca, in what is now Malaysia, in 1511. Using the intelligence they gathered there, they made it to the promised land: the tiny Banda Islands, the world's only source of nutmeg and mace, which they reached the following year. Nutmeg is the pit of the nutmeg tree's fruit, and mace, which commanded and still commands a higher price, is the delicate red aril which comes between the pit and the fruit's husky exterior. Chaucer extolled "nutemuge put in ale . . ." and it remains an essential part of Coca-Cola's secret formula.

After filling their holds, the Portuguese began their return. One ship ran aground, stranding its crew on a remote island. Hearing of a strange race of white men in his parts, the sultan of Ternate, the most powerful of the clove isles, sent for them—and so the Europeans found the last secret source of spice.

Look out from the expansive verandah of the sultan's palace in Ternate and one of history's great microcosms lies before you. Dominating one side is Gamalama, the island's temperamental volcano. Opposite it stands its equally fickle twin on the island of Tidore. The two spits of land, not a mile apart, are now almost unknown beyond their immediate vicinity. But five centuries ago their names were uttered with breathless excitement across Europe as their rulers, ancient rivals, played the new great powers off against each other with promises of limitless wealth.

Dark, husky aromas swirl through the palace as incense made specially of local spices finds its way into the thick tropical air. The place is overflowing with gifts from distant customers: priceless Chinese vases, exquisitely carved Indian daggers, fine Venetian glassware, all of them evidence of the influence these rulers once wielded. Ask politely, and you might be allowed to gaze—from a respectful distance, and only after much ceremony—at the sultan's magical crown, its hundred sparkling gem-stones hanging heavy like ripe peaches. You are not the first impressionable tourist here. Francis Drake gushed about the palace, especially its 400-strong harem. And it seems that it's still good to be the king: one of the gifts on display is an enormous modern settee, helpfully labelled "Lazy chair: for the sultan to take naps."

For much of the 16th century, Spain and Portugal tried to win control of the trade in cloves that made such a lifestyle possible. This meant entangling themselves in the long-running rivalry between the rulers of the two islands, who were in-laws. The European powers would build alliances and forts in one place and then the other, only to find themselves kicked out or caught up in endless intrigues and feuds. After decades of this Machiavellian palaver the Portuguese emerged as the top European player in the clove market, but they never really made it a monopoly. Indeed, they allowed the Dutch, who were growing increasingly anxious for a piece of the action, to be their chief distributors in the north and west of Europe. After Spain gobbled up Portugal in 1580, though, the trade changed again. The Spanish tightened control of the market to which they now had exclusive access, cutting the Dutch out of the picture and raising prices across the continent.

Convinced that they had to find a way to control the source of the spices, the Dutch got their act together. In 1602 they formed the Dutch East India Company (the *Vereenigde Oost-Indische Compagnie,* VOC), an association of merchants meant to reduce competition, share risk and realise economies of scale. Other European countries also formed East India companies—everyone from Portugal to Sweden to Austria had a go—but none was ever as successful in the spice trade as the VOC. By 1670 it was the richest corporation in the world, paying its shareholders an annual dividend of 40% on their investment despite financing 50,000 employees, 30,000 fighting men and 200 ships, many of them armed. The secret of this success was simple. They had no scruples whatsoever.

The secret of this success was simple. The Dutch had no scruples whatsoever.

The VOC's first conquest was the Banda archipelago. Unlike the sultans of the clove islands, who relished the attention lavished upon them by their European suitors and the opportunities for mischief that came with it, the fiercely independent Islamic merchants of the Bandas had never allowed Spain or Portugal to build forts on their islands: they insisted on their freedom to trade with all nations. This independence proved their undoing, since it encouraged the VOC to put the nutmeg trade first on its order of business.

For a taste of Banda's romance nothing beats a trip to Run, an explosion of nutmeg trees in the middle of a turquoise sea. Reaching it after a night aboard ship is a magical experience; scores of dolphins dart about your bow-wave as the first glints of sunrise streak across the sky. It feels much as it must have done when English adventurers first claimed the place, making it the country's first colony anywhere. Not much of a colony, it must be said: the island is so small that even a modest fishing vessel can come ashore only at high tide. Yet this seemingly insignificant toe-hold in nutmeg-land so exercised the Dutch that they traded away a promising young colony on the other side of the world to secure it. That island was New Amsterdam, now better known as Manhattan.

The purchase of Run demonstrates the VOC's persistence; it does not do justice to the company's cruelty (normally, but not exclusively, meted out to non-Europeans). Its most successful head, Jan Pieterszoon Coen, had earlier convinced the reluctant Bandanese of his firm's God-given right to monopolise the nutmeg trade in a more typical style: he had had every single male over the age of fifteen that he could get his hands on butchered. Coen brought in Japanese mercenaries to torture, quarter and decapitate village leaders, displaying their heads on long poles. The population of the isles was 15,000 before the VOC arrived; 15 years later it was 600.

When they turned to the clove trade the Dutch had no time for the squabbling politics of Ternate and Tidore. The VOC uprooted all the Sultans' clove trees and concentrated production on Ambon, an island where its grip was tight. By 1681, it had destroyed three-quarters of all nutmeg trees in unwanted areas and reorganised farming into plantations. It imposed the death penalty on anyone caught growing, stealing or possessing nutmeg or clove plants without authorisation. It drenched every nutmeg with lime before export, to ensure that not one fertile seed escaped its clutches. Yet high on its hillside Afo lives to tell its tale.

Climb through the dense, aromatic forests that cover the steep slopes of Ternate's volcano, and you will find this living testament to the ultimate futility of monopoly. Nearly 40 metres tall and over 4 metres round, Afo is the world's oldest clove tree, planted in defiance of the Dutch ban nearly four centuries ago. Despite the VOC's extreme precautions, Afo's sister seedlings, stolen in 1770 by an intrepid Frenchman (curiously, named Poivre), ended up flourishing on the Seychelles, Réunion and especially Zanzibar, which later became the world's largest producer of cloves. By the end of the 18th century the emergence of these rivals had broken the Dutch monopoly for good.

By that time the VOC was already a hollow mockery of its original ghastly self. As early as the end of the 17th century, careful analysis of the books shows that its volume of trade was reducing every year. Even a monopoly so ruthlessly enforced could not help but leak, and the VOC's overheads were huge—tens of thousands of employees, garrisons, warships. Decades of easy rents had created a corrupt and inefficient beast. By 1735, dwindling spice income had been overtaken by textiles in the company's profit column. In 1799, the most vicious robber baron of them all met its final end. The VOC went bankrupt.

The demise of the VOC was not just a pleasing comeuppance. It was evidence that, in just two centuries, Europeans had changed the spice trade forever. The spices that were once limited to tiny islands in hidden archipelagoes were being grown around the world and in large quantities. Trade routes that spanned oceans were becoming commonplace and, as such, competitive. The Dutch did their best to buck the trend, destroying their stocks so blatantly that, according to one observer, the streets of Amsterdam were "flooded with nutmeg butter". But it was all in vain. Spices were no longer that hard to come by. Monopolies gave way to markets.

Those markets remained rich in romance; the allure of the trade, its role as a cultural crossroads, its many rival players, its uncertainties and its opportunities for smuggling (even relatively cheap spices carry a lot of value for a given weight) kept the spice bazaars of Kerala, Ambon and Rotterdam fascinating. And lucrative, too; though no one could control the overall flow of spice any more, information could still be rushed ahead fast enough—or sequestered behind long enough—for people in the know to make a killing. Now, though, the information itself has started to flow freely. "There just aren't so many secrets any more," reflects a spice trader in Rotterdam. "The farmers in Vietnam are walking around with mobile phones. They know the market price as soon as I do."

Hot Chile

"Oh Blessed Incomparable Chile, ruler of all things . . . I give thee thanks for my digestive health, I give thee thanks for my very life!" Thus the Transcendental Capsaicinophilic Society, one of the worrying number of cults devoted to *capsicum:* chiles or "red" pepper.

If it sounds as if they are on drugs then so, in a way, they are. Paul Bosland of the Chile Pepper Institute in New Mexico reckons they and all chile-heads are high on endorphins, painkillers released by the body to block the sting of the capsaicin which gives chiles their bite.

The addicts are spread all over the world. Travelling on the back of the European spice trade, America's chiles have since colonised every corner of the earth so thoroughly that everyone thinks they have always been around. Even the top man at the Indian Spices Board refuses to accept that chiles are an import, pulling dubious sanskrit references from the Vedas to bolster his point. His clinching argument? "Indians can go months without touching black pepper, but not a day goes by that we don't eat chile peppers."

This is fast becoming true everywhere else, too. Americans' consumption of chile has doubled over the past two decades; they now use the spice in almost everything. Salsa now outsells ketchup as America's top condiment. But black pepper still gets all the glory as the world's most important traded spice. Unlike its fickle namesake, red pepper grows like mad all over the place. So though there may be a great demand for it, no one makes much money out of trading it. Bad news for traders, good news for foodies.

Such traders are now caught in a trap. Their space for bargaining and trade, opened up with the end of monopoly production, is being hemmed in by ever more powerful purchasers—the food giants and spice multinationals. In an age of free-flowing information these buyers can bypass the markets and go directly to the source. From Jew-town, still the key pepper entrepôt, to Rotterdam, London and New York, the main international markets, spice traders are a dying breed. One industry veteran reckons that only a fifth of the trading concerns that flourished 30 years ago are still in business.

Their problems stem from men like Al Goetze. Meet him in his office near Baltimore, at the staid headquarters of McCormick, the world's largest spice firm, and his conservative suit and dry manner might lead you to mistake him for a stuffy corporate type. But to his admiring colleagues he is "a modern day Marco Polo."

Procurement managers at food-processing firms were once content to purchase spices through brokers, never leaving the comfort of their air-conditioned offices. Mr Goetze hits the road. He and his men have travelled to nearly every country on earth that grows spices, again and again. McCormick has set up joint-ventures or wholly owned subsidiaries in over a dozen key spice-producing countries in recent years.

Once the reason for going to the source was price. Now, Mr Goetze says, quality is what matters. Both American and European regulators, prompted by increasing consumer awareness of food safety, have been cracking down hard on impurities. Mr Goetze points to an unlikely assortment of objects in a display case: stones, rusty nails, giant cockroaches, plastic beach sandals. All were crammed into bursting burlap bags and sold to McCormick with its spice. Big processing firms and marketers, frightened that such stuff—or, worse, microscopic impurities that come with it—might make it to the dinner plates of litigious customers, are going straight to the source to clean things up.

Stones, rusty nails, giant cockroaches, plastic beach sandals, all crammed into bursting burlap bags and sold with the spice.

Alfons van Gulick, the head of Rotterdam's Man Producten, the world's biggest and most influential spice-trading firm, is understandably unimpressed: "McCormick should stick to polishing its brand and selling, rather than telling countries how to produce spice." But the people for whose products McCormick and Man Producten compete have an interest in Mr Goetze's strategy. The Indian Spices Board is already helping members improve standards and obtain seals of approval such as ISO certification. The hope is that, over time, producers can go downstream and capture more of the fat margins that come with the "value-added" processing now done in rich countries.

Industry analysts are sceptical about vertical integration. In other commodities it has not been much of a success. Cutting out the middleman may pose unexpected problems for conservative multinationals, unfamiliar with the culture and risks involved in going upstream. And then there is volatility, on which middlemen thrive and which farmers and multinationals dislike. Asked whether the trade has lost its mystery, one animated trader replies "Mystery? I experience it every day when I try to figure out what is going on with prices in this market!"

Producers hate this, and have made various attempts to iron out the market's ups and downs. The International Pepper Community—which includes India, Indonesia and Brazil among its members—has tried for decades to form a producers' cartel to boost prices, without any success. Price fixing by vanilla growers in Madagascar succeeded for a while, but then Uganda flooded the market with cheaper beans. Indonesia and Grenada, the top producers of nutmeg, managed to boost prices for a few years by limiting supply, but cheating quickly scuppered the arrangement. Quiet talks are underway between top cardamom producers in India and Guatemala, who produce nearly all the world's output, to restrict supply; it may work for a while, but not for long.

Every decade or so, an ambitious individual trader tries to do with money what the producers cannot do by agreement. To corner the pepper market would offer huge riches, and so people regularly have a go. Half a century ago, it was an Armenian; a decade ago, an American. Now it appears that a shadowy Indonesian tycoon may be making a play for at least the white pepper market. But history teaches that such grandiose efforts at monopoly face an uphill struggle. And though it may be possible to milk them for a while, the modern day economics of the trade ensure that they cannot last. The spice trade, once the stuff of legends, has become a market much like any other. And a taste of luxury beyond the dreams of almost every human in history is available to almost everyone, almost everywhere.

After Dire Straits, an Agonizing Haul across the Pacific

It was only a generation after Columbus that Magellan's tiny fleet sailed west, via his strait, then on around the world.

SIMON WINCHESTER

Balboa found the ocean. Then, in their droves, explorers emerged to circle and probe and colonize it, but first, in that most daring of all endeavors, to cross it.

No one could be sure how wide it was. No one could be sure where lay the Terra Australis Incognita, which Ptolemy had postulated and which Mercator would argue was a necessary balance for a spherical world—without it the whole planet might simply topple over, to be lost among the stars. No one knew the weather or the currents or the winds. But one small certainty spurred the would-be circumnavigators onward. It was that the Spice Islands, the Moluccas, lay at the farthest side of whatever might lie beyond the waters, pacific or unpacific, that Balboa had discovered.

Traders buying nutmegs and cloves from Arabian merchants had known about the Spice Islands for centuries; in the 1200s Marco Polo knew roughly where they were, for he saw junk traffic in the ports of North China loaded with spices and manned by crews who had come from the south. In 1511 a Portuguese expedition led by Antonio d'Abreu actually discovered them by moving eastward, after passing the tip of Africa, to Malacca, thence down the strait and past the immense island of Borneo to the confused archipelago where nearly all known spices grew in wild profusion. To reach their goal, d'Abreu's men had gone halfway round the world from Europe to the Orient.

The geographical fact they established was of great political and imperial importance. Since 1494, when the Treaty of Tordesillas was signed, all of the unknown world to the east of an imaginary line that had been drawn 370 leagues west of the Cape Verde Islands would belong to Portugal. Everything to the west of that line would belong to Spain. So far as the Atlantic and the Indian oceans were concerned, there was no problem; but what about the other side of the world? Conquest, squatter's rights, annexation, force majeure—these cruder tools of geopolitics might well dictate its eventual position. Thus the Moluccas, if discovered by going eastward around the globe, would belong to Portugal—at least by the logic of

some explorers. But the Moluccas claimed by a party going westward might belong to Spain. So while d'Abreu and his colleagues went off eastward, even braver or more foolhardy men, carrying the banner of Castile, were determined to discover—heroically and, as it turned out for many of them, fatally—the way to reach this same Orient by traveling westward across the vast unknown.

There is thus a nice irony in the fact that the man who undertook the seminal voyage, and did so in the name of Spain, was in fact Portuguese. He was born Fernao de Magalhaes, and the Portuguese—"He is ours," they insist—rarely care to acknowledge that he renounced his citizenship after a row, pledged his allegiance to King Charles I (later to become Emperor Charles V) and was given a new name: Hernando de Magallanes. The English-speaking world, which reveres him quite as much as does Iberia, knows him as Ferdinand Magellan.

He set off on September 20, 1519, with a royal mandate to search for a passage to El Mar del Sur, and thus to determine for certain that the Spice Islands were within the Spanish domains. He had not the foggiest notion of how far he might have to travel. For all Magellan's 237 men in their five little ships knew, Balboa's Panama and the northern coast of South America, which Columbus had sighted in 1498 on his third voyage, might be the equatorial portions of a continent extending without a break to the Antarctic pole, making the southern sea they sought quite unreachable from the west. Johann Schöner's globe of the world, then the best known, placed Japan a few hundred miles off Mexico. The historian Lópex de Gómara asserts that Magellan always insisted that the Moluccas were "no great distance from Panama and the Gulf of San Miguel, which Vasco Núñez de Balboa discovered." Magellan would rapidly discover precisely what "no great distance" was to mean.

The five vessels that would soon make history—the *Victoria,* the *Trinidada* (the *Trinidad*), the *San Antonio,* the *Concepción* and the *Santiago*—were small, the largest being 120 tons, and hopelessly unseaworthy. ("I would not care to sail to the Canaries in such crates," wrote the Portuguese consul in Seville, with obvious pleasure. "Their ribs are soft as butter.")

They set sail from the Guadalquivir River under the proud corporate title of the Armada de Molucca, amply armed but hopelessly provisioned, with crews composed of men of nine different nationalities including a lone Englishman. There was one Moluccan slave, Enrique, who would act as an interpreter if the crossing was accomplished. There was a journalist, too, Antonio Francesca Pigafetta, who may also have been a Venetian spy. In any case, Pigafetta's diaries remained the source for all future accounts of the voyage; he had joined the ships, he said, because he was "desirous of sailing with the expedition so that I might see the wonders of the world."

The sorry tales of sodomy and mutiny, of yardarm justice and abrupt changes of command, and of all the other trials that attended the armada on its path south and west across the Atlantic do not belong here. The truly important phase of the journey starts on February 3, 1520, when the vessels left their anchorage near today's Montevideo and headed south. No charts or sailing directions existed then. The sailors were passing unknown coasts, and confronting increasingly terrifying seas and temperatures that dropped steadily, day by day.

They began to see penguins—"ducks without wings," they called them, *patos sin alas*—and "sea-wolves," or seals. Seeking a way to the Pacific, they explored every indentation in the coast off which they sailed, and with depressing regularity each indentation—even though some were extremely capacious and tempted the navigators to believe that they might be the longed-for straits—proved to be a cul-de-sac. They spent much of the winter, from Palm Sunday until late August, in the center of a chilly and miserable bay at what is now Puerto San Julian. The winter was made doubly wretched by an appalling mutiny and the consequent executions and maroonings that Captain-General Magellan ordered; by the wrecking of the *Santiago,* which he had sent on a depth-sounding expedition; and by the realization of the dreadful damage done to the remaining ships by the chomping of those plank-gourmets of the seas, teredo worms.

But one important discovery was made at Puerto San Julian: these southern plains were inhabited by enormous nomadic shepherds who herded not sheep, but little wild llamas known as guanacos, and who dressed in their skins. Magellan captured a number of these immense people—one pair by the cruel trick of showing them leg-irons and insisting that the proper way to carry the shackles was to allow them to be locked around their ankles. Magellan's men also liked the giants' tricks: one, who stayed aboard only a week but allowed himself to be called Juan and learned some biblical phrases, caught and ate all the rats and mice on board, to the pleasure of the cook and the entertainment of the men. Magellan called these men "*patagones*"—"big feet"; the land in which he found them has been known ever since as Patagonia.

By late August the fleet set sail again. Two men had been left behind, marooned for mutiny by Magellan's orders. They had a supply of wine and hardtack, guns and shot, but when other, later expeditions entered the bay, no trace of them was found. They may have been killed by the giants; they may have starved

to death. All that the men of the armada remembered were their pitiful wails echoing over the still waters as the ships sailed out of the bay into the open sea, and then south.

By the time the flotilla had reached 50 degrees south latitude (not far from the Falkland Islands), the men were restive. Their artless plea now was: If the expedition wanted to reach the Spice Islands, why not turn east toward them and pass below the Cape of Good Hope, as others had? Magellan, sensible enough to know this would make a nonsense of the whole plan to render the Spice Islands Spanish, refused. But he promised that if no strait was found by the time they had eaten up another 25 degrees of latitude, he would turn east as they wished. The murmurs stilled. The Captain-General clearly had no idea of the utter impossibility of navigating at 75 degrees south latitude, for on that longitudinal track his ships would get stuck fast in the thick ice of what is now the Weddell Sea, hemmed in by the yet unimagined continent and the unendurable cold of the Antarctic.

The Captain-General Sights a Virgin Cape

On October 21, 1520, Magellan sighted a headland to starboard. Cabo Virjenes, which today is equipped with a lighthouse that flashes a powerful beam and a radio direction beacon, is an important navigation point on the South American coast. It marks, as Magellan was soon to discover, the eastern end of the strait that bears his name—the tortuous entrance, at long last, to the Pacific.

Ranges of immense, snow-covered mountains crowded into view; there could be, Magellan must have thought, no possible exit. Still, he ordered the *San Antonio* and the *Concepción* into the headwaters of the bay—only to be horrified when he saw them being swept into a huge maelstrom of surf and spindrift by unsuspected currents and winds. But he had no time to dwell on such miseries, for an immense storm broke over his own ship, the *Trinidad,* as well as the *Victoria,* alongside. Men were hurled overboard. One vessel was dismasted; the other nearly turned turtle several times. The storm went on and on and on. When relief finally came to the exhausted crews, the only recourse, it seemed, was to turn tail and head for home. The expedition was over, an abject failure.

Yet just at that moment (one occasionally suspects that the mythmakers have been at work on the story) the lookout sighted sails on the western horizon. They were indeed what they could only have been: the two scouting vessels had returned. Not shattered and aground, they were safe and sound. The joy Magellan must have felt at realizing his men were still alive was, however, as nothing when, as the *San Antonio* and the *Concepción* drew closer, he saw their yardarms hung with bunting, music being played, and the crews dancing and singing.

As an account of the long voyage puts it, "Suddenly, they saw a narrow passage, like the mouth of a river, ahead of them in the surf, and they managed to steer into it. Driven on by wind and tide they raced through this passage and into a wide lake. Still driven by the storm they were carried west for some hours into another narrow passage, though now the current had reversed, so what appeared to be a great ebb tide came rushing towards them. They debouched from this second straight into a broad body of water which stretched as far as the eye could see toward the setting sun. . . ."

By tasting the water and finding it salty, and then making sure that both the ebb tides and flood tides were of equal strength (tests that argued against this body of water being a river), the captains of the scout ships realized they had, indeed, discovered the way through. Magellan, believing that his ultimate goal was within his grasp, brushed aside the persistent doubter's view that he should, despite the discovery, turn back *eastward* for the Moluccas. "Though we have nothing to eat but the leather wrapping from our masts," he declared, "we shall go on!"

The Strait of Magellan is as darkly beautiful as it is useful. Before I first visited the strait I supposed, wrongly, that since its latitude to the south is more or less the same distance from the Equator as Maine's latitude is to the north, the coastline would also be vaguely similar. But it is much starker, more hostile, more grand. Heading west, as Magellan did, the land begins flat, and wind reduces such trees as there are to stunted survivors. Even today the strait is not an easy place for sailing vessels: ". . . both difficult and dangerous, because of incomplete surveys, the lack of aids to navigation, the great distance between anchorages, the strong current, and the narrow limits for the maneuvering of vessels," says the pilot manual.

"A Cargo of Falsehood against Magellan"

For Magellan and his men it was a nightmare. The currents were treacherous. Unexpected winds, now known as williwaws, flashed down steep cliffs, threatening to drive the little fleet onto the rocks. He lost another ship; though he did not know it at the time, the *San Antonio* had turned tail and was heading back to Spain, "bearing a cargo of falsehood against Magellan." She also took away supplies vital for all of the fleet—one-third of the armada's biscuits, one-third of its meat and two-thirds of its currants, chickpeas and figs. The men began begging to turn back.

Days passed. Finally, on November 28, 1520, *Trinidad, Victoria* and *Concepción* passed beyond the horrors of the strait, and sailed westward into an evening that became, suddenly, magically serene. We are told that "the iron-willed Admiral" broke down and cried. Then he assembled his men on deck. Pedro de Valderrama, the *Trinidad*'s priest, stood on the poop deck and called down on the crew of all three remaining vessels the blessing of Our Lady of Victory. The men sang hymns. The gunners fired broadsides. And Magellan proudly unfurled the flag of Castile.

"We are about to stand into an ocean where no ship has ever sailed before," Magellan is said to have cried (though it has to be emphasized that there is no hard evidence that he did so). "May the ocean be always as calm and benevolent as it is today. In this hope I name it the Mar Pacifico." And just in case it was not Magellan who first uttered the name, then perhaps it was Pigafetta: "We debouched from that strait," he later wrote, "engulfing ourselves in the Pacific Sea."

The European Dawn Breaks on the Pacific

The concept of the Pacific Ocean, the greatest physical unit on Earth, had been born. Balboa had seen it. D'Abreu had ventured onto its western edges. Magellan had reached its eastern periphery. Now it was up to the explorers to try to comprehend the enormity of their discovery. But before they could do that, Magellan had to sail across it. This was his determined aim, and the aim of those who sponsored his venture.

So the Captain-General ordered the sails set to carry the shrunken, but now at long last triumphant, armada northward. He thought it might take three or four days to reach the Spice Islands. It was a savage underestimate—a tragically optimistic forecast, based quite probably on the terrible inability of long-distance navigators to calculate longitude (an inability that insured that not a single estimate then available to Magellan was even 80 percent of the true size of the ocean).

Not that anyone suspected tragedy as they breezed to the north of Cape Desado. Far from it. Once the armada had reached the lower southern latitudes, the winds began to blow balmily and unceasingly from the southeast. They were trade winds, just like those well known in the southern Atlantic and Indian oceans, and they were pleasantly warm. Their effect produced nothing but splendid sailing: no undue swells, no angry squalls, no cyclonic outbursts. Just endless days and nights of leisured running before a steady, powerful breeze. "Well was it named Pacific," wrote Pigafetta later, confirming his master's choice of name, "for during this period we met with no storms."

And for weeks and weeks, simply by wafting before the winds with sails unchanged, the fleet managed to miss every single one of the islands with which the Pacific Ocean is littered. Magellan's course, sedulously recorded by his pilot, Francisco Albo, shows him—almost uncannily—leading his vessels past the Juan Fernández Islands, past Sala y Gómez and Easter islands, past Pitcairn, Ducie, Oeno and Henderson and, indeed, past everything else. His astrolabe, his crude speed recorder, his hourglass (a watchkeeper would be flogged for holding it against his chest, since to warm it made the sand flow faster, the hour pass more quickly, the watch be more rapidly over) served Magellan admirably: he plotted the likely course to the Spice Islands, and his ships took him there, more or less.

Any deviation could have caused disaster. Had he strayed just 3 degrees north of Albo's recorded track, he would have hit the Marquesas; 3 degrees south, he would have come to Tahiti. He was a hundred miles off Bikini Atoll. He passed within half a day's sailing of razor-sharp coral reefs—thundering surfs, huge spikes and lances that would have ruined his ships forever. At this distance in time, it seems as if some guardian angel had Magellan's tiny fleet under benevolent invigilation for days and nights too numerous to count. Yet this providence had a less kindly face. Six weeks out of the strait, Magellan's men began to die. In the monotony of a long, landless passage, what proved unbearable was the lack of food aboard the sea-locked ships.

Much of the stores had already gone, carried off on the treacherous *San Antonio*. Such food as the three ships carried began to rot under the soggy tropical airs. The penguins and seals they had killed and salted in Patagonia started to turn putrid; maggots raged through the ships, eating clothes and supplies and rigging; water supplies turned scummy and rank. Men began to develop the classic symptoms of scurvy—their teeth loosened in their gums, their breath began to smell horribly sour, huge boils erupted from their shrunken frames, they sank into inconsolable melancholia.

In January men began to die. One of the Patagonian behemoths whom Magellan had persuaded aboard was, despite his immense physique and power, the first to go; he begged to be made a Christian, was baptized "Paul" and then died. By midJanuary a third of the sailors were too sick to stagger along the decks. Their food was limited to scoops of flour stained yellow by the urine of rats, and biscuits riddled with weevils.

The depression and deep anxiety afflicted Magellan too. At one point he flung his charts overboard in a fit of rage. "With the pardon of the cartographers, the Moluccas are not to be found in their appointed place!" he cried. The fleet did, in fact, strike land in late January—a tiny island they called St. Paul's, and which seems to be the minute atoll now known as Pukapuka, in the French Tuamotu group. (Four centuries later, Pukapuka was the first island to be spotted by Thor Heyerdahl aboard the balsa raft *Kon-Tiki* after his long drift westward from Callao in Peru.) They stayed a week, replenishing their water butts and feasting on turtle eggs. They left in an optimistic mood; surely, they surmised, this island must be the first of a vast skein of atolls and lagoons stretching to the now close Moluccas. But it was not to be; the ships had barely traversed a third of their ocean. Soon the hunger pains, the racking thirst and the sense of unshakable misery began anew, and the dying began once more.

After Meals of Leather—Land!

More and more terrible the voyage steadily became. By March 4 the flagship had run out of food completely. Men were eating the oxhides and llama skins used to prevent the rigging from chafing (not too bad a diet—so long as the crew's scurvy-ridden teeth hung in). The smell of death, the knowledge that it was both inevitable and impending, gripped Magellan's sailors. And then dawned March 6, when a seaman called Navarro, the only man still fit enough to clamber up the ratlines, spied what everyone was waiting for—land.

A great cheer went up. Cannon were fired. Men fell to their knees in prayer. A squadron of tiny dugouts sped from shore to meet the Spaniards. Magellan had reached the islands he first called Las Islas de las Velas Latinas and later, after much of his cargo had been filched, Las Islas de Ladrones, the Islands of Thieves. He had made his landfall at what we now call Guam. It was March 6, 1521. Magellan had crossed the Pacific. A voyage the Captain-General had supposed might take three or four days had, in fact, occupied three and a half months.

The fleet stayed in Guam for only three days—to rest, make minor repairs and take on food (such as the "figs, more than a palm long," which must have been bananas) and fresh water. Then Magellan set off, still toward the Moluccas, standing down for the southwest and to the Philippines, islands of which all travelers to these parts had often heard, but which no European

had ever seen. Though the Spice Islands, it must be recalled, were the armada's prescribed goal, the official mandate and ambition of Magellan was to discover, name and seize in the name of Spain the immense archipelago that lay north of them.

The only Briton on the expedition, Master Andrew of Bristol, died on this last, short passage. He was never to see the islands that, a novelist was later to write, were "as fair as Eden, with gold beaches, graceful palms, exotic fruits and soil so rich that if one snapped off a twig and stuck it into the ground it would start straightway to grow."

Magellan made his landfall on March 16 on an island at the southern end of the large Philippine island of Samar. Two days later, the first contact was made with Filipinos, though the name "Philippines" was not to be given to the place until 1543, when explorer Ruy López de Villalobos named one after the Infante, later to become King Philip II, the Spanish monarch whose reign made the words "Spanish Armada" infamous. (The name "Philippines" caught on later to mean the entire island group.) The significant moment came two days later still, when the ships sailed down the Gulf of Leyte and the Surigao Strait, where, more than four centuries later in World War II, one of the world's last great naval battles was fought, and Adm. William F. Halsey reduced the Japanese Imperial Navy to vestigial strength.

Once through the strait, Magellan landed at the island that guarded its entrance, Limasawa. Eight inhabitants sailed out to the *Trinidad* in a small boat. On orders from the Captain-General, his Moluccan slave, Enrique, hailed them. In a moment that must have seemed frozen in time, it became clear that the men in the approaching boat understood the words of the Moluccan perfectly.

Their language was being spoken to them by a man on a huge ship that had come to them from the east. The linguistic globe—even if not necessarily the physical globe—had been circumnavigated. A man who had originated in these parts had traveled across Asia and around Africa to Europe as a slave, and had now returned home by the Americas and the Pacific. Enrique de Molucca may well have been, strictly speaking, the first of humankind to circumnavigate the world; he was never to be honored for so doing.

Nor, by the unhappy coincidence of ill-temper and wretched misfortune, was Ferdinand Magellan ever to be able to savor his own triumph. Just six weeks after landing he was dead, cut down on a Philippine island in a skirmish that is as unremembered as the place in which it happened is unsung—a flat and muddy little island called Mactan, where an airport has now been built to serve the city of Cebu.

The circumstances of the Captain-General's end, however, are riven into every Iberian schoolchild's learning, even today. Despite his crew's objections, Magellan insisted on exploring. He was pleased at the relative ease with which the people took to Christianity. (It is perhaps worth remembering that the Catholic faith, which Magellan and his priests brought to Samar and Cebu and northern Mindanao, flourishes there still today. The Philippines, in fact, is the only predominantly Christian country in Asia, and the influence of the church contributed significantly to the recent overthrow of President Ferdinand Marcos.)

But the successful sowing of the seeds of Christianity were to be Magellan's undoing. His horribly inglorious end came in late April. The precise circumstances were chronicled. Magellan had demonstrated what he felt was his superior status to the local raja of Cebu, and had made Christians of him and all his followers. But significantly, the rest of the Philippine nobility did not go along. Many local junior rajas objected, especially the minor raja of Mactan, a man named Cilapulapu and now known to all Filipinos simply as Lapu Lapu. He declared that he was not going to pay fealty to this Christian interloper, come what may. He cared little enough for the raja of Cebu, let along the Cebuano's newfound foreign friends.

The Spaniards soon got wind of this rebellious mood, and on April 27 Magellan and 60 of his men paddled across the narrow strait to Mactan, in an attempt to bring Lapu Lapu to heel. "You will feel the iron of our lances," Lapu Lapu was told by Magellan's interlocutor. "But we have fire-hardened spears and stakes of bamboo," replied a defiant chieftain. "Come across whenever you like."

The Last Stand on Mactan Island

The waters at the northern end of Mactan are very shallow and degenerate into warm swamps. A selected 48 of the Spaniards, dressed in full armor, had to wade the last few hundred yards to do battle with the Mactan warriors. They fought for an hour, thigh-deep in the water. Then Magellan plunged his lance into the body of an attacker and was unable to withdraw it quickly enough. It was a fatal delay. Another islander slashed Magellan's leg with a scimitar. He staggered. Scores of others crowded around him as he fell, and as Pigafetta was to write, "thus they killed our mirror, our light, our comfort and our true guide."

It is worth remembering that Fernao de Magalhaes was a native Portuguese—of whom it used to be said, because they were such energetic explorers, "they have a small country to live in, but all the world to die in." There is a monument near the spot where he fell, a tall white obelisk, guarded solicitously for the past 15 years by a man with the splendid name of Jesus Baring. There are two accounts of the event, one engraved on either side of the cross. Señor Baring derives much amusement from showing his occasional visitors—and there are very few, considering how globally important this spot should be—how markedly they differ.

The one on the monument's eastern side—the side that pedant geographers will recognize as marginally nearer to the Spanish Main—records the event as a European tragedy. "Here on 27th April 1521 the great Portuguese navigator Hernando de Magallanes, in the service of the King of Spain, was slain by native Filipinos. . . ." On the other side, by contrast, it is seen as an Oriental triumph—a heroic blow struck for Philippine nationalism. "Here on this spot the great chieftain Lapu Lapu repelled an attack by Ferdinand Magellan, killing him and

sending his forces away. . . ." Baring points to the latter and roars with laughter. "This is the real story. This is the one we Filipinos like to hear!"

Lapu Lapu is thus the first, and to many Filipinos the greatest, of Filipino heroes. These days his memory is being revived, his exploits retold, his adventures made the stuff of comic strips, films and popular songs. Each April there is a full-scale reenactment of the Battle of Mactan on the beach, with an improbably handsome Cebuano film star playing the part of the seminaked hero and, when I was last there, the Philippine Air Force officer Mercurion Fernadez playing the role of the armor-clad Magellan. The two sides struggle gamely in the rising surf until that epic moment when Officer Fernandez contrives to collapse into the shallow sea and grunts his last. The assembled thousands then cheer. Such is Filipino pride in the raja of Mactan that there are firebrands—in Manila as well as in Cebu—who believe their country should shed its present name, a reminder that it is a colonial conquest, and be reborn as LapuLapuLand.

Little more needs to be said of the tiny armada now, save to note what most popular historians choose to forget. The *Concepción* was scuttled; the flagship *Trinidad*, which tried to make for home via the Pacific once more, was blown north as far as Hakodate in Japan, captured by a Portuguese battle group and became a total loss in the Spice Islands, which had been its original goal. But one of the ships, the doughty little *Victoria*—at 85 tons she was the second smallest of the original five—did make it back to Spain.

The *Victoria* scudded home under the charge of Juan Sebastian d'Elcano, previously the executive officer of the *Concepción*. She made Java. She made it round the top of Africa, through the waters where freak waves sometimes cause modern oil tankers to founder. She made the Cape Verde Islands, where the crew realized that despite meticulous log-keeping, they had lost an entire day from their calendar: the concept of crossing the international date line was unknown—and profoundly unimaginable—to them.

On September 6, 1523, the *Victoria* made the harbor of Sanlucar de Barrameda, from where she had set off almost exactly three years before. Juan Sebastian d'Elcano had brought just 17 men back with him: 237 had started out. Circumnavigation, it happened, was a most costly business.

But well rewarded. D'Elcano was given an annual pension and a coat of arms as handsome as it was aromatic: a castle, three nutmegs, 12 cloves, two crossed cinnamon sticks, a pair of Malay kings bearing spice sticks, and above all, a globe circled by a ribbon emblazoned with the motto *Primus Circumdedisti me.* "Thou first circumnavigated me."

SIMON WINCHESTER is the author of eight books that combine history and travel, including *The Pacific* (Hutchinson), from which this article was adapted.

From *Smithsonian*, April 1991, pp. 84–95. Copyright © 1991 by Simon Winchester. Reprinted by permission of the author via Sterling Lord Literistic.

The Significance of Lepanto

GREGORY MELLEUISH

Since September 11, 2001, there has been quite an outpouring of books dealing with the historical relationship between Islam and the Christian West. This has included a number of surveys of the history of that relationship, some emphasising conflict and bloodshed and others the sometimes harmonious association that at times existed between the two civilisations. New studies of the Crusades have emerged, including the first complete history of the movement since Runciman's classic work, in the shape of Christopher Tyerman's *God's War.*

The Battle of Lepanto has a major place in the symbolism of the Western-Islamic relationship, and Niccolò Capponi's recently published *Victory of the West: The Story of the Battle of Lepanto* treats the battle as a major encounter between the Islamic Ottoman empire and the forces of Western Christendom.

Lepanto was the last great battle that could be described as a simple clash between Christendom and Islam. Fought on October 7, 1571, it saw the fleet of the Ottoman empire pitted against an alliance of Spain, Venice and various other minor players to form a Holy League under the leadership of Don Juan of Austria, the illegitimate half-brother of Philip II of Spain.

The battle was the response of the Christian powers to the invasion of the Venetian possession of Cyprus. At stake was control of the Mediterranean. If the Ottomans had won then there was a real possibility that an invasion of Italy could have followed so that the Ottoman sultan, already claiming to be emperor of the Romans, would have been in possession of both New and Old Rome. The Pope could have become as much a tool of the Ottoman sultan as his Orthodox counterpart the Patriarch of Constantinople already was.

Yet, as Capponi points out, the Holy League was hardly a model of Christian solidarity. The Spanish and the Venetians had different strategic objectives—the Spanish were concerned primarily with Italy, North Africa and the Western Mediterranean, while Venice was anxious to recover Cyprus and protect its interests in the eastern Mediterranean. The Spanish were not keen for a battle that might lose them precious resources, particularly as Philip II, with interests as well in northern Europe, was usually on the verge of bankruptcy. The Spanish were also concerned that the Venetians were in the process of cutting a deal with the Ottomans. Just a few days before the battle there was a conflict between the Spanish and Venetians that almost tore the fleet apart. Nevertheless the alliance held and the League fleet scored a stunning success.

The League's victory, as one might expect, did not translate into Christian hegemony of the Mediterranean. The Ottomans soon repaired their losses and the Venetians, heavily dependent on trade with the Ottoman empire, soon sued for peace, including paying an indemnity. If anything the Battle of Lepanto confirmed the status quo in the Mediterranean. The Ottomans had reached the limit of their power with only a few small territorial gains, such as Crete conquered from the Venetians in the mid-seventeenth century, waiting to be made. The cultural shape of the lands around the Mediterranean was confirmed with a largely Islamic East and South staring across the waters at a Christian North and West. The Ottoman empire, like the ancient Roman empire and the Byzantine empire before it, was left with the task of defending its ever diminishing borders over the next three centuries. When it did finally "fall" after the First World War the ramifications were enormous, and we are still attempting to cope with them from Bosnia to Iraq.

For the people of Western Europe the Battle of Lepanto was an enormous psychological boost because it demonstrated that the "Turk" could be beaten.

For the people of Western Europe the Battle of Lepanto was an enormous psychological boost because it demonstrated that the "Turk" could be beaten. The aura of invincibility surrounding the Ottoman empire was broken. Lepanto was very easy to interpret in terms of Christendom versus Islam because it was one of those rare occasions when the religious division of the combatants was so clear-cut. Of course, in the wider world of strategic alliances the situation was far more complex. The French often supported the Ottomans against the Spanish and Hapsburgs, while the Orthodox Christians of the Eastern Mediterranean generally preferred the tolerant rule of the Ottomans to attempts by the Venetians to impose Catholic bishops on them.

But there are other ways of considering Lepanto. One is to interpret it in terms of a dynamic innovative West pitted against the "stagnant" East. The League won because it used innovative tactics. The usual form that galley warfare took was to ram the enemy ships and then take them by storm. The Venetian ships attempted a new and different tactic. Using a larger and modified form of galley known as galleasses, they filled these ships with cannons and attempted to blow as many of the Ottoman galleys as possible out of the water. League ships carried many more cannon and its troops made much greater use of firearms. Many of the Ottoman troops preferred to use bows, although these were not necessarily inferior to the clumsy arquebus of that time. Capponi has a very good grasp of the military dimensions of Lepanto, and although this is sometimes tedious for those with little interest in strictly military matters, a grasp of such matters is crucial if the battle is to be understood.

If the League had kept to the established "rules" of naval warfare of the time they would probably have lost the battle. In the sixteenth century the Ottoman empire was much more powerful than its rivals in Western Europe but its power was founded on the adaptation of the traditional institutions of Islamic civilisation. This meant in particular the janissaries, the use of slave soldiers and slave administrators as the core of the Sultan's power. This gave the Sultan a loyal and efficient bureaucratic-military machine, although the cost was that this machine tended to behave like the praetorian guard of the Roman empire and to push the Sultan into war to satisfy its desire for plunder.

The state machinery of much of the West was much more ramshackle and less centralised. They relied heavily on Italian bankers and on the wealth of Italy. Nevertheless both the Emperor Charles V and his successor Philip II of Spain had to deal with the constant threat of bankruptcy.

In the longer term, however, the future belonged to the new commercial instruments of the West rather than to the bureaucratic machinery of the Ottomans. In her study of seventeenth-century Crete, *A Shared World,* Molly Green demonstrates that the commercial techniques and practices used by the Venetians were much more sophisticated and developed than those of the Ottoman regime that replaced them in mid-century. It was also the case that the Ottomans were slow to take to make use of printing, with the "printing revolution" that swept the West in the sixteenth century not really taking off in the Islamic world until the nineteenth century.

Even if the Ottomans had won it was unlikely that they would have established hegemony over Western Europe. True, they would have dominated the Mediterranean in the short term and it is likely that they would have been able to conquer Southern Italy and even take Rome. But the history of Byzantium from Justinian onwards suggests that this would have been the limit of their conquests. The Ottomans failed to take Vienna in both the 1520s and the 1680s partly because the supply lines into Central Europe were too long.

In any case it is clear that by the 1570s the dynamic that had driven the earlier Ottoman conquests had largely exhausted itself. Despite defeat at Lepanto they remained in control of Cyprus but that was the extent of Sultan Selim's conquests. In the seventeenth century they were able to wrest Crete from the Venetians but that was the last of their European conquests.

This suggests that Lepanto is better understood in terms of the dynamics of imperial expansion than some desire by Islam

to subdue and conquer the world. The Ottoman empire came into being because of the decaying state of the Byzantine empire in the Balkans and Anatolia, a decadence aggravated by the conquest of Constantinople in 1204 during the Fourth Crusade. The Ottomans succeeded because they defeated their possible rivals, such as the Serbs, in battle.

They did so because they possessed what Ibn Khaldun in his *Muqaddimah* called *asabiya* or a strong sense of social solidarity. According to Ibn Khaldun, barbarians are able to conquer an established settled civilisation because they have a strong sense of their social solidarity that is grounded in the harshness and necessity of nomadic life. However, having conquered a settled society the invaders in turn are conquered by the comfort and soft living of that society until, with their *asabiya* decaying they, in turn, are conquered by another group of uncorrupted barbarians.

Linking social solidarity to imperial success was not limited to Islamic theorists. In his explanation of the worldly success of the Roman empire in book five of the *City of God,* Augustine, drawing on Sallust's *War with Catilene,* argued that empire had shifted to the West and Rome because the Romans possessed a high level of virtue. By virtue he meant the capacity to place the common good above personal gain, a virtue that he saw was destroyed particularly by the sin of avarice.

Sallust emphasised the simple lives of the uncorrupted Romans, and attributed their success to the "eminent merit of a few citizens" before "the state had become demoralised by extravagance and sloth". These ideas were to form the basis of the Western ideal of republicanism and republican virtue that still resonates in our contemporary world.

Now this analysis of history made enormous sense in both Asia and Europe for a long time. Rome, and the Roman empire, had to face an almost continuous set of threats, beginning with the Celts, then moving through to the Germans, Huns, Avars, Arabs and Turks. The Ottoman Turks simply delivered the *coup de grâce* to what had become little more than a living corpse. China built its "great wall" to protect itself from nomadic predators, while the damage inflicted by the Mongols on the settled Islamic world, including the sack of Baghdad, was staggering.

The argument that it was a strong sense of social solidarity that grows out of what could be described as a lifestyle founded on poverty has, I believe, powerful explanatory power. A settled civilisation, by creating a measure of comfort and a settled way of life, makes itself a target for those living outside their boundaries who are drawn by what it has to offer.

In his recent study *War & Peace & War,* Peter Turchin has built on the idea of *asabiya* to emphasise the importance of social co-operation as means of building strong states. He quotes a number of examples of small determined bands being able to overthrow political entities that, on paper, looked far more powerful. Alexander the Great and his superbly drilled Macedonian phalanx is perhaps the best known of these examples.

For Turchin, co-operation rather than competition is the key to success for any state. Moreover, Turchin maintains, it is the replacement of co-operation by competition within a state that leads to the evisceration of the social energy provided by co-operation. Turchin points to the way in which population growth, particularly amongst social elites, leads to a savage competition for resources and a weakening of both social and state power. Such states become the potential victims of those who have maintained their *asabiya*.

By the 1570s the élan or social energy of the Ottoman empire had begun to dissipate. Over the next 250 years the empire slowly became the "sick man of Europe" as certain regions established their de facto autonomy. According to the sociology of Ibn Khaldun this should have resulted in the next group of socially solid barbarians conquering and replacing them, just as they had previously conquered the Byzantines.

And yet this did not happen. One reason for this was that the Qing Chinese empire in the eighteenth century successfully conquered and subdued the last of the great nomadic empires of Eurasia. For the first time in millennia no barbarian horsemen, no Huns, no Avars, no Mongols, surged across the great plains of Eurasia to sack and pillage Europe, China and the great civilisations of the Islamic world and India.

When a new barbarian empire emerged powerful enough to threaten the Ottomans, and by this I mean the Russian empire, it was successfully checked by the jealousy of the other European powers. It was also into this world of decadence, of empires that were not revitalised by new sets of barbarians, in the Middle East, in India and in China, that the European empires were able to make such inroads from the eighteenth century onwards.

L epanto was not the victory of Christianity over Islam, nor is its significance to be considered primarily in religious terms or as a clash of civilisations. Of course that does not mean that was not how it was viewed in a celebrating Europe, including Protestant England, and in the many paintings that have come down to us as representing the battle. Yet across the centuries Lepanto also looks like an exercise in futility, a scene of blood, gore and human misery that, at least on the surface, settled so little.

It was the last major naval battle that involved galleys rowed by banks of oarsmen. And it was won, somewhat against expectations, by the side that was willing to experiment with the use of overwhelming firepower in an attempt to blow the enemy ships out of the water rather than use the time-honoured practices of hand-to-hand combat.

In many ways Lepanto can be considered to be a clash of two different types of empire viewed as forms of polity and expressions of political culture and economic practices. On the one hand there was the traditional "plunder empire" as represented by the Ottomans that sought conquest for the sake of plunder in the shape of precious goods and slaves. Selim had sought to conquer Cyprus, as there was an expectation that a

Sultan should keep his janissaries happy at the beginning of a reign by providing them with a prize to conquer. There was little difference between the motives that led the Romans to expand their empire and those of the Ottomans.

The new European empires, as represented by Spain and Venice, were not uninterested in conquest and plunder, especially when one considers the behaviour of Spain in the Americas. But they were also in many ways quite different from the older territorial empires of Eurasia of which the Ottoman was one of the last representatives. And the difference lay in their concern with commerce and trade. Venice did not really want war with the Ottomans because it ruined her trade with that empire, and as soon as possible after Lepanto sought to re-establish that trading relationship.

Lepanto can be seen as symbolic of that transition, described by the nineteenth-century French liberal philosopher Benjamin Constant, from the age of war to the age of commerce. Or as others might say, it can be considered as the birth of modernity. Even the overwhelming use of firepower can be found in the pages of Constant as a feature of the utilitarian approach to warfare favoured by commercial nations. The irony was that the somewhat ramshackle empires of sixteenth-century Europe, with their disorganised finances and administrative apparatuses much inferior to those of the Ottomans, would within 300 years come to dominate the world not because of their superior *asabiya* or virtue but because of their capacity to create modern efficient institutions far superior to the slave bureaucracy of the Ottomans, and because of their ability to deliver superior firepower.

This new European and commercial form of empire supplanted an older, more traditional imperial form. What this meant was that the old rules of empire, of an imperial expansion dictated by the need to conquer to attain booty and slaves and a decline governed by the need to protect its settled possessions from new predators, would give way to a new set of rules. These are the rules of the export and import of capital, as described by Niall Ferguson in his recent studies of the English and American empires.

Nevertheless it is appropriate that scholars such as Turchin direct our attention to the significance of *asabiya* and the importance of the idea of social cooperation as a foundation of a stable and powerful state. It is also important that the story of Lepanto should recover its place in the historical consciousness of the West. Capponi's highly readable and scholarly account does help to achieve that goal. But it should not be read as yet another episode in the seemingly endless war between Christianity and Islam. Rather it should be seen as a battle in which an emerging form of state and empire was able to show its mettle against the last powerful traditionalist empire.

From *Quadrant*, April 2008. Copyright © 2008 by Quadrant Monthly. Reprinted by permission.

Test-Your-Knowledge Form

We encourage you to photocopy and use this page as a tool to assess how the articles in *Annual Editions* expand on the information in your textbook. By reflecting on the articles you will gain enhanced text information. You can also access this useful form on a product's book support Web site at *http://www.mhcls.com*.

NAME: DATE:

_____

TITLE AND NUMBER OF ARTICLE:

_____

BRIEFLY STATE THE MAIN IDEA OF THIS ARTICLE:

_____

LIST THREE IMPORTANT FACTS THAT THE AUTHOR USES TO SUPPORT THE MAIN IDEA:

_____

WHAT INFORMATION OR IDEAS DISCUSSED IN THIS ARTICLE ARE ALSO DISCUSSED IN YOUR TEXTBOOK OR OTHER READINGS THAT YOU HAVE DONE? LIST THE TEXTBOOK CHAPTERS AND PAGE NUMBERS:

_____

LIST ANY EXAMPLES OF BIAS OR FAULTY REASONING THAT YOU FOUND IN THE ARTICLE:

_____

LIST ANY NEW TERMS/CONCEPTS THAT WERE DISCUSSED IN THE ARTICLE, AND WRITE A SHORT DEFINITION:

We Want Your Advice

ANNUAL EDITIONS revisions depend on two major opinion sources: one is our Advisory Board, listed in the front of this volume, which works with us in scanning the thousands of articles published in the public press each year; the other is you—the person actually using the book. Please help us and the users of the next edition by completing the prepaid article rating form on this page and returning it to us. Thank you for your help!

ANNUAL EDITIONS: World History Vol. 1, 10/e

ARTICLE RATING FORM

Here is an opportunity for you to have direct input into the next revision of this volume.
We would like you to rate each of the articles listed below, using the following scale:

1. **Excellent: should definitely be retained**
2. **Above average: should probably be retained**
3. **Below average: should probably be deleted**
4. **Poor: should definitely be deleted**

Your ratings will play a vital part in the next revision.
Please mail this prepaid form to us as soon as possible.
Thanks for your help!

RATING	ARTICLE	RATING	ARTICLE
	1. Stand and Deliver: Why Did Early Hominids Begin to Walk on Two Feet?		23. Vox Populi: Sex, Lies, and Blood Sport
	2. Gone but Not Forgotten		24. Woman Power in the Maya World
	3. Out of Africa		25. Secrets of a Desert Metropolis: The Hidden Wonders of Petra's Ancient Engineers
	4. Mapping the Past		26. It Happened Only Once in History!
	5. First Americans		27. Ancient Jewel
	6. Dawn of the City: Excavations Prompt a Revolution in Thinking about the Earliest Cities		28. What Is the Koran?
	7. The Dawn of Art		29. The Dome of the Rock: Jerusalem's Epicenter
	8. Prehistory of Warfare		30. First Churches of the Jesus Cult
	9. Writing Gets a Rewrite		31. Women in Ancient Christianity: The New Discoveries
	10. Poets and Psalmists: Goddesses and Theologians		32. The Survival of the Eastern Roman Empire
	11. The Cradle of Cash		33. The New Maya
	12. How to Build a Pyramid		34. The Ideal of Unity
	13. Indus Valley, Inc.		35. The Arab Roots of European Medicine
	14. Uncovering Ancient Thailand		36. The Age of the Vikings
	15. Empires in the Dust		37. The Fall of Constantinople
	16. Black Pharaohs		38. 1492: The Prequel
	17. Messages from the Dead		39. The Other 1492: Jews and Muslims in Columbus's Spain
	18. China's First Empire		40. The Far West's Challenge to the World, 1500–1700 A.D.
	19. Beyond the Family Feud		41. A Taste of Adventure: Kerala, India, and the Molucca Islands, Indonesia
	20. In Classical Athens, a Market Trading in the Currency of Ideas		42. After Dire Straits, an Agonizing Haul across the Pacific
	21. Alexander the Great: Hunting for a New Past?		43. The Significance of Lepanto
	22. Sudden Death: Gladiators Were Sport's First Superstars, Providing Thrills, Chills, and Occasional Kills		

ABOUT YOU

Name

Date
_____

Are you a teacher? ❏ A student? ❏
Your school's name
_____

Department
_____

Address   City   State   Zip
_____

School telephone #
_____

YOUR COMMENTS ARE IMPORTANT TO US!

Please fill in the following information:
For which course did you use this book?
_____

Did you use a text with this ANNUAL EDITION? ❏ yes ❏ no
What was the title of the text?
_____

What are your general reactions to the Annual Editions concept?
_____

Have you read any pertinent articles recently that you think should be included in the next edition? Explain.
_____

Are there any articles that you feel should be replaced in the next edition? Why?
_____

Are there any World Wide Web sites that you feel should be included in the next edition? Please annotate.
_____

May we contact you for editorial input? ❏ yes ❏ no
May we quote your comments? ❏ yes ❏ no